KEYNES

Recent Titles in
Contributions in Economics and Economic History

KEYNES

A Critical Life

David Felix

Contributions in Economics and Economic History, Number 208

GREENWOOD PRESS
Westport, Connecticut • London

Library of Congress Cataloging-in-Publication Data

Felix, David, 1921–
    Keynes : a critical life / by David Felix.
      p.   cm. — (Contributions in economics and economic history,
  ISSN 0084–9235 ; no. 208)
    Includes bibliographical references and index.
    ISBN 0–313–28827–5 (alk. paper)
    1. Keynes, John Maynard, 1883–1946. 2. Economists—Great Britain—
  Biography. 3. Keynesian economics. I. Title. II. Series.
  HB103.K47F444   1999
  330.15'6—dc21
  [B]   98–30494

British Library Cataloguing in Publication Data is available.

Library of Congress Catalog Card Number: 98–30494
ISBN: 0–313–28827–5
ISSN: 0084–9235

First published in 1999

Greenwood Press, 88 Post Road West, Westport, CT 06881
An imprint of Greenwood Publishing Group, Inc.

Printed in the United States of America

The paper used in this book complies with the
Permanent Paper Standard issued by the National
Information Standards Organization (Z39.48–1984).

10 9 8 7 6 5 4 3 2 1

Copyright Acknowledgments

The author and publisher gratefully acknowledge permission for use of the following material:

Excerpts from unpublished writings of J. M. Keynes copyright © The Provost and Scholars of King's College, Cambridge 1998.

Excerpts from the correspondence of John Maynard Keynes with Duncan Grant and Oswald T. Falk are printed with permission of The British Library.

Excerpts from the correspondence of Lytton Strachey copyright © 1998 The Strachey Trust are printed by permission of The Society of Authors on behalf of The Strachey Trust.

Excerpts from a letter of George H. W. Rylands to Maynard Keynes are printed with the permission of Dr. Rylands.

Excerpts from the diaries of John Neville Keynes are printed with the permission of the Syndics of Cambridge University Library.

Excerpts from the following correspondence: Lytton Strachey to Leonard Woolf, 2 February 1906; John Maynard Keynes to Lytton Strachey, 20 June 1906; Lytton Strachey to Leonard Woolf, 21 June 1906; and Lytton Strachey to Leonard Woolf, 27 May 1909, are printed with the permission of the Berg Collection of English & American Literature, The New York Public Library Astor, Lenox and Tilden Foundations.

Excerpts from a letter of Professor Arthur C. Pigou to John Maynard Keynes, June 1940, are printed with the permission of John Johnson (Authors' Agent) Limited on behalf of the author's estate.

Excerpts from the correspondence of David Garnett with John Maynard Keynes of 15 November 1915, 22 March 1918, and August 1940 are printed with the permission of Richard Garnett.

Excerpts from the correspondence of Vanessa Bell with Maynard Keynes are printed with the permission of Angelica Garnett.

Excerpts from Clive Bell's letters to John Maynard Keynes are printed with the permission of Anne Olivier Bell.

Excerpts from *The Collected Writings of John Maynard Keynes* are reprinted with the permission of Macmillan Ltd.

For Georgette

Contents

Preface: A Double Life

The title of this volume is a double entendre, the *Life* meaning both Keynes's life as it was lived and for which he was responsible, and his life as it is here written, for which only the writer is responsible. I am making two points, the first banal and the second, a precision. Any great person lives a critical life by definition, his or her greatness showing itself by its *critical* role in great developments. In writing Keynes's life, to go on to the second point, I take a critical position, unlike the other biographers, but it is not to be mistaken for hostile. Rather, it is, as I believe I show, sympathetic while refusing to slip into partisanship or hagiography. This approach derives from the sense that all persons are humanly flawed and that greatness derives its character from the flaws as well as from the excellences.

The association of individual greatness with great developments is a self-evident fact of history. *Uniquely* fitted for the circumstances, the great person relates to them uncannily and expresses their essence in his or her functioning. A few examples can illustrate what I am trying to say.

Alexander the Great represented the leap from the Greek polis to the super-state. Drawing on the barbaric energy of his own Macedonians and the thought and skills of the Greeks, he conceived of a ruthless Greek-Asiatic ecumene and took advantage of the weaknesses and divisions of his world to advance much further than could the Macedonians, Greeks, Persians, and the neighboring peoples of themselves at the time. The aristocratic demagogue Caesar represented the transition from an aristocratic republic to an authoritarian empire responsive to its bread-and-circuses masses, although it took a minuscule Caesar to complete the process. Abraham Lincoln was uniquely right for his role in eliminating slavery, a function in which a ruthless legalism was central. He recognized that this peculiar institution simply could not be permitted to shackle the nation morally and operationally and, uncompromising about it after all the historic compromises, maneuvered ruthlessly to that end. It required the bloodiest war in American history, but he had the moral courage to accept the consequences even as he used his legal skills to avoid the crippling responsibility of initiating action. Given his easy forgiveness and refusal to hate, his profound personal humanity permitted the healing, however painfully, to begin in a restored union. To Alexander, Caesar, and Lincoln can be added the names of many others who compressed an enormity of history in their lives; for example, Charlemagne, Frederick II of the Holy Roman Empire, Frederick the Great of Prussia, Bismarck of Germany, Popes Innocent III and John Paul II, William the Conqueror and Elizabeth I, Louis XIV and Napoleon, Peter the Great and, despite a contemporary fall in market value, Lenin. These were pure *leaders*.

Keynes belonged to another, more complex, more difficult class of greatness, the thinker-leader, in whom these contradictory characters are in continual conflict. In history, the closest parallel to Keynes is Karl Marx, however different their styles. With deep instinct guiding superb intellection, each undertook political action but achieved his ends by generating ideas and communicating them in his writings, ultimately in one classic book. In Keynes's case the reader will see how precisely he fit his circumstances and how triumphantly he overcame resistance at a series of critical points in the economic history of his nation, the advanced part of the world, and the world generally. If I do not detail Marx's magnitude in these pages, I note that at the end of World War II Keynes and Marx divided the world between them.

This book is companion to my *Biography of an Idea: John Maynard Keynes and* The General Theory (1995), a study of Keynes and his economics. In that volume, I made an aggressive critique of the pure theory of *The General Theory*. Loyal Keynesians, preferring to appreciate the elegance of Keynes's thought, find this interpretation alienating. I believe this life will further show that his greatness is not diminished if the theory, limited to its ideational self, is shown to be in error. It was, as that first volume claims to demonstrate, true to the practical needs of the *political* economy in which it was conceived and projected. In fact the contradictions between thinker and leader were crucial in making Keynes so effective. The thinker, constrained by obdurate reality, was forced to deceive himself and others; the leader, constrained by his intellectual fastidiousness, was unable to exercise pure power. The dual personality commanded reality in the long run more powerfully than pure leaders, who were eventually deserted by fashion, while finding intellectual formulae that were socially acceptable as the pure ideas of pure thinkers were not. This life, critical as it is, permits me to complete the story of Keynes's greatness.

I continue to draw benefits from the help of several economists, and I here extend the thanks published in the first volume without, however, committing them to approving my interpretations. To these names I add R. M. O'Donnell, a profound student of Keynes's philosophy and economics, whom I had the pleasure of joining in research in the Modern Archive Centre of King's College, Jacqueline Cox, the centre's hospitable and most knowledgeable and helpful archivist, and Robert Skidelsky, who invited me to tea at Tilton, which he has lately inhabited, and so permitted me to breathe the air of the country home of Baron Keynes of Tilton. I am also grateful to Dr. Benjamin Brody for professional insight into the psyche in general and Keynes's in particular.

These institutions and their staffs were my major research resources: the Modern Archive Centre, with its Keynes Papers and copies of the Charleston Papers, and the Lamont Library of Harvard University with its microfilm of the Keynes Papers, the Cambridge University Library, the British Library in London, the Public Record Office, formerly in London and now in Kew Gardens, and The New York Public Library and its Berg Collection.

Introduction: Private and Public

"The Child is father of the Man" probably sounded as much a commonplace when Wordsworth first said it[1] as it does today, but John Neville Keynes's meticulously phenomenological, pathetically human diary documents the truth of that commonplace in the life of his son, further supported by the evidences the articulate son provided early and late. John Maynard Keynes the Man had been able to unite his characters as thinker and leader; similarly, he kept his identity with the Child he had been. Of course there were strains in both cases.

Here, we see that the private Keynes unmistakably inhabited the public Keynes. When we pursue the boy cyclist on Cambridge's Harvey Road, incidentally noting an accident there deforming a finger, we see him later elevated but recognizable in the British emissary on a flying boat over the war-roiled Atlantic. The immovable player in Eton's Wall Game later refuses to budge when the united establishment commands. He makes love and plays politics in the same style, promiscuously up to a point but responsibly. The child wonders who invented time and the undergraduate philosophizes about it with sophisticated, borrowed erudition. The child breathes economics and logic in the household air and never stops thinking logic and economics until he changes the world's thinking and economics. Despite the strains of living two or more lives, John Maynard Keynes is integral.

In John Neville's diary we can trace the origins of John Maynard's greatness—and its cost. Here is an early record of the younger Keynes's ill health and a suggestive relation to his compulsion to gain ascendancy over others. The father is a capable scholar and administrator but, hampered by anxiety, limits his own achievement and leaves room for the son to achieve more while generating that compulsiveness. Thus, we see a loving, proud, considerate, and supportive father righteously thrashing a child over a period of two or three years, imprinting him with rage, but a limited, unconscious anger, which develops as a rage to succeed and, intermittently, to punish or subvert, privately or publicly.

His parents were not the only witnesses of the epiphanies accompanying, if not preceding, the Child. The headmaster of Maynard's elementary school force-fed him with mathematics, Latin, Greek, and Milton's *Samson Agonistes*, and his wife, observing that Maynard commanded general knowledge besides such specifics as mathematics, called him a ''genius.'' She was predicting the ability of the future Keynes to rise above his economist competitors, beginning with his father, and gain substantive effects; the point was to set economics in a broader context of knowledge and experience than the others commanded. Consistently, at Eton, preparing for Cambridge University, Maynard would specialize in both mathematics and classics, the latter extending to medieval Latin poetry. So armed and stiffened further by his unwillingness or incapability to admit error, the boy was always the winner in family debates, and the young man made Bertrand Russell, the philosopher has testified, feel foolish in their dialectical encounters. Accompanying his outstanding abilities, the certainty and the arrogance came early.

In the great affairs of belief or action, science excepted but philosophy included, history awards the triumphs not to those most nearly right, but to the possessors of boundless wills and the total conviction of being right. It was that sheer certainty that permitted the inflexibly willed Luther and Calvin to establish orthodoxies while the rejects of history began and ended as heretics. Kant got his victorious certainty by turning Hume's confident skepticism inside out. Hegel built another world philosophy on the silly theses that thinking will make it— whatever it is—so, and that something need not be itself. Napoleon's will and confidence covered over egregious, deadly errors, his plunges, for example, into the disasters of Egypt, Spain, and Russia. Like Karl Marx before him and Milton Friedman after, the mature Keynes erected a more or less economic ideology on the willed certainty of a nature formed in childhood as much as on his indubitable, equally precocious, genius.

But the affairs of the heart are more vital than those of knowledge or state. We take as given the centrality of love in every sentient being and inquire how the intimate related to the professional in Keynes, who rings intriguing changes on both. For two decades from his adolescent awakening we see Maynard as active, often gutter-cruising homosexual—and thereafter as happy, settled benedict. Obligingly, Maynard Keynes shows clearly how his inner child affects the economist, civil servant, policymaker, and statesman. Although secure in his superiority, the lover of street boys will sympathize, if not quite empathize, with the working classes. As policymaker he will work amicably with trade-union leaders who reject his neoclassical economics. Himself then rejecting the wisdom of his various fathers, he will then cast away that economics and construct his new model of the economy, his General Theory, in a populist, if not proletarian, sense. The elitist endures as tribune.

We see Maynard Keynes moving productively, only successfully, in a fluent, if not always geometrically straight line, from his childhood home through boarding school, university, junior government office, back to university as don, back to government as high-level civil servant, on to business and politics—and to integrating a wide range of professional activities. At the same time, he will be winning a circle of friends and entering into his extended family of Bloomsbury aesthetes where, again, private and public will jostle each other synergetically, if at times bruisingly for all. His friends, many of them pacifists, will belabor him for doing the government's dirty work and seek his help with that dreadful government. Guiltily, responsibly, affectionately, but sometimes arrogantly, he will oblige with overwhelming energy and efficiency. He will help get them excused from military service and secure government funds to stock Great Britain's National Gallery with an opportune purchase of great art they doubt he can appreciate.

In his country idyll, with his wife sunbathing naked in the garden, Keynes writes his *General Theory* and creates a working farm with numerous pigs. From his don's power center he creates an ideological school to further his economic policy and a builds a theater to display his Lydia's talents and nourish her self-esteem. Enriching economic theory and profiting symmetrically, he exploits the business world to finance his ease and his political influence, the latter further to translate his theory into practice.

Keynes's greatest tour de force of many will be to establish a profound union with a funny, earthy dancer, a great personage in her own right, who will ease, if not reduce, the compulsions that drive him so far and, striking at his vulnerable health, kill him too soon. Bonifying the somewhat abbreviated life left to him, this ultimate relationship will strengthen the inner man to permit him to carry out his lifetime mission of improving the world. Private and public.

NOTE

1. In William Wordsworth, "My heart leaps up when I behold" (1807), *The Oxford Dictionary of Quotations,* 4th ed. (Oxford, 1992), 745. That poetical leap continues: "A rainbow in the sky: / So it was when my life began; / So is it now I am a man; / So be it when I shall grow old, / Or let me die!" Wordsworth then arrives at "The Child is father of the Man" but descends in the final couplet: "And I could wish my days to be / Bound to each other by natural piety."

CHAPTER 1

Fathers (and Mothers) and Sons (and Daughters)

The effects of fathers on their sons are inescapably pervasive but John Neville Keynes (1852–1949) had a remarkably specific influence on John Maynard Keynes (1883–1946) both in a positive and a negative sense. On the positive side, one need only be aware, in this introductory acquaintance with them, that each was a Cambridge University don who wrote significant works in logic and economics. As for the negative, the father's achievement was bounded by his two scholarly fields and educational administration, while the essence of the son's career was its boundlessness. Emphasizing the father is not to minimize the mother's influence, which was equally, although covertly, powerful. It is true that, to use an economist's idiom of importance to Maynard later, Neville's intimacy with him might seem to have "crowded out" a comparable intimacy with Florence Ada Keynes. Yet, although she loved her three children deeply and more than supportively, she was rather distant in all her relationships and never properly exercised the feminine prerogative, at least in that late Victorian period, of letting her feelings overflow. Neville's, however, were subject to constant leakage. This exchange of the conventional paternal and maternal variances in closeness and emotive roles, constituting a reversal of the Oedipal situation, had to leave its imprint on all the children.

The first-born, himself providing a partial buffer, experienced the parental radiations more immediately than the other children. Geoffrey Langdon Keynes, a perceptive third child, suggested the depths and variances in Maynard's bonds to Neville and Florence: "His relations with my father were very close and he

John Neville Keynes, father of John Maynard Keynes, in 1905. Photo courtesy of Milo Keynes.

Florence Ada Keynes, mother of John Maynard Keynes, in 1905. Photo courtesy of Milo Keynes.

was devoted to my mother throughout his life.''[1] Geoffrey and Margaret, the middle child, were similarly devoted to Florence but only Margaret, who took the initiative herself, seems to have reduced much, if not all, of the slight distance between child and mother. Maynard would develop his character in terms both of the intimacy and the lack of it which he experienced at home.

Neville, who was born in Salisbury, one hundred miles southwest of Cambridge and site of the splendid cathedral, was the only child of an older (b. 1805), loving father and a considerably younger (b. 1820), more than loving mother.[2] John Keynes, a splendidly self-made man, had first built up *his* father's brushmaking manufactory but then found it more rewarding to exploit his hobby of flower growing. He prospered as producer of dahlias and roses, expanded his operations into other businesses and banking, and achieved the ultimate distinction of the mayoralty of Salisbury—not long, however, before his death in 1878. John Keynes had been benign but demanding. Neville, the only child of his second marriage (there was a daughter from the first), endured pressures that were all the more intense because they were expressed in a frame of love and concern also lavished on Neville by his father's unmarried sister and (until her death in her nineties in 1869) by John Keynes's mother. Everything impelled Neville agonizingly to rise above his father's level of successful man-in-trade to the distinction of a university don.

John Keynes and John Neville Keynes represented a revival of the family fortunes. According to researches Maynard himself made in Eton's well-stocked library, the Keynes name derived from the locality of Cahagnes in Normandy. Although the family had achieved prosperity after participating in the Norman conquest, it lost its position by clinging to Catholicism, producing a number of Jesuit priests, and then lapsing into nonconformity. Neville Keynes appeared almost precisely at the moment when nonconformity, while providing personal discipline and force, was no longer a bar to entrance into Cambridge or Oxford universities and only a moderate handicap in British society. His eldest son, particularly, would inherit his luck in timing. As his diaries show, Neville won his success at the price of chronic depression, pervasive anxiety, and numerous psychosomatic complaints. Maynard would reverse the inheritance of anxiety into vaulting confidence but could avoid neither the depression nor ailments that were much more seriously somatic.

John Keynes, encouraged by Neville's obvious competence, sent the eleven-year-old off to a school that could prepare nonconformist boys for appropriate careers. After leading his matriculation class in mathematics and doing almost as well in classics, Neville spent two years working even harder, up to twelve hours a day, at University College, London, and went on to win a scholarship in mathematics at Pembroke College, Cambridge.[3] The only problem was that, aware of not being a first-rate mathematician, he hated the subject. A year later, he escaped into moral sciences, which comprehended moral and political philosophy, psychology, and his best subjects, logic and economics. In December 1875, now twenty-six, he placed first in the moral science tripos (honors examination), impressed the great Alfred Marshall as possessing "a very clear mind,"[4] and won a six-year fellowship at Pembroke. (Fellows are elected members of a given college corporation as scholars, teachers, or administrators—or a combination thereof; all fellows are dons but some dons, although functioning like fellows, lack the designation and privileges of the elect.) Before that period was up, Neville had established himself as a Cambridge University don for life.

In the next few years Neville finished defining himself professionally and personally. He accomplished the first by lecturing successfully on logic and economics and entering into the university administration, and the second, by marrying Florence Ada Brown, who had been a student in Newnham, one of the two women's colleges (Girton was the other) founded at Cambridge during that period. Neville happened to be lecturing at both, but he formally met Florence at the home of a mutual friend toward the end of her first year, when she was eighteen. He promptly pursued the acquaintance but had to wait proper Victorian intervals for proposal and marriage, the first, one year after their meeting and the second, more than two years after that. She was twenty-one and he not quite thirty when they married on 15 August 1882. Maynard was born on 5 June of the next year. The parental situation was functionally and psychically perfect for the nurture of John Maynard Keynes, economist and practicioner of various other professions, all intricately related.

Florence contributed no less than Neville to their son's formation. Her father, John Brown, was a superb preacher, doubtless influencing Maynard's negative judgment of most preachers he endured. Dr. Brown was the author of church histories and the standard biography of John Bunyan, his predecessor as nonconformist pastor in Bedford, twenty-five miles southwest of Cambridge, by two centuries, a Yale College honorary doctor of divinity, and, like Neville, indeed more so, a great Liberal and supporter of William Gladstone. His redoubtable wife, Ada, herself daughter of an exemplary pastor's wife, set up a school, like her mother, to give *her* daughters a proper education, hence Florence Ada's impulsion toward Newnham and another daughter's (as well as a son's) into the practice of medicine. For twenty years Ada Brown found herself teaching children of friends. Florence, eldest child of six, spent two years helping her run the school back at Bedford after leaving Newnham and before marrying Neville. To the children of Neville and Florence science and scholarship were inescapable. Margaret was a special case. While refusing to compete with her brothers on her own, she married a Cambridge University physiologist and future Nobel laureate. Another element in their heritage, to which all three submitted, was service to others.

Neville and Florence were persons of extraordinary and almost perfect tact and consideration, qualities evident during the rigors of courtship. Their consideration, however, did not extend to the point of permitting themselves to be victimized by excessive claims on them. Each had to set limits on the affections of Neville's widowed mother, who made a point of telling him before the wedding, "You are *everything* to me."[5] He had, however, anticipated that by taking her to Italy for a kind of honeymoon in the reverse mode: "The Campanile! The Uffizi Gallery!!! . . . The Pitti Gallery!!!"—and could conclude that the trip "had been a great satisfaction to me in so far as I have been able . . . to manifest my love towards her."[6] Florence, for her part, had to oppose a firm negative when Anna Keynes indicated she would like to live with the couple.[7] (Anna Keynes did move from Salisbury to Cambridge, but after failing to achieve a second-best choice, residence next door to them, settled satisfactorily for all within the range of a slow fifteen-minute walk.)[8] When the children were growing up, Neville would take them to visit her on Sunday afternoons, where he "relieved the possible tedium of family conversations by reading to us from Dickens," as Geoffrey chose to remember, or, as Neville confessed, "disgraced myself, as I sometimes do, by falling asleep."[9]

Florence had to use all her tact to contend with both son and mother before she and Neville achieved their notable equilibrium. Neville's anxiety had released itself during the long engagement, and he sometimes questioned his worthiness of her and, as a logical consequence, the constancy of her love for him.[10] Geoffrey granted that during this time his father "sometimes tortured himself."[11] Accurately sensing that she loved him less than he loved her, Neville was also exquisitely torturing his fiancée. One month after Maynard was born, Anna Keynes, exercising her license as mother-in-law, suggested that Florence was "a little undemonstrative," Neville recorded, but he immediately insisted parenthetically "(my darling is not so to me now)" and permitted himself to be satisfied by the felicities and comforts of marriage. He conceded her right to defend herself against "implicit criticisms which Mother does rather keep on about." It was then that Florence had succeeded, with rare "tears in her eyes," in fending off Anna Keynes's establishment next door to them.[12] Repeated references in Neville's diaries document his deepening love for Florence and his growing dependence on her. Two months before Maynard's birth, he reflected their physical happiness with a fugue on his "pleasure when in the morning I see her wake smiling at finding me lying by her side . . . see her wake . . . with a smile of welcome on her face."[13] Vouchsafed such blessings, he could accept, whether he acknowledged it or not, the distance Florence kept about herself. Husband and wife provided a fundament strong enough to support Maynard's genial and Geoffrey's and Margaret's nicely proportioned achievements.

The family residence at 6 Harvey Road was one of six pairs of identical, semi-detached, four-storied, steep-roofed houses newly built for married dons on land owned by Gonville and Caius College. Named for the discoverer of the circulation of blood, a distinguished alumnus of the college, Harvey Road is a short street of some two hundred yards on what was then the southern outskirts of Cambridge, and a brisk twenty-five-minute walk to Neville's eventual university offices. (Geoffrey Keynes would publish a prize-winning life of William Harvey as well as a bibliography of his works.) Resolutely utilitarian, the houses were built to accommodate prosperous, philoprogenitive families with visiting relatives and friends and an appropriate staff; the Keynes family had three servants plus a governess when needed. Geoffrey, sensitive about such matters, was apologetic about his home's lack of "special charm or character," which, with its William Morris wallpaper and reproduction of Raphael's *Virgin and Child*, "suited our inexacting standards."[14] Maynard, taking it as a given and lacking an aesthetic sensibility despite his picture collecting and other art concerns, seems never to have felt such distress. The house was constructed of dark, mottled, yellow bricks made from the local clay, dreary on first view. Longer acquaintance finds the bricks softened into friendly, staunch arrangements of hospitality. (While carrying out research in Cambridge I lived in a flat carved out of the basement scullery area of another of the houses, one sitting catty-cornered across the street from No. 6. Reviewing my notes, I looked across a flower-bordered garden where real robins murdered worms in obedience to Darwinian law.) Neville and Florence could furnish their home with the help of more than one hundred wedding presents, including three tea services, cases of fish knives and unqualified knives, an oil painting, a hand-painted table, an ecritoire, and a "china jar for the hall," this last a gift of Miss Helen Gladstone, the prime minister's daughter and principal of Newnham College.[15] Returned from their honeymoon, they stayed with friends until the house, in the final throes of construction, was ready for occupancy on 11 November 1882.[16] Neville saw to it that they had no reason ever to move. For Maynard and the other children No. 6 Harvey Road incorporated the solidity and security of their family.

Neville Keynes was a classically handsome, small man, five feet, six inches tall, a half-inch taller than Florence[17] and a half-dozen inches shorter than his sons would be. He seemed determined to remain small and circumscribed, but grew, however modestly, well beyond that. In his middle age, photographs show that he gained honestly in distinction. Florence, classically but severely handsome herself, also gained in distinction while softening into thoughtful (sad?) comeliness. Neville was a first-rate scholar and administrator—and a great, if problematic, father—the father, one must not forget, of a lifelong prodigy.

A consolidator of reform but not a reformer, Neville had arrived at the critical moment to benefit from a series of characteristically piecemeal English reforms that gradually opened up Cambridge University to progress and long-excluded groups of the population. Even though he was an economist, he opposed Alfred Marshall's efforts to create a separate tripos for economics (with politics as accompanying minor subject). Furthermore, despite his romantic and professional associations with Newnham College, he found it premature to grant degrees to women.[18] (Florence, after two years, had simply passed an examination on a modest level before returning to her mother's side.) It had been only in 1871 that Parliament removed the religious tests for admittance to degree study at Cambridge University, thus permitting Neville to enter it in the first place. Until 1882 the archaic university provisions forbade marriage by the fellows at the price of losing their positions. In that year, while he was enduring his long engagement, new statutes were passed allowing fellows to marry—although at the newer price of accepting six-year limits to their fellowships. For Neville, it meant formally separating from Pembroke College in August 1882. Given his proclivity for expecting the worst, this might have given him pause in proceeding with the wedding despite a comfortable annual income of £600 and numerous prospects that were opening up for him. In early 1881, before stepping into a professional void, however, he was offered the position of assistant secretary of the Cambridge Local Examinations Syndicate at an annual £200. (In connection with extension lectures the examinations were a method used by the university to set standards for the schools, another expression of reform.) Encouraged by Marshall, Neville had applied for the prestigious but poorly paid chair of political economy at University College, London, vacated by the great W. Stanley Jevons, but withdrew from his candidacy when the Cambridge appointment opened up. With these positive and negative decisions he had picked general administration over the theorizing and teaching of economics (and logic), without, however, eliminating them. Before the end of 1881, also, he had committed himself to the construction of the Harvey Road house. For the rest of the decade Marshall, who valued his scholarly abilities and needed talented people to create the right economics establishment for Britain, tried to reverse Neville's decision.

Modestly, Neville went "from strength to strength,"[19] including well-contained teaching and scholarly projects. In 1883, the year Maynard was born, Neville's distinction as senior moralist and his lucid lectures won him a university lectureship in the moral sciences, which he would hold until 1911. The new position itself provided an annual £50 plus students' fees, but, more important, it established Neville in a solid and responsible teaching post keeping him face-to-face with living, learning students. In 1883, also, the salary of his examinations position was increased to £250. (In 1887, four years later, he declined a raise to £300 because it would demand more work than he was willing to give in return.)[20] At the begining of 1887, he recorded a capital of £16,800 and an annual income running at upward of £1,000.[21] In 1890, he could specify that his income was £1,467 and his savings, £400. Inexorably, in 1900, his capital had reached £24,000 and, in 1908, £38,000.[22] His administrative responsibilities increased and branched out.

Inevitably, by way of consummate tact and dogged committee work, Neville was directing himself toward the administrative center of the university. In the Syndicate, on 25 March 1891, meanwhile, he rose from assistant secretary to secretary with wider duties, his salary increasing to £500, with annual increments of £25 toward a maximum of £700. A year later he permitted himself this much satisfaction from a sense and appreciation of power: "I certainly like the feeling that I am master at the Syndicate Building. My old interest in the work is kept up and increased."[23] In 1892, also, on 7 November, he was elected second on the list of eight candidates, four of them successful, to the university's Council of the Senate, its principal governing body. The significance of that step is suggested by his receiving "congratulations on attaining cabinet rank."[24]

Less than six months later, in April 1893, he became the Council secretary and a central figure in the university administration. (*Also* in November 1892 he had been co-opted into the Newnham Council and appointed to the Press Syndicate overseeing the Cambridge University Press.)[25] The effective head of the university is the vice-chancellor. (The chancellor is figurehead, thus the Princes Albert and Philip in their respective centuries.) The chief administrator under the vice-chancellor is the registrary; Neville's diaries indicate, and Geoffrey Keynes was sure, that his father "propped up for several years the work of the . . . registrary."[26] Neville propped up vice-chancellor as well. On 2 October 1894, in one of a number of such indications, Neville quoted the incumbent vice-chancellor to the effect that he " 'owe[d] more . . . to . . . Dr. Keynes than any other . . . member of the Senate. . . . All the members are able to appreciate his work . . . but only the vice-chancellor can estimate how many mistakes he would have made [without] the help of one whose memory, judgment, and industry are unfailing.' " In his long service, Neville similarly helped a succession of vice-chancellors, who, in those days, were usually limited to two-year terms. (Now it is at least five years.) On 2 November 1896, this modest man recorded that, as secretary of the Council, "I carried two motions and was rather pleased with myself." On 8 November, one week later, he could reassure himself: The Conservatives would not "oppose me, on the ground that I was indispensable on the Council whatever my particular views might be." The next day he was reelected.[27] In 1910, Neville became registrary while remaining Council secretary, a fact that would further substantiate the value of his pre-registrary work. He would resign in 1925 at the age of seventy-three.

Man and office were well matched. Given the wealth and self-sufficiency of the individual colleges (a maximum of twenty-three in Neville's time; thirty-one recently) and the poverty and limitations of the university administration, his function required exquisite persuasion rather than the exercise of direct power. The inaudibility of criticism suggests his success. In 1942, celebrating John Neville's ninetieth birthday and his and Florence's diamond wedding anniversary at a King's College luncheon, the famous John Maynard—*Lord*—Keynes apostrophized him: "For thirty-three years he was one of the best administrators there ever was." Slipping into affectionate and sentimental hyperbole, he asserted, "During those years this university was a better place . . . than it has ever been before or since."[28] The younger Keynes was passing silently by the disinclination of his father to make the university a better place for women students and economic science as well.

Neville's diaries show his opposition to Marshall's ambitions for economics to have been personal and long-enduring. A diary entry of 11 May 1886 found Marshall "narrow and egotistical," while Neville sympathized with the philosopher Henry Sidgwick, who led the resistance to Marshall and remained an immovable obstacle as long as he lived. On 31 January 1902, a year and a half after Sidgwick's death, Neville noted that Marshall was resuming his campaign: "I want to nip it in the bud if possible." That was the year that Maynard, like

Neville before him, matriculated at the university as an unenthusiastic student of mathematics. In 1903, a year too late for the entering student, the economics (and politics) tripos was established. Women students had to wait until 1948 for the university to grant them degrees. Neville made the university a better place, one might amend, for those who qualified according to its still retrograde standards.

Whatever his limitations, Neville was no mere administrator. After a false start during his Pembroke fellowship period, he had gone on to write two books that were both sterling contributions to scholarship. He had to transcend the misfortune of having got entangled in Alfred Marshall's tastes and ambitions. Marshall had encouraged him, in 1877, to write the book-length essay, ''The Effects of Machines on Wages,'' for a newly established university prize. This exercise in the inductive gathering of facts and statistics was not an appropriate subject for a master, as he would prove, of deductive logic; Neville expeditiously produced a substantial manuscript that failed to win the prize and disappeared without a trace.[29] For the period his only publication appears to have been an article on logic in the philosophical periodical, *Mind*, in July 1879.[30] On 5 July 1883, precisely one month after Maynard was born, having meanwhile been named head lecturer on logic at Girton College, Neville noted that he was ''beginning to write small book of Problems and Exercises in Formal Logic.''[31]

With his impeccable judgment and luminously clear mind, Neville easily defined and attained his objectives. On 18 August, less than six weeks after he began, he had formulated 216 questions. leaving a projected 53 to write. A month less a day later he had achieved 373 questions, with ''none'' remaining. He specified that he had ''nearly but not quite finished the book''; he was working on a ''General Solution.''[32] On 22 November he recorded having sent the complete manuscript to the publisher; on 13 February 1884, its publication.[33] His other book, while sharing all the excellences of the first, was not so swiftly produced.

Alfred Marshall was heavily responsible for the creation—and its lenteurs— of Neville's *The Scope and Method of Political Economy*.[34] Marshall had arranged that Neville give a series of weekly lectures on the subject at Oxford for the summer term (April to June) of 1885; once again, economically, Neville proposed to write up his lectures and turn them into a book. He began on 28 March of that year.[35] He had to be careful, however, not to invade Marshall's domain as Britain's commanding economist. Rather, as Neville knew, his project, by outlining the correct thought process, was to support Marshall's project, which was to secure his command by laying down what was to be thought. Neville was still working on his first chapter eighteen months later.[36] He completed a draft by 1888, but Marshall wanted much more attention paid to the Germans: more delay, because in the circumstances, counsel was command. (Neville, furthermore, did not know German, but Florence, who did, could help him.) He was also expending his time collegially reading and commenting on the draft of Marshall's *Principles of Economics*,[37] the massive foundation of partial equilibrium analysis and, more generally, of neoclassical economics in Great Britain. On 24 July 1890, he tersely noted having Marshall's newly published "book to hand"; it was a "very handsome volume." Neville's book was published on 17 January 1891.[38]

While Marshall erected a grand synthesis of economics, Neville Keynes had laid down the principles of thinking in general and in economics. Accurately if not expansively, Marshall wrote him that the logic was a " 'beautiful specimen of thorough Cambridge work and likely to be of very great service.' " Léon Walras, the great creator of *general* equilibrium analysis and a grander synthesis than Marshall's, wrote a "charming note," saying of the political economy that he was "frappé de votre connaissance approfondie . . . et du jugement sur et délicat."[39] Both Neville's books were received with almost universal praise and, each going into four editions, widely used.

The first book built the most exquisitely precise syllogisms on a sturdy foundation of clear sense; the second applied the same approach to economics while carefully balancing the rigors of deduction with due regard, despite Neville's strength in deductive logic, to the wealth of materials contributed by inductive findings. As late as 1915 Neville could note, "Both my books have been selling quite satisfactorily." He could happily add, referring to his son's first published work, "Maynard's book appears to be sold out."[40] The only defect of Neville's books lay in their self-evident character, once properly understood—but only then. The "most modest man imaginable" in Geoffrey Keynes's fair estimation,[41] his father had constructed two monuments of unobtrusiveness so perfect that their author was virtually forgotten. He was, however, well remembered by Joseph A. Schumpeter, the brilliant economist and erudite historian of economic thought, who was a contemporary of Maynard's. Schumpeter credited Neville's political economy with resolving most of the "methodological issues" troubling English economics "in a spirit of judicial reasonableness and to the satisfaction of the profession."[42] The logic book should be required reading for all college students, and the political economy for all economics students. Seriously taken, they would reduce much of the nonsense that passes for elevated or profound wisdom in academia. Maynard Keynes devoted his best thought to overthrow these expressions of Neville Keynes's best thought, but, given the absolutely different life purposes of father and son, this is to the discredit of neither.

If Neville was modest, he did not undervalue himself. Indeed, he had carefully delimited and defended his sphere of action and kept to it for the rest of his life. In his scholarship he had been a completer and a summarizer—in the first instance, of Aristotelian logic, and in the second, of the methodology of the new science of economics. He had nothing more to say except for a few precisions limited to revising his logic book thoroughly and to contributing a few articles to the *Dictionary of Political Economy* of his friend Inglis Palgrave; he wisely kept his silence. He could go on working hard and quietly as administrator while continuing as lecturer for some years. Unlike many able fathers, he left Maynard all the space a son needed to become the greater man (and provided his two other children with the nourishment to become first-rate persons and achievers).

Neville had to withstand extreme pressure to keep to the identity he chose for himself. From 1884 to 1889 Marshall, enlisting Florence Keynes as well as powerful university personages, tried to make him a greater figure in the institutionalization of Marshallian economics. At the end of 1884, before Marshall left Oxford to assume the professorship of political economy at Cambridge the next year, he urged Neville to lecture on economics as his replacement at that other university—with the prospect of a professorship there in perhaps three years. On a visit to Cambridge, accompanied by his economist wife, Marshall moved Florence to write a letter to Neville expressing more ambition for him than he had himself: "Of course, we should both very much dislike the thought of leaving Cambridge—but your work must be considered first of all—& you might have more congenial work at Oxford. . . . And as long as we had each other & the boy we could get on anywhere."[43] Marshall had emphasized, as Florence told Neville, that he was wasting his time on Local Examinations " 'while there is such a fine career there for the right man.' " After noting this in his diary Neville objected definitively, as he thought, "I cannot at present feel that my chances of success at Oxford are sufficient to warrant me giving up what I have at Cambridge." Marshall shouldered his way past Neville's refusal. He pursued his first effort with two letters and two telegrams, and when they failed to budge Neville, got him, at least, to take the weekly, one-term lecture assignment at Oxford that led to his political-economy book.[44] Neville found Oxford "handsomer and more imposing" than Cambridge and the master (head) of Balliol College liked his lectures. In two letters in June 1885 Marshall, having got Neville physically in Oxford, tried to keep him there, proposing that he accept the master's offer of three more such one-term assignments, with the professorship always in prospect. Neville returned a double negative.[45] When Oxford's professor of political economy conveniently died, in January 1888, Marshall seized the opportunity to impel Neville to compete for the post; Neville was probably relieved to lose out to an economic historian.[46] Marshall persisted. In 1887, when the creation of the *Economic Journal* as the profession's organ in Great Britain was in progress, a colleague urged Neville to take the editorship; he refused. Noting this in his diary, he added, "Alfred Marshall, however, pressed me very strongly . . . to reconsider the question." Reluctant to give up other work for it, he refused again.[47] In 1888, Marshall returning to the charge, Neville countered that it would "worry me beyond measure."[48] Ten months later he recorded Marshall's last effort and, anxious obstinacy having defeated unfeeling persistence, his own ultimate refusal.[49] Marshall would get his way— with Maynard.

However tactful and modest, Neville could assert himself aggressively for principle and himself in critical circumstances. In May 1882, shortly before he married Florence, he had a "serious row" with the head of Pembroke College. It was just after the "Phoenix Park murders," the assassination of the chief secretary for Ireland and his deputy as agents of Prime Minister William E. Gladstone's policy. Neville had wanted to "enter a bottle of Champagne in honor of Gladstone," who was attempting, in the face of such violence, to grant Home Rule to Ireland. This was the gesture of a loyal Liberal to defend Gladstone, although Neville actually deplored the idea of Home Rule. His action enraged the master of Pembroke: " '[H]e is responsible for these murders.' " This was precisely what Neville was denying. His account, quoting himself, continued, " 'I am pained and disgusted to hear you talk like that.' Master: 'You will not make the entry in the fine book.' Keynes: 'I am doing so.' " "Of course we hardly spoke during dinner."[50]

In his own interest Neville, like a successful general, preferred to avoid committing himself to an action unless he could could put overwhelmingly superior forces into the field and be sure to win. Even then, with his profound pessimism, he was never sure. In late 1887 friends, on the strength of his logic book and his fine teaching, were urging him to apply for a doctorate. (In English academia then it was a rare distinction, granted only for exceptional contributions; his son never got it.) Less confident than his friends, Neville refused to make the attempt. It was only after the reassuring reception of his political economy, on 3 May 1891, that he risked an application. On 9 June he got his D.Sc.[51] He approached the registraryship in the same manner.

As the year 1910 opened Neville was "feeling v. much depressed and dreaded[ed] the burden of the coming term." Surely the main reason, although he mentioned another as well, was "the registraryship question."[52] He knew that the registrary was dying and that, having done most of the man's work for years, he was, in all his modesty, the logical successor. On 28 January he noted forebodingly that his man was "very ill." There was nothing for it but to position himself appropriately to avoid the humiliation of failure as much as to achieve an earned consummation. In March he speculated that Trinity College would propose a candidate; that was threatening, because, as he later specified, Trinity men had held the registrary position for eighty years.[53] For most of 1910 the ghost of a Trinity candidate flitted through his consciousness, although, as it turned out, he was the only person who took it seriously. Unobtrusively, Neville began his campaign. Preparing to go to Hungary on holiday later that month, he dined with a close friend in June and discussed modalities if the registrary died while he was away. Formidably, he had told one hesitant candidate that he intended "to stand" and got his assurance that he would therefore not.[54] After an "enjoyable [trip] with many novel experiences," Neville returned to find the registrary successively "v. ill again," much better physically but afflicted with "all kinds of hallucinations," and then "clear in his mind but . . . v. ill."[55] On 15 September another possible candidate withdrew; word came that the registrary would resign on 1 October; Neville began to write letters requesting support. On Sunday, 18 September, he recorded: "Wrote hard all day with Florence's help." She was writing the addresses while he composed the letters. They continued in this manner for several days. He later noted, "I shall have written with my own hand not much short of 1,000 letters."[56] Meanwhile he organized a support committee among his university friends. By 20 September, after many positive indications, he was cautiously reporting on the absence of a Trinity candidate and indeed of all competition. On 24 September, he was secure enough to take Florence away for a week of golfing. On 1 October, the registrary's resignation in hand, the Council of the Senate fixed the date of the election of a successor, the vice-chancellor taking the occasion to praise Neville's work as Council secretary: "I am glad that Florence and Margaret were in the Senate House." Neville was thinking of organizing a second support committee although wife and daughter thought it unnecessary. Two days later he decided that the "safest course" was nevertheless to "issue a second committee list." That night he had a "rather violent attack of diarrhea," for him the frequent accompaniment of strain.[57] He was presently "depressed at the idea of leaving the Syndicate Building," where he had reigned over Local Examinations so contentedly and so long. On 12 October he was elected registrary without opposition: "It is delightful the extreme cordiality with which my election appears to be received by everybody."[58] He never gave further evidence of ambition.

In Maynard's celebration of his father, which will require more note than this second reference, he proceeded to mention Neville's later "withdrawal, gradual, very gradual, to his dear wife and the bosom of his family."[59] Florence, meanwhile, was moving acceleratingly outward, perhaps to equilibrate the modesty of ambition that prefigured her husband's withdrawal. Her first movements were modest and in the form of enriching her personal culture. In 1885 she attended Alfred Marshall's first lectures as professor of political economy at Cambridge.[60] She was still very much a mother, unhappily obeying the doctor to wean Margaret in three months and, two years later, much more happily nursing Geoffrey more than six months. Neville found her "so cheerful and happy.... Nursing seems to suit her."[61] In 1888, mother and leader, she presided efficiently over a mothers' tea meeting of two hundred.[62] She was, as ever, the companiable, supportive wife, Neville finding her "perfect" on their seventeenth wedding anniversary in 1889: "Every year I love her more and feel more dependent on her."[63] In 1890 she was working up her German to help with Neville's political economy.[64] By that year she was a member of the Charity Organization Society, which provided small pensions for the worthy indigent. In 1891 Neville recorded her "giving her women a lecture on the first year of a child's life. Her lectures always seem to be a great success."[65] The next year she gave readings from John Bunyan, her father's subject, at the Cambridge Railway Mission.[66] In 1895 Neville remarked on her "wonderful progress with her Italian," but more forebodingly, "She has consented, rather against my wish, to be secretary of the Charity Organization Society." Two years later he wanted her to give up or reduce her work with the society: "too much to do and too many things to worry her."[67] The worry was his.

Fairly launched, Florence became an increasingly active leader in Cambridge social work and, inevitably, community affairs generally. In the early 1900s she helped establish a juvenile employment agency and a residence for tuberculosis sufferers. Almost always in good health, in contrast to Neville, she joined him in submitting to an attack of influenza in early 1907 and, while he recovered quickly, endured a year and a half of relapses into feeling poorly.[68] In March 1907, nevertheless, she successfully ran for a seat on the Board of Guardians, which oversaw the Poor Law administration; in 1910 she was reelected without opposition.[69] Beyond Cambridge, in 1912, she took part in forming the National Union of Women Workers, which she chaired for a period, while going on to serve as the president of the National Council of Women in 1930–31. One of her rare failures occurred when the Cambridge Conservatives opposed her as vice-chair of the Board of Guardians, an action that Neville found "very disgraceful."[70] She was also giving lectures on such subjects as voluntary aid, state relief, and unemployment, a complex of problems pointing specifically to eventual concerns of Maynard.[71] In October 1914, the first woman elected to it, she ran unopposed for a seat on the Cambridge Borough Council.[72] By that time she was extremely busy with the new demands of the World War, Neville continually complaining that she was overexerting herself and suggesting that she was not paying him quite as much attention as a loving husband needed. At the end of 1915 he found "Florence . . . full of business of various kinds." With the war taking away most of the university's students, Neville listed the lowest number of hours he had worked in any year since beginning as administrator: "not unnaturally the easiest year I have had."[73] The war, which depressed Neville profoundly while challenging Florence, marked the beginning of his withdrawal and decline even as she expanded her activities. Neville's diary stops at the end of 1917. Perhaps that was part of his decline. In 1932 she became Cambridge's first woman mayor.

In 1902, to Neville's eventual regret, Florence got a bicycle as a birthday present. (Seven years earlier Maynard's birthday bicycle collided with a hansom cab and the little finger of his right hand was injured and slightly deformed.[74]) Neville himself, complaining about the problem of getting on and off a bicycle,[75] appears never to have mastered it. Florence, however, found it ideal for attending to her diverse duties scattered over Cambridge's flat terrain. (Despite narrow streeets and automobiles, the bicycle remains a favored form of locomotion today, particularly for university students, who are not permitted to operate automobiles in town.) Between 1912 and 1915, with increasing apprehension, Neville recorded Florence's experience of a round half-dozen bicycle accidents causing a "strained foot," bruises, and vein damage.[76] In 1914, regarding the damaged vein, his diary entry insisted, "I feel quite clear that she must not bicycle in Cambridge any more." That was not quite a command and Florence persisted. In October 1915, making him "more anxious about her bicycling," her arm was "rather badly hurt" and, five weeks later, she had another "tumble." In 1916 they found a compromise formula: "Florence says she can't get through her work unless she bicycles a little; but she promises it shall be as little as possible."[77] No counterforce could halt the progress of Florence Ada Brown Keynes, total wife and mother (if a bit distant) and total feminist (even if she never recognized the fact).

Whatever distractions, Neville and Florence created a warm, enlivening, and utterly secure home for their children. To the south were open fields; to the north, the lively university town with many other adults and children like themselves. Harvey Road itself was populated with a concentration of academic families. Neville and Florence were fluently hospitable, receiving an unending train of guests staying overnight, a week, or even longer. On Sundays, Neville carved the roast for family, particularly Florence's siblings and their children, and friends, including increasingly numerous friends of the children.

Engaging in a succession of hobbies and games, surely diversions from a more demanding use of his time, Neville contributed a wealth of amusements to life at home. He had been an excellent chess player as a boy and young man, a sport which failed to interest any of the children, however; he let it slip away for other activities, although not before his thirty-seventh year, when he defeated a former national amateur champion in a London match.[78] He had once collected stamps and was encouraging three-year-old Maynard to do the same. By February 1887, "Maynard [was] much interested in his collection of stamps." In March Neville found him already more sophisticated on the subject. Later that March he noted, "In my old age I have actually begun stamp collecting again."[79] (He continued thus into his nineties; Maynard dropped stamps in his early teens.)[80] By 1895 Neville had eight thousand stamps, which Maynard valued at £2,000 and which Neville insured for £600. Their catalogue value was £4,865 seven years later.[81] If interesting Maynard in stamps brought Neville back to them, the nine-year-old Geoffrey, a science-minded collector, was himself responsible for initiating his father's pursuit of butterflies. (Geoffrey also dug out and classified Pleistocene bones in a river bed near Cambridge.) From 1905 Neville and Geoffrey undertook seven entomological expeditions into the Swiss and Tirolean Alps, the Pyrenees, and Hungary. In 1911 Florence went along to the Tirol and enjoyably, Neville thought, caught more than one hundred butterflies herself. At home father and son carefully mounted their specimens in proper cabinets Neville ordered for the purpose; the collection was kept for the grandchildren and then donated to the university's zoological museum. Geoffrey has documented his "gratitude to my father for giving me so much enjoyment."[82] If Neville dropped chess, he entered into whist and bridge, and organized the Harvey Road Book Club.[83] A fair athlete, he played tennis and became a committed golfer after a friend "gave Florence and me our first lesson in golf" on 20 September 1892.[84] Florence occasionally joined Neville, but, more often he got Maynard to play, although his son was, in the judgment of a university classmate, the second worst golfer he knew.[85] A few years after Neville's introduction to the game, he played in the rain on one occasion, incidentally accompanied by Maynard, instead of attending two committee meetings. He washed away his guilt with an easy confession: "I felt very wicked."[86] He set a balanced example of work and play, but Maynard would upset that balance in his own life.

Theirs was a reading and writing family. Neville and Florence read the classics and the better contemporary novels, and even Ibsen's plays. Florence frequently read aloud to Neville while he arranged his stamp collection; and both read to the children. When apart (the children beginning quite young) everybody in the family wrote to everybody else, although in the earlier years Florence was content to let Neville do most of the writing for her. The family letters, like Neville's diaries, yield almost no indication of the nastier feelings, no envy or jealousy, no sense of any child's feeling neglected or cheated. On his parents' example Maynard took little advantage of his status as the brightest and firstborn and supported rather than bullied the younger ones. Not quite six, he commented reflectively, "Geoffrey and Margaret are quite the most precious things in the house." After Margaret, following Maynard, had gone off to boarding school, Neville noted, "We miss Maynard and Margaret very much." A week later: "Geoffrey is very much amused because we read Maynard's and Margaret's letters so many times: 'Curious old creatures.' "[87] They were all nice to each other almost all the time.

It is true that, as Geoffrey remembered in his high old age, he felt that he "lived under the shadow of a far more forceful and intellectual character" in Maynard. Yet he did not much exaggerate by saying that their parents, with their "lovable aura of perfect integrity and goodness," were "always ready to further any worthwhile interests as soon as they discerned them."[88] Neville's entry into Geoffrey's entomology went even beyond this. At the age of three Geoffrey decided he would be a doctor; from that moment his parents unhesitatingly encouraged him to do so. That moment became an episode in the doubtless often recounted family history: his mother found him studying a book with diagrams of blood circulation—appropriate reading on Harvey Road. The real test of parental understanding was Margaret.

After Geoffrey had won a prize at Rugby and closed some of the distance between Maynard and himself, Margaret commented cheerily that she was "glad to hear about Geoffrey." Referring to herself, she remarked, "It is unfortunate to be the one brainless one of the family."[89] That was an expression of security, not self-denigration; the mature Geoffrey characterized her as a "strong personality with much originality and humor."[90] The only child who seems ever to have failed a test, she required an extra year to make good her failure to win her certificate on completing her studies at Wycombe Abbey, her boarding school. Neville recorded the failure and the success without comment.[91] Daughter of one of the first students of Newnham, she was evidently never pressed to qualify for it, never subjected to insidious comparison, except of her own humorous doing, while her brothers got the encouragement fitting their potentials. Happy in a special relationship with her mother and in a series of friendships, Margaret was allowed her identity, with skills in crafts and in such pleasurable pursuits as hockey, lacrosse, rowing, and riding, this last begun with a series of

Margaret (age 4), Geoffrey (age 2½), and Maynard (age 6) Keynes in 1889. Photo courtesy of Milo Keynes.

lessons as a birthday present.[92] About the hockey, the fifteen-year-old Etonian Maynard, perhaps paternally, certainly reflecting his own competitive spirit, wanted to know, "How are you . . . compared to the other girls?"[93] He was blandly ignoring the fact of his athletic inferiority, compared to her. In her first year at Wycombe Abbey she found almost everything "awful fun" in a letter beginning exuberantly, "My dear dear dear Mother" and demanding, "I should like another of those big nice letters."[94] After she left school, her parents sent her off to Germany to learn the language at least, but then she was called back to teach bookbinding for a term.[95] Resettled at Harvey Road, inexigently, she followed her mother into social work, in 1907 entering the Juvenile Employment Exchange, which Florence Keynes had helped found. In 1911 Margaret wrote a "most appreciated" paper, "The Problem of Boy Labour in Cambridge," which Maynard, while as proper don demanding clarification on two points, fraternally and perhaps professionally found "extraordinarily good."[96] After marriage and motherhood she would return to social work, this time dealing with the elderly, and become a borough councillor in a town near London. She was later appointed a member of a royal commission concerned with social and industrial policy. In 1937, regarding this last, Maynard could helpfully write her to introduce herself as his sister to Ernest Bevin, the labor leader (and future foreign secretary), with whom he had cordially worked on industrial policy.[97] Actually, while or because favoring him, Neville was harder on Maynard than on Margaret or Geoffrey.

The story of Neville and Maynard, with its intensities of intimacy and emotion, penetrated beyond the general familial niceness into disturbing ambiguity. The membrane between father and this child was thinner than between Neville and spouse or other child, and a great complex of feeling, thought, and example passed through with little inhibition except tact, but tact cannot impede the more insistent communications. As already mentioned, Neville overflowed with depression and ailments. He also expressed himself in dutiful-pleasurable Victorian cruelty.

Anticipating their first child, Neville found, "We are so happy" and wondered, "Are we *too* happy? Do we need the discipline of suffering?" He had to dilute the happiness with doubt. Five days after his birth, "I felt rather depressed. The thought haunted me that Maynard might not grow up sturdy in mind and body." Neville was in fact right about the body. A half-year later, with his logic book in process of publication, "I began the New Year with a headache, and felt generally rather depressed."[98] The depression, along with similarly expressive ailments, accompanied Neville through the years. He had long suffered from odd facial aches; on 16 April 1884, drastically, all his upper teeth were pulled, relieving that distress. Other distresses followed. On 1 February 1885, he recorded "shooting pains in my chest and back lately" and wondered how long he had to live. He could not tell Florence, then ready to give birth for the second time. It was a very brief labor, which, however, exhausted her, and the doctor frightened Neville by speculating about possible

heart failure. He proposed tragically, "I would a hundred times more die myself." On 5 January 1886, he remained in bed until midday with a "bad nervous
headache"; the headaches continued through the years, interspersed, as he noted
later in 1886, with "my customary bilious attacks." At the end of February
1887, as part of his meticulous record-keeping, he calculated having worked
222 hours: "That is my best month's record." He was feeling better lately: "It
seems to suit me." But in May he endured "rheumatic pain" in his shoulders,
followed by back pains, with the rheumatic pain—"rather bad"—reappearing
in November.[99] His headaches were often in the migraine class, "megrims" he
called them, sometimes accompanied by diarrhea. In 1912, well established as
registrary, he endured a "violent" migraine attack making him "unable to see
at all next day" and leaving his eyes "still queer" two days later.[100] Psychic
agony could exceed these pains.

On 18 August 1907, Neville's mother died. He felt terribly guilty for having
failed to express his love to her sufficiently, he thought. He wept every morning.
Exceptionally, "It tries Florence a good deal." He vowed, "But this shall be
the last time." Two and a half months later Neville was still "feeling terribly
depressed. Florence . . . urges me to fight against it. But it seems beyond my
control."[101] This was when she was suffering her extended period of ill health.
If sad events caused Neville's depression, so did the blessings and triumphs. On
24 April 1896, he noted "a great many congratulations" on the success of a
conference he had organized: "And yet I feel somewhat depressed." In this
fashion he endured into his ninety-eighth year.

Unusually in the case of a first child, Neville had wanted a girl. He wrote his
mother, "This was rather a blow." Inaccurately, "They say that the boy is the
image of me. It's ugly enough." This impression of ugliness seems, as will be
evident, to have been communicated to Maynard. "I have thrown over the work
I had for today," Neville continued, "Florence is beginning to nurse the child
herself. They look happy together." The next day, confronting and waving away
his first impression, "I am already getting very fond of him notwithstanding his
ugliness. . . . I could sit and look at him for hours."[102] The desired girl was
forgotten, or rather, conflated into this entrancing boy, and the real girl child
was received almost casually. A year later Florence was pregnant too soon,
Neville thought, with what he now easily expected to be that girl: "We did not
want the little sister quite so soon."[103] Margaret, born on 4 February 1885, was
not as seductively bright and interestingly problematic as Maynard, with his
early evidences of fragile health to confirm Neville's dire premonitions.[104] Indeed, "She looks fat and strong with a neck and back like a young bull."[105]
On Maynard's second birthday, five months later, Neville could not forbear to
record, "We love that boy more than ever."[106] In one entry the next month,
Neville contrasted Maynard's intriguing distresses, so like his own, with Margaret's rather cloying excellences: "Maynard feels the heat and is a little crabbed. Margaret is very good & sweet." He might go on to assert emphatically,

"I am getting *very* fond of little Margaret" and "Little Margaret is now a most bonny child."[107] In no way did that threaten Maynard's position.

The father–son relationship ramified variously until it was time for Maynard to leave for Eton at the age of fourteen. Neville and Maynard had joined in more and more activities: stamp collecting, chess and backgammon, golf, visits to the theater—and work. Maynard experienced and, on occasion, joined in discussions on questions of logic with W. E. Johnson, Neville's expert friend, when Neville was revising his first book.[108] Although he was acutely sensitive to noise and disturbances, Neville nevertheless established Maynard's desk in his study, and for years both labored companionably and efficiently together at their separate tasks. On 14 April 1897, Maynard bicycled to Bedford to spend a few days at his grandparents' home; three days later Neville anticipated what was to come: "I miss Maynard very much. It is not merely the stamping, but altogether." After the summer, "I shall never again have the dear boy so much with me."[109] Immediately before the Eton scholarship examinations, Neville recurred to the thought: "It is a grief to me to think that the dear boy will not ... do his work very much longer with me in the study. I like to see his books arranged opposite me; and I like all his little ways."[110] "Little ways" was anachronistic: at the beginning of the year Maynard was almost at Neville's height; by early June he had gained three inches.[111] Maynard's establishment at Eton would permit the intimacy to be maintained at a degree sufficiently satisfying for Neville while tolerable for the boy himself. That intimacy deserves a second viewing before he leaves home. The years of working together had strengthened the father–son, and weakened the mother–son, bond. Neville had profoundly conditioned Maynard in the conveniences and security of homoerotic relations. It seems inevitable that he act out that conditioning in the single-sex ambiance of Eton.

Affected in another way by his close contact with Neville, Maynard lived dramatically under the lifelong threat of ill health, the threat later taking the form of a cardiac condition that ultimately killed him. In February 1919, while the thirty-five-year-old Maynard Keynes was at the Paris Peace Conference as principal Treasury representative, reports of his undergoing a serious attack of influenza "were beginning to alarm" a friend in London until a letter from him provided reassurance that he was not "at death's door. ... You have such a habit of almost dying, my dear Maynard, that one of these days one fears you will do it tout de bon."[112] The friend was percipient. Perversely, he survived that attack, although many millions died then in the world's greatest epidemic.

Maynard had begun life small, scrawny, and fragile, "the little shrimp," Neville fondly and fearfully called him.[113] On 7 April 1886, when he was not quite three and Margaret, fourteen months old, Neville found his weight to be thirty pounds, compared with twenty-seven for her: "There ought to be much more difference."[114] At fourteen years, as mentioned above, Maynard began to shoot up toward his eventual height of six feet. This placed additional strain on his health. For his first three years he had suffered from Neville's chronic complaint of diarrhea. Thereafter into maturity Maynard endured "feverish attacks," unexplained onsets of high temperatures, and, for all of his life, frequent colds or, as in 1919, more debilitating attacks of what appeared to be influenza. All this prepared the way for the heart problem.

Neville's diary is a continuing report of Maynard's lapses from normal health, much like his own but worse, if not more frequent. Neville and Florence were up the whole night of 27–28 December 1884, because a vague but frightening illness had befallen Maynard; he did not recover for a week.[115] In February 1885 he endured four or five days of fever and coughing.[116] It was in the summer of that year that he was "crabbed" because of the heat that did not disturb Margaret. In 1886, while his health seemed better despite his laggard growth, another warning signal appeared: "Maynard's stammering rather troubles us. He is an excitable little man."[117] Although it gradually declined, the stammering continued into early manhood. On 4 August 1887, "Maynard continues poorly." The next day, "Maynard kept in bed all day." Three days later, "Maynard has got over his feverish attack. But he is very thin and eats hardly anything." In contrast, Geoffrey, four and a half months old, was flourishing without the crying they had experienced with Maynard; result: "capital nights."[118] (I was not able to consult Neville's diary for 1888.) In the first half of 1889 Maynard got through whooping cough, "a succession of his ordinary feverish attacks" ("but he is lively as a cricket"), and a spell of pains in the heart region.[119] These last did not recur and were forgotten. Other distresses appeared.

In late January 1889 the five-and-a-half-year-old boy entered the kindergarten of the Perse School for Girls. By October his parents were "rather worried about Maynard lately." He had been having "dreadful twitchings about his eyes."[120] A teacher suggested he be removed from school and kept " 'absolutely idle for a time.' " The family doctor, agreeing, diagnosed a "slight form of chorea" (St. Vitus' Dance).[121] Maynard returned to the kindergarten, but was removed again, in January 1891, Neville confiding no reason in his diary, but a governess carried on at home. After a year he entered St. Faith's Preparatory School, where he would prepare successfully for Eton. Although two years younger than the class average,[122] Maynard found the work enjoyable. The ambitious schoolmaster, given a receptive pupil, heaped too much work on him too fast, Neville thought, but his repeated adjurations were too half-hearted to have much effect on the man.[123] In the fall of 1893, more effectively, Maynard was removed from St. Faith's for a term and sent to his grandmother Brown in Bedford, where she reopened her school for him. That relieved the stress but Neville complained that Maynard was "not quite up to the mark. Perhaps Florence pays too much attention to his ailments; but at Bedford they go to the opposite extreme . . . laughing at him when he professes himself not well."[124]

Back at St. Faith's, Maynard enjoyed a remission from most of his ills and, now easily mastering the work, went to the head of his class. Approaching entry into Eton, however, he suffered a chill and "feverish attacks," arriving there three days late.[125] When Neville visited him two weeks later, he found him with a bad cold, and on Maynard's first holiday home, he also arrived late, having been "rather seedy for some days."[126] Indeed Eton, although much improved from its rigors (and horrors) of the earlier part of the century, was still ill-heated and drafty, as Maynard complained, and, weakened by his swift growth, he suffered a series of colds as well as his fever "periodicals," as he began to refer to them.[127] Nevertheless he became an outstanding student and engaged enthusiastically in such strenuous sports as rowing and the Wall Game, "the most brutish and least elegant mutation of football,"[128] which was played not infrequently on a field of mud. And so it went: intermittences of ill health but great achievements and many normal schoolboy activities.

As in his arrival at Eton, ill health continued to strike down the young and older Maynard Keynes at crucial moments in his crowded, achieving life. At the beginning of 1914 he took a holiday from his intense labors and the concomitant fatigue as a member of a governmental commission and bolted for the casinos of the French Riviera. On 14 January Neville got a telegram followed by a postcard from him saying he was ill, possibly with diphtheria (which was soon confirmed). Two letters of Maynard's addressed to his mother, which may have arrived later, specified a temperature of 103 and a doctor's "gloomy view." The family specialist for medical matters and emergencies generally, she left for France that evening, arriving the following midnight, "a horrid journey—in such cold weather," Neville commiserated in Cambridge. Too infectious to be approached for the moment, Maynard wrote his mother, "I feel ashamed to have brought you here." Nevertheless right reason could see much need for her: "However, I shall be very glad to have you, and I believe one is really more in need of comfort when convalescent than when moribund."[129] Mother and recovering son returned to Cambridge on 30 January. Three weeks later Maynard was suffering from paralysis of the soft palate as a lingering effect of the episode but back at his various activities.[130] On 11 June 1915, Florence found herself again nursing Maynard, now in the Treasury and befallen by acute appendicitis. It was acute enough to require an emergency operation the next day on the kitchen table of his London flat. Functioning also as his secretary, she remained in London to see that he had properly recovered—and on 23 June a new distress was diagnosed: pneumonia. The effects were grave enough to keep him out of his office at the Treasury until August, Neville also coming to London and, like Florence, also doing his son's secretarial work.[131] The effects also included damage to Maynard's heart, which, Roy Harrod wrote, "were to have serious consequences twenty-two years later."[132] (Actually, it was sooner than that, but not recognized at the time.) In Paris in 1919, after recovering from his influenza earlier that year, Maynard took to his bed in May out of exhaustion and protest against the peace terms, but he rose to write his notorious *Economic Consequences of the Peace* and enter upon a more elevated career, more accurately, complex of careers. In the 1920s his health was better, although with the usual colds and influenza. In late October 1931, after attacks of tonsillitis *and* influenza, he suffered a more ominous onslaught of "the most dreadful pain in my chest" and related symptoms, all suggestive of angina pectoris but not diagnosed as such.[133] He probably ignored slighter recurrences, but began feeling similar pain, along with breathlessness, in the summer of 1936. (He had published his *General Theory of Employment, Interest and Money* in February.) In May 1937 he suffered his almost fatal heart attack but rose again, and energetically denying that he was a cardiac invalid, made six exhausting as well as otherwise dangerous wartime trips to the United States as financial negotiator and joint architect of the future international monetary order. He had his ultimate heart attack on Easter Sunday 1946.

Maynard Keynes's ills, like Neville's, had their psychic side in the form of depression and related humors. The boy's twitching and stammering were signals of distress. While insisting that Maynard was "normally cheerful, witty, and full of self-confidence," Geoffrey Keynes appended that he "occasionally had fits of adolescent depression, what he called 'natural sadness.' "[134] Young Maynard had precocious skills in rationalization; it was not natural at all. Neville recorded a few instances of this "sadness," but the first one I found, describing the ten-year-old boy, suggests that they had begun much earlier and were habitual: besides enduring a "feverish attack," the boy was "more depressed than usual."[135] When Maynard as university student dropped in at 6 Harvey Road for tea, "I thought he seemed just a little depressed." At the end of his undergraduate period, a year later, "Maynard is tired and depressed. We are worried about him."[136] Quite possibly it was depression (and Neville's proximity) that made Maynard reject Alfred Marshall's encouragement to continue his postgraduate study of economics in Cambridge, and instead enter government service. "I could probably get employment here. . . . But," he wrote a friend in an uncharacteristically and dramatically desperate mood, "prolonging my existence in this place would be, I feel sure, death."[137] Another friend found him at a low point in October 1914 after a soon repaired failure to find a position in the wartime Treasury and the breaking up of a communal house shared with friends. "[F]earfully lonely in his [new] rooms," he had sagged into depression and was "bitterly" reflecting on a lost love.[138] Thereafter the depressions appear to abate, the maturing Keynes usually managing to keep too busy to have the leisure for them. (The 1914 episode emphasizes what could happen when, exceptionally, he had that leisure.) He was a hard worker like his father, but unlike him, became compulsive, setting no bounds to his activities. While lifting those activities to the level of world-historical importance, that characteristic became thus a substitute pathology, with its private, non-negotiable price.

Depression, as Nietzsche and Freud analyze it, is a result of unvented anger and aggression. Maynard had something about which to be angry and someone with whom to be angry: humiliating chastisement and Neville. This is not to deny another possible factor: depression as effect of insufficient maternal loving. Of course Florence loved her son deeply, but did her somewhat distant persona communicate it?

Besides striking and slapping him, Neville whipped the boy. I have found four instances reported in the diaries over a period of three years, when Maynard was two and a half to five and a half.[139] ("Whipped" is Neville's—and Florence's—term; they did not specify the instrument.) There may well have been more occasions—in his biography Robert Skidelsky fixes the whippings (along with "frequent slappings") from "Maynard's second to seventh year"[140]—but these four exercises in the inflicting of pain and humiliation are enough to form a hard core of obscene Victorian horror in the father–son intimacy and in the life of the family. Although I did not find mentions of a whipped Geoffrey, always the "good" child, the spirited Margaret, at the age of a little over two and a half years, got at least one unqualified whipping.[141]

Florence opposed the whippings in specific instances and, implicitly, on principle. When one of them took place in her absence, she wrote, "I do not think I should have let you whip him, husb[and], if I had been at home." She pointed out that the active boy—Neville being hypersensitive to noise and other disturbances of his train of thought—had been kept in the nursery all day: "I don't wonder that he gets restive."[142] Another time she expressed herself more pathetically. Occurring on 7 September 1887, the episode, as Neville recounted it in his diary, is powerfully illustrative:

The little shrimp was naughty this morning & had to be whipped. He preserved his equanimity during the preliminaries. But he soon began to cry bitterly & then my heart smote me. Florence was nearly crying. He told her afterward that it stung him so & made him feel warm down there. I think it did him good. He was good for the rest of the day. He is a dear affectionate little man & kissed his hard-hearted father very affectionately soon after the punishment was over.

Perhaps Neville regarded Maynard's attitude this time as salutarily improved from that of the first whipping; "I whipped the little man because he would not go upstairs properly. He wept & looked very reproachful, but would not say he would be a good boy." In the year and a half since then Maynard had learned the limits of defiance.

One might try to imagine oneself as this two-and-one-half and four-year-old boy, whom his loving father had long convinced of his great value but suddenly hurt and, worse, humiliated. The punishment comes suddenly. The agent of punishment is this huge benign presence become magically, monstrously strange. Consider again the boy feeling "warm down there" and later kissing the destroyer of his dignity. Surely Maynard got a sense of orgasmic action that was more than punishment, surely Neville felt something more pleasurable than the satisfaction of doing his disagreeable duty. For some, spanking, known on the Continent as "the English vice," is a favorite form of sexual experience in the giving and the receiving. Three days after this episode Neville was "feeling capitally well, & my play at tennis is satisfactory."

Neville frequently shouldered past factors that should have exonerated the perpetrator, thus Maynard's restiveness from having been cooped up in the nursery all day. His last recorded whipping occurred on the day he entered kindergarten. Margaret's chastisement took place when, as Neville himself reported, she had become "troublesome" in the absense of her nursemaid.[143]

Sigmund Freud wrote a suggestive but frankly tentative essay, "A Child Is Being Beaten" (1919), about a fantasy reported by patients suffering from hysteria or obsessional neuroses. "The fantasy has feelings of pleasure attached to it," he reported; it had an "almost invariab[e] . . . climax [of] masturbatory satisfaction." His patients, however, "were very seldom beaten in their childhood." At all events the beatings were not the rule.[144] Yet this appended qualification permitted occasional whippings like Maynard's. In any case he *lived* the fantasy and continued it as fantasy variously. Thus, from Eton, where he had been beaten three times in one term, he would inquire of Geoffrey whether his brother had also been caned on his "natural cushion" at *his* boarding school. In purer imagination the middle-aged Keynes conceived of the philistine world kicking the bottom of Albert Einstein, a sympathetic acquaintance of 1926, with whom he clearly identified. Certainly being beaten preoccupied Keynes over an extended period at least intermittently. Other effects on the beaten child were more important.

The whippings stopped. The monster disappeared. Maynard found himself effectively closer—working in the same study—with an unremittingly affectionate, responsive, and tactful father anticipating as well as satisfying his needs and velleities. Neville seems to have made all decisions in his son's interest even when against his own. Thus he supported Maynard's departure from the university to enter the India Office although surely preferring that he stay, and when Maynard proposed to quit it to return to Cambridge, questioned that reversal—"I have argued with him in vain"—while refusing, despite Maynard's apparent demand for it, to impose a decision on him. A father's delicacy could hardly have been more exquisitely refined. Neville thought that Maynard would give up the idea if he expressed a definite opinion but refused to take "so decided a position." Nevertheless, Maynard "will be throwing up a certainty & taking risks. That fits in with his scheme of life, not with mine."[145] Properly, Maynard himself made the decision that suited his taste for risk-taking and Neville's carefully repressed desire.

The child-whipper showed great tolerance of the adolescent's irregularities and accepted the young adult's as given. Perhaps therapeutically, Maynard, on holiday from Eton, got into the lifelong habit of keeping to his bed late in the morning. (As an adult he did much of his work mornings in bed.) Indeed, when he was back at Cambridge as a student, Neville went to his rooms at King's College to waken him for the honors examination that Neville too apprehensively thought he might have slept through. Later, Neville rented a London flat and staffed it with Florence, Margaret, and, sometimes, himself to ease Maynard's passage through the civil-service examination. Neville wrote the index for Maynard's first published book, and conscientiously and encouragingly read the proofs of another early work, a study in logic rejecting the principles of his own 1884 work. How could one stop loving so loving, tactful, *and* useful a father? In his biography Donald Moggridge noted the various whippings in one sentence as "instances of disciplinary problems" and went on to address the increasing father–son intimacy.[146] In *his* biography Robert Skidelsky, mentioning the privileges enjoyed by the adolescent Maynard as well as the intimacy, would have "[t]he whippings long forgotten."[147] To this one can venture: if so, all the more important.

The anger—the rage—Maynard felt was expressed variously, covertly, and unrecognized by either when it approached Neville himself, openly and sometimes outrageously when directed against others. Consider another part of Maynard Keynes's celebration of his ninety-year-old father: "[E]legant, mid-Victorian, highbrow, reading Swinburne, Meredith, Ibsen, buying William Morris wallpaper, whiskers, modest and industrious, but rather rich, rather pleasure loving, rather extravagant within carefully set limits, most generous, very sociable, loved entertaining, wine, games, novels, theatre, travel. . . ."[148] The patronizing, faintly contemptuous note is clear enough. In another, no less hostile sense, the social scientist had clamped John Neville Keynes to the microscope's plate and lectured learnedly on the creature's magnified characteristics. Maynard never attacked Neville, but in 1911 told this "rather rich" person that he was "in favor of the confiscation of wealth," and in 1917, speculating on the dire effects of the war, wrote his mother (who had by then superseded Neville as chief correspondent of the two): "The abolition of the rich will be rather a comfort and serves them right anyhow."[149] More broadly, although he was an orthodox exponent of neoclassical economics and setting out himself to become rich, he nurtured unintegrated populistic-socialistic sympaties that would slowly merge with his economist's professional thinking. He found other seniors easier to attack than Neville.

Easily expressing contempt in the third person for father figures, from adolescence Maynard was as easily insulting—"rude," in English idiom—in second-person encounters with others. He did not directly attack Alfred Marshall but enjoyed despising him in a measured way, a sentiment uninhibited by Marshall's patronage of his career after he gave up on Neville. Maynard assured one friend that he might be a "very great man," but was "rather a silly one in his private character," and, on another instance, corrected Roy Harrod's respectful attitude: "He was an utterly absurd person, you know."[150] If Maynard could still write an exquisitely just obituary article on Marshall, his satirical portraits of David Lloyd George, Woodrow Wilson, and Georges Clemenceau, representative fathers of their countries at the Paris Peace Conference, are classics of mockery. Earlier, at a Treasury discussion, he had told Lloyd George, who, as chancellor of the exchequer then, had expatiated on the financial situation in France: "With the utmost respect, I must, if asked my opinion, tell you that I regard your account as rubbish."[151] About almost anyone else one would hesitate to repeat so unlikely a story, but, from an early age, Maynard had communicated such sentiments directly to the offending (in his eyes) party. While still at St. Faith's, thus at fourteen or younger, he formalized his detestation of another boy in a " 'commercial treaty' " with him, according to Geoffrey Keynes, providing that the boy "not approach [him] nearer than fifteen yards."[152] At Eton, while enjoying cordial relations with nearly all the masters, Maynard found one of them intolerably boring, however, and affected him in this manner: "Rather a provoking boy. . . . Reads notes when he should be attending to the lesson. Apt to talk to his neighbors unless severely repressed."[153] Not much later the master had a breakdown and left Eton. Roy Harrod, Keynes's protégé long before becoming biographer, granted, "There was something freezing and terrible about Maynard's [rudeness]." Inaccurately, he excused it as "employed selectively against victims deserving punishment."[154] Not so: while Keynes sometimes used it to blast through foolish opposition to a good action, it was frequently gratuitous. Isaiah Berlin first met Keynes when he found himself sitting next to him in the King's College dining hall and became the victim of his a priori crossness. After finding the menu unsatisfactory, as if Berlin were responsible, Keynes inquired into his presence there. When, as Berlin recalled, he said he was giving a paper afterward on pleasure, Keynes returned, "Pleasure? What a ridiculous subject." He then lapsed into silence.[155] More accurately, Harrod concluded on Keynes's rudeness, "It was not usually meant to be unforgivable, but was often not forgiven."[156] Sir Kenneth Clark, the art historian, worked with Keynes on the Arts Council, which Keynes, in his last years, directed to the nation's great cultural benefit. Clark explained the limits of their relations: "Although [he was] a kind man, I have seen him humiliate people in a cruel way."[157] Keynes had a great store of anger on which to draw.

The evidence suggests that a thick blanket of shame had been flung over the boy's anger, blocking all normal outlets and causing it to seethe for the rest of his life. Probably when they were eight and four years old, in any case at a late and self-conscious age for Maynard, he and Geoffrey were circumcised, a favorite Victorian means to inhibit masturbation.[158] One can imagine the suggestiveness of such an operation on this acutely aware, *whipped* boy. Certainly this castrationlike bloody attack on his tender masculinity related itself in his mind to the previous delicti that had caused him to be punished in a way that had "made him feel warm down there." All this could have made Maynard vulnerable to the thought that, as his father's first viewing saw him, he was ugly, indeed disgustingly repellent. In all probability the boy heard the story of Neville's early impression; he was well prepared to believe in his ugliness and uncleanliness. The six-year-old boy could then believe that he himself was the originator of the idea, Neville recording, "Maynard has quite made up his mind that he himself is remarkably ugly. He thinks no one was quite so ugly."[159] Almost twenty-three, Maynard explained to a friend his failure to press his suit on a potential lover: "My dear, I have always suffered . . . from a most unalterable obsession that I am so physically repulsive that I've no business to hurl my body on anyone else's." He had an acute sense of its a priori nature: "The idea is so constant that I don't think anything—certainly no argument—could ever shake it." He rephrased, "Well it may be lunacy but I can't help it."[160] The boy Maynard was not ugly at all. Rather, his early photographs show an elfin attractiveness much more intriguing than the perfect prettiness of both Margaret and Geoffrey. True, the Etonian with the downy upper lip is unappetizing, but that is the ugly-duckling phase that describes his contemporaries as well. The young man was neither handsome nor ugly. The face was an interesting, irregular assemblage of scoop nose, sensual lips, short chin, and grenadiers's mustache. With his stature and exquisitely modulated, impeccably accented voice, preceded by his reputation for cleverness and accompanied by an interested spirit, he could be impressive and even attractive. Whatever his triumphs, Maynard Keynes *felt* for much of his life at least that he was a vile body committing the unspeakable. He proceeded to commit more of it.

Surely the whippings and the unexpressed, hence boundless, shame of circumcision pointed the way toward Maynard's unabashed homosexuality. Anterior to these factors was the reversed Oedipal situation at home: the feminine emotiveness of Neville, the more manly restraint of Florence, and exclusively affecting Maynard, his period of working in his father's study. Maynard's siblings themselves gave suggestive indications of homosexuality.

Before her marriage at the rather late age of twenty-eight Margaret had entered into an intense relationship with Eglantyne Jebb (1876–1928), nine years older and the niece of a Cambridge classical scholar. Eglantyne began working with Florence Ada Keynes in the Cambridge Charity Organization Society in 1903 and would later organize an international children's aid society. Meanwhile, in 1907, Florence Ada suggested that Englantyne engage Margaret, who had not found her vocation, as her assistant. According to her biographer, Eglantyne was "irresistible . . . both to men and women. . . . The younger woman soon fell under her spell and . . . threw herself . . . into social work."[161] From mid-1910 to 1913, Neville's diaries carried at least sixteen references to Eglantyne, often as Margaret's house guest or traveling companion. He was noncommital except for calling her "a very bright and interesting visitor."[162] "It was during these years that her friendship with Margaret took on its most exalted form. They wrote to each other every day. . . . It was a deep and genuine love." In August 1912 Archibald Vivian Hill, a young fellow of Trinity and a physiologist (who would become a Nobel laureate), joined a committee dealing with juvenile labor; Margaret was the committee's secretary. "His name begins to crop up in Margaret's letters. . . . In March 1913 . . . Margaret writes to Eglantyne that she is the luckiest woman because she is going to get the best husband in the world having already the best friend and the best parents and brothers."[163] They were married on 18 June, Neville's diary noting six days earlier, "Eglantyne has come to stay with us until after the wedding." Reporting on the engagement to a friend (and former lover), Maynard had written that Margaret was "in the highest state of elation, the family well satisfied, and even the Sapphist not notably obstreperous." About the "Sapphist," " 'She's much too sensible,' Margaret said to me, 'to make a fuss.' ''[164] Margaret's first child of four, born a year after the wedding, was named Mary Eglantyne (but always called Polly, even professionally).

Geoffrey, for his part, gave a teasing hint of his nature in mentioning the bisexual poet Siegfried Sassoon: ''Our friendship had been a sober affair, not passionate in any sense.''[165] This suggests other friendships that had indeed been possibly passionate; Geoffrey had made a close friend of the poet Rupert Brooke at Rugby (where Brooke's father was headmaster). A biographical study of Brooke found heterosexual posturing in teasing relationships with women, but more sincere homosexual and homoerotic behavior.[166] After two vain proposals to a Newnham student, who equally vainly preferred Brooke to him, Geoffrey, just thirty years old and like the other Keyneses a determined person, but within limits, successfully proposed to Margaret Darwin, daughter of the Cambridge-astronomer son of Charles Darwin. Like his sister Margaret, mother of two boys and two girls, Geoffrey had four children, but they were all boys. Like Maynard, Margaret and Geoffrey were subject to the sexual confusion emanating from their parents, but less thoroughly and directly, and equally subject to the homoerotic atmosphere of their boarding schools. Under such influences a homosexual phase is quite common—followed by the conventional heterosexual longings, marriage, and children.

Maynard's situation at 6 Harvey Road was extreme, Neville having introduced him to the painfully physical and psychic aspects of a father's love. Beginning to express its consequences at Eton, he would be an incessantly active homosexual for two decades. The wonder is that he would turn away from such a life and become a happy benedict. But, on second thought, one must credit in his case, as in Margaret's and Geoffrey's, the more ''normal'' aspects of their family's ambiance—and the impulsion to live them out as well. That homosexual character, however, would widen the terrain on which Maynard functioned and make him receptive to heterodox forms of thought and action in general and in economics. John Maynard would rebel against John Neville with the materials his progenitor had endowed him. Thus the (Maynard) Keynesian Revolution.

NOTES

1. Geoffrey Keynes, *The Gates of Memory* (Oxford, 1981), 19.

2. Much of the family background from John Neville Keynes's diaries (hereafter JNK Diary), Cambridge University Library, which, with gaps, extend from 1864 to the end of 1917; the Keynes family correspondence in the Keynes Papers, Modern Archive Centre, King's College Library (KP, MAC, KCL—hereafter KP; a microfilm of the KP has been made available to subscribing libraries); Milo Keynes, ed., *Essays on John Maynard Keynes* (Cambridge, 1975), and, besides Geoffrey Keynes's account, Florence Ada Keynes, *Gathering Up the Threads* (Cambridge, 1950). I have also drawn on *The Collected Writings of John Maynard Keynes*, 30 vols., (hereafter *CW*), managing eds.

Sir Austin Robinson and Donald E. Moggridge (London, 1971–89); Robert Skidelsky, *John Maynard Keynes*, vol. 1: *Hopes Betrayed 1883–1920* (New York, 1986) and vol. 2: *The Economist as Saviour 1920–1937* (London, 1992) (hereafter *JMK*, 1, 2); D. E. Moggridge, *Maynard Keynes: An Economist's Biography* (London and New York, 1992; hereafter *MK*); Roy Harrod, *The Life of John Maynard Keynes* (London, 1951; hereafter *The Life*); and Charles H. Hession, *John Maynard Keynes: A Personal Biography* (New York, 1984).

3. Geoffrey Keynes, *Gates of Memory*, 13.

4. Letter to JNK from a tripos examiner, quoted, Skidelsky, *JMK*, 1: 12.

5. JNK Diary, 21 February 1882.

6. Ibid., 17, 18, 24 January 1882.

7. Ibid., 7 February 1881.

8. FAK succeeded in opposing this with "tears in her eyes," ibid., 8 July 1883. On 4 August JNK recorded that his mother had definitely given up: "I am sorry to say."

9. Geoffrey Keynes, *Gates of Memory*, 5; JNK Diary, 12 February 1899.

10. JNK Diary, 1881–82 (e.g., entries, 15 January, 23 July 1882). Many of the pages for the period are suspiciously missing.

11. Geoffrey Keynes, *Gates of Memory*, 16.

12. JNK Diary, 8 July 1883.

13. Ibid., 4 April 1883.

14. Geoffrey Keynes, *Gates of Memory*, 17.

15. Clipping pasted into JNK Diary, 16 August 1882.

16. Ibid., 8, 11 November 1882.

17. According to JNK's measurements, ibid., 21 November 1886.

18. Ibid., 31 January 1902; 26 March 1892.

19. Roy Harrod, *The Life*, 9. Skidelsky disagrees: *JMK*, 1: n. 58.

20. JNK Diary, 4 May 1883; 21 February 1887.

21. Ibid., 5 January 1887.

22. 3 January 1900; 3 January 1908.

23. Ibid., 14 March 1891; 26 March 1892.

24. Ibid., 8 November 1892.

25. Ibid., 11, 24 November 1892.

26. Geoffrey Keynes, *Gates of Memory*, 14.

27. JNK Diary.

28. "Xerox of JMK's Remarks," KP, Personal Papers (hereafter PP)/20.

29. Skidelsky, *JMK*, 1: 13–14.

30. Moggridge, *MK*, 12.

31. JNK Diary, 15 June, 5 July 1883.

32. Ibid., 17 September 1883.

33. J. N. Keynes, *Studies and Exercises in Formal Logic* (London, 1884; 4th, rewritten, enlarged ed., 1906).

34. J. N. Keynes, *The Scope and Method of Political Economy* (London, 1891; reprint, 4th ed. [1917], 1955).

35. JNK Diary.

36. Ibid., 23 September 1886.

37. Alfred Marshall, *The Principles of Economics* (London, 1890; 9th variorum ed. with 2nd vol. of notes, index, 1961).

38. JNK Diary, 17 January 1891.

39. Ibid., 16 February 1884; 22, 23 January 1891.

40. Ibid., 1 October 1915.

41. Geoffrey Keynes, *Gates of Memory*, 14.

42. Joseph A. Schumpeter, *History of Economic Analysis* (Oxford, 1954), 824.

43. Dated 17 December 1884, quoted, Skidelsky, *JMK*, 1: 60, from letter in the possession of Polly Hill (granddaughter of Neville and Florence).

44. JNK Diary, 18, 22, 29, 31 December 1884; 12, 31 January, 10 February 1885.

45. Ibid., 17, 18 June 1885.

46. Skidelsky, *JMK*, 1: 62–63. This was the missing year of the diary.

47. JNK Diary, 15 February 1887.

48. Ibid., 21 April 1888, quoted, Skidelsky, *JMK*, 1: 63.

49. JNK Diary, 6 February 1889.

50. Ibid., 10 May 1882.

51. Ibid., 27 November 1887; 5 May, 9 June 1891.

52. Ibid., 14 January 1910.

53. Ibid., 2 March, 12 December 1910.

54. Ibid., 13 June 1910.

55. Ibid., 10, 27 August, 7 September 1910.

56. Ibid., 15 October 1910.

57. Ibid., 1, 3 October 1910.

58. Ibid., 8, 12 October 1910.

59. KP, PP/20, as above.

60. JNK Diary, 24 April, 11 May 1885.

61. Ibid., 4 May 1885; 26 October 1887.

62. Skidelsky, *JMK*, 1: 57.

63. JNK Diary, 15 August 1889.

64. Ibid., 1890 passim.

65. Ibid., 25 March 1891.

66. Ibid., 28 March 1892

67. Ibid., 22 February 1895; 6 February 1897.

68. Ibid., 3 March, 23 April, 5 May, 16 July 1907; 7 May, 23 September 1908.

69. Ibid., 25 March 1907; 24 March 1910.

70. Ibid., 18 April 1917.

71. Ibid., 9 November 1909; 6 February 1910.

72. Ibid., 9, 22 October 1914.

73. Ibid., 14, 31 December 1915.

74. Ibid., 12 June 1895; Hession, *John Maynard Keynes*, 13.

75. JNK Diary, 3 October 1896.

76. Ibid., 1, 24, January 1912; 7 February 1913; 14 July 1914; 14, 31 December 1915.

77. Ibid., 29 October, 4 December 1915; 2 May 1916.

78. Ibid., 27 March 1889.

79. JNK Diary, 12 February; 12, 20 March 1887.

80. About John Neville, aged 90, ''more dim and shambling,'' but profitably spending £750 for stamps, letter, Geoffrey to Maynard, 14 June 1943, KP, PP/45/167; about Maynard, Geoffrey Keynes, ''The Early Years,'' in Milo Keynes, ed., *Essays on John Maynard Keynes*, 30.

81. JNK Diary, 30 June 1895; 30 March 1902.

82. Geoffrey Keynes, *Gates of Memory*, 24–25; quotation, 25. JNK Diary, 25 July 1911.

83. JNK Diary, 8 December 1883.

84. Ibid., 20 September 1892.

85. C. R. Fay, "The Undergraduate," in Milo Keynes, ed., *Essays on John Maynard Keynes*, 37.

86. JNK Diary, 28 October 1899.

87. Ibid., 4 March 1889; 24 January, 1 February 1899.

88. Geoffrey Keynes, *Gates of Memory*, 19.

89. Quoted, JNK Diary, 25 July 1902.

90. Geoffrey Keynes, "The Early Years," 31.

91. JNK Diary, 29 September 1902; 28 August 1903. It was known as the Higher Local Certificate. Earlier she had failed in history, ibid., 3 March 1899, the first (and only) failure I have seen recorded about any Keynes child.

92. Ibid., 9 February 1901.

93. Letter, 3 February 1899, KP, PP/45/144.

94. Quoted, JNK Diary, 10 February 1899.

95. Ibid., 4 July 1905.

96. Ibid., 25 January 1911; JMK to Margaret Keynes [Hill], 12 February 1911, KP, PP/45/144.

97. Letter, 12 July 1937, KP, PP/45/144.

98. JNK Diary, 18 February, 10 June 1883; 1 January 1884.

99. Ibid., 5 January, 4 April 1886; 28 February, 20, 28 May, 18 November 1887.

100. Ibid., 20, 23, 24 December 1912.

101. Ibid., 18, 22 August, 2 November 1907.

102. Letter copied into ibid., 5 June 1883; ibid., 6 June 1883.

103. Ibid., 15 June 1884.

104. E.g., ibid., 12 December 1884, when Neville and Florence found him very ill and remained awake that night. He had not recovered until 3 January 1885.

105. Ibid., 9 February 1885.

106. Ibid., 5 June 1885.

107. Ibid., 5, 28 July, 18 October 1885.

108. Roy Harrod, *The Life*, 8.

109. JNK Diary, 17 April 1897.

110. Ibid., 28 June 1897.

111. Ibid., 21 January, 12 June 1897.

112. Clive Bell to JMK, 2 February 1919, KP, PP/45/25.

113. E.g., JNK Diary, 5 June 1886 (Maynard's birthday): "I wish he weighed more the little shrimp."

114. Ibid.

115. Ibid., 28 December 1884; 3 January 1885.

116. Ibid., 24 February 1885.

117. Ibid., 5 May 1886.

118. Ibid., 4, 5, 8 August 1887.

119. Ibid., 21 April, 8, 9, 10 June 1889.

120. Ibid., 30 October 1889.

121. Ibid., 5, 11 November 1889.

122. Ibid., 26 March 1893.

123. Ibid., 11 February, 30 March, 30 April, 2 May 1893.

124. Ibid., 2 January 1894.

125. Ibid., 19, 20, 21, 25 September 1897.

126. Ibid., 17 December 1897.

127. E.g., JMK to FAK, 21 March 1899, KP, PP/45/168.

128. Richard Ollard, *An English Education: A Perspective of Eton* (London, 1982), 40.

129. JNK Diary, 14, 15, 16, 21 January 1914; notes, JMK to FAK, incorrectly dated 3, 4 for 13, 14 January and "Thursday" (15 January), 1914.

130. JNK Diary, 22 February 1914.

131. Ibid., 11, 12, 13, 22, 23, 26 June, 1 July 1915.

132. Harrod, *The Life*, 202.

133. JMK to Lydia Keynes, 25 October 1931, KP, PP/45/190.

134. Geoffrey Keynes, "The Early Years," 30.

135. JNK Diary, 19 September 1897.

136. Ibid., 7 July 1904; 4 May 1905.

137. JMK to Lytton Strachey, 23 November 1905, KP, PP/45/316.

138. Vanessa to Clive Bell, 2 October 1914, quoted, Skidelsky, *JMK*, 1: 294.

139. The whippings, JNK Diary, 27 January, 3 June 1886; 7 September 1887; 22 January 1889. As noted previously I did not see the 1888 diary, which might have recorded other instances.

140. Skidelsky, *JMK*, 1: 65.

141. JNK Diary, 23 September 1887.

142. Letter, composed in April, referring to one of the above whipping instances, quoted, ibid., 3 June 1886.

143. Ibid., 10, 23 September 1887.

144. Sigmund Freud, "A Child Is Being Beaten: A Contribution to the Study of the Origins of Sexual Perversions," in *The Standard Edition of the Complete Works of Sigmund Freud*, tr. James Strachey, vol. 17 (1917–1919; London, 1955), 179–204; quotation, 179.

145. JNK Diary, 1 March 1908.

146. Moggridge, *MK*, 23.

147. Skidelsky, *JMK*, 1: 72.

148. KP, PP/20.

149. Quoted, Skidelsky, *JMK*, 1: 241. Letter, 24 December 1917, KP, PP/45/168; also, *CW*, 16: 265.

150. Quoted, Harrod, *The Life*, 177, n. 177.

151. Quoted, ibid., 201.

152. Geoffrey Keynes, "The Early Years," 29.

153. Report by R. A. H. Mitchell, July 1900, KP, PP/21.

154. Harrod, *The Life*, 31.

155. Isaiah Berlin, quoted, Noel Annan, "Portrait of a Genius as a Young Man," *New York Review of Books*, 35 (19 July 1984).

156. Harrod, *The Life*, 31.

157. Kenneth Clark, *The Other Half: A Self-Portrait* (London, 1977), 27.

158. According to an interview with Geoffrey Keynes, 6 September 1979, Skidelsky, *JMK*, 1: 66, 412.

159. JNK Diary, 11 May 1889.

160. Letter, JMK to Lytton Strachey, 11 March 1906, KP, PP/45/316.

161. Francesca M. Wilson, *Rebel Daughter of a Country House: The Life of Eglantyne Jebb* (London, 1967), 103, 109.

162. JNK Diary, 30 May, 13 June ("a very bright . . ."), 25 November 1910; 18 March, 11 May, 4 June 1911; 22, 26 July, 28 August, 20 November, 12 December 1912; 18, 25 January, 9 February, 10 April, 12 June 1913.

163. Francesca M. Wilson, *Rebel Daughter*, 113–14.

164. Letter to Duncan Grant, 12 February 1913, British Library (hereafter BL), Add. MSS 57931.

165. Geoffrey Keynes, *Gates of Memory*, 234.

166. Paul Delany, *The Neo-pagans: Rupert Brooke and the Ordeal of Youth* (New York, 1987), 7, 78–80, 139, 147, 160–61, 173–78, 197.

CHAPTER 2

Training

By 1897, with his position as secretary of Cambridge University's Council of the Senate consolidated, John Neville Keynes insensibly shifted his diary's emphasis away from his concerns and toward Maynard's. It signaled the change in its account of the wait for the telegram announcing his son's acceptance at Eton as a scholarship student. Identifying with Maynard and, as always, pessimistic, Neville reacted to a delay of a few hours by giving up hope. (The ebullient Margaret, with healthier instinct, ''still maintained the belief that it would be all right.'') For Neville, ''This was the most delightful telegram I ever received. My own successes never gave me anything like the pleasure that this has done.''[1] Of course his dignity would require accession to the post of registrary, achieved in 1910, but, beyond that, he could rest on Maynard's triumphs as his own.

Eton, so much more altitudinous than Neville's noncomformist academy, was a nurturer of prime ministers, a promise of public acclaim. Neville was directing his son toward the great world he himself, clinging to his Cambridge-bounded anxieties and hobbies, was avoiding. The great public school meant a powerful reinforcement of Maynard's long evident ambition to know and excel—and his less apparent drive to lead and dominate. Whatever covert distresses Neville had caused his eldest son, he had also provided all his children, as Geoffrey has testified, a grand wealth of happy domestic experience at 6 Harvey Road, a reserve to be exploited for a lifetime. At home, as we have seen, Maynard had started out enveloped in love, respect, enlivening interests, and appropriate pleasures. The private Maynard Keynes would confront public life on equal terms.

Maynard began well at Eton and rose above that. In the spring of 1901, in the fourth of his five years there, Samuel Gurney Lubbock, his tutor, reported that he "seems to improve visibly every half [term]." Indeed, he "combines admirably the lighter and more solid qualities of the intellect."[2] This was well and even prophetically observed: if Neville might be doubtful of those lighter qualities, the essence of Maynard's future success would derive from his ability to combine the substantial and the nimble. Now, although the boy had already won a vast array of prizes, he was approaching the ultimate series of examinations that would determine the more or less impressive character of his entrance into university life. Trusting that they could avoid the worst by continuing to expect it, Neville intensified the attention he gave to Maynard's studies. A week after Lubbock's report Maynard was home on a brief vacation, but "working steadily about three hours a day under my direction. I feel quite like a trainer, as if I were training him for a race or a prize fight."[3] Exactly; but this had been going on since his son was able to talk and walk. But Maynard was his own co-trainer, indeed, *pace* Lubbock et alia, the leading co-trainer.

The child had quickly shown himself intelligent and ready to learn. On his first birthday Neville reported him "nearly" walking; he was "cute and understands a good deal." A half-year later, "Maynard now knows twelve animals by name. He says so prettily his few little words,—'Mama, Papa, Boy,' " the latter for himself.[4] His first-term report from the Perse School's kindergarten, when he was almost six, found "promise in mental work," although his insecure health had required twenty-one absences.[5] At six the boy impressed both parents with his verbal skills and even philosophical curiosity. Neville observed, "Maynard's tongue is regularly on the go. If he can't think of anything sensible to say, he talks nonsense."[6] In her family memoir Florence recalled Maynard's inquiring into the nature of things. "Who invented time?" he asked. "How did things get their name?" Having learned about the function of the brain, he proposed, "Just now it's wondering how it thinks. It ought to know." More pragmatically, "He never failed to be ready with an excuse or an argument in support of his own views."[7] Indeed, in Geoffrey's memory, Maynard had "the reputation in the family of having always been able to get the better of them in any argument."[8] At St. Faith's, his preparatory school, Maynard showed a marked capacity for mathematics. The headmaster's wife, less restrained than his future tutor, unqualifiedly characterized him as a "genius," moreover possessing, beyond the specific talent in mathematics, notable "general ability."[9] Maynard had long taken much of the initiative in the training process.

Very early the child showed a professional attitude. Complaining that he "seems to get so little done," he wanted to stay on at the kindergarten later in the day.[10] Removed from the kindergarten to be given home lessons, he proved "an enthusiastic pupil, longing for the lessons to begin."[11] At St. Faith's from January 1892, at eight and one-half and two years younger than the average,

Maynard needed little time to catch up with his seniors. Two months after he began there, "Maynard is now greatly rejoiced because he is no longer bottom in his class."[12] On sober evaluation Neville thought his son more advanced than he himself had been at that age.[13] In April of 1892 Ralph Goodchild, the demanding headmaster of St. Faith's, allowed that Maynard had "done fairly well for his first term." Indeed, he was "decidedly above the composition of his class."[14] A month later Neville could note, "Maynard . . . to the top of his class this week."[15] By August Goodchild had unequivocally defined Maynard as "the brightest boy in his division," but ominously, in view of Maynard's vulnerable health, wanted him to develop his ready capabilities more considerably and do evening work as well. Neville and Florence resisted the thought: "[H]e should not be unduly pressed forward."[16] The parental adjurations had little effect. At the end of the year Maynard arrived "top" in the examinations and, handicapped by his frequent absences, second to a twelve-year-old in the term's work.[17] For the moment, defeated by ambitious schoolmaster and their son, Maynard's parents withheld their protest about excessive work. In fact, early in 1893 all the Keynes children were started in French at home.[18]

Early in 1893 Maynard produced a warning signal in the form of a nettle rash. By 11 February Neville, noting such school assignments as quadratic equations and long Latin-prose works, was again expostulating that it was too much; Florence had to help the boy with his homework. Later in the month, with the rash still bothersome, Neville arranged that Maynard be relieved of homework; he promptly slipped to seventh place in his class of ten.[19] A month later Maynard was contending with Euclid, quadratics, Ovid, Latin prose, and John Milton's *Samson Agonistes*. Neville, with another headmaster supporting him in judging the boy "pushed on a good deal too fast," asked Goodchild not to follow his plan of adding Greek as well. Two days after that, the schoolmaster, ignoring that opinion and starting Maynard on Greek, Neville weakly recorded: "We shall probably have to put a stop to this."[20] His parents succeeded in putting a stop to "this" by removing Maynard from St. Faith's and placing him under his grandmother Brown's tutelage for a term. Even if, as Neville had noted, Maynard's health became, if anything, worse, the break was followed by reassuring developments. Back home, somewhat recovered under his mother's closely observant eye, Maynard commenced a series of successes at St. Faith's that continued straight through Eton.

The boy's stay with his grandparents produced another constructive educational effect: On 2 October 1893 Neville had noted, "Maynard now writes to me every Sunday." They were "nice little letters . . . something to look forward to on Monday mornings." It would be easy for the Eton student to resume that Sunday habit. Father and son were to pay requisite attention to the quality of the son's prose expression: more early professionalism.

At St. Faith's during the second half of 1894, as Neville's diary registered, "Maynard has been enjoying his examinations [30 July]. . . . handsome prize . . . first in his class . . . great pleasure to us, especially as he had been doing his

work with so little effort [31 July]. . . . Maynard is in high glee because he is
to have two hours special mathematical teaching four days in the week'' (8
October). Maynard was also spending a half-hour on German daily after tea
with the new German governess (9 October). Maynard was first in his class in
examinations and term work, Goodchild reporting, '' 'really brilliant work, but
lacking [as other teachers and his grandmother Brown also said at the time]
perseverance in the face of difficulty . . . but am persuaded he will make his
mark . . . when he has got his growth' '' (21 December). The next year Neville
found Maynard's annual ''examinations . . . rather exciting,'' with first place
shifting continually among him and two other bright boys, but Maynard ending
in first place; he was more robust and found the work easy. At the end of 1895
Maynard was overpoweringly first, with 1,365 marks against 1,043 for the
runner-up (20, 30 July, 19 December).

Maynard's ''decided taste for mathematical work,''[21] which Goodchild had
discovered earlier and vigorously encouraged, gave him a great advantage: ''one
of the cleverest boys he had ever had at his school'' (19 December 1895). In
April 1896 Goodchild was reporting that with Maynard ''work that may take
two hours is finished in less than half the time given.'' Moreover, making up
for his carelessness in full flight, Maynard ''corrects [his mistakes] when I am
looking them over before I have seen them myself.''[22] There was a price. Four
months later Goodchild had to report on Maynard's stammering—''increased
hesitation in speech,'' as he euphemistically put it—granted it was connected
with the school work, and agreed again to relieve him of homework for a period.[23] Nothing, however, threatened Maynard's premier position. In the summer
of 1896, before his last year at St. Faith's, he was put in charge of the mail at
home while his parents took a holiday in Scotland: ''Maynard has been acting
as my private secretary while I have been away.''[24]

At the end of 1896 Goodchild reported that Maynard had made great progress
in mathematics and was ''head and shoulders above all the other boys.'' His
marks, at 2,456, had widely exceeded the 1,684 of his nearest competitor. His
best subjects were virtually all of his subjects, Goodchild mentioning trigonom-
etry, algebra, Latin translation and verse, German, and Greek. The headmaster
was kind and apologetic about Geoffrey, who had started at St. Faith's and was
eighth in his class ranking: ''[H]is work as far as it went, was good. . . . I feel
that we have hardly done him justice.'' Geoffrey was, at least, ''worthy of being
Maynard's brother.''[25]

If Maynard's record indicated an Eton candidacy, Goodchild feared that even
with his aptitude in mathematics he might not be strong enough against the
intense competition and recommended another school. While that might accord
perfectly with Neville's pessimism, he was encouraged by a more confident
Florence to be bravely ambitious for his son. Eton, moreover, was particularly
advantageous in more than one way. The chief attraction, besides the school's
nonpareil prestige, was the Eton scholarships for fifteen boys each year. The
point was not the money for the prosperous Neville. Indeed, he recorded on

New Year's Day of 1897, "Audit of securities very satisfactory."[26] Of course he never undervalued the cost factor, but it was the other elments associated with the scholarships that were determinant. The seventy scholarship boys, institutionalized as an elite, lived together as *Collegers* in College, a separate house in the school itself. (The seven hundred fee-paying aristocratic or wealthy boys lived in houses scattered in the town of Eton as *Oppidans*, from *oppidanus*, of a town.) Just large enough in number to form a critical mass and defend themselves against the Oppidans, the Collegers, exceptionally, were respected for being bright and studious. Geoffrey, who would do well at the somewhat less distinguished Rugby, was known as "studious Keynes," a pejorative there, he recalled.[27] Eton would be ideal for his consciously thinking, unathletic brother, who, moreover, would find friends appropriate to his qualities and needs, as he had not in Harvey Road and St. Faith's.

In mid-January 1897 Neville and Florence called on Goodchild to discuss Maynard's prospects. The headmaster could easily predict great things. Neville's feelings rose upward without limit: "I am already too proud of the dear boy. My pride in him and my love for him feed each other."[28] Preparing for the Eton scholarship examinations, Neville naturally did everything to maximize Maynard's chances. Engaging special tutors, he got the boy up at 7 A.M. to work before breakfast, a habit that Maynard would later reverse into lifelong late rising. A week before the examinations Neville was "depressed" and "nervous." On Sunday, 4 July, the day before Neville, Florence, and Maynard went off to Eton for the three-day test period, Neville was "in a fearful state of worry," although Florence was "more philosophical." Maynard, undisturbed, allowed himself to be roused at 6:15 A.M. in their Eton hotel on Tuesday, 6 July, for Latin composition—and walked confidently back into the hotel before Neville could depart to fetch him. He broke off early from at least two other examinations, Latin and Greek grammar, and Greek translation. There followed the interminable wait for the results. On Sunday, 11 July, Goodchild, despite earlier expectations, expressed himself pessimistically after inspecting Maynard's examinaton notes, Neville recording himself again as fearful. On Monday Neville chronicled: "Another bad night. . . . Maynard himself is a little depressed." Neville seemed to be instructing his son in the perverse pleasures of being depressed. But resisting his father's example, "[H]e is certainly more hopeful than Florence and I now are." However, "as the afternoon wore on we gave up the little hope that remained in us (except Margaret). . . ." Then the "delightful" telegram arrived at 5:30 P.M.: "A marvelous change in the situation. . . . I had been very depressed all day, but now felt quite a different person." Geoffrey was "fired with the ambition to go and do likewise." Maynard had made "bad mistakes in his Classics," but his mathematics, in which he tied for first place, had been a great help. On Wednesday, at a garden party, "Florence . . . received so many congratulations that . . . it seemed like a triumphal procession."[29]

Beginning with his insertion into College, Eton and John Maynard Keynes

were extraordinarly well met. It might seem that King Henry VI had founded
the school in 1441 with Maynard in mind, but that could be equally true of the
sixteen Etonians who became prime minister out of the thirty-nine achieving
that rank between 1721 and 1927.[30] For Maynard the match extended to his
future at King's College, since Henry had established the two institutions as
sister foundations, King's accepting students only among Eton graduates until
the mid-nineteenth century. Eton and King's were perhaps the best achievements
of the last of the Lancastrians, the mild, intermittently mad, and eventually
murdered son of Prince Hal become the bellicose Henry V. Near Windsor Castle,
Eton was a favorite of the Tudor, Stuart, and Hanoverian kings, George III
becoming a particular patron and mourned to this day in the black suits the boys
wear. The school took root in the late medieval chaos of the War of the Roses
and flourished despite the Civil War of the seventeenth century. Later, however,
falling into stasis, it lagged well behind the great progress of the nineteenth
century until close to its end. During the earlier part of the century school life
was a brawl among the boys and between boys and masters, bullying of the
smaller boys in the first instance and, in the second, beating (cane on clothed
bottom) or flogging (birch on bare bottom). Until 1846 the Collegers were
locked into the Long Chamber, where, unless the noise provoked punitive in-
vasion, they relieved the cold and other physical horrors with odd violences and
pleasures. One Colleger (and future master), arriving in 1851, restrained his early
reminiscences: "I will say nothing about the moral and social aspects . . . because the less said about them the better."[31] By then, however, most of the
Collegers, except for the fifteen most recent arrivals temporarily placed in cu-
bicles in Chamber, were provided with individual bed-sitting rooms, "an *immense* luxury to Aldous Huxley even a half-century later.[32] Reform, meanwhile,
reduced the classical command of the curriculum by as much as half, with
mathematics in second place, distantly pursued by history and modern languages. A boy and his tutor, as the case of Maynard with the responsive Gurney
Lubbock, could also variously stretch these proportions. More reform was necessary to make life agreeable for Maynard, and the benign Francis Hodgson,
provost from 1890, said, "Please God I will do something for those poor boys,"
and put a stop to the residual evils.[33]

Precisely prepared by Neville, Maynard overleaped his anticipatory fever and
the resultant lag in arriving at Eton, and launched himself directly into efficient
achievement. Working his way through the entrance examinations, he established himself uncomplainingly in his Chamber cubicle, and five days later Neville noted, "A capital letter from Maynard telling us just what we want to
know." He was "getting on and feels quite settled down." Florence had taken
Maynard to Eton, but Neville went there a fortnight later, on Saturday, 9 October, to see for himself and found reassurance in talks with Lubbock and two
of the boy's masters. Maynard had a "bad cold" but was otherwise all right.[34]
On Monday he addressed a letter exceptionally to his mother. Neville was
crowding her out now in the epistolary manner, Florence writing some months

later, "Father is such a good correspondent that I generally leave the letter writing to him."[35] Maynard began, "Dear Mother, To my great surprise I have come out top . . . in the fortnightly order. . . . My cold is very much better." He then arrived at the reason he was writing her: "The pears are delicious and I should like a hamper containing the following—Tongue, Sardines, Cheese, Pears, chocolat creams, Honey, Strawberry Jam. . . ." (Eton's provisions were still notoriously meager and unappetizing.) Neville wrote, "My dear Maynard, We are greatly delighted at your position in the fortnightly order. It is a capital beginning and will encourage you to do your best to get a thoroughly good place at Trials at the end of the term." He advised: Don't put off work and be forced to use a crib; perhaps study with another boy *if* permitted. How was Maynard getting on with the *Odyssey*, the "problem paper," his Latin prose and verse, and Greek prose?[36]

Appropriate to ambitious father and son, Eton had gathered in numerous prizes over the centuries and, by a ranking fixed every two weeks, established a precise system of calibrating performance. Ambitions whipped on and denial impossible, the boys knew exactly where they stood throughout the school year. Maynard won prizes in fourteen of the fifteen terms of his five years, missing out only in the second term of his first year. The total was thirty-nine, including all the major prizes in mathematics and classics, his area of competence. He also won the history prize in his fourth year; a parvenu among the subjects, it was not so richly endowed with such rewards. In addition Maynard was named nine times for "distinction" of performance and his work was "sent up" six times, that is, collected and held by the school as a model of excellence.[37] He would finish with a series of ultimate prizes and win recognition as the top Colleger in his final year. At the beginning of this performance Geoffrey remarked sympathetically, "Poor fellow, he can't help it."[38] Maynard began in June 1901, at the end of his fourth year, by winning the Tomline examination in mathematics, with £32 in books, went on in July to write thirty papers for the Cambridge Higher Certificate (the same test his mother passed in leaving Newnham) and thus captured the Chamberlayne Prize, a £60 scholarship at a university of the candidate's choice for a postgraduate year as well as three undergraduate years, and, in December 1901, a Cambridge University scholarship providing £80 annually plus free tuition and rooms at King's College until he got his BA. This last was a particular accomplishment and also reconfirmed Maynard's fate as a Cambridge person.

In these final months at Eton Maynard had been consulting intensely about his various options with Neville, Lubbock, various masters—and himself. It was possible to take the Cambridge University examination in one or two subjects. Maynard had been one of eight out of some 150 candidates who prepared two subjects, in his case, classics as well as his forte of mathematics. (He was taking the King's College examination, since as sister foundation King's offered "closed scholarships" for Etonians only; it was an extra security that appealed surely more to Neville than Maynard.) Achieving second place among all the

candidates for the ten scholarships available, Maynard was granted a more generous open scholarship, "a special distinction," on the basis of his two examination subjects. As Neville proudly wrote him, "Again congratulations."[39]
Neville deserves a substantial part of the credit.

Fluently, as in a loop of continuous conversation, Maynard wrote home every
Sunday from Eton. On 8 May 1898, during his first spring there, Neville wrote,
"Your letter was, as it always is, very welcome. You know we quite look
forward to Monday mornings!"[40] On a Wednesday morning a year and a half
later Neville noted, "Still no letter from Maynard; so I telegraphed & received
a telegram in reply—'Letter posted at usual time. Will write.' "[41] Maynard had
absently forgotten to address the envelope.[42] In that letter of May 1898, besides
expressing his pleasure in Maynard's last letter, Neville had got down to business. This was at the end of the only term in which Maynard had not won a
prize; the letter had faithfully reported on his failure and listed who had won.
Neville demanded more information, "You did not tell us what your marks
were. . . . Do you know how much you were behind the three who got prizes?"[43]
Neville got to know the capabilities of Maynard's main competitors, while his
son was able to provide more reason for parental pleasure. Two months later
he dashed off a postcard reporting his capture of the Junior Mathematical Prize,
Neville responding feelingly, "I had rather set my heart on your getting this
prize."[44]

Neville mixed generous praise into his maximal demands. Toward the end of
Maynard's second year he writes, "Your letters . . . are even more interesting
than usual. We are quite satisfied with your position in the mathematical examination." He inquires how Maynard compared with two other boys, one of
them, (Alfred) Dillwyn Knox, a close friend as well. "Knox seems to be the
coming mathematician."[45] Perhaps influenced by his father's modesty, Maynard
avoided the appearance of boasting. Thus Neville could write him a month later
that he was "very much pleased to hear that you have . . . got the Chemistry
Prize notwithstanding your anticipation to the contrary." A week and a half
after that, congratulating Maynard on five "distinctions," Neville writes, "You
make more of your defeats than of your victories."[46] During Maynard's fourth
year, responding to news of another prize, Neville threw up his hands, "These
things seem to come to you whether you will or not."[47] Geoffrey had had the
same thought much earlier.

But leaving nothing to chance, Neville had plotted out grand strategy and
precise tactics. In his third year Maynard had won the Senior Mathematical
Prize, calling up congratulatory letters from both Florence and Neville. Maynard
had evidently written that it was a near thing, and his mother reminded him
supportively that he had rowed in a race the same week. In *his* letter, Neville
began, "We rejoice. . . ." He then took occasion to refine the last strophes of
Maynard's Eton career: "You must make a special effort to get the Tomline
next year." He reasoned correctly, "As Capron has now been beaten by Knox
there is no reason why he should not also be beaten by you." He added, "Work

up carefully for the Extras Exam[n] on the 28th: that too is important in its way."[48] Demanding as he was, Neville was guiding a force in his son that called it up. He had the tact not to go beyond that. Before Maynard left Eton, without consulting his own choice, Neville had envisioned a course that would lead Maynard either to an academic or a governmental career: "I suppose he will take his Tripos [honors examination] in 1905, & his C. S. [Civil Service] exam[n] in 1906, so that leaves a good margin for a fellowship dissertation."[49] Sensitive to Maynard's developing abilities and tastes, Neville's prediction was precisely correct on all three counts, including the timing. Within that general course, however, major details had to be resolved. Maynard himself began the process at Eton.

The boy presented a seductive challenge to his teachers. (There was one exception, the master Maynard found so boring that he became insolent.) Gurney Lubbock, Neville's inspired and well-researched choice as tutor, helped shape Maynard's program and also taught him appropriate subjects. At the end of the first term, Lubbock, a first-class tripos graduate of King's College in classics, wrote Neville suggestively, "I gather that mathematics is his fate, but he has done really well all round."[50] Three years later G. H. Hurst, the mathematics master, said he "shews much promise," but granted that the boy himself was "a little diffident about his capacity for mastering the higher portions of the subject." With his vested interest, Hurst was refusing to "anticipate any great difficulty."[51] Maynard knew better, as did other masters. In the next term H. E. Luxmoore, Eton's most distinguished classicist, emphasized the difficulty. Commending "admirable work in almost everything," he expressed the "hope that the more accurate sciences will not dry the readiness of his sympathy and insight for the more inspiring and humane subjects: his little essay on *Antigone* was not like the work of one made for mathematics. He has a well furnished and delightful mind."[52] Maynard's general abilities and the disagreements among his seniors gave him the opportunity of choice.

With his lively curiosity about almost everything, Maynard launched himself enthusiastically in various directions. At first he leaned against Eton's emphasis and got permission to do more mathematics at the cost of extra work in classics.[53] But then he resisted another effort of Hurst to increase his mathematics work even more.[54] When Maynard concentrated on his Tomline examination in mathematics, however, he had to reduce the time for his classical studies. After that he could right the balance and successfully undertake the double mathematics-classics university examination. Through it all he was developing more confidence in his own judgment. Indeed at Eton he began to judge his superiors more severely than they judged him.

Maynard's interests at Eton accurately prefigured the range of the mature man. We have seen that he could do well in chemistry. Sensitized further by the Boer War, which broke out in 1899, he plunged into history and quickly developed a thoughtful political perspective. About a British defeat he writes Neville after first mentioning his fortnightly ranking, "But we console ourselves with history which makes our losses seem puny." Comparing the casualties to those of a battle in the Peninsular War, he concludes sagely, "Seventy men killed in a battle is terrible for their families but it is a tiny loss for a nation of thirty million."[55] Maynard had discovered *Realpolitik*.

A series of essays in 1900–1901 show the youth's increasing sophistication. In the first he concluded that Pope Julius II was prince more than pope, "not a bad man or a politician more unscrupulous than the diplomacy of his age demanded." About the spread of Lutheranism Maynard distinguished between secular and religious issues while even-handedly evaluating the economic and social effects of Henry VIII's spoliation of the English churches. Toward the end of 1900 he won the Richards English Prize with an essay on the character of the Stuarts. He began with a Tacitus quotation and continued in a stately, Latin-influenced, Gibbon-mimicking style quite different from his usual straightforward expression, thus "the curse of the house was weakness of will . . . conscience . . . mind . . . body. . . ." The essay ended, "It is easy to love the Stuarts . . . right to pity them, but . . . impossible to admire them." Scamping the political and social realities, Maynard had indulged himself in the collective ad hominem. An egregiously impressive effort, it deserved the prize for the wrong reasons. A half-year later, writing plainly again, he found in Oliver Cromwell "all the essential qualities of a great commander—an iron will, a cool head, and a power of instant decision."[56] Here Maynard stood securely on political bedrock.

History led Maynard further astray, beyond usefulness to his Eton career. He spent frequent Sunday afternoons researching the Keynes family genealogy in the Eton library. It was he who traced its origins to Cahagnes in Normandy. Perhaps the research was a political act. As scion of a nonconformist family the young and the mature Keynes looked upon himself as a member of a meritocratic elite, compared with the aristocrats. Now demonstrating his Colleger ability to beat the Oppidans at their own game, he would become an expert at establishing his ascendancy over selected others.

Like all great achievers, young Keynes often engaged in activities of great but covert value to his career. Besides his genealogical excursions, Maynard permitted Gurney Lubbock to lead him into the esoteric pleasures of medieval poetry. One result was an essay on Bernard of Cluny, a twelfth-century monk who wrote the long poem *De Contemptu Mundi*. In his last term Maynard read the essay to the Eton Literary Society and subsequently revised and reread it to more mature audiences. Both versions show a greater desire to like the author and poem than Maynard could truly feel. He could only quizzically contemplate Bernard's attack on the world's vanities and arbitrarily see him as a forerunner of the Renaissance. In the second version Maynard had to concede, after mentioning "metrical details which have amused me," that "[p]erhaps it is at its best mere rhetoric, at the worst, inferior doggerel."[57] The essay was a limiting case. Influenced by a sympathetic teacher, he had tried to extend his sympathy to spiritual and aesthetic experience, both beyond him. Although he never penetrated the first and by then had cast it casually aside, he would always yearn to enter into the life of art and always fail. In a letter to his father he mentioned reading Robert Browning's *Ring and the Book* and, bypassing its quality, debauched into a discussion of the length of long poems. The future economist and connoisseur of statistics reported that the Browning work had 21,116 lines, compared with William Morris's *Earthly Paradise* (40,000 lines), Edmund Spenser's *Faerie Queene* (35,632), and the *Aeneid* (9,896).[58] A cricket ground was at the end of Harvey Road, and at home, with similar statistical interest in an activity for which he had little competence, "Maynard spent many hours watching the players and keeping records of their scores."[59] The classicist Luxmoore, in his sensitive appreciation of Maynard, had, however, entered one negative. He thought "highly of his powers—except in the direction of imagination. His verse composition is very wooden."[60] But even Keynes's failed yearning would have its usefulness, thus his adept chairmanship of the British Arts Council among many other mature activities related to art.

Given his opportunity of choice, how would Maynard begin to define himself? At the end of his Eton period he indicated it both precisely and approximately by his choice of two subjects for his university scholarship examination. He would be both specialist and generalist, and if this seemed to slip into the excluded middle, he would furnish powerful rebuttals. As he prepared to enter King's College, Maynard Keynes had positioned himself flexibly for his plural futures.

An important part of Maynard's development at Eton was a process of broader socialization. At home his relationships outside the family were light and lightly dropped, but he quickly made the Collegers a newer family. In mid-course he wrote his sister, now at her boarding school, "One seems to have . . . two extremely different lives, one at home, and the other at school and when you are living one of them, the other one doesn't seem much more than a dream."[61] In January 1901 he was elected to College Pop, the debating society, and exercising his new historical and political judgment, exuberantly joined in the debates. Although he had not quite eradicated his stammer, he could write his father in February 1902, his last year, "I spoke twice and find that by now I have no modesty when on my legs before a strange audience." He could report that he had been elected president of the Eton Literary Society, which he had revived (and before which he read his paper on Bernard of Cluny). He had also been elected to the management committee of School Stores, "chiefly as a person competent to cheque the financial affairs. I am finding like you when I am appointed to a committee I am invariably made to do all the work."[62] Maynard could still easily identify with Neville while suggesting he would also do otherwise.

In that last year, while he was gathering in his last bounty of prizes, Maynard achieved a pure eminence that he could never again quite match. Three months before the letter about debates and committees, he reported to Neville on the Eton Society, familiarly called Pop (not to be confused with the debating College Pop). The Eton Society was the school's most exclusive social club, which helped govern it and, moreover, was dominated by Oppidans and athletes. Frankly excited, "You will scarcely believe me," he wrote. "I have been elected to Pop."[63] As a member of Pop, he could add to the sartorial elegance of the black Eton suit, white shirt, and white tie, a colored vest, "a perfect dove of a waistcoat, lavender with pale pink spots," as he later informed his mother, a rolled umbrella, and other distinguished appurtenances. Now his father suggestively replied, "It is fortunate that you are naturally of a modest disposition as your head would be turned by all the honors that are being piled upon you one after another."[64] And this was before Maynard's great prizewinning round of 1902.

The unathletic Maynard even distinguished himself in sports despite frequent colds, his fever "periodicals," the measles, "liver attacks," boils on his knees, and "twitching of the facial muscles."[65] Lacking coordination, he gave up on cricket after a few lamentable performances. He rowed enthusiastically, but was presently "supplanted in the boat by another, so my violent exercise is over," he wrote his mother. "It was disappointing at first, but now I find it a great relief."[66] He refused to stay away, however, and managed to win his boating colors, although he was later remanded to the boat for "poor oars."[67] He engaged in other sports with varying success, but also won his colors in the Wall Game, which he enjoyed despite or because of the mud and exhaustion. His size was an advantage and, with his will to win, he was often able to keep possession of the ball under a mass of enemy players. An article in the local newspaper on a Colleger–Oppidan game said that "for the losers" Keynes was among the half-dozen players who "were good." The Etonian flavor, if not the sense, of the game is suggested by this account: "[A]fter the sixth bully the Oppidans . . . got the ball down to the chalk line of their opponents' calx, where a bully was formed . . . and J. K. Henderson attained a shy for the Oppidans."[68] To his schoolmates Maynard would be outstandingly "normal."

Maynard won respect although he lacked the charm for easy popularity. He was independent enough, moreover, to risk unpopularity. While reflecting on the Boer War as a history student, he refused to be caught up in the jingoistic spirit it aroused. He consulted with his parents, but clearly indicated what advice he preferred: "[T]he head gave us a stirring oration on the Volunteer movement." It was the "duty of all to get what military training they could" by joining the Eton volunteer corps. "Am I to join? I am not keen and the drills will be a nuisance." On the other hand, "It will be unpleasant to be the only nonshooter." Florence replied the next day that although it was all right if he yielded to the consensus, "in fact we prefer you shd. not." Maynard could then report that "without your letter which amounted to a refusal, I should have been impelled to be engulfed in this marvelous martial ardour that has seized the school." While many of his friends had joined, "I wavered a little and hey presto! it was done—or rather it was not done."[69]

At Eton Maynard made three close friends whom he kept in his life afterward and established other more distant but enduring relationships. There was Dil or

Dilly Knox, his main rival in mathematics and also a classicist, his first friend—
and, according to his meticulous record, first lover. Before becoming a remarkable cryptographer in World Wars I and II, he would join Maynard at King's
College as student and then fellow in classics. A closer friend in his last year,
but not a lover to that friend's subsequent regret, was Bernard Swithinbank, a
tall, handsome, poetic, and vague classicist, who would override Maynard's
objections to go out to Burma and become a leading civil servant there. The
second lover was the handsome, younger Daniel Macmillan, later director of his
family's Macmillan & Co., publishers (and brother of Harold, the future prime
minister, whom Maynard found even more handsome).[70] In Eton's homoerotic
atmosphere, as generated by masters with more or less affinity for boys, and
boys in their sexually exigent years, Maynard began two decades of life within
the bell jar of a homosexual world.

A few letters suggest the character of Maynard's initiation. In a letter of 1905
to Dil Knox, which he evidently had not sent, he wrote that since "the curious
incidents that marked our last two years at Eton, there has been a kind of
affection between us."[71] He also mentioned the "incidents" to Bernard Swithinbank, as he wrote to a later lover in 1908: "I told him about Dil and me long
ago at Eton. . . . I've never seen anyone so much surprised—and so jealous. . . .
Apparently he had longed to do likewise himself and had never dared."[72] To
another friend and lover Maynard remarked on "the astounding . . . goings on
of my circle during my last year at school. . . . Walks in which the doctrine of
the Resurrection of the body alternated with the problem as to whether a kiss
shd. be followed up by a cop[ulation]."[73] It does not appear that Maynard made
a conscious connection between these "goings on" and the whippings he had
experienced at home plus the canings he underwent or witnessed as praeposter,
senior student responsible for discipline, at school. His diary, which he lacka-
daisically kept for a half-year at Eton, mildly records his three canings in the
final term of his second year, one of them inflicted, he insisted, "absolutely
unjustly." He made a joke of caning in a letter to Geoffrey, inquiring if his
brother had yet been "beaten . . . on your natural cushion?"[74] Or was it a joke?
At King's College he would resume the more pleasurable goings on in earnest.

At nineteen Maynard was a fully defined person, sexually determined at least
for an extended period and intellectually fully competent to understand, consciously or unconsciously, the essentials of his existence. European primary and
secondary schools teach their students much more than do American schools.
At the age of an American university junior Maynard was better equipped to
manage information and to think than the average American graduate. If he
lacked much science and if some of his mental stock was more decorative than
functional, thus his command of classical languages and texts, he had exercised
his mind well and learned to write freely and efficiently. He would become his
own director of studies at the next stage of his education.

On 1 October 1902 Maynard settled into King's College in a manner suggesting that it was their joint, inevitable fate. A medium-sized college, it had

about 150 students and thirty dons then in a university of some three thousand students. Although it emphasized teaching rather than scholarship, its teaching was highly regarded and brought its prestige close to the level of such larger and more scholarly colleges as Trinity and St. John's. One of Maynard's first friends there recalled their meeting on the staircase in the shabby students' residence on King's Lane known as the "Lane," later more descriptively as the "Drain." (It was torn down in 1967 and replaced by a handsome structure that the maturer Keynes funded.) Maynard invited Charles R. Fay, later a distinguished economic historian, to tea: " 'My name's Keynes. What's yours?' " Maynard had improved on his surroundings: "He had a mustache and a fancy waistcoat, a beautifully carved desk, and a wicker basket." He presently told Fay, "I've had a good look round this place and come to the conclusion that it's pretty inefficient." He may already have begun projecting the improvements he would personally carry out. In Fay's memoir he surveyed, not too hyperbolically, Keynes's career beyond King's College: "[N]one of us forsaw . . . that, before he was finished, he would be running the world."[75]

King's College would be the Archimedean point from which Keynes would exercise his world leverage. Except for a two-year interruption he would maintain his residence there, while adding sites in London and Sussex, for the rest of his life. He could not have made a more appropriate choice than King's. The college is a range of architectural splendor based on its chapel, which the city guide asserts without contradiction "is the most magnificent building in Cambridge, dominating the city by its size and beauty."[76] "Chapel" is technically correct but misleading. It is, not by chance, the size of a cathedral, Henry VI having conceived it to match Eton's chapel and that chapel was expressly projected to be longer than Salisbury Cathedral. Eton's great chapel was never built, but King's College Chapel was completed in 1515. Its length, at 289 feet, is all the more imposing because no transept interrupts it, while its eighty feet of height also works imposingly. But its late-Gothic allure enchants as well, with the chapel's great serrated pinnacles at its four corners and more modest ones fixed along the four sides of the roof line. Inside one looks up, up to the weblike tracery of the fan-vaulting—astonishing, heavenly!—the last, supreme touch of the Tudor masons. The choir, its younger members wearing top hats and Eton jackets, is renowned. Although the secure atheist Maynard Keynes was weakly musical, he liked, sometimes accompanied by guests, to slip into the chapel to listen to it at eventide. The chapel's eastern front faces the street, called King's Parade for a few hundred feet in the college's proximity. (Farther north the street changes its name to accommodate Trinity and then St. John's Colleges.) The pinnacle motif is taken up by the screen, a wall with Gothic apertures and an exorbitantly ornate gatehouse that runs southward parallel with King's Parade from the chapel to the college dining hall. Extending from the dining hall westward is a range of buildings that includes the library and the provost's lodge. Another college structure, the three-storied classic Fellows Building (1724–32), all harmony and restraint, extends from the southwestern corner of the chapel to the other college buildings and joins with them and the screen to form the college's luxuriously spacious front court. On the other side of the Fellows Building a great lawn falls away toward the threadlike River Cam, also called the Granta. The Cam flows behind several of the colleges on its looping way through Cambridge, and their back lawns join with the King's College lawn to form "the Backs," inviting to outdoor lounging in good weather. The languid Cam is perfect for punting (or, better, yet, being punted), a fine way of enjoying a balmy day and the university's architectural treasures. If Maynard's sensibilities never achieved aesthetic or musical heights, he could not help responding gratefully to such generous gifts. It did not matter that he was, for his first year, placed away from the grand front court in mean lodgings reached through a cramped, mean side court and an underground passage. As his new friend Fay could see, young Keynes was at home.

In his concern for efficiency Maynard might have pointed out, if he had anticipated his own professional knowledge or drawn upon his father's, that King's College was a remarkably uneconomic enterprise. Such an enormous plant for two hundred faculty members and students! Certainly it made more sense than the pre-reform establishment of a half-century earlier, when their numbers barely reached seventy. Then, most of the faculty treated the college as a rest home and the students needed no more energy to depart with their BA's. Even today, with five hundred undergraduate and graduate students, the King's College population could be accommodated in the satellite campus of an American community college. (All of Cambridge University today has some fifteen thousand students.) Yet, like the other colleges, this beneficiary of five centuries of royal, aristocratic, and, more lately, plutocratic favors, has contributed immeasurably to the nation over those centuries in the form of spirit, culture, and more or less well-trained talent. Young Keynes slips easily into the line of succession.

Under his own guidance Maynard immediately established a pattern radically different from his Etonian modus operandi. If Gurney Lubbock had adjusted his curriculum to his affinities and if his father had exhorted or manipulated rather than commanded, Maynard had kept discipline. At King's he shattered the given structure. He did begin to meet regularly with a supervisor of studies, but the man is just a name in the record; he seems to have had no effect on what Maynard studied. Maynard also had a coach in mathematics, a capacity of considerable distinction, and he did apply himself to mathematics, but within limits he himself set. On 9 October 1902 Neville observed, "Maynard is settled at King's. It seems strange having him in Cambridge, and yet not with us." Almost immediately he found himself contemplating his son's recalcitrance in mathematics, Maynard informing him that he did not propose to concentrate on it.[77] Maynard had found a natural competitor in his lodgings, one William Norton Page, who joined him in undergoing the ministrations of the mathematics coach. Disdainfully, he told Neville that Page was working eight hours day, but that he was keeping up with Page on a maximum of six hours. He found Page, only a mathematician, a bore and a precise example of what not to be. Helplessly, Neville wrote, "I feel he ought to get in more than he does after dinner." Two days later Neville had Maynard joining the Apennine Literary Society, one of the many clubs at the college, to begin an extensive exploration of extracurricular activities. Before the end of October Neville found matters worse: "I am afraid the boy is not doing much work this week."[78] A month later Maynard had tea with his parents and announced that he would give up rowing, which he had continued at King's, but with the satisfaction of having seen his boat win a race. *But*, "The boy has joined another debating society, and can now [enter] up to five debates a week." Neville protested, "It is too much." Furthermore, pursuing another interest, "He is still spending his substance at David's" (the Cambridge bookseller).[79] In mid-December Maynard was devoting three morning hours to his mathematics and his evenings to working up an essay on Peter Abelard for the Apennine Society. He was radically readjusting, while maintaining, his specialist-generalist orientation. The mathematics, for which he would be tested in the tripos after three years, constituted the irreducible core of his objectives as undergraduate, but he constricted it within his other interests, intellectual and scholarly, literary, rhetorical and political, athletic, hedonistic and amatory, and social.

Maynard and Neville continued to agonize over the mathematics. One might wonder why Neville encouraged his son in this direction after Neville himself had found the subject a torture and escaped into the moral sciences. Why, given Maynard's broad interests, had Neville not raised that possibility? His diary and the other sources offer no definite answer, but Maynard had a proven and recognized mathematical capacity; that promised more security to a fearfully security-minded person. Despite his own pain in the past Neville remained anesthetized to Maynard's pain in the present. As for Maynard, he found it difficult to break completely with a vested interest and an established pattern; the mathematics might well have its value and meanwhile he had his other burgeoning interests to impassion and distract him. One possibility was not immediately open, namely economics, except as part of the moral sciences, and Neville had his responsibility for that. We should recall that the economics tripos, which he had opposed, was not established until a year after Maynard entered King's. Looking ahead to his projected postgraduate year, however, one could envision the economics as an eventuality. Yet Maynard's general program, including his nonacademic activities, overwhelmed the value of this or that detail. With hindsight one can see that his decisions or avoidances of decisions were all fundamentally correct. He may not have needed all that mathematics, although it gave him an easier fluency in managing his eventual economics. On the other hand, his career demonstrated the wide and deep uses of the apparently irrelevant, including interests for which he had no affinity. Joined with his real talents they would put him in touch with a great range of experience—would permit him to overleap the limits of any profession and achieve his unique greatness. Neville, had he foreseen it, would have been all the more appalled.

Mathematics, whatever its excellences, became a source of joint depression for father and son. Early in Maynard's second term Florence found him "rather depressed" about it. "He says he is coming to the conclusion that it is his worst subject." At the end of his first year, in mid-June 1903, Neville was "feeling very much depressed and worried about Maynard's future, whether we did the right thing in letting him read mathematics." Neville fled into wishful thinking: "No doubt if he would work regularly six hours a day it would be all right." (A month later he could at least record that his son was in new rooms in the main court with a view of the wondrous chapel.)[80] At the beginning of the next year Maynard "is as late as ever in the mornings, but," Neville comforted himself, "he often sits up workng till nearly two A.M." Approaching his final undergraduate year, "Maynard is working at mathematics in the mornings and at Burke . . . in the evenings."[81] Maynard was competing for the university essay prize and duly won it with his essay on Edmund Burke's political ideas. For Neville that could be reason for pride, but not comfort.

Before the tripos, beginning on 15 May 1905 and comprehending two four-day periods, Maynard wrote dispiritedly to Bernard Swithinbank, "I am soddening my brain, destroying my intellect, souring my disposition in a panic-stricken attempt to acquire the rudiments of the mathematics."[82] A few days later Neville noted, "Maynard is tired and depressed. . . . We are worried about him." Neville announced himself also "feeling very tired and depressed." It was "partly . . . due to worry about Maynard. I think he is going to do badly, and I am oppressed by the idea that I ought not to have encouraged him to read mathematics. He has throughout found the subject irksome." In the interval between the two sets of examinations, "I have Maynard on my mind, and my thoughts are constantly reverting to him in season and out of season."[83] Accepting the part of a gentleman's gentleman, Neville was appearing at Maynard's rooms every morning to get him up on time. One morning he found Maynard in his bath less than a half hour before the examination was to begin. Emerging from the tripos, predicting his position on the list of honors in mathematics, "Maynard sees himself himself as high as twelfth Wrangler." Neville, however, appended as forebodingly as a Greek chorus, "[B]ut I am afraid he is too sanguine."[84] The next day was Maynard's birthday and Florence signaled it in a letter: "[I]t is natural that I should think of you . . . today. I hope for—and expect—success this time as so often before, but whatever the result may be next week, I shall be proud of your university career and satisfied that you have spent your time well."[85] As usual Neville's fearfulness threw off his judgment, while Maynard's feeling for his situation, his mother concurring, was correct, indeed precisely so.

On 13 June 1905 Neville could write, "Maynard is bracketed [paired] twelfth with one other." Maynard's first-year neighbor Page, for all his concentration, was minimally better as eighth Wrangler, also bracketed. Neville loyally made the best of it. With well wishes divided between congratulations and condolences, "On the whole we are satisfied." Reflexively, however, he regretted:

"[T]he boy might have done better had he devoted himself more exclusively to his mathematics." Against this, firmly, Maynard "maintained that he is glad he gave no more time to mathematics, even though it would have meant a much better place on the tripos list."[86] He had his postgraduate year in which to improve his situation, but, more important, he had been training himself more fittingly for his eventual career(s).

A month later, reflecting on the tripos results, Neville noted, "We have not yet decided whether Maynard shall take Part II of the moral sciences tripos or of the economics tripos."[87] So, at last, the moral sciences became a postgraduate option at least, while economics was now available as well. Although Neville did not mention it in the diary entry, the civil service, which he had had in mind since Maynard's last year at Eton, was also an option. For his specialist-generalist son, who was turning his back on his specialty of mathematics, the situation was not too disagreeable. By this time he was already investigating economics as another possible field, but also he intuitively demanded the time and experience to make a choice in the frame of the affinities he was still in process of discovering in himself.

Before the end of June 1905 Neville's diary had noted, "Maynard now working assiduously on Marshall's *Principles of Economics*."[88] Whatever the purpose—the moral sciences or economics tripos, or the civil service examination—Maynard, his father's son, immediately felt a deep affinity here. Two days later, rising out of the frustrations of an inconclusive love affair, Maynard wrote to Swithinbank, "The ease with which one recovers and takes refuge in political economy . . . is terrifying and humiliating. . . . [F]or the last few days a reactionary love of knowledge has entirely filled me."[89] He would, however, soon demonstrate that he could devote himself to the two kinds of love simultaneously. Now economics was more than comfort. A week later he wrote Lytton Strachey, a Trinity College student and newer friend, that he was reading "masses of economics." He had "discovered someone whom I had not realized to be very good—namely [W. Stanley] Jevons. I am convinced that he is one of *the* minds of the century. He has the curiously exciting style of writing which one gets if one is good enough."[90] Maynard had settled into King's for three weeks of hard reading in economics. He was also spending time with Arthur C. Pigou, a young economics lecturer and protégé of Alfred Marshall's. Empathizing with Pigou's scandalous love of undergraduates, he helped check the proofs of his new book on labor relations and provided "valuable help," Pigou acknowledged, on its mathematical appendix.[91] Pigou would become an important and benign presence in Maynard's professional life. After a mountain-climbing expedition in the Alps, another conscientious foray into the always strange world of sport, Maynard returned to King's and economics in September 1905. By October, according to recently discovered documents, he had read more than a score of major economic writings from David Ricardo to Jevons, Marshall, and beyond. At that time, on 12 October, he attested to his serious interest in economics—and the limits to it. Filling out an application to attend Marshall's lectures, he appended a list of books he had read, but also specified: "I shall not be able to devote the whole of my time to economics as I intend to enter for the civil service examination in Aug. 1906."[92] The mathematics student of modest accomplishment was confronting embarrassing riches in career possibilities.

While attending two months of Marshall's lectures during the fall of 1905 Maynard wrote two dozen essays, some quite long (e.g., thirty-four and forty-six pages), for Pigou as well Marshall. His subjects included the marginal utility of labor, pension systems (Maynard emphasizing the moral need "to remove the widespread *causes* of distress"), Ricardo's "invariable . . . standard" of value, monopolies, the rationale of export duties (about which Maynard, as a Liberal believer in free trade, felt "very doubtful"), index numbers, trusts and railways, and "Pure Economic," this latter a survey of economic theory beginning with a "Note on Elasticity in Symmetric Curves." Here was a blaze of talent that teased Marshall with a second chance to enlist a reluctant Keynes in his crusade. About a comparison of railway service in two countries, Marshall began, "The answer is good," noted that Keynes had more to say, and raised his valuation to "a brilliant answer." On another paper he had already accepted young Keynes into the profession: "I trust that your future career may be one in wh. you will not cease to be an economist." He repeated, "I should be glad if it could be that of economist." That did not prevent his disputing and correcting passages where he thought Maynard had gone too far or missed the point, but the great man treated him as a colleague capable of equally valid judgments. About a paper on pricing under monopoly and competition Marshall scrawled on the back of the page, "I repeat what I said before, that I shd. immensely like to see you become a member of some economic staff, & especially of this." Resignedly, he added, "But I know the world is large."[93]

Marshall's flattering respect nevertheless had its effects along with Maynard's recognition of his taste for economic reasoning. To Lytton Strachey, resettled in London, he wrote seriously as well as jokingly on 15 November 1905, "I find economics increasingly satisfactory, and I think I am rather good at it. I want to manage a railway or organize a trust or at least swindle the investing public."[94] After a week he was less secure about his prospects as economist: "Do you think there is anything in it.[*sic*] I doubt it. I could probably get employment here. . . . But prolonging my existence in this place would be, I feel sure, death. . . . I suppose I shall drift."[95] If "death" was too dramatic, "drift" described his situation perfectly. For another moment Maynard had lapsed into a fit of depression. Some of his friends, like Strachey, had left, and his postgraduate year seemed lonely despite remaining friends and a family in residence. Perhaps the presence of his family, particularly of Neville, was beginning to oppress him. Uncharacteristically indecisive and hating it, Maynard nevertheless resisted the impulse to make a decision before he was ready.

Three days later Neville noted, "Maynard looked in. . . . I am afraid Marshall is endeavoring to persuade him to give up everything for economics." Moreover, Neville exclaimed, "Maynard himself has this afternoon broached the idea that he would give up reading for the Civil Service!"[96] This was only a momentary caesura. Lytton had replied to Maynard, "Oh, no, it would surely be mad to be a Cambridge economist. Come to London, go to the Treasury, set up house with me. The parties we'd give. . . ."[97] In the event Maynard spent four days in London as Lytton's guest in mid-December and on 18 December Neville recorded, "Maynard is now at home and working at psychology. His last idea is to give up the economics tripos so as to concentrate on preparation for the C. S. exam[n]."[98] Later, in May 1906, Marshall tried to reverse this reversal, but having invested heavily in cramming for the civil service examination by then, Maynard could easily keep to his plan.[99] Marshall's determination, part of his greatness, and Maynard's talents, continuing to unfold toward *his* greatness, did not permit that to be the end of it.

Since Maynard went on to become an economist, it might seem that the civil service represented a wasteful career detour. Yet his scope as economist comprehended much more than economics. His life at King's College prefigured this accurately. Between the mathematics, which he was letting slip, and the economics, at which he had impressively arrived, he had compacted a number of other career-enhancing learning activities.

Maynard had alighted running at King's College and never stopped. After a month he had written to Swithinbank:

Immediately after [dining] hall I went to a Trinity essay society and heard a most brilliant satire on Christianity [by Strachey: evidently his first experience of Strachey]. From there I went to an informal philosophical debating society of interesting people where I stayed till nearly twelve; I then went to see Monty [Montagu R.] James [bibliophile and biblical scholar who would become King's College provost, 1905–18] where I stayed till one; from there I went on to another man with whom I talked till half past four. At half past seven I got up and read the lesson in Chapel. I had four hours' work that morning, and rowed half a course in the afternoon. In the evening I went as a visitor to the Political Society to hear a paper on the Jesuits. . . . The President of the [Cambridge] Union has put me on the paper to speak.[100]

Early in his second term, besides dutifully attending to his mathematics, Maynard sought other intellectual nourishment in the lectures on ethics by the philosopher G. E. Moore, who would have an important influence on his thought, and another philosopher, J. E. McTaggart, who would have a passing effect on it. In the name of a remarkably idealistic empiricism Moore was attacking the Hegelian idealism of McTaggart. Toward the end of his second year, in April 1904, "Maynard looked in to dinner," Neville recorded. His son, gourmet of ideas, was attending the lectures of the mathematician and idealist philosopher Alfred North Whitehead "three times a week *solus*"—thus evidently as Whitehead's total audience. Maynard found them "interesting, but," Neville silently objected, "they will pay very little, if at all, for the tripos."[101] If one looks beyond the tripos, which Maynard *solus* was doing, they paid.

The undergraduate and graduate student read much on his own. During the Easter vacation of 1905, just before the mathematics tripos and paying not at all for it, Maynard listed these readings, inter alia: Plato's *Symposium*, *Phaedrus*, and *Republic*; Aristotle's *Politics*, Henry James's *Sacred Fount*, Herbert Spencer on education, Thomas S. Moore on Albrecht Dürer, Gilbert Murray's translation of *The Trojan Women* of Euripides, Henri Poincaré's *Science et hypothèse* in translation, and Shakespeare's *Sonnets*. In June, following the tripos, he listed *Romeo and Juliet*, H. G. Wells's *Modern Utopia*, and a work of Maxim Gorky. Preparing for Marshall's lectures he devoted July to economics, but in August read Jane Austen and the first twenty chapters of Edward Gibbon's *Decline and Fall of the Roman Empire*. From September to the end of 1905 his notes record more economics, but also Shelley, Hume, the economic historian Arnold Toynbee, Oscar Wilde's *Dorian Grey*, Thorstein Veblen's *Theory of Business Enterprise*, and *King Lear* as well as the *Sonnets* again. From January to May 1906, while preparing for the civil service examinations he listed some seventy works, many in history and philosophy, but also more Shakespeare and a novel of Robert Louis Stevenson.[102] At the same time, as mentioned here already, he was processing these materials, his lectures, and other intellectual fodder into writings.

Maynard expended a great part of his mental energy writing essays of his own choice. The essay on Peter Abelard (1079–1142), begun before the end of his first term at King's College, suggested that the medieval period he had explored at Eton was not his mind's natural habitat. Bernard of Cluny, as examined in his Eton essay, represented an ascetic's pure faith. In forty-six pages Maynard now found more in common with Abelard as an engaged member of his society and the incorporation of reason's moderation: "the first light out of the darkness of medievalism."[103] Maynard's exposure to McTaggart's philosophy led to an extended metaphysical *jeu d'esprit*, "Time," for another literary society, the exotically named Parrhesiasts, evidently read on 8 May 1913.[104] Referring eruditely to Newton's conception of time, Maynard argued that it was infinite and hence lacking a logical starting point. He leaped to the conclusion that the world was purposeless and goalless, while "time and change are delusions, and . . . the universe is present in a timeless, changeless perfection." That led obscurely "to the question of the explanation of good and evil . . . upon which Dr. McTaggart is at present lecturing." Disarmingly, Maynard confessed at the end, "We have clearly tied ourselves into knots in every direction, and the question . . . is consequently unproven." The essay was a game with other persons' ideas, and if Maynard had failed to advance beyond them, he had shown the skills of an apprentice thinker and potential teacher. This was true of his other writings: dexterity rather than originality.

In a new flow of essays, some two dozen in less than a decade (these not including the economics essays for Marshall), Maynard moved on to an intellectual style and position from which he would never depart. G. E. Moore provided the precise inspiration, indeed the logical matrix, in his *Principia Ethica*, published in the fall of 1903.[105] A nourishing social context was provided by the Cambridge Conversazione Society, a discussion society founded in 1820, of which Moore and Maynard, the latter since February 1903, were both members. Others included the mathematician-philosophers Whitehead and Bertrand Russell, the novelist E. M. Forster, and Maynard's friend, Lytton Strachey.

Moore provided a religion for the group in the form of an ethical philosophy to replace a discarded Christianity. Although the members, who mockingly called themselves Apostles, thought they had left religion behind, they maintained a guilty faith in its basic propositions. Thus Moore's aim was to achieve goodness, a barely secular translation of sanctity. He employed metaphysical formulae to relate the somewhat Dechristianized good to good feelings, seen as approximations of happiness, and good appearances, thus beauty. The good and its analogues were Platonic or Kantian essences (Moore had written his dissertation on Kant) and constituted the primal life materials. Impure realities could be analyzed and their parts separated out, but the essences themselves could not be further broken down. Hence—Moore hurled himself with intimidating authority over the nonsequitur—the good was indefinable. "If I am asked, 'How is the good to be defined?,' my answer is that it cannot be defined, and that is all I have to say about it."[106] The Apostles, Maynard prominently among them, assigned themselves the endless task of deciding what Moore and they themselves really meant.

Our concern here is not so much what young Keynes thought, as how he thought, in the process of training himself to function professionally as economist, policymaker, and politician, inter alia. Since Moore's ultimate realities were indefinable, unerring intuition was necessary to penetrate to them. Confident that he had it, Moore was adept in his use of the "accents of infallibility," as the mature Keynes put it.[107] Maynard, *his* confidence erected upon parental love and young achievement, easily followed in security of intuition and accents.

Maynard moved swiftly from seeing Moore's *Principia Ethica* as a "stupendous and entraordinary work, the *greatest* on the subject,"[108] to correcting the master. Incidentally raising the question of probability, the book led to Keynes's dissertation, later published as *A Treatise on Probability*.[109] Moore had argued that the existing rules of moralists as guided by the law of probability were the best way to determine if one was committing good instead of evil. Addressing the issue in three essays for the Apostles, the first read to them in January 1904, Maynard countered that Moore was applying the wrong laws of probability, namely mathematical frequency, instead of the relevant ones, which had to do with the grander subject of belief as developed by Aristotle, Leibniz, and Locke. Just before writing the essay, according to Neville's diary, Maynard had been studying mathematical probability.[110]

In an early, thinly covert sign of rebellion against his father, Maynard proposed to correct that estimable logician on probability along with Moore: "[T]he logic books, though sometimes plausible, are not really adequate."[111] It is typical of Keynes, early as well as late, that he could combine unabashed criticism with disarming admissions. Thus he concluded, "I do not claim to put forward any precise definition of probability and I hope the society [the Apostles] will be able to give me something more convincing."[112] Another essay on Mooreian problematics, written in the summer of the next year, mixed extravagance, administrative ambition—and pure presumption. Maynard proposed a "catalogue raisonée of fit objects and good feelings" as a kind of Mooreian cosmography. It would comprise 150 volumes: "Moore himself might be employed (at a small but sufficient salary) to write it under direction." The bibliophilic Keynes, immediately providing direction, specified the use of Baskerville type and, as "essential preliminary . . . a search through the cellars of France for the silver type aforesaid."[113] Maynard could be as silly as he frequently found his seniors.

Other essays ranged irregularly around the landscape of a competent, interested, and irregularly stocked mind. Essays on "beauty" showed great dialectical skill combined with a pathetic failure of aesthetic apprehension. One began disarmingly perhaps by confessing "to feign certainty . . . that one's mind is certainly without." It made no reference to a given object, but another did actually mention specific works of art, thus "the difference between Botticelli and Degas, between Venus of Milo and the Balzac of Rodin."[114] The difference remained unarticulated and invisible. Once again young Keynes showed his limits.

Within his limits Maynard could be outstanding. His ninety-nine-page essay of 1904 on Edmund Burke was superior to anything else he had written and suggested his expanding potentials. Keynes's ultimate statement—his greatness—would consist of a fusion of thought and action; the essay commended a similar fusion in Burke. At the same time, conceding the defects of their similar positions, he could easily identify with Burke: "The whirl and the interest of affairs, the strength of his domestic affections and of his political passions, conspired together to defeat any early ambitions . . . to shine as an exponent of pure political theory." To pass from Burke to Keynes one need only exchange "political" for "economic" in the last phrase. Pragmatically, Maynard tried to excuse in Burke a "preference of peace over truth," as if the two were logically opposed. In any case he was easily excusing politic mendacity. On the other hand, "the great political ideals," as shown by the French Revolution, which Burke had so profoundly and prophetically analyzed, might be "madness and delusion [but had] provided a more powerful motive force than any Burke has to offer." His man taught "wisdom [but not] the essentials of leadership."[115] Through Burke's thought and experience, the young man had glimpsed the boundary of good sense in politics and demonstrated his own mature political wisdom.

An important ingredient in the Burke essay's reasoning was the writer's political experience. On 10 October 1902 Neville himself had nominated the newly matriculated Maynard for membership in the Cambridge Union, and by 4 November his diary reported on his son's maiden speech in the university debating society: "He felt nervous and he says it was the bravest thing he ever did. He thinks he was coherent." The unabashed Eton orator had realized that Cambridge demanded a higher performance level; he did not communicate his stage fright and quickly regained his Etonian confidence. A university publication found that he had "interesting opinions even on a dull subject at late hour. He speaks a little fast."[116] The Union president was Edwin Montagu, a member of a Jewish family prominent in Liberal politics, and Montagu became an early patron of Maynard's. In return, in January 1906, the graduate student campaigned for Montagu in the general election, a great Liberal victory. Meanwhile, after serving as secretary, Maynard succeeded Montagu in the Union's presidency. Maynard also soon joined the university's Liberal Club and became its president as well. In his second term he also carried out a successful political action in King's College. With John T. Sheppard, another Apostle and future colleague, he opposed the establishment of a college mission in a parish of the Church of England in South London. Both members of dissenting families, they eloquently objected that the scheme should be on a nonsectarian basis; the eventual resolution was to organize a boys club in Cambridge itself.[117] G. M. Trevelyan, the Cambridge University historian who often took Maynard for exhausting walks, got it half right when, futilely opposing his entry into the civil service, he argued, "You are born to be a politician."[118]

The range of subjects on the civil service examination conveniently addressed the generalist in young Keynes. In December 1905 he commenced his readings, beginning with psychology and, in January, continuing with Greek philosophy. That did not prevent his campaigning for Montagu that January and, in the early spring, spending more than 1 month on a continental holiday, accompanied, however, by utilitarian reading material. The holiday included two weeks as guest of Mary Berenson, the American wife of the art connoisseur Bernard Berenson and sister-in-law of the Apostolic Bertrand Russell. One week was occupied making a motor tour of Tuscany, the party also including an Oxford undergraduate and Mary Berenson's daughters Ray and Karin by an English husband she had left for Berenson. After Maynard and the other student spent a conscientious ten-day study interval in Siena, they were guests for a week at the Berenson villa I Tatti near Florence. During the first week Maynard had reported to Lytton, "The boys vary amazingly from place to place," but almost all were "physically repulsive." At I Tatti he declared himself "fallen in love with [the eighteen-year-old] Ray a little, but as she isn't male I haven't had to think of any suitable steps to take." As for their host, "Bernard B. is, I am sure rather a bad man, but we've hardly seen him." In Siena Maynard had been studying history for six hours a day, but self-defeatingly: "I've never come on any subject that is so easy and cloys so quickly."[119]

For the examination in London from 2 to 24 August 1906, Neville organized a major family operation, renting a flat in South Kensington and expediting

Florence and Margaret there: "The pianola goes with them."[120] Later, Neville and Margaret changed places.[121] Maynard was the second of 104 candidates. Defeated for the first-choice Treasury post, he accepted an India Office clerkship as the only satisfactory second choice. His training was over. His career began on 16 October 1906.

Maynard's marks as well as the subject variety of the examination further emphasized his capabilities as a generalist. He insisted on being "enraged" at the results, which he found skewed. As he wrote to Lytton Strachey, "I have done worst in the only two subjects of which I possessed solid knowledge—mathematics and economics."[122] He later insisted that he knew more economics than his examiners.[123] This is possible, given his considerable readings for Marshall. Furthermore, one can easily imagine that his risk-taking mind, which Marshall, although appreciating, tolerantly corrected, put off less competent intelligences. In any case his ranking in economics itself, seventh out of 104, was not bad at all, particularly because he had been competing with candidates who had concentrated on the subject. The question of mathematics, his tripos subject, is less disputable. He was eighteenth in the "mathematics" part and seventh in "advanced mathematics"; he had been wise to have fled the subject. On the other hand, he was first in political science, and logic and psychology, and second in moral and metaphysical philosophy and in English composition. He was twentieth and twelfth in the two periods of English history examined,[124] due, quite possibly, to his cavalier attitude to the subject. If the civil service could well use such general competence, it was too much for the kind of work required. As he would almost immediately discover, he was overqualified for his post and bored with its mediocre demands on him. An important part of his ability, however, was the fact that he could make the most of almost any experience. He would be able to adjust the balance between generalist and specialist at his ease. The India Office, although their association was brief, would be another critical success in his career.

NOTES

1. JNK Diary, 12, 13 July 1897.

2. Letter quoted, ibid., 4 April 1901. The Eton year was divided into three "halves" or terms.

3. Ibid., 11 April 1901.

4. Ibid., 5 June, 14 December 1884.

5. Report for term ending 17 April 1889, Perse Girls' School, KP, PP/21; JNK Diary, 14 April 1889.

6. JNK Diary, 20–21 July 1889.

7. Florence Ada Keynes, *Gathering up the Threads*, 64.

8. Geoffrey Keynes, *Gates of Memory*, 20.

9. As Neville recalled much later, JNK Diary, 16 July 1902.

10. Ibid., 8 March 1889.

11. Ibid., 21 January 1891.

12. "He is a good deal the youngest," Neville emphasized, ibid., 14 March 1892.

13. Ibid., 29 March 1892.

14. Report, 14 April 1892, KP, PP/21.

15. JNK Diary, 28 May 1892.

16. 7 August 1892.

17. Ibid., 19 December 1892.

18. Moggridge, *MK*, 26.

19. JNK Diary, 11, 21, 26 February 1893.

20. Ibid., 30 April, 2 May 1893.

21. Report to parents, 2 August 1894, KP, PP/21.

22. Report to parents, 4 April 1896, ibid.

23. Report to parents, 18 August 1896, ibid.

24. JNK Diary, 16 July 1897.

25. Ibid., 17, 22 December 1897; letter, Goodchild to JNK, 24 December 1897, KP, PP/21.

26. JNK Diary.

27. Geoffrey Keynes, *Gates of Memory*, 101.

28. JNK Diary, 12 January 1897.

29. Ibid., 26 June, 4, 6, 11, 12, 13, 14 July 1897.

30. Richard Ollard, *An English Education*, 182. For much of the foregoing see ibid. Also, Christopher Hollis, *Eton: A History* (London, 1960); Oscar Browning, *Memories of Sixty Years at Eton* (London, 1910); Sybille Bedford, *Aldous Huxley: A Biography* (New York, 1985; 1st ed., 1973), 27–31, 88–92.

31. Browning, *Memories*, 16.

32. Aldous Huxley, arriving in 1908, quoted, Bedford, *Aldous Huxley*, 30.

33. Quoted, Ollard, *An English Education*, 54.

34. JNK Diary, 30 September, 9 October 1897.

35. FAK to Maynard, 19 July 1898, KP, PP/45/168.

36. Letters, Maynard to FAK, JNK to Maynard, 11, 14 October 1897, ibid.

37. Calligraphed listing of Maynard's prizes, KP, PP/21.

38. Quoted, Skidelsky, *JMK*, 1:97.

39. JNK to Maynard, 14 December 1901, KP, PP/45/168.

40. Ibid.

41. JNK Diary, 7 November 1900.

42. JNK to Maynard, 11 November 1900, KP, PP/45/168.

43. Ibid.

44. 21 July 1898, ibid.

45. 18 June 1899, ibid.

46. 21, 31 July 1899, ibid.

47. 4 February 1901, ibid.

48. FAK, JNK to Maynard, 16, 17 June 1900, ibid.

49. JNK Diary, 14 January 1902.

50. Letter to JNK, 7 December 1897, KP, PP/21.

51. Report by G. H. Hurst, December 1900, ibid.

52. Classical Report, H. E. Luxmoore, Lent 1901, ibid.

53. JNK to Maynard, 9 December 1898, KP, PP/45/168.

54. Maynard to JNK, 14 May 1899, ibid.

55. Maynard to JNK, 17 December 1899, ibid.

56. The essays, Early Creative Writing and Notes, 1897–1901, KP, PP/31.

57. 2 AMS [autograph manuscript signed] Essays on Bernard of Cluny, KP, PP/33.

58. 1 July 1900, KP, PP/45/168.

59. Harrod, *The Life*, 13.

60. Classical Report, Michaelmas 1900, KP, PP/21.

61. 2 February 1900, KP, PP/45/144.

62. Maynard to JNK, 27 January 1901, 9 February 1902, KP, PP/45/168.

63. Maynard to JNK, 15 December 1901, ibid.

64. Maynard to FAK, 2 May 1902; JNK to Maynard, 17 December 1901, ibid.

65. JNK Diary, 1892–97, and KP, PP/45/168 passim. The "twitching," as reported by a friend, JNK Diary, 26 November 1898.

66. Letter, 26 July 1900, KP, PP/45/168.

67. Maynard to JNK, 12 May 1901, ibid.

68. Photocopy of article in *Windsor & Eton Express*, 7 December 1901, attached to letter of Maynard to JNK, 9 February 1902, KP, PP/45/168.

69. Maynard to JNK, FAK to Maynard, Maynard to JNK, 29, 30 January, 4 February 1900, ibid.

70. Knox ("ADK") is listed for 1901 and 1902, and Macmillan ("DM") for 1902 on one of three lists of young Keynes's sexual activities, but Swithinbank is not on any list. The three lists, KP, PP/20A. More on these activities of JMK's, ch. 4.

71. 25 December 1905, KP, PP/45/174, labeled as "[unsent?]."

72. Letter to Duncan Grant, 22 December 1908, BL, Add. MSS 57930.

73. Letter to Lytton Strachey, 27 March 1905, KP, PP/45/316.

74. 3 July 1899, KP, PP/35; 20 September 1901, KP, PP/45/167.

75. C. R. Fay, "The Undergraduate," in Milo Keynes, ed., *Essays on JMK*, 36–38.

76. *A Jarrold Guide to the University City of Cambridge* (Norwich, 1992), 10.

77. JNK Diary, 15 October 1902.

78. Ibid., 18, 20, 30 October 1902.

79. Ibid., 26 November 1902.

80. Ibid., 18 February, 16 June, 14 July 1903.

81. Ibid., 9 January, 9 September 1904.

82. 18 April 1905, KP, PP/45/321.

83. JNK Diary, 4, 19, 22 May 1905.

84. Ibid., 25 May, 2, 4 June 1905.

85. KP, PP/45/168.

86. JNK Diary, 13 June 1908.

87. Ibid., 16 July 1905.

88. Ibid., 28 June 1908.

89. 30 June 1905, KP, PP/45/321.

90. 8 July 1905, KP, PP/45/316.

91. Letter, Maynard to Lytton Strachey, 20 July 1905, ibid; Moggridge, *MK*, 83.

92. Quoted, Moggridge, *MK*, p. and n. 95.

93. AMS economics essays marked by Professors A. C. Pigou and A. Marshall . . . examination papers . . . 1905, KP, University Affairs (hereafter UA)/3. Marshall comments on papers of 9 November, 31 October, 9 November 1905.

94. KP, PP/45/316. Harrod made too much of the joke by eliding the reference to swindling, followed by Skidelsky, who scolded Harrod for the elision.

95. Letter, 23 November 1905, ibid.

96. JNK Diary, 26 November 1908.

97. Letter, 27 November 1905, KP, PP/45/316.

98. JNK Diary.

99. "[I]f you went in for the Tripos, merely re-reading Economics in the ten days before it, you would *probably* get a first class," Marshall to Maynard, 2 May 1906, *CW*, 15: 2.

100. 13 November 1902, KP, PP/45/321.

101. JNK Diary, 23 January 1903, 28 April 1904.

102. AMS lists of books read . . . 1905 . . . 1906, KP, UA/24.

103. 2 AMS drafts, 1 incomplete, of an essay on Peter Abelard, KP, UA/16. Quotation from complete draft.

104. KP, UA/17.

105. G. E. Moore, *Principia Ethica* (Cambridge, 1962; 1st ed., 1903).

106. Ibid., 6.

107. Maynard, in his memoir of 1938, *My Early Beliefs, CW*, 10: 438.

108. Letter to Swithinbank, 7 October 1903, KP, PP/45/321.

109. *CW*, 8 (first published in 1921).

110. JNK Diary, 19 December 1903. In his *MK*, Moggridge has questioned (131–36) the dating of Keynes's first essay on Moore's ethics, but his argument depends on reasoning too subtle for this writer. The date of January 1904 is accepted by Skidelsky in *JMK*, 1, O'Donnell in *Keynes: Philosophy*, and the KP archivist in the archive catalogue.

111. "Ethics in Relation to Conduct," KP, UA/19, 15.

112. Ibid., 17.

113. "Miscellanea Ethica," written 31 July–19 September 1905, KP, UA/21, 7, 8.

114. Untitled essay on "beauty" read 30 April 1904, KP, UA/19, 8; "A Theory of Beauty," written 23 August–5 October 1905, KP, UA/23, 32.

115. "The Political Doctrines of Edmund Burke," KP, UA/20, 81, 10, 85, 86.

116. *Granta*, quoted, JNK Diary, 9 November 1902.

117. JNK Diary, 1 February 1903; letter, Maynard to Swithinbank, 5 February 1903, KP, PP/45/321; Moggridge, *MK*, 68–69.

118. Letter, 1905 (?), quoted, Harrod, *The Life*, 99.

119. Letters, 2, 15 April 1906, KP, PP/316.

120. JNK Diary, 28 July, 1 August 1906.

121. Ibid., 24 August 1906.

122. Letter, 4 October 1906, KP, PP/45/316.

123. Harrod, *The Life*, 121.

124. Editorial note on the rankings, *CW*, 15:3.

CHAPTER 3

Functioning

Young Keynes's abilities and interests easily—too easily—flowed into his India Office work. He found a service flat nearby in the Westminster government district of London and entered his duties on 16 October 1906. With marvelous bureaucratic irrelevance he was first placed in the Military Department, where he occupied himself with arranging the shipment of ten young Ayrshire bulls from the Yorkshire port of Hull to Bombay. He appears to have carried out his assignment efficiently enough, although his imaginative recommendation to provide the bulls with the companionship of heifers to give them a "better chance of becoming acclimatized" was evidently disregarded.[1] He later improved on the story, dropping the heifers, to say that all he had accomplished in his twenty-one months in the India Office was to achieve the shipment of one pedigreed bull to India.[2]

His superiors insisted on finding Keynes more impressive than he found them. They twice offered him a promotion to a resident clerkship and he demurred each time because it would interfere with his free time. Besides his work on the probability dissertation, which he openly pursued in the office during the frequent slack moments, "I find the idea of sacrificing any of my out of office freedom repellent. I am, for instance, almost always away from London for weekends."[3] At the beginning of March 1907, between these two proposals, forgiving his recalcitrance and stubbornly appreciating his talents, his superiors transferred him to the more appropriate Revenue, Statistics and Commerce De-

John Maynard Keynes in 1908 at age 25. Watercolor by Gwen Raverat in the National Portrait Gallery, London. Photo courtesy of Milo Keynes.

partment. The private Keynes was successfully asserting himself in discharging his public responsibility.

"I like my new Department," Maynard wrote to Lytton Strachey on 7 March. "I haven't much to write at present, but there is an excellent system by which everything comes to me to read and I read it." Keynes the generalist found "quite absorbing, Foreign Office commercial negotiations with Germany, quarrels with Russia in the Persian Gulf, the regulation of opium in Central India...." Boastfully, he continued on 18 April, "I have really been almost overworked.... I really believe that I have written every dispatch in the Department this week."[4] In May and December, however, he was writing his mother, "I have not done one minute's work yesterday" and "I have not averaged an hour's office work a day this week so that I am well up to date with the dissertation."[5] In Cambridge on weekends and dining with the London population of Apostles and other friends during his evenings, he worked on it chiefly in his gentlemanly office hours, which totaled twenty-seven weekly—five hours from 11 A.M. (eminently satisfactory to a late sleeper) on weekdays and two hours on Saturday. The other friends included members of the Bloomsbury group, then a little over a year old and hardly aware of itself as a group, in which the Apostolic Lytton was a leading figure. Another Bloomsbury member was Duncan Grant, Lytton's cousin and temporarily his lover, who would become Maynard's in 1908, indeed the greatest love of his life. Despite these distractions, young Keynes was so efficient when the India Office had something for him to do that he kept his superiors more than content.

In his new department less than three weeks, Keynes produced a recommendation on "The Position of the Jute Trade" that demonstrated a remarkable command of that complex position. He had to deal with the character of monopoly, domestic trade and exports, the danger of foreign competition, the problems of corruption generally and product adulteration specifically, and the delicate balance of governmental control and freedom of enterprise. He was judicially supporting the recommendation of a local official that quality control to prevent adulteration should be attempted through easily applicable export measures, thus without interfering with domestic operations and arousing the resentment of the jute growers. His department head cautiously agreed with Keynes but, uncomfortable about taking the initiative as Keynes wanted, left the final decision up to the Government of India.[6] Another memorandum of Keynes won compliments from the head of the India Office, Secretary of State for India John Morley, but again bureaucracy limited its practical effects. As Maynard wrote Lytton, "He did not say whether he had reversed the damned committee [dealing with the question] and agreed with me."[7] In his earlier letter to Lytton happily reporting on his new department, he had added, "Yesterday I attended my first Committee of Council. The thing is simply government by dotardry; at least half of those present showed manifest signs of senile decay." A half-year later, on 13 September 1907, he drew the appropriate conclusion. "I'm thoroughly sick of this place and would like to resign," he wrote Lytton. He was "bored nine-tenths of the time and rather unreasonably irritated the other tenth whenever I can't have my own way." He had futilely attempted to reopen the case of a person guilty of one improper action but censured for another—against the bureaucratic wisdom that it was not worth the trouble to connect censure with crime: "All my thoughts are on Probability."[8]

It was one of its many values that the experience as civil servant was concentrating young Keynes's mind about a career wonderfully, if not completely. He could follow the strong thread of the dissertation out of the bureaucratic labyrinth and back to Cambridge. A month after his letter to Lytton, Maynard began expending three weeks' leave there to pursue his probability studies. After a week at 6 Harvey Road, "Maynard has now gone into rooms at King's. He wants to have another taste of college life," Neville recorded.[9] By mid-December Maynard had completed and submitted the dissertation for the King's College fellowship elections of the following March.

Maynard was not necesssarily committing himself to career or scholarly specifics. If elected, he could treat his fellowship as a general qualification in government work and choose to be a nonresident fellow. He presently dispensed himself of that alternative. This was when Neville emphasized the value of the security of the civil service. On 5 March 1908 Neville had to note that Maynard proposed to write to the friendly Arthur Pigou, who was a fellowship elector, that he would take up residence at King's upon election.[10] Consistent with the dissertation, however, Maynard still regarded himself as a logician with an interest in statistical theory. How this would sit with Pigou and his chief, Alfred Marshall, remained mysterious.

Astonishingly, shockingly, the results of the election, which took place on 17 March 1908, appeared to render the question moot. Maynard had experienced one of his rare failures. He had not been elected! The implications, however, were only moderately negative. Among the electors, Neville's logician friend, W. E. Johnson, was favorable, but the Apostolic A. N. Whitehead, although Pigou later got him to soften the judgment, had found the dissertation "muddled and of very mediocre value."[11] On that 17 March Neville noted, "We feel very much disappointed and depressed," but the next day could take comfort. He was informed that the deciding factor was not the quality of Maynard's work; one of the candidates had succeeded because it was his second and last chance. Maynard had a second chance and his prospects were excellent.[12] The other successful candidate, it might be mentioned, had not needed charity to win election; he was Maynard's boring mathematical classmate, W. H. Page. Humiliation aside, Maynard could take heart. As always he refused to recognize defeat. In the summer he commenced revising the dissertation.

Alfred Marshall, given his second chance with a talented Keynes, resolved all the outstanding questions. He had never lost his appreciation of the younger Keynes's qualities and took neither the subject of the dissertation nor its failure seriously. He wanted young Keynes as economist and, in any case, could engage only an economist. On 3 April 1908 Marshall wrote him this cautious but precise scenario: on its meeting in June the university's Special Board for Economics and Politics would meet and *might*, if Keynes agreed, name him as lecturer in economics. Marshall indicated some, but surely not all, of the factors making for uncertainty.[13] When Maynard wrote Neville, then on holiday in the south of France, Neville waited until he was back in Cambridge to reply—and, noting Marshall's communication of uncertainty as well as desire, mentioned possible negatives.[14] Maynard, confident that he could manage the economics, let logic and statistical theory limit themselves to his dissertation and other writings, at least for the while, and wrote his father, "Nothing would suit me better than this."[15]

The resolution of the various questions justified Marshall's uncertainty but not Neville's pessimism. Marshall was resigning as professor of political economy at Cambridge University before the end of April. Still ambitious for economics, he proposed to maintain his influence. The key player for both Marshall and young Keynes was Arthur Pigou, whom Marshall wanted as his successor. But Pigou was barely past thirty and Marshall, for the good of economics in Cambridge and Britain, would ruthlessly elevate him over three seniors. While still remaining a great power in academe, Marshall could not be absolutely sure that his will would be done. On 30 May 1908 Pigou's succession to his chair was indeed confirmed. On 3 June the Special Board met, incidentally electing Neville as its chairman, and established two supernumerary lectureships in economics, one of them going to Maynard.[16] Marshall's plan was fulfilled in every detail.

Immediately at home in the university, no longer trammeled by administrative inhibitions, young Keynes exploded in a burst of multiple, intricately if sometimes distantly related, activities that would characterize the rest of his life, professional and personal. Indeed, as his start on the probability dissertation showed, he had anticipated his academic work almost from the moment he got through his civil service examination. In March 1908, even before he left the India Office, a statistical journal had published his review of an analysis of a London district's social and industrial problems. In September and December 1908, the *Economic Journal* carried two successive notes of his on index numbers, a subject, connected to his ideas on probability, which he would fruitfully pursue.[17] Meanwhile, on holiday from 17 August to 23 October 1908 after departing the India Office in July, he worked so assiduously on probability that the dissertation revisions were well in hand; he could give some thought to his lectures while actually beginning a major article on the economy of India.[18] (This was also the most nearly perfect moment in his life, an idyll on the Orkney Islands off Scotland with Duncan Grant, recently become his lover. The intense part of the affair would endure a year and a half before proceeding through restrained discontents into an enduring friendship.) Disposing of his Westminster flat in November, Maynard suffered a case of influenza severe enough to put him into a North London hospital, his mother's doctor-sister "look[ing] after him."[19] The influenza checked his stride only briefly. Returning to 6 Harvey

Road still "very weak" on 16 November,[20] he resumed work on his dissertation soon enough to submit it in early December. He spent much of the rest of the month writing—and discussing with his father—the overwhelmingly authoritative "Recent Economic Events in India," which was published in the *Economic Journal* of March 1909.[21] Supportive of the Indian administration, it was most pleasing to his former superiors. That was also true of four letters he published in *The Economist* from February to May 1909, which discussed Indian trade statistics expertly and also defended the principle of free trade.[22] He had given himself very little time to prepare his lectures, but managed two weeks in London in the reading room of the British Museum, where he worked on them and checked statistics for the India article. All the odd bits and pieces of all these undertakings fit easily into a coherent whole.

On 31 January 1909, on the authority of "several sources," Neville's diary recorded that "Maynard's lectures appear to be a great success," and on 9 February that they "appear to be very much more popular than Meredith's." H. O. Meredith, five years Maynard's senior, held the title of Girdlers' Lecturer in Economics. (In 1911 he would depart Cambridge for the professorship of economics of Queen's University, Belfast—to be succeeded by Maynard as Girdlers' Lecturer.) A year after Maynard began teaching, on 27 January 1910, he wrote his father on stationery headed "King's College Cambridge," "My stock exchange class yesterday numbered 52! and there wasn't even standing room."[23] Compulsively, young Keynes plunged into more activities, while opportunities, in recognition of his evident talents, sought him out for still more. Inevitably, that led him to a number of critical points in economic science, teaching, and college and university administration—and beyond.

Almost from the day he began his lectures, Keynes could be confident he would be elected a fellow and his status regularized. On 21 January, two days after he gave the first one, Neville's diary recorded information coming to him that Whitehead, the most severe critic in 1908, had become favorable. On 5 Feburary Whitehead himself met Maynard in the street and told him that "the new version has now convinced and converted him on a fundamental point" of his previous disagreement.[24] In his formal comment "Whitehead, although still entering criticisms, regarded the [revised] dissertation as a 'contribution . . . of great importance.' "[25] It remains unclear how much of this revision of an original acutely negative judgment was due to the revisions and how much to the persuasions of such Keynes supporters as Arthur Pigou. With the fellowship election, unnecessarily, as it would turn out soon enough, Keynes was assured of six years at King's. He would also draw the annual fellowship dividend of £120. His supernumerary position as lecturer had been established as a professor's charity, £100 annually (for each of the two such lecturers), which Marshall had personally provided and which Pigou had agreed to continue. Neville had matched that with a paternal grant to give Maynard a basic income equal to his India Office salary. To that Maynard could add per capita lecture fees and income from private coaching. Before the end of the year he had twenty-four pupils and found himself working too hard. He complained to Duncan Grant, to whom he was writing frequently and fondly at the time, that he had become a "machine for selling economics by the hour," but announced that he was giving a party that evening and looking forward to lunch with the Fabian leader Sidney Webb the next day.[26] A few days later Neville noted, "Maynard says that he is rolling in wealth, and that including the £100 I give him has an income of £700 a year."[27] He would reduce the coaching next year. Maynard's reported income precisely equaled the income Neville would only begin to receive the next year as registrary (but not including the income from inherited capital). The young lecturer's and the mature administrator's annual incomes compared with £53 for the average wage earner and £130 for the average salaried person.[28] Maynard was indeed working hard. By 1913 he had given ten different courses, including, for four years, "Principles of Economics," normally Pigou's course. This arrangement doubtless reflected the easy relations between the two. Secure as "the Prof." and creator of welfare economics, Pigou could let the brilliant Keynes radiate as he would.

So established, young Keynes proceeded efficiently in various directions. In 1910 he became director of studies for Trinity College's economics undergraduates. His election to the endowed position of Girdlers' Lecturer at the end of that year fixed his tenure as lecturer for five years at least, but in June 1911 he became college lecturer in economics, a permanent position. In October of 1911, Marshall, making good his repetitive failure with Neville, achieved the appointment of his twenty-eight-year-old son as editor of the *Economic Journal*. Although an advisory committee was set up in view of his youth, Keynes functioned with such decisiveness that the committee faded away by 1919. (In 1913 he became secretary of the Royal Economic Society, of which the journal was the official organ, energetically managing its finances and occupying himself over the years with the publication of two major scholarly series, the works of David Ricardo and the economic writings of Jeremy Bentham.) Reading one hundred article submissions a year and assigning himself reviews of books that interested him, he more than adequately filled out his patchy, if capably thought through, economics background. Unlike the previous, less aggressive editors, the young Keynes, strong-minded but supremely professional and usually tolerant of other views, immediately made himself a power in the world of economic science. Marshall had very soon seen his judgment validated. In April 1911, Neville won the distinction of an honorary fellowship of Pembroke College and Marshall paid him the two-edged compliment: "Among your many honors there is perhaps none greater than that of being the father of J. M. Keynes."[29] Neville was modest enough to be flattered.

Of course the younger Keynes plunged into administration. In November 1909, joining his father on it, he was elected to the Special Board for Economics and Politics, becoming its secretary the next year. His industry rebutted any possible charges of nepotism. Even more appropriately he moved toward financial administration. Almost immediately after being elected a fellow he became

one of the three inspectors of accounts of King's College, to be further elevated
to its Estates Committee two years later. The inspectors' duty was to join the
provost in examining the work of the bursars; the provost since 1905 was Montagu R. James, the fellow bibliophile whom the fresher Keynes had got to know,
as he had recounted to his friend Bernard Swithinbank, in 1902. James, who
nurtured hopes of reform, lighted on Keynes as a natural lieutenant to that end.
The three annual inspectors' reports from 1909 demanded a more profitable
employment of the sums held on current account. In November 1910 James
asked Keynes if he would be prepared to become a bursar. Too secure to be
eager Keynes returned that he was agreeable provided it did not interfere with
"more serious occupations."[30] In 1912, in the face of bursarial resistance,
Keynes joined his old Eton friend Dil Knox, now also a King's fellow, and the
economic historian John H. Clapham in organizing an attack on the bursarial
administration. At the Congregation, the annual meeting of the college's fellows,
the reformers carried motions demanding a reduction of the college balance and
a reform of staff working conditions, but failed with a motion to increase the
fellowship dividend by £10. In 1913 Keynes became a member of a committee
threateningly established to consider the first bursar's resignation. The bursar,
however, held fast, and James himself gave up, resigning in 1918 to go to Eton
and an easier provostship. But in November 1919 Keynes became second bursar
and immediately, overwhelming the new and weaker first bursar, whom he
would succeed five years later, seized control of its finances and proceeded to
make the college much richer.

Unlike the India Office administration, a university could easily permit and
exploit individual initiatives going well beyond its table of organization. In January 1909, the month he began lecturing, Keynes wrote out the outlines of eight
papers, two monographs, two treatises, and two textbooks. In their imaginative
range they comprised a burst of pure genius if they meant anything substantive
to come, as indeed they did, even if the specific projects were not carried out.
Keynes was pursuing or would pursue the subjects in one form or another, thus
probability, statistical methods, index numbers, monetary theory, economic crisis
theory in general, and the problem of the "long run."[31] Also in 1909, on 22
October, he started his Political Economy Club for the university's dozen or so
abler economics students on the model of the Apostolic Conversazione Society
and the other university discussion societies.[32] One of his future protégés and
collaborators summed up the effect: "Through his club Keynes knew intimately
. . . all the best of each generation of Cambridge economists. . . . And through
the club we insensibly acquired certain elements in Keynes's own approach to
the problems of economics."[33] Appreciating its elegance and clear sense, he was
teaching pure Marshallian, that is to say, neoclassical economics; he would continue to do so into the 1920s.

In these years, young Keynes was developing two styles of functioning, the
practical and the perverse. He demonstrated the practical in his flexibly realistic
use of applied economic theory to government, economy, and institutions in the

situation of India. The perverse described his pure theorizing as concentrated in his probability dissertation. In both he was a virtuoso. Marshall, a reforming, near revolutionary in his time, might have approved Keynes's spirit, if not his specifics.

Interrupted by the Indian project and the World War, *A Treatise on Probability* did not appear until 1921 but was almost completed in 1914 and showed Keynes already at the topmost level of his powers of pure intellection.[34] Almost five hundred pages long, ten of its thirty-three chapters speckled with abstruse equations of symbolic calculus, it began by fusing a pair of noncompatible subjects and proceeded determinedly and artfully to argue a complex set of nonsense propositions derived impossibly from them. The basic subjects were the two probabilities that Keynes, in somewhat Hegelian fashion, split from the integral word *probability*. Actually, probability is a homonym, the first meaning being "frequency," the important mathematical field for concerns ranging from insurance to physics, and the second having to do with degrees of belief, as situated in epistemology. (Recent scholarship calls the first aleatory and the second, epistemic probability, thus the probabilities of chance and knowledge.) This latter has a distinguished, if minority, adherance, having been suggested by Aristotle, developed by Leibniz in his dissertation, and articulated by Locke, as quoted by Keynes, " 'Probability is likeness to be true.' "[35] A tiny group of philosophers continues to speculate seriously and perhaps profitably about epistemic probability or probability-as-belief. Keynes's primal error was to see a relation between it and aleatory probability, thus probability-as-frequency.

Keynes set probability-as-belief to conquering probability-as-frequency. He argued correctly enough that knowing was more basic than counting, but he failed to recognize that knowing was prior not only to frequency but to all other experience. Using his symbolic notation, he attacked frequency variously; indeed he devoted much more space to it than to probability-as-belief, ten to twenty times as much, depending on how one defines the ambiguities. He questioned the sense of insurance actuarial tables, for example, stating that all frequency could do was to "assert a characteristic of a *series* of propositions, rather than of a particular proposition."[36] He was demanding that the insurer predict the next accident—the individual instance. But, by definition, frequency calculates with plural instances. This is an early example of Keynes's donnish debating technique: give the opponent an impossible task and grade him as failing.

In developing his probability-as-belief Keynes divided knowledge between certainty and partial belief, the latter, as expressed mathematically, running the gamut from fractionally less than the figure one to zero. Most thinkers reject this radical scission and take their knowledge integrally. In any case Keynes's conception subsumed an insoluble problem, which became evident when he verbally translated his zero as the position of "impossibility." For impossibility is just as certain as the certainty expressed by the figure one. The Cambridge philosopher Richard B. Braithwaite, a student friend of Keynes who wrote the introduction to the *Collected Writings* volume reprinting the treatise, recognized the problem by silently discarding impossibility in his interpretation and, instead, using the term *certainty of falsehood* for zero.[37] He only emphasized it the more. Such questions bring up larger ones.

Keynes was trying to situate his inquiry within the limits of logic. Yet his subject was knowledge or belief, thus a problem in epistemology. He began by trying arbitrarily to finesse the subject. Disarmingly, he explained, ''I do not wish to become involved in questions of epistemology to which I do not know the answer.'' He preferred to concentrate on ''the particular point of philosophy or logic which is the subject of this work.''[38] He cannot be so excused.

The book threw up many other problems. Keynes used the words *knowledge* and *belief* interchangeably, although belief can be based on faith and not the facts and reason of knowledge. Following G. E. Moore, who gave him his first impulse toward probability, he refused to define his terms, beginning with probability itself. Like Moore, he was justifying intuition, *his* intuition, as the ultimate arbiter of the (inescapably epistemological) truth. Thus the trained mathematician Keynes, although making deft use of his mathematics in the dissertation and his economics generally, frequently minimized its value; he always put his intuition above it. With his seamless confidence he would never give up his faith in his ability to cognize objective reality intuitively.

In its indefinables the treatise broke out beyond the specificity and objectivity of Neville Keynes's *Formal Logic*. Maynard Keynes simply rejected the obedience demanded there to an ''objective reference . . . outside the state of mind which constitutes the judgment itself.''[39] Yet, at the end, Maynard fell away from his absolute certainty. Disarmingly again, granting that frequency might be more valid than he had previously argued, he admitted having ''pressed on a little faster than the difficulties were overcome.''[40] The reader might now ask how much belief in the treatise's propositions could be retained. Yet the performance had been impressive while shaping the skills Keynes would apply to economic reasoning.

The treatise had the surplus value, as suggested in the author's admissions, that it encouraged him to drop logic as a central concern and concentrate on the economics he was finding increasingly challenging and rewarding.

More practically, ''Recent Economic Events in India'' and Keynes's published letters on Indian policy strengthened his connection to the India Office for the good of both parties. The article itself demonstrated the luminous intelligence of a first-rate professional in command of expressive statistics and familiar with Indian agriculture, trade, currency, and finance. It brought Keynes a note on 30 March 1909 from John A. Godley, his old chief as the permanent undersecretary: ''I sincerely hope you will continue to keep an eye on Indian affairs, and write about them as opportunities occur.''[41] Keynes did not have to be asked to oblige.

Establishing a valuable new relationship at the India Office, Keynes had drawn on Lionel Abrahams, financial secretary and creator of India's financial system, for the article. This led to a visit by a group of India Office people with

Alfred Marshall, who discussed India's financial system for an exhaustive six hours.[42] Marshall approving the system, Abrahams wrote Keynes in great relief, "I may slumber in peace."[43] In 1910, to Abrahams' renewed relief, Keynes wrote a review in the *Economic Journal* opposing a pamphleteer's demand for a change in the reserves backing the Indian currency.[44] Keynes then consulted with Abrahams for six lectures on "Currency, Finance, and the Level of Prices in India" he had been asked to give at the London School of Economics. He repeated them in Cambridge in early 1912 instead of his regular course, "Company Finance and the Stock Exchange."[45] Also publishing letters defending India Office policies, he developed his ideas further and in November 1912, interrupting his work on probability, began expeditiously to write what became *Indian Currency and Finance*, his first published book. By January the proofs were beginning to come back. The book and the attendant circumstances placed him at another critical point in his professional life.

In the first week of November 1912, meanwhile, two issues, essentially separate but suggestively related by rumors of scandal, troubled the financial administration of India. The major issue, already anticipated by the pamphlet Keynes had criticized, was the character of India's currency and finances. The other issue concerned the operations of Messrs. Samuel Montagu & Co., a firm of bullion brokers that had been secretly buying silver on behalf of the Government of India for its gold standard reserve. This was a normal enough procedure, but scandalmongers prompted questions in the House of Commons. The latter problem affected Keynes personally because the family of his old Cambridge Union patron Edwin Montagu, now parliamentary undersecretary of state for India, was associated with the bullion firm. On the request of Abrahams, happy about his start on the Indian currency book but confronting the urgencies of the situation, Keynes published a richly detailed letter deprecating the "ungenerous and ill-founded charges" in the London *Times* of 14 November.[46] Enough questions had been asked in Parliament and press, however, for the Royal Commission on Indian Finance and Currency to be created early in 1913 "to inquire into the whole financial management of the India Office."[47]

Keynes was a splendid candidate for the commission's secretary, but between March and April 1913 the proofs of his book, and, he thought, Montagu's patronage got him promoted to the commission itself.[48] Not yet thirty, he was the youngest of the ten commissioners, and, generating a sixth of their questions, the most active.[49] His book, giving him a solid foundation for his commission work, was published on 9 June 1913. Like that of the India Office, his aim on the commission, with the book's assistance, was to defend the Indian financial order, which he had found appropriate and even advanced, and to suggest an additional progressive element in the form of a state bank.

The objective of the critics was to achieve the transformation of what Keynes called the gold *exchange* standard, regnant in India, to a pure gold standard. That would mean holding the gold standard reserve exclusively in gold and not partially in coins and liquid investments. The critics also wanted a gold currency introduced into the system. In a letter to the *Times* Keynes had earlier argued that the full backing of the Bank of England's gold reserves was entirely sufficient and that the changes would be "a wanton extravagance," with the gold currency draining off into hoardings.[50] An aggressive examiner, Keynes was able to show the weakness and, often, the self-interest in the statements of the gold-standard advocates.[51] Combined with the practical wisdom of Lionel Abrahams, young Keynes's donnish command of theory helped swing the consensus toward support of the India Office position.

At the same time Keynes could move to his positive proposal. Between the two periods of testimony, from 5 June (Keynes's birthday) to 6 August and 23 October to 14 November, the young financial expert was charged with designing the state bank in consultation with an India-based British merchant. After the last session Keynes then found himself intricately engaged in drafting changes in the final report, writing his mother on 20 December 1913, "The last three days have been about the most exacting to character and intellect that I have ever been through and I feel rather a wreck."[52] The sum might well have undermined his health; it was then, in early January, that Florence Keynes found herself rushing to succor her son on the French Riviera, where diphtheria had overwhelmed his quest for recreation. While slowly recovering, he fought a hard and mostly unsuccessful battle by mail and then in person to make the paper currency supply in India more flexible, a sound but minor reform. His proposal for a state bank was too breathtakingly advanced for most of the commissioners and relegated to a neutrally informational annex to the report proper. But the commission's inquiry had dissipated the suggestions of scandal, while the India Office's financial administration, gold exchange standard included, was fully vindicated. As for the state bank, authority incorporated in Marshall was "entranced by it as a prodigy of constructive work," as he wrote to Keynes,[53] although real need impelled its creation in principle, whatever differences in detail, as the Reserve Bank of India in 1935. The sum was a substantial success for Keynes and the India Office.

Indian Currency and Finance was an impeccable exercise in applied economics—and more. The book and the report's annex on the state bank were both technical marvels: expert in finance, business, government, empire, and colony; working documents that immediately became part of the functional and historical reality they were describing. The book's specifics included a masterly detailing of India's currency and financial mechanism, thus the purchase and sale of Indian Council bills in London, the regulation of the note issue, and the management of reserves and cash balances. The Keynes who flirted with Fabian socialism and rebelled against the constraining logic of his father was also present in the book—shockingly. Accepting the gold standard as a fundamental verity—and justifying India's gold exchange standard because consistent with it—he was willing to go dangerously beyond it. He argued that the gold-standard system was rare and fragile, that the leading nations were paying a three-quarter of a percent premium on gold during the comparative calm of November 1912.

"The time may not be far distant when Europe, having perfected her mechanism of exchange . . . will find it possible to regulate her standard of value on a more rational and stable basis," he predicted.[54] He would continue to be of two or more minds about gold, the outbreak of the World War calling up another series of contradictory opinions.

Keynes was immediately led to select an appropriate opinion on gold among his ambivalences on Sunday, 2 August 1914, a day after Germany had declared war on Russia and two days before Britain entered the war. That opinion was strongly suggested to him by Basil Blackett of the Treasury, who had gotten to know Keynes when he replaced him as secretary of the Indian commission. In a letter that the British Post Office delivered that day (Sunday delivery being a convenient custom—at a premium), Blackett asked Keynes to advise in the developing financial crisis and signaled, mentioning the leading bankers, an indication of the kind of advice he wanted, "The joint stock banks have made absolute fools of themselves and behaved very badly."[55] Never fond of banks and bankers, Keynes could easily agree with the Treasury (and the Bank of England) and against the joint stock banks (also called clearing banks). At issue were two questions; how to protect the financial system in general, thus the banks and other financial institutions, and, specifically, should this protection include suspension of external gold specie payments, in other words, departure from the gold standard, as was the case with all the other major combatant nations. Keynes's various comments and accounts, influencing the historical record subsequently,[56] have altered the real proportions of the financial crisis. Dramatically, contradicting his long-term thinking, he made gold the essence of the matter.

Responding with his sure instinct to the situation, Keynes had set out for London immediately on receipt of Blackett's letter. He found the train service inadequate and pressed his new brother-in-law, owner of a motorcycle with a sidecar, into service.[57] (The athletically fit Margaret Keynes Hill had occupied that sidecar the year before on an 1,800-mile honeymoon trip to the north of England and Scotland.)[58] After joining Blackett for tea at 6 P.M. that Sunday, Keynes produced a 5,000-word memorandum late the next day "on my instigation," as Blackett's diary recorded, "on the disastrous character of any policy leading to suspension of specie payments."[59]

If Blackett of the Treasury had picked him, Keynes's response picked the Treasury as the right place—the central point—for his war service, his memorandum locating himself in the heart of the Treasury's culture of financial responsibility. Under the circumstances, it was natural that the joint stock banks should take self-protective measures against excessive gold losses that could cause immediate hurt to other members of the financial community. Thus some banks were beginning to call in loans and to draw gold from the Bank of England. It was also natural that the Treasury, composed of civil servants concerned about the general welfare and unthreatened themselves, should demand that the bankers relent in their protective actions and patriotically run the risk of bankruptcy. Keynes, practiced in success, found it easy to be ruthless, a quality that success often requires. Ruthlessly discarding qualifications, he cast the joint stock bankers in the role of villains.

In his memorandum of 3 August Keynes wrote, "The recent heavy drain of gold from the Bank of England has been mainly due to a fit of hoarding on the part of the joint stock banks."[60] In other comments he was more severe. His father, whom he was keeping informed, later demurred, "Surely the maintenance of our banking system is the most important point of all," he wrote. "You . . . seem to me to be a little hard on the banks." Loyally, characteristically, Neville acknowledged, "But of course you know a great deal more . . . than I do."[61] He could, however, cite Maynard to himself, his son having denounced the bankers as having "completely lost their heads" in a letter to him at the height of the crisis, but parenthetically interjecting, "I doubt if a single director of the Bank of England is solvent today."[62] The danger was real enough and the younger Keynes's memorandum had gone on to suggest means of saving the bankers along with the country's other economic agents.

As the memorandum clearly explained, the country was nevertheless not in immediate danger of heavy gold losses, thus was not being objectively forced off the gold standard. Nor had the joint stock banks, whatever their derelictions, formally recommended suspension of gold payments, although they may have been moving toward an idea that many reasonable persons entertained. Adamant against it, the Treasury blamed the joint stock banks, Keynes's memorandum reflecting its opinion, for demands for gold from the Bank of England that were making that possibility more likely.

The essence of the financial problem lay in the existence of £350 million in bills of exchange outstanding, two-thirds issued to foreigners,[63] while international communications were disrupted. Keynes's memorandum put it precisely: "So far from other countries being able to draw from us, the most formidable difficulties which now face the money market arise out of the fact that foreign countries are not able to meet their immediate liabilities to us."[64] A 1976 study influenced by Keynes's interpretation described the result: "Thus the clearing [n.b., joint stock] banks' theoretically liquid assets—bills, loans to the bill market against bills, and loans to the stock exchange—all ceased, within a few days, to be liquid."[65] Drawn into the same danger of bankruptcy along with the joint stock banks were the acceptance houses (merchant banks), which had "accepted" the bills of exchange, and the discount houses, acting as middlemen between buyers and sellers of the bills. Hence the gold-standard question was a matter of long-term theory, capable of being comfortably postponed. But something had to be done immediately to save the banks and discounters. Actually, despite acute differences in details, Keynes and the Treasury agreed in general with the joint stock bankers on the character of the problem and how to solve it.

With some justification, given the ambiguities, Keynes's memorandum had reversed the order of urgencies and concentrated its argument on the gold-standard question, thus the problem that was not urgent. Then, agreeing with the bankers, Keynes proposed that the internal problem be resolved by "some form of emergency paper currency" beyond the limits set by the nation's (slender) gold reserves. His strategy for recovery, however, made maintenance of the gold standard its centerpiece, thus "maintain specie payments, so as to meet foreign demands, while"—to reduce the drain, at least—"making it extremely difficult and inconvenient for the ordinary man to get gold." His ultimate argument was classical: "The *future* position of the City of London as a free gold market would be severely injured if at the *first* sign of emergency specie payment is suspended." He was willing to grant, "A point may conceivably come when such a measure cannot be avoided."[66] Whatever hindsight might say, it was a masterly argument of itself and as a rationale of the Treasury position. And it worked. Blackett's diary recorded for 5 August: "[David] Lloyd George . . . has clearly imbibed much of Keynes's memorandum and is strong against suspension."[67] Blackett's (and Harrod's and most other accounts) failed to mention another persuasive defender of the gold standard, Walter Cunliffe, governor of the Bank of England, a big game hunter who proposed to "meet the situation 'like lions.' " At the same time he seemed to be preparing for a retreat, granting that the Bank's reserves were "low" and wondering "if we have to suspend" without cooperation by the bankers.[68] His leonine attitude, however, got greater publicity—and a peerage for him. Cunliffe's power and prestige surely outweighed Keynes's marvelous logic with Lloyd George. On 5 August the chancellor told the House of Commons that specie payments would be maintained. And so Britain committed itself to the gold standard for better or worse.

A great deal more had to be done. The House of Commons then empowered the government to postpone payments by the financial institutions for six months and provide an emergency currency. Moratorium and (paper) money saved the situation. On Friday 7 August, after a bank holiday from 3 August, the banks opened and reasonably normal business resumed. Keynes meanwhile, on 5 August, produced another memorandum that discussed cautious and subtle ways of relieving the acceptance houses.[69] The government's policy took a different direction and he later opposed as wasteful what actually was done. This was a series of other measures continuing into early September, which offered generous loans to the threatened institutions and made the Bank of England the nation's creditor of the last resort, in effect the British taxpayer. The sum provided the necessary security until burgeoning war expenses created a new, and more nearly real, threat to the nation's finances.

Perhaps Keynes's first memorandum was too classically a Treasury statement. The Treasury's sternly responsible civil servants too often frustrated Lloyd George by telling him he could not do what he wanted to do. Keynes was used and discarded, the chancellor installing a friendly editor and statistician as special adviser promising more obedient service. Disappointed and perhaps humiliated, but resiliently hopeful, Maynard wrote his father on 14 August, "My work with the Treasury has finished for the present. I am amusing myself by

writing a financial history of the last fortnight.'' He was also thinking of ''bringing out a small book in September.'' He did a lot more than that, although the
book never appeared. Early in 1914, after finishing with the Indian commission,
he had resumed work on the probability book, Neville reading the proofs and
returning one set on 16 August. On 25 August, on holiday in Cornwall in
southwest England, Maynard wrote Neville that he was working on an article
for the *Economic Journal*: ''I have entirely given up Probability.''[70]

The younger Keynes's amusement was part of a deadly serious campaign for
a Treasury post. Over the next five months he variously addressed Britain's
financial and general economic situation. He wrote three major articles—for the
September and December issues of the *Economic Journal* and the November
Quarterly Journal of Economics—and also several memoranda for key personnel, three letters published in *The Economist*, and two newspaper articles.[71] He
was winning wide publicity, and the close attention of people in government,
for his expertise. In the first *Economic Journal* article he continued to attack
the leading bankers, accusing them of ''endanger[ing] . . . the system . . . by running on the Bank of England.''[72] It was a simplistic denunciation of understand-
able efforts to remain solvent. Besides that, in letters to his father and Marshall,
he wielded the ad hominem, telling the first, ''The bankers completely lost their
heads and have been simply dazed,'' and the second, mentioning the two leading
bankers, ''The one was cowardly and the other selfish.''[73] The first charge was
simply false, the bankers having anticipated the crisis with a plan originating as
far back as mid-1913, which the Treasury had refused to address because it
emphasized the paucity of British gold reserves. As previously mentioned, far
from dazed, they then produced a second plan during the acute part of the crisis,
an ad hoc recommendation of an emergency currency that was adopted in essence and also offered to sacrifice some of their gold reserves to support the
Bank of England, the government finding it expedient to do without this latter.[74]
The banker Keynes called cowardly communicated his sentiments vigorously
enough to win a slight retraction in the second *Economic Journal* article.[75] Was
Keynes too ''harsh'' on the bankers' conduct? He granted, ''Perhaps this was
so.'' But, with a statesman's reluctance to admit he was wrong, he concluded
the article by retracting much of his retraction in the last sentence and resumed
recriminating with ''bankers inclined to haggle when they should be constructing . . . —when all should have been thinking of the state.''[76] However unfair,
the articles were superb exercises in the analysis of swiftly changing, chaotic
economic developments, and the *Bankers' Magazine*, although questioning the
writer's ''practical touch with financial affairs,'' nevertheless ''heartily commended'' the first article for its critical perspective.[77] One of the recipients of
Keynes's memoranda was Montagu, now financial secretary at the Treasury. On
Tuesday, 5 January 1915, Keynes wrote his father, ''I have been offered a
position in the Treasury. . . . No time for details as I have a very heavy piece
of work to do . . . by Friday when Lloyd George . . . sails for France.''[78] He
thought Montagu had got the post for him; he also thought that Montagu, besides

helping him previously, also assisted his next step further upward.[79] But he had been operating in a manner that inspired such support.

In December Maynard and his mother had planned to visit Geoffrey at Versailles, where he was functioning as a surgeon in a military hospital. Florence, however, felt unwell, and Maynard went alone,[80] taking the occasion to study French finances in Paris. His first duty, the "heavy piece of work," on his return to the Treasury was the memorandum, "Notes on French Finance," completed expeditiously the day after he wrote Neville and two days before Lloyd George departed with it. Maynard's functioning continued to be as apposite.

Keynes's apposite memoranda and his instinct for bureaucratic survival and success combined to project him quickly into another leverage point. In January, in addition to his paper on French finances, he also produced one on wheat prices for the Secret Committee of the cabinet, of which he became secretary, and a plan to buy Indian wheat below the world market price.[81] Survival, however, was a first necessity. He had been assigned as assistant to Lloyd George's adviser, the man whose installation had spoiled his first chance for a Treasury position. The expert, in process of losing the chancellor's ephemeral favor, had been shunted to an another office distant from the Treasury. Keynes, taking advantage of an alternate place in the office of the friendly Basil Blackett, dropped the man and made himself available for such assignments as wheat prices and pure finance.[82] On 29 January 1915, on embossed Treasury stationery, he wrote to his father that he would not be coming to Cambridge; "I *am* to go to Paris. . . . It's a most select party:—Lloyd George, Montagu, the Governor of the Bank of England, and me. . . . I wish I hadn't a cold coming on."[83] Once again Montagu had helped. Lloyd George had objected to the company of the Treasury's joint permanent secretaries with their talent for seeing the negative, and Montagu had suggested the swiftly responsive Keynes.

The party was attending the Inter-Ally Conference of 2–5 February on credits, these to be chiefly supplied by Britain, to finance their joint war operations. Before leaving the country, Keynes had grasped the full significance of the conference and on 30 January put it into a memorandum. Urgently recommending that France and Russia ship gold to England as partial collateral for the credits, he began bluntly: "The following points are worth bargaining for."[84] With this, Keynes, "a temporary civil servant of genius," in the judgment of a British historian of the period,[85] began to construct the financial control system over which he would presently rule. His reign would endure two years and two months—until the United States, entering the war, would become the creditor of the last resort, but he would continue to bear huge responsibilities for the rest of the war and beyond. "From one point of view this was the height of his career," Harrod wrote justly.[86] Never again would Keynes function in so pure a situation, where he would be so totally in command—in power and sense— of a central segment of reality. Greater achievement would require an admixture of impurities.

A series of promotions and adjustments consolidated Keynes's position. After

a change in the government in mid-1915 he was moved to the Treasury's No.
1 (or Finance) Division, while he got a new chief as chancellor of the exchequeur
in Reginald McKenna, a sensible Liberal politican, with whom he established
an easier rapport than with Lloyd George. On 1 September of that year he
succeeded Basil Blackett, dispatched to the United States on financial negotiations, as deputy to the head of his division. Keynes managed the finances of
Britain's needier allies with such decisiveness and efficiency that his superiors
were happy to let him function as freely as possible, except for enlisting him
elsewhere in emergencies. He was developing a charisma that made him a personal center of action, reporting to his mother, "Half the office seems to drift
to my room unless I drive it determinedly away."[87] In February 1917 the Treasury recognized his central position by making him head of the new A Division,
split off from No. 1 Division, as his own fief, dealing with all questions of
external finance and numbering seventeen by war's end. He was subordinate
only to Joint Permanent Secretary Robert Chalmers and the chancellor, now the
Conservative leader, Bonar Law, who had succeeded McKenna in another government change and who similarly, if not so personally, valued his work.[88] One
emergency situation had him accompany the chief justice, Lord Reading (another Jewish Liberal politician), to the United States on a six-week excursion
beginning 4 September 1917 to clear the financial conduits. It was his first
experience of the country and although the trip meant another successful operation for him, it was also a humiliating lesson, which as an economist increasingly in advance of his times he sensitively registered, of the passing of Britain's
primacy and the arrival of America's. Residing pleasantly with Lord and Lady
Reading in Washington, Keynes made himself so useful that Reading kept him
an extra ten days beyond the week originally granted and asked for still another
ten days. Bonar Law, however, found his presence even more useful for a conference with the French that had been postponed pending his return.[89]

Keynes's usefulness was his chosen cross. Trained in compulsion, he sought
overwork. At the India Office he had filled out his office time with work on
probability. Now, however, he always had too much to do. In its gentlemanly
way the Treasury gave him a free day to edit his *Economic Journal*. By October
1915 Keynes admitted he was so busy with his war that he needed help and
brought in the former editor, F. Y. Edgeworth, as joint editor, but he never
relinquished his prime responsibility. Nor did he demur when requested to give
a series of six lectures on war finance at University College London in November and December that year. On 3 November he was writing his mother, "I'm
desperately hard worked this week."[90] It would be a frequent refrain, Keynes
desperately seeking an occasional free weekend to defend his vulnerable health.
Of course the hard work had its effects in the form of frequent colds and attacks
of influenza. The appendicitis followed by pneumonia in mid-1915 may have
been another such effect; he needed two months to recover, a blessing in that
that he could build up a margin of health against future overwork. Stress added

extra emphasis to the sheer labor as Keynes found himself engaged in heart-straining battles over policy.

The stress encouraged Keynes's tendency to launch into insult. It was at his first international conference, in February 1915, that he told Lloyd George that he was talking rubbish. His relations with Lloyd George remained difficult, moreover, because he never concealed his view that, besides talking rubbish, the war leader was also a "crook."[91] On a trip to the United States, perhaps reacting to Britain's position as supplicant, Keynes was "rude, dogmatic, and disobliging" to the Americans, achieving "a terrible reputation for his rudeness here." This came from his friend Blackett, who was on duty there.[92] Keynes treated his compatriots in Washington even worse, according to the British ambassador, who reported Keynes insulting two members of his staff into silence and treble notes respectively: "really too offensive for words."[93] When Bonar Law was chancellor, he was also not spared, Keynes writing his mother that at tea with his chief he had "attacked him violently on the Irish question. He had very little defense to put up."[94]

However crucial Keynes's original memorandum of 3 August 1914 had been, his work from 1915 led him elsewhere and responsibility for keeping on the gold standard had to rest with prime minister, chancellor, and permanent secretaries. As expert subordinate and creative memoranda-artificer, however, he had more to contribute, and he produced three additional memoranda defending the original logic, one each year into 1917, when the question became temporarily more or less moot with the U.S. war declaration on 6 April. He was also further exercising his skill in occupying both sides of a given issue. Before he produced these memoranda reiterating the orthodox doctrine, his second *Economic Journal* article of 1914 had played with the iconoclastic thought introduced in his *Indian Currency and Finance* and he again mocked the faith in gold. He proposed that one "melt the reserve into a great golden image of the chief cashier and place it on a monument so high that it can never be got down again." He looked forward to the day when "gold is deposed from its despotic control."[95] By the spring of 1915, Britain's trade balance had swung over into the passive and responsible persons began to suggest that, after all, one should depart the gold standard. Once again representing the Treasury culture, Keynes now argued (6 November 1915) that it would harm the country's ability to attract foreign balances then and after the war. He repeated similar arguments in memoranda on 1 February 1916 and 1 January 1917.[96] Early in 1919, after the cessation of U.S. aid, Britain gracefully and almost imperceptibly slipped off gold. Keynes would deplore the return in 1925 and celebrate the ultimate departure in 1931. In 1939, consistent in his inconsistency but reluctant to admit having been wrong, he produced a memorandum as guidance in the new world war and argued that quitting gold in 1914 "would have destroyed our credit and brought chaos to business."[97] Would it indeed?

As Keynes alternately put it, the gold standard was mostly illusion, the gold itself only the glitter given off by real productivity. Britain's wealth consisted of its people, institutions, and industry: they would have continued, gold standard or not, to attract foreign credits and maintain financial order. In the early 1920s, while Britain was off the gold standard, its productivity and stability brought in too great an influx of foreign funds and lifted it back onto the gold standard, *hélas!*—to express Keynes's sense at the time. Actually, long before 1919 the pound had been selling at substantial discount in New York, sign of a de facto departure from gold. The country's ability to remain formally on the gold standard had been an archaic skill, as useful to the war effort as playing whist. But the game had been harmful because it imposed unnecessary constraints on the war effort.

Keynes used his great skills in another questionable game. Beginning in mid-1915 he rationalized the Treasury's policy of a classical balance between the civilian and the war economy as against a policy of all-out war, whatever the economic distortions. Supporting his new chief, Reginald McKenna, his memoranda warned that the terrific expenditures would be self-defeating. But McKenna and the other cabinet members were resisting the imposition of conscription and trying to wage war in nineteenth-century style, with volunteer forces and subsidized allies to do most of the fighting. Lloyd George, ascending through the positions of munitions minister and secretary of war to become prime minister by 6 December 1916, was ruthless enough to understand that this was no gentleman's war—and the nation agreed. If Keynes's arguments for archaic warmaking enraged him, Lloyd George knew that this don was still an invaluable civil servant. In February 1917 Lloyd George punished Keynes by striking his name from the Treasury's recommendations for Companion of the Bath (CB), but did not prevent his promotion to head of A Division. Typical of the Treasury culture and governmental culture generally, the Treasury put Keynes's name forward for a CB again, in May, and Lloyd George stayed his hand.[98] If he had known about other actions of Keynes, he might not have been so temperate.

Appalled by the slaughter and affected by his Bloomsbury friends, who turned inward into pacifism and conscientious objection, Keynes hoped for a negotiated peace. Using the cover name "Politicus," he published a letter and an article advocating it in January and April 1916.[99] It was hardly correct—or prudent—for a responsible civil servant. Like his friends, Keynes refused to recognize the force of nationalism, which dominated the thinking of the ordinary citizen on both sides. Meanwhile, ineluctably, indeed, genially efficient, although fundamentally responsible as Bloomsbury was not, Keynes served superbly, if reluctantly, in Lloyd George's all-out war. In return, Lytton Strachey, representing Bloombury and allied with the fellow pacifist Bertrand Russell, chastised his friend for achieving "the maximum slaughter at the minimum expense."[100] Guiltily, Keynes accepted the punishment.

Whatever the frictions, Bloomsbury, enriching his life and making it more meaningful, was another variously supportive family. Willy-nilly, it helped him function more effectively. Bloomsbury also initiated his introduction to the powerful of Britain. On 2 July 1914 Ottoline Morrell, a great hostess, fortuitously arranged a dinner party, which included Keynes, to introduce Bloomsbury denizens to Herbert H. Asquith,[101] prime minister until the war and Lloyd George overwhelmed him. Montagu, as has already been seen, was also important to Keynes's governmental career. Keynes went on to specify that he had introduced him "to the great ones," who included, in his memory, Lloyd George and Reginald McKenna, while placing him next to Margot, Asquith's equally political wife, at dinner. Montagu also got him invited to "private dinners" of the secretaries of important government leaders "who exchanged the secret news and discussed . . . the big problems of the war."[102] The Asquiths and the Morrells had country houses near each other in the Oxford area, and, with his wit and his bridge playing (the latter a profitable inheritance from Neville), Keynes became a welcome guest at both residences. He was also a frequent guest at the McKennas' country place. But his major recommendation was his sheer usefulness, McKenna, as we have seen, depending on his memoranda, and Asquith learning to appreciate the "clever young Cambridge don" as secretary to the cabinet's Secret Committee.[103] The sum made Keynes genially effective in functioning within the immediacy of events and in thinking beyond them to anticipate and improve the future.

Keynes's support of the limited-war party had not removed him from the center of decision making but success and the prospects of peace began to do so. As economist, as a human being bereft of chauvinism and war hatred, he began to resist the impulsion to make the Germans pay for all the horrors. It was natural that the economist be drawn into the financial peace planning, and as early as 2 January 1917 Keynes helped write a memorandum noncommittally speculating on the German capacity to pay.[104] Approaching war's end, his A Division was made responsible for Treasury policy on the indemnity. Keynes produced a preliminary memorandum for the department that tried, coolly using irony, to set limits on fantasies about the sum. He suggested that $2.5 billion (£500 million), equal to a fourth of its annual national income, could be extracted over the years "without crushing Germany," while a figure approaching $10 billion meant "crushing Germany."[105] In the official Treasury memorandum of mid-November 1918, yielding to the pressures for a greater figure, he was willing, however, to contemplate the crushing figure as an objective—"if effected without evil indirect consequences." He could not resist adding the caveat, "If Germany is to be 'milked,' she must not first of all be ruined."[106]

Lloyd George had meanwhile removed the Treasury from ultimate responsibility for the indemnity in favor of the very political Committee on Indemnity. The British election of mid-December confirmed the need to temper professional judgments about Germany's capacity to pay with responsiveness to a popular explosion of vengefulness. The indemnity committee then recommended $120 billion, a dozen times the Treasury's figure. Lloyd George later wrote that the recommendation was a "wild and fantastic chimera,"[107] but appointed two members of the committee to the inter allied Reparations Commission to deal with the problem under that euphemism at the Paris Peace Conference.[108] Keynes arrived in Paris on 10 January 1919, ten days before the conference began, as the chief Treasury representative with a long list of titles and functions. He had risen to the rank of acting principal clerk (equivalent to assistant secretary today), subordinate only to the permanent secretaries. His annual salary was £1,200; it would presently be raised to £1,500, retroactive to 1 January, two and a half times his starting salary.[109] He was the impotent representative of an impotent government department.

For two months, excluded from the substantive problem of reparations, Keynes transformed himself—one thinks of his mother and sister—into an international social worker. He busied himself trying to expedite the shipment of food into a starving Germany. The German representatives resisted various allied exactions before shipments could be sent, and Keynes tried to mediate in the brutal and desperate bargaining. His diplomacy with the Germans and his battles with unforgiving French representatives led to a formal resolution at a meeting of the allied Supreme War Council on 8 March. It was a small adjustment quite possibly saving some lives and requiring still more negotiations. In a memoir read to his Bloomsbury friends two years later, he could end the story happily: "The food trains started to Germany."[110] A little later Lloyd George found it expedient to bring Keynes and the Treasury back into the reparations issue.

The prime minister knew better than to trust the financial judgment of his representatives on the Reparations Commission, but he also knew they were closer to popular opinion than he was himself. On 17 March they proposed German annual payments rising to $3 billion by 1926, half of the Committee on Indemnity's figure and equivalent to one quarter of the country's national income. It was still a crushing impossibility, but, appearing to be a great concession, more mischievous and potentially destructive. Maneuvering against his own monstrosities, Lloyd George requested alternative plans, one from a committee of experts—and one from Keynes. He found the two new proposals offensively mild but the effect was useful confusion: all three plans vanished into it.[111]

Keynes, straining against what he saw as disastrous decisions, was encouraged to try again. On 28 March the conference leaders, seeing that public opinion and financial sense were too far apart, agreed to leave the reparation figure out of the peace treaty for a future determination. Although Keynes knew that the eventual figure would also be impossibly enormous, he seized on the opportunity to produce a new plan for the interim period. Possibly Lloyd George found it useful as a bargaining counter against unrelenting French insistence on an exorbitant reparation sum and the bland U.S. assumption that their wartime allies would begin to pay their huge war debts. Keynes, given his opportunity, emphasized the constructive in his plan's name, "Scheme for the Rehabilitation of European Credit and for Financing Relief and Reconstruction," but it became known, to the extent that it was known at all, less effectively but more flatteringly as the Keynes Plan. The terms would have Germany issue $25 billion in bonds, to be retired partly in cash and partly by reconstruction work in war-devastated areas, the bonds to be guaranteed by the leading allied governments. Associated with the plan would be an allied agreement to reduce all inter allied war debts.[112] The latter motif repeated more moderately an original idea of total and general war-debt cancellation that Keynes had brought up when the Treasury was drafting its memorandum of mid-November on the indemnity, that is to say reparations.[113] The Keynes Plan was granted a moment of official reality.

On 12 April, from a Bloomsbury outpost in the country, Keynes wrote his mother that he had been flown back to England to present his plan: "The state of Europe is very desperate—the economic system jammed and the people without hope." Five days later, in desperate hope, he reported to her from London, "I have been kept about here until today getting through the cabinet a *grand scheme for the rehabilitation of Europe.*"[114] Keynes knew better. The plan's excellence condemned it. President Wilson rejected it quickly, pointing out that the Congress would not approve a U.S. guarantee for the German bonds. He did not have to emphasize that the United States would not give up its war-debt claims.[115] Keynes had run hard against two immovable objects: allied, particularly French (and Italian), reparation demands and U.S. war-debt obduracy, the one reinforcing the other. Furthermore, he could see that the Americans, disenchanted with European realities, were withdrawing from Europe. At least he had proved to himself that the suicidal course could not be altered.

On 14 May, back in Paris, Keynes economically wrote the same letter to his mother and Duncan Grant while adding specifics for either. To both he wrote, "I've been utterly worn out, partly by work partly by the depression at the evil round me."[116] On 19 May he wrote to his superiors in London that he would resign.[117] On Sunday 1 June, again writing a double letter to his mother and Duncan, he told them that "misery" and "prolonged overwork" had overwhelmed him: "I gave way last Friday and took to my bed suffering from sheer nervous exhaustion." More energetic than most healthy persons, he was "rising only for really important interviews" and a successful effort to "achieve some improvement" for wretched Austria.[118] On 5 June, his thirty-sixth birthday, he wrote Lloyd George, "I am slipping away from this scene of nightmare. I can do no more good here." He had lost the hope that "you'd find some way to make of the treaty a just and expedient document. . . . The battle is lost." He was leaving in two days.[119]

Keynes's terrific competence as economist and his humanity, causing this psychic and physical suffering, had removed him from government. He could no longer function in it. Probably better than anyone else, he could see how bad the situation was; indeed, prophetically, he could envision greater future horrors than the late war. The tidying up of the wretched details could be left to lesser persons.

Before the end of June, denouncing that peace and confirming his isolation from power and direct influence, Keynes began writing his notorious *Economic*

Consequences of the Peace. He would have none of the responsibility for the dreadful consequences. He was sure that events would eventually overtake his vision. Meanwhile there would be a period in the wilderness, but it would be a well-furnished wilderness. He had his base in King's College, the university, and the *Economic Journal.* He had No. 6 Harvey Road and Bloomsbury. He was known as a devilishly clever don and Treasury man. He was receiving golden offers. He had a plan for becoming rich.

NOTES

1. Draft minutes by JMK, dispatch of Ayrshire bulls, 18 October 1906, India Office, KP, India Office Clerk (hereafter IA/2); Anand Chandavakar, *Keynes and India: A Study in Economics and Biography* (London, 1990), 12; editorial note, *CW*, 15: 3.

2. According to W. M. Page, his contemporary in mathematics at Kings College, Harrod, *The Life*, 122.

3. Letter to Permanent Undersecretary John A. Godley, 3 October 1907, *CW*, 15: 3–4.

4. KP, PP/45/316.

5. Letters, 9 May, 6 December 1907, KP, PP/45/168.

6. Keynes's covering note, reply by Thomas W. Holderness, and Keynes's recommendation, all dated 19 March 1907, *CW*, 15: 4–11.

7. Letter, 13 July 1907, KP, PP/45/316; quoted, *CW*, 15: 4.

8. KP, PP/45/316.

9. JNK Diary, 19 October 1907.

10. Ibid.

11. Quoted, R. M. O'Donnell, *Keynes: Philosophy, Economics, and Politics* (New York, 1989), 15.

12. JNK Diary, 17, 18 March 1908.

13. Letter, *CW*, 15: 13.

14. Letter, 23 April 1908, ibid., 14.

15. Letter, 21 April 1908, KP, PP/45/168.

16. Keynes's pre-war lecture schedule, *CW*, 12: 689. Two sets of his early lecture notes, ibid., 690–783.

17. The review, *CW*, 11: 174–77; the notes, ibid., 178–82.

18. Letters, JMK to JNK, 13, 27 September 1908, KP, PP/45/168.

19. JNK Diary, 11 November 1908; other notes on his condition, 13, 16 November.

20. Ibid., 16 November 1908.

21. Ibid., 25 December 1908; the article, *CW*, 11: 1–22.

22. The letters and editorial commentaries, *CW*, 15: 17–28.

23. KP, PP/45/168.

24. Letter, JMK to Duncan Grant, 5 February 1909, BL, Add. MSS 57930.

25. O'Donnell, *Keynes: Philosophy*, 15.

26. JMK to Duncan Grant, 10 October 1909, BL, Add. MSS 57930.

27. JNK Diary, 7 November 1909.

28. Moggridge, *MK*, 187.

29. Quoted, JNK Diary, 29 April 1911.

30. Letter, JMK to Duncan Grant, 24 November 1910, BL, Add. MSS 57930.

31. R. M. O'Donnell, "The Unwritten Books and Papers of J. M. Keynes," *History of Political Economy* 24 (Winter 1992): 769–817.

32. Letter, JMK to Duncan Grant, 24 October 1909, BL, Add. MSS 57930.

33. E. A. G. Robinson, "John Maynard Keynes 1883–1946," *Economic Journal* 57 (March 1947): 27.

34. Reprinted as vol. 8 of the *CW*. Detailed analysis, Felix, *Biography of an Idea*, 28–36; extensive analysis, O'Donnell, *Keynes: Philosophy*, 1–154. O'Donnell takes the treatise's theses seriously, but maintains and concedes his "general silence on evaluation," 5.

35. *CW*, 8: 87.

36. Ibid., 444.

37. Ibid., xvii.

38. Ibid., 10.

39. J. N. Keynes, *Formal Logic*, 2.

40. *CW*, 8: 467.

41. Quoted, editorial note, ibid., 15: 17.

42. Letter (cited above on founding the Political Economy Club), JMK to Duncan Grant, 24 October 1909, BL, Add. MSS 57930.

43. Letter, 31 October 1909, quoted, *CW*, 15: 39.

44. *Economic Journal*, September 1910, ibid., 11: 23–26.

45. Editorial note, 15: 65.

46. The article, ibid., 91–94; quotation, 94.

47. Editorial note, ibid., 95.

48. Correspondence on the original and enhanced offers, ibid., 97–98; Keynes's idea about Montagu's role, JMK to Lydia Lopokova, 16 November 1924, KP, PP/45/190.

49. Editorial note, *CW*, 15: 100.

50. Published, 26 October 1912, ibid., 89.

51. E.g., Minutes of Evidence, 5, 17, 26 June, 11 July 1913, ibid., 101–27.

52. KP, PP/45/168.

53. Letter, 9 March 1914, *CW*, 15: 268–69; quotation, 268.

54. *CW*, 1: 17, 71. Another view of Keynes and the India Office, Amiya Komar Bagchi, *The Presidency Banks and the Indian Economy* (Calcutta, 1989). Keynes was "that pillar of the India Office establishment," rationalizing the "extraction of the surplus from the Indian economy" (105, 15). In fact Keynes was a kindly (and patronizing) imperialist, believing that Great Britain ruled India better than the Indians could.

55. Dated 1 August 1914, quoted, editorial note, *CW*, 16 (*Activities 1914–1919: The Treasury and Versailles*): 3.

56. E.g., account of the crisis in R. S. Sayers, *The Bank of England 1891–1944*, 3 vols. (London, 1976), based on vol. 16 of Keynes's *CW* (also drawn on in these pages) and on interviews, but at that late date not with any of the actual subjects, n. 68. A more balanced view in E. V. Morgan, *Studies in British Financial Policy, 1914–1925* (London, 1952), which quotes Keynes's criticism but also *The Times History of the War*, the latter saying that the joint stock banks, object of Keynes's heaviest attacks, had "lent every assistance" in the crisis (30, n. 30).

57. Editorial note, *CW*, 16: 3.

58. She had gained "half a stone. . . . I have never seen Margaret look better or bonnier," JNK Diary, 20 July 1913.

59. Quoted, Harrod, *The Life*, 197.

60. "Memorandum against the Suspension of Gold," *CW*, 16: 7–15; quotation, 12.

61. Letter, 30 August 1914, KP, PP/45/168.

62. Letter, JMK to JNK, 6 August 1914, ibid.

63. Morgan, *Studies in British Financial Policy*, 3, 8. His review of the crisis, 3–32.

64. *CW*, 16: 8.

65. Sayers, *The Bank of England* (cited above), 1: 71.

66. *CW*, 16: 7, 12, 10.

67. Quoted, Harrod, *The Life*, 197.

68. Account by the economic historian Sir John Clapham, printed in Sayers, *The Bank of England*, 3: 31–45; quotations, 36–37. Sir Felix Schuster, a leading banker, and Prime Minister Asquith thought Cunliffe was leaning toward suspension at one point, Moggridge, *MK*, 239, n. 239.

69. "The Proper Means for Enabling Discount Operations to Be Resumed," *CW*, 16: 16–19.

70. KP, PP/45/168.

71. The articles, *CW*, 11: 238–328; the other writings (reprinted or summarized), ibid., 16: 20–57.

72. Ibid., 16: 253.

73. Letter to JNK, 6 August 1914, KP, PP/45/168; letter to Marshall, 10 October 1914, excerpted, *CW*, 16: 30.

74. Sayers, *The Bank of England*, 1: 64; see also account by Clapham, ibid., 3: 33.

75. Editorial note, *CW*, 16: 31–32.

76. Ibid., 11: 328.

77. Editorial note quoting *Bankers' Magazine*, ibid., 16: 31.

78. KP, PP/45/168.

79. JMK to Lydia Lopokova (cited above), 16 November 1924, KP, PP/45/190. This was not inconsistent with the fact that, as Harrod wrote (*The Life*, 201), he was brought in as an assistant to Sir George Paish, the financial adviser of Lloyd George, who found himself overworked.

80. JNK Diary, 7, 10, 18 December 1914.

81. "Wheat Prices," *CW*, 16: 57–66; supporting memorandum and editorial notes, ibid., 82–92, 78, 82.

82. Keynes's account in a note to Bonar Law, Skidelsky, *JMK*, 1: 299.

83. KP, PP/45/168.

84. *CW*, 16: 67; memorandum, "Russia," ibid., 67–71.

85. W. N. Medlicott, *Contemporary England 1914–1964* (London, 1976; 1st ed., 1967), 49.

86. Harrod, *The Life*, 206.

87. Letter, 29 December 1916, KP, PP/45/168.

88. Details, editorial note, *CW*, 16: 223–24.

89. Editorial note and excerpt from a Reading letter to Law: "I am parting from Keynes with the greatest reluctance—he has been my mainstay here in finance," ibid., 264–65.

90. KP, PP/45/168.

91. Letter to FAK, 14 April 1918, ibid.

92. Quoted, editorial note, *CW*, 16: 264.

93. Quoted, Skidelsky, *JMK*, 1: 342.

94. Letter, 22 April 1918, KP, PP/45/168.

95. *CW*, 11: 313–14, 320.

96. Ibid., 16: 143–49, 162–77, 215–22.

97. "Notes on Exchange Control," 24 September 1939, ibid., 210–14; quotation, 211.

98. Letters, JMK to FAK, 11 February, JMK to JNK, 25 May 1917, KP, PP/45/168.

99. *CW*, 16: 157–61, 179–84.

100. Quoted, Holroyd, *Lytton Strachey*, 2: 172.

101. JMK to FAK, 2 July 1914, PP/45/168. Keynes had evidently met Asquith earlier, JMK to JNK, 13 August 1913, ibid., but the Morrell party had a more lasting effect.

102. JMK to Lydia Lopokova, 16 November 1924 (cited above), PP/45/190.

103. Asquith quoted, Roy Jenkins, *Asquith* (New York, 1964), 345.

104. Editorial note and memorandum, *CW*, 16: 311–34.

105. "Notes on an Indemnity," 31 October 1918, ibid., 338–43; quotations, 342.

106. "Memorandum by the Treasury . . . ," ibid., 344–83; quotations, 378, 375.

107. Quoted, Lloyd George, *Memoirs of the Peace Conference* (1939), editorial note, ibid., 336.

108. One of the two was the temporarily unemployed Lord Cunliffe, who had led the Bank of England, alienating his own staff in the process, in a conflict with the Treasury. He demanded the dismissal of Permanent Secretary Robert Chalmers and Keynes, but Bonar Law, instead, worked Cunliffe's dismissal. The other was the Australian prime minister.

109. Salary and functions, JMK to FAK, 16 March 1919, PP/45/168. About the functions: "Deputy for the Chancellor of the Exchequeur . . . with full power to take decisions [etc.] All of which sounds rather grander than it is."

110. "Dr. Melchior: A Defeated Enemy," *CW*, 10: 425–26.

111. Harrod, *The Life*, 235–46; Philip M. Burnett, ed., *Reparation at the Paris Peace Conference* (New York, 1940), 1: 689–92.

112. *CW*, 16: 429–31, 431–36.

113. Editorial notes and Keynes's proposal, ibid., 417–19.

114. JMK to FAK, 12, 17 April 1919, KP, PP/45/168.

115. Wilson's letter of 3 May 1919, quoted, editorial note, *CW*, 16: 441.

116. JMK to FAK, *CW*, 16: 458; JMK to Duncan Grant, BL, Add. MSS 57931.

117. The letter, to Permanent Secretary John Bradbury, is missing, but Austen Chamberlain, who had succeeded Bonar Law as chancellor in January, referred to it in a letter of 21 May appealing to Keynes to stay, editorial note, *CW*, 16: 458–59.

118. JMK to FAK, *CW*, 16: 470; JMK to Duncan Grant, BL, Add. MSS 57931.

119. *CW*, 16: 469.

CHAPTER 4

"A Kind of Affection" (and a Sense of Responsibility): Keynes in Love

Underlying the public responsibilities of his functioning and creating terrific tensions lay the private exigencies of Maynard Keynes's nature. We have seen the overt expression of some of this in his opposition to conscription and all-out war. But such actions as his briefing of Chancellor of the Exchequeur Mc-Kenna and his composition of persuasive memoranda, however, cannot convey the depth of his feelings. One must find the private man in the public function-ary. The wonder is that he kept his personal quarrels with government policy so well controlled. It is also another aspect of his genius.

If Keynes's emotionally charged opinions might have surprised his superiors, it should be recognized that they were also fallible humans with sometimes questionable personal and public aims. Lloyd George had scandalously taken advantage of his position to gain financial advantages and was known as the "Goat" for his incessant womanizing. Asquith, his predecessor as prime min-ister, had entered into ambiguous, surely close relations with a comparably young friend of his daughter; indeed she resolved the ambiguities by suddenly evoking and accepting a marriage proposal by Edwin Montagu, Keynes's patron. Some of the cabinet ministers wanted a negotiated peace; in France, which took the war more angrily than Britain, two like-minded members of that cabinet were arrested as putative traitors, one of them spending two years in prison. Keynes's private agenda remained, by and large, successfully private.

Much of Keynes's personal policy derived from, or related to, his principled, romantic homosexuality as reinforced by the similar or analogous moeurs of

John Maynard Keynes (right) and Duncan Grant in 1912 (Vanessa Bell photograph album). Photo courtesy of the Tate Gallery Archive, London.

other members of Bloomsbury. Nor would he be content with merely escaping punishment unscathed. With Lytton Strachey he had projected ideas for liberation from legal sanctions and, on his own as a Liberal ideologue, would later take a rather daring public position on sexual freedom.

But then, on second view, Maynard Keynes was not that extreme. In the end, he would establish a new orthodoxy for political economy, whereas the lover of men would spend his maturer years as a happily married man.

In an evidently unsent letter to Dil Knox, we might recall, young Keynes of King's College had memorialized, at least to himself, "a kind of affection" arising from "the curious incidents that marked our last two years at Eton."[1] The incidents were sexual. The biographer of Dil and his three brothers had "Dilly and Maynard . . . calmly undertak[ing] experiments, intellectual and sexual, to resolve the question of which things are necessary to life. Pleasure, like morality and duty, was a psychological necessity, which must therefore be accepted, but without much fuss."[2] The early death of their mother had discouraged the Knox boys from placing much weight on feelings, but Maynard had been more fortunate. Unafraid to write the word "affection," if not so temerarious then as to attempt the unambiguous "love," Maynard would commit his feelings as far as they would go. It was natural that as recorder of the scores on the cricket field near Harvey Road and the number of lines in notable long poems, he would keep an exact record of the activities those feelings inspired. He showed part of that record to James Strachey, Lytton's youngest brother (by seven years), future analyzand and translator of Sigmund Freud, who expostulated to Lytton, "His statistics make me gasp."[3]

Some years later, in 1920, Lytton himself remarked to a friend about Keynes, "With his curious typewriter intellect, he's also so oddly and unexpectedly emotional."[4] The emotion was as authentic as the statistics. If the latter recorded wholesale lust, young Keynes's letters, illuminating the amatory register, document intense singular love as well.

Maynard and Lytton had joined as best friends and theorists of the Higher Sodomy, which they proclaimed superior to heterosexuality, with its mediocre female partners and mind-distracting children. Yielding to Lytton's three years of seniority, Maynard was at first content to accept his ascendancy as he had done with Montagu in Cambridge University politics. In their letters Lytton and Maynard spun out their theory from a free translation of G. E. Moore's *Principia Ethica*. The goodness Moore had sought also could be found, Lytton amended, in feelings for beautiful young men. Lytton was an even more prolific letter writer than Maynard, sometimes sending him three a day. Their letters fell thicker and faster for the year from October 1905, when Lytton departed Cambridge for London, to the next October, when Maynard followed, although the correspondence had been lively before and would remain so into 1908. Like Marx and Engels, the revolutionaries Strachey and Keynes carefully saved their letters as guides to their followers in implementing their theory. "Our time will come about a hundred years hence," Lytton wrote Maynard, "when preparations will have been made . . . so that at the publication of our letters, everyone will be finally converted.''[5] Like Marx and Engels guiding their revolution, these two later leaders could enjoy the considerable immediate benefit of communion and mutual support.

The two friends saw themselves as older unattractive mentors of younger ''beauties.'' We know where Maynard got the false view of himself as ugly. Lytton's self-image was more accurate. A wavering lath of six feet, one inch,[6] he had a huge head, bespectacled eyes, equine teeth, and an aggressively over-sized nose. (He later softened his physiognomic effect by the addition of a rich brown beard.) His voice, perpetually breaking, wavered betwen the treble and the bass. If Maynard was often ill, Lytton, suffering a range of ailments from deranged digestion and fainting spells to indiscriminate breakdowns, was never well. In these years Lytton's situation in life, like his voice, swung between the absurd and the impressive. He had a slapdash earlier education under the dis-tracted attention of his mother (who had ten surviving children, out of thirteen born, to contemplate) and the inattention of an elderly father (who in his younger days had been a general, a great administrator in Queen Victoria's India, and a scientific spirit who had helped found Indian meteorology). Lytton fell fortu-nately into Trinity College and, like Maynard, found friendly affinities in Cam-bridge University's discussion societies. Entering the Apostles after two years, unlike the prodigy Maynard, he soon became secretary, however, and with his literary culture and wit, became their spiritus rector. Again, unlike the smoothly successful Maynard, Lytton, prone to self-defeating behavior, tripped himself up more often than he succeeded. He won the Chancellor's Medal for a long poem, but achieved only second-class honors in his history tripos and, after three graduate years, wrote a dissertation deemed unremarkable. Having failed to win a fellowship, crushed, mourning his lost Cambridge paradise, he had to retreat to a bed sitting-room in the Strachey home in the Bayswater section of London.

Lytton's situation was not as bad as his exorbitantly self-deprecating imagi-nation made it. All along, making crabwise progress, he had been deepening his literary culture, which was his half-recognized strength. In his last two years in Cambridge he had published a half dozen review articles in two respectable British journals. In London he was writing an article every six weeks; after two years the *Spectator* engaged him to contribute an article a week, and he produced seventy-five competent and sometimes scintillating efforts in the next nineteen months.[7] In May 1918, outshining Maynard's long-established brilliance, he would publish the book that would revolutionize the art of biography in England and make him a famous and prosperous author.

In Lytton's last year in Cambridge, meanwhile, the balance of power shifted to Maynard. In November 1904 Lytton discovered Arthur Lawrence Hobhouse, a Trinity freshman, whom he described appreciatively as ''look[ing] pink and delightful as embryos [Apostle candidates] should.'' So he informed Leonard Woolf, the fellow Apostle who had earlier joined him in vetting the embryo

Keynes. Woolf was now a recent arrival as colonial officer in Ceylon (Sri Lanka today), when he would serve Lytton as correspondent-confidant for nearly seven years. "I'm rather in love with him," Lytton volunteered, "and Keynes, who lunched with him today . . . is convinced that he's all right."[8] Within a fortnight, however, Lytton told Maynard, still his chief confidant, "Hobhouse and I are beginning to quarrel. I believe I don't like his nose."[9] Lytton reversed direction immediately when he heard, on 2 February 1905, that Hobhouse had been injured in a bicycle accident, as he immediately wrote Keynes. He found the victim in bed being read to by friends: "So dreadfully shattered—you've no idea. . . . Oh, dear. The appearance. He was flushed, embarrassed, exquisite. I fled after three seconds cursing everything and everybody . . . wondering . . . how many people his bedroom will be able to hold."[10]

Maynard, quickly attracted to the embryo, easily outmaneuvered Lytton. Before the end of the month, he had taken over Hobhouse and successfully sponsored him into the Apostles. "Lytton was left to brood abjectly over 'my own unutterable silence—my dead, shattered, desiccated hope of some companionship, some love.' " For a few weeks Lytton hated Maynard. On 25 February he attacked Maynard at a Society meeting, explaining, " 'For it is one of his queer characteristics that one often wants . . . to make a malicious attack on him. . . . He is a hedonist and a follower of Moore; he is an Apostle without tears.' "[11] Except for the tears, which Maynard unashamedly spilled on occasion, this was acutely true, and others would similarly attack him. Lytton had also left out the major reason: Maynard's infuriating ability to get what he wanted—his sheer power and success. Maynard, meanwhile, could mollify his friend by suffering a defeat.

Preparing for his honors examinations, Maynard had efficiently woven Hobhouse into his study program. In April, taking his mathematics books with him, he spent three weeks visiting with his new Apostle. The result was frustration and worse, as Maynard reported to a happier Lytton: "That episode is over." At the moment Maynard and Lytton seemed to have exchanged characters, Maynard referring to "the violence of the various feelings I have been through" and the "phenomenal troubles . . . which brought their depression with them." He was "more madly in love with [Hobhouse] than ever," but "I have discovered I am within an ace of being in love with you."[12] Their correspondence resumed more thickly than ever.

In August 1905, while striving to finish his ill-fated dissertation, Lytton experienced a new epiphany. Writing Maynard from the country, where his family had rented a house for the summer, he announced, "I've managed . . . to catch a glimpse of Heaven. Incredible. . . . I want to go into the wilderness, or the world, and preach an infinitude of sermons on the text—'Embrace one another,' Oh yes, it's Duncan."[13]

Duncan Grant was a cousin on the maternal, Scottish side of the family. His parents fixed in India, he had lived for extended periods with the Stracheys. Born 21 January 1885, he was not quite twenty when Lytton discovered him as lover, and everyone agreed with Lytton that he was a beauty. Of middle stature, he had his mother's perfect features, enhanced by thick, dark hair, blue-gray eyes, and lips that were "incomparably lascivious,"[14] a quality Lytton found commendable when not associated with Maynard. The adolescent Duncan had shown a pronounced talent for painting and very little else, as if anything else mattered. Arithmetic and other mental disciplines had no effect on him, but he was intelligent where it mattered, about art and people. He had the natural charm, passivity, and self-centeredness of an infant: the perfect love object.

At first the course of love ran too smoothly for Lytton, who could best appreciate happiness in the future or past. He insisted on heaping more love and intensity on Duncan than their object could endure, with its self-protecting tenderness and short attention span. Ecstasy was also hard on Lytton's tender physical system; later in August he reported, "A letter from Duncan and a violent attack of constipation."[15] Befallen by heaven in August, by October he had succeeded in disturbing its tranquility. On 13 October he reported at length to Maynard, "Things are smoothed over. . . . I realize that the relation is a trifle lopsided. There is distinctly something of the lovee about his affection, if not about his lust." Forebodingly he wrote, "And I can't help feeling that the latter is liable to lapse in time." Lytton, however, was not contracting the world down to Duncan alone. Overusing the adjective, he preferred the insight that Dil Knox had "no serious bottom, only a lascivious one. . . . Hobby floats before me in a golden mist." About Maynard's frustrated friend, Bernard Swithinbank, "Oh Swithin, Swithin! I long to press your hand! Isn't he beautiful[?]" Closing, he could joyously tell Maynard of the receipt of an "undoubtedly superb" letter from the writing-shy Duncan, "a filth packet stuffed with pearls. Adieu!"[16] Perhaps an uneven course of love was more gratifying.

Maynard was sage and supportive. From a hotel in Switzerland, where he was undertaking his Alpine expedition, an enjoyable but unrepeated experience in his busy life, he had commended his friend for having overcome his "prejudice against incest." Maynard saw that "better feelings seem to have supervened. I hope he is a real person."[17] He also mentioned Hobhouse in a manner that could soothe the sting to Lytton's amour propre. First, on 31 July, while he was still at King's College, he reported progress: "For months I courted him and he turned a cold cheek." That unavailing, "For three weeks I have cultivated a demeanor of the utmost apparent coldness. I have rated him and jeered at him. . . . And tonight he comes round and declares he is in love with me. . . . Heavens!"[18]

Absorbed with Duncan, Lytton could empathize. In Maynard's original letter encouraging the Duncan affair, he had begun, "About Hobhouse . . . we have had two glorious days." But suggesting frustration rather than consummation, "He does not understand what the thing means." From Vevey, irrelevantly, he recommended, "Here might one live with his favorite catamite for £100 a year . . . unconstipated and unconcerned." He added, "ALH may call on you tomorrow."[19] Hobhouse did so. On 7 September Lytton reported that they had discussed constipation and sex, Hobhouse complaining of the first and of the second, "He says he is repulsed by it." Lytton echoed Maynard, "Poor thing, he doesn't seem to understand much."[20] With Hobhouse declared irrelevant, a general peace descended on Lytton and Maynard. But they were not quite done with Hobby.

Later in October, following Lytton's new accomodation with Duncan, Maynard sought to confirm that state of affairs: "I see much better than before how things lie—and they are superb. . . . You are appropriate to each other. I am in love with your being in love with one another." In the character of a counselor in love relations he cautioned, "Don't oppress him with excessive demands. And don't . . . think any kind of disaster [is] on the brink." Lytton returned, "You're very kind and encouraging." Continuing with a soupçon of the negative, he was encouraged to rise to the positive: "Last night he seemed so very stand-offish. But today I've seen him twice & each time very happily." Lytton rose further, launching himself toward transcendence: "Oh, dear, let's become Chinese & spend our days besides rivers smoking opium . . . with an occasional lyric or two, & an occasional kiss. Let's dream of calm interminable heavens . . . abolish time, and forget that we have ever lusted, and die smiling. Your GLS."[21] But Lytton could not restrain his importunities and other counterproductive behavior.

One factor helped keep the Lytton–Duncan relationship in being: absence. Lytton, a witty, considerate, asked-back guest, was continually shuttling among numerous refuges from the gloom of the Strachey residence. Duncan had arrived at the point where he could profitably learn from the French masters, and, perhaps at a hint from him, was presented with an opportunity to do so. First, however, at the beginning of January 1906, Lytton and Duncan spent a five-day interlude in the country, which Lytton had dreaded as too much of a good thing but during which he enjoyed an insecure bliss. He assured Maynard that Duncan was "a *genius*—a colossal portent of fire & glory."[22] In February, continuing his overseas confidences, he informed Leonard Woolf that the only important things in life were "when Duncan would have his next erection & whether it's pleasanter to feel his buttocks or look into his eyes."[23] Later in February the pair found themselves traveling to Paris, but only, fortunately or not, to separate. Duncan stopped there to begin his learning; he would remain in Paris, except for two visits back home, until mid-1907. A sister of Mrs. Strachey, thus aunt of both and even-handedly generous, had invited Lytton to her villa in Menton, in the south of France, and had presented Duncan with £100, which was financing his Paris stay. After two months of healthy boredom and too few communications from Duncan, Lytton got a cataclysmic letter from him in April: Hobby had come to Paris and he and Duncan had fallen in love. "It's a complete shock, and I'm still gasping," he wrote Maynard.[24] He returned to a room in Duncan's Paris hotel, where he collapsed, and his sister Pippa (Philippa) came from England to steady his tottering steps homeward when he was capable of tottering. Duncan visited the patient kindly but without altering matters. After a delay lengthened by a railway strike, Lytton returned home in May, committed, despite the shock, to more reviews and subject to more invitations. He comforted himself variously. In July he reported, "This morning I had a little flirtation with one of my delightful nephews."[25] About Hobby he had fraternally written Maynard, "If I was very wicked I should urge you to lure him on & . . . then turn & rend him. . . . Of all prostitutes, the spiritual ones are the worst."[26] The Duncan–Hobby affair underwent the predictable vicissitudes; Duncan lapsed into inconstancy and Hobby was too fearful of his mother's discovering matters to be a rewarding lover. By the end of 1906 it had dissolved. Before then Maynard won satisfaction of a kind. His amatory record notes his own success with Hobby finally in 1906, thus during the period of the Hobby–Duncan affair, but that would represent an ending rather than a beginning. When Duncan returned to London in 1907, he resumed his affair with Lytton, who contented himself at a lower level of bliss, recrimination, and apprehension. At the time Maynard, employed at the India Office until the summer of 1908, was also in London.

Lytton had introduced Duncan to Maynard in October 1905, right after his return to London from Cambridge.[27] Inevitably, they fell in love. Certainly it would have happened even if Lytton had not been so persistently self-defeating. To Duncan Maynard was a powerful, practical figure, a source of secure masculine initiative and much less oppressive than Lytton. To Maynard Duncan was a beauty and an artist, adorable as both. In June 1908 Lytton went up for three weeks to Apostolic Cambridge, which was enormously restorative after the rigors of London, its springtime lawns star-spangled with attractive young undergraduates. The affair started or intensified after he left. Lytton learned about it on his return to London in early July.

"It came as an explosive shock," Michael Holroyd, Lytton's bigrapher, wrote, "a kind of death."[28] But Lytton lived multiple lives. He had already experienced the loss of Duncan to Hobby and risen above it emotionally and professionally. In one vital sense it was worse; Lytton had to reconstitute his life without his lover of nearly three years, whatever the interruptions, but also without his counselor and best friend, however rivalrous, Machiavellian, and lacking in resonant empathy. Maynard's "common sense was enough to freeze a volcano," he had earlier complained.[29] The episode, however, proved that Maynard could be just as emotional as Lytton, indeed more deeply so, if not so wildly and confidingly. Nor was Lytton embarrassed for lack of sympathetic counseling. Besides Leonard Woolf in Ceylon he could draw on, among others, his brother James, now sufficiently matured as Trinity undergraduate ensconced in Lytton's old rooms and possessing the *Einfühlungsvermögen* that would make him an early psychoanalyst. Pillowed by family and friends, Lytton found his situation not as wretched as he had apprehended, while Maynard bared a vulnerable heart to endless wounding.

Blind to the end, Lytton had taken Maynard and Duncan to lunch in London in July and only then, capturing a whisper between them, faced the unimagined inevitable. Although Lytton, more at home in chaotic situations, expressed himself in a statesmanlike variety of dissimulation, Maynard reacted feelingly and frankly. From his Westminster flat, just before giving it up, he wrote Duncan the next day, "Dearest Duncan, Lytton has been. He begins, 'I hear that you & Duncan are carrying on together.' " Maynard continued, "I feel quite shattered by the interview." He recognized Lytton's defensive deceptions: "He takes the cynical line—much interested as a student of human life." Lytton had known better than to pretend totally: "But it gave him, as he said, a turn." Maynard recurred to his own sense of weakness: "Oh, dear, I don't know what to think of the interview & feel ill & rather distraught. I wish there was no one else in the world but you. . . . Come early tomorrow."[30]

Lytton was practicing the arts of dissimulation with such abandon, as he swung between pain and rage to resignation and empathy, that he was deceiving himself more than he did Maynard and the others engaged in his drama. Nor could he avoid clear-headedly mocking himself at the same time. To his brother he confided his deepest pain: "Things are spectral to me now. . . . Oh! There are cruelties in the world." He succumbed to disgust: "He has come to me reeking with that semen."[31] Maynard insisted on approaching Lytton, begging, "Please don't be unsympathetic and don't if you can help it, hate me."[32] Hating him passionately at the moment, Lytton responded with sovereign graciousness: "You must believe that . . . I don't hate you and that if you were here now I should probably kiss you, except that Duncan would be jealous, which would never do!"[33] Maynard responded gratifyingly by return post, "Your letter made me cry."[34] Lytton pursued Maynard with gifts, "three most lovely books," Maynard wrote Duncan. "[I]t is too good of him."[35] Lytton provided a synoptic version of the event and his feelings to Leonard Woolf.

Recollected in tranquility, in the family's ancestral abode in Scotland almost two months after the denouement, the event took on an autumnal softness of edge. Now Lytton slipped into other deceptions. In a letter to Leonard he reviewed a variety of details since his previous communication, thus his three weeks in Cambridge ("It was happiness!") and Maynard's resignation from the India Office. He arrived at the affair: "Of course I was jealous, and cynical, and kind; & now I seem to myself to be indifferent. There were some amazing scenes—tears in floods, and kissings to match." Maynard and Duncan were now off on "their honeymoon. . . . I shouldn't be surprised if they were to ask me to join them, and I were to do so." A few days later Lytton reported resignedly from London, "Keynes's love affair isn't in the least wearing out. Idyllic letters come. . . . I walk out . . . and brood over conceivables. I linger in theatres among glimpses of exquisite young men." At the end of October he wrote that he had stayed with Maynard, who had just returned, in his new, half-furnished rooms at King's: "It was horrible. His futility. . . . I shuddered, I lusted, I dreamt of the past, of Duncan, of all the impossibles, and he remained unmoved."[36] Lytton essayed to move Maynard.

During the rest of 1908 and early 1909, abetted by James, Lytton undertook a mostly imaginary campaign to convince Maynard and their Apostolic friends

of Maynard's horridness and to isolate him. In his more negative moods Lytton
had dubbed Maynard "Pozzo di Borgo," suggesting Machiavellian villainy, and
on 14 February 1909 in effect told James the kind of report he would like from
him: "I've been feeling rather uneasy about the Pozzo man." G. E. Moore had
found Maynard "very depressed & silent. . . . I can't help feeling rather guilty."
Trying to substantiate his brother's dire thoughts, James reported the next day
from Cambridge, "Popular opinion seems to be smashing him." But James's
account of 15 February, after having Maynard tearful again at the thought of
Lytton's anger, lacked other data and conceded, "He has *such* compensations.
I'm certain he still feels quite fixed about Duncan."[37] This was, furthermore, a
few days after Maynard's brilliantly successful start as economics lecturer. Ten
days earlier Lytton had anticipated and improved on James's report in a triumphant letter to Leonard: "As for poor Keynes, he's quite absolutely sunk . . .
the unveiled collapse. . . . And by God I think he deserves his fate. Looking
back I see him, hideous & meaningless . . . a malignant goblin gibbering over
destinies that are not his own. The moral is never put your penis in a French
letter [condom] that's cracked." Lytton's imagination, however, recoiled from
this image: "What's curious is that he, at this moment, must be imagining . . .
that he's reached the apex of human happiness—Cambridge, statistics, triumphant love, and inexhaustible copulations." Desperately, Lytton envisioned
Pozzo's "existence [as] the merest shell . . . until one day it shivers into smith-
ers."[38] Intelligent enough to realize what he was doing, Lytton went on retouch-
ing his image of Maynard to enhance its absurdity.

So seized by his imagination, Lytton felt better and, a kindly person at bottom,
became virtuously charitable. Of course he did not want to lose Maynard as a
friend. "Maynard . . . seems to me more and more an almost tragic figure," he
wrote James presently. "I'm afraid he must be dreadfully in love—how could
even he avoid that in the circumstances?" The approaching vote on Maynard's
second submission of his dissertation would be a good moment to give him
desperately needed reassurance. "The more I consider this, the more certain it
seems to me that I'm the only person who can support him."[39] When the news
of Maynard's success arrived, Lytton wrote him, "I was very glad to hear of
the fellowship. . . . I've been wanting to write you for some time . . . only to say
you must think of me as your friend." Pozzo did not rise to the occasion, but
rather plunged to its depths. "I was *very* glad to get your letter," he began
promisingly, but he went on, "Tonight for the second time I dined at their High
Table. The food is excellent but, by God, one feels the don. I play the part
admirably . . . but I should like to rape an undergraduate in the Combination
Room, just to make them see things . . . in their true light."[40] It was enough to
freeze a range of volcanoes.

Within the bounds of his love for Duncan, Maynard showed himself to be as
vulnerable and agonized as Lytton too easily felt for himself and wished for
him. Maynard would not and could not, in Lytton's manner, escape into a new
landscape or move on to find other sufficiently lovable love objects, as he soon

would do. By mid-1909, however much passion he had expended, Lytton had fallen completely out of love with Duncan, he told his brother, perhaps accurately.[41] For Maynard, Duncan was the great love of his life, whatever amatory adventures before, during, and after the affair. Nor did his ultimate and substantial love change this. Accepting every despair and humiliation, he invested himself totally in Duncan. He could not, however, yield the professional Keynes, committed to an increasing range of responsibilities, together with that personal Maynard.

If various distractions would interfere only too soon, Maynard and Duncan would at least have the opportunity to spend a long holiday in which to express and receive love without interference. It was the perfect moment. Duncan was not bound to a schedule and Maynard, having just left the India Office, was free for almost all of the summer and most of the fall of 1908 before settling in as lecturer in Cambridge. Duncan provided the physical frame. Expert at being patronized, he had now been invited by a rich friend of his mother's to the Orkney Islands, north of Scotland. It remained only to attach Maynard to the invitation, easily possible if, as they chose, they found their own accomodations.

Their correspondence began with businesslike notes to "Dear Duncan" from "Yours . . . J. M. Keynes," thus on 5 June, his twenty-fifth birthday, which he left unmentioned.[42] Maynard became intimately, lingeringly chatty in a letter to "Dearest Duncan" from "JMK" on 10 July, five days before the "Lytton-has-been" letter. He would maintain salutation and tone with Duncan for the rest of his life. In the 10 July letter he gossipped about James Strachey, the poet Rupert Brooke (a friend of Geoffrey Keynes) and Rupert's brother Justin, the economics student and a future Keynes protégé and colleague Gerald Shove, and "other beauties also . . . a crowd of the loveliest undergraduates." He demanded, "Why are you not a Cambridge undergraduate, damn you, instead of a wretched Londoner[?] Come, and I will make King's Chapel into a studio for you and you shall paint all the beauties of the age, and live on salmon mayonnaise, while Justin shall wait on you and Rupert shave you and Gerald tie up your bootlaces and I shall kiss you and we shall live happy and virtuous for ever."

Maynard continued on 24 July: he was moving into his rooms in King's the following day, "Dear Duncan, good night . . . Your most loving JMK," and, on 26 July, "My rooms . . . look at the best view in the world . . . the river and backs beyond. . . . So I lie on my window seat wishing you were with me." Similar sentiments were repeated almost daily, but by 3 August Maynard was complaining about a gap in Duncan's letters and on 4 August, "I am getting into the most miserable condition . . . depression has descended and of course it has fixed on you. . . . Dear Duncan I shan't be really happy again until I see you." On 5 August he celebrated Duncan's first letter from the Orkneys, "There was your packet for me to kiss and read. Do please arrange for me to come north at the earliest possible moment. . . . I love you too much and I can't now bear to live without you." Duncan evidently did nothing to speed Maynard's departure. Rather, on 14 August, Maynard was unhappy about his "noncommittal postcard." On Saturday, 15 August, Maynard got a telegram "which is devilish," proposing that he delay his trip—or worse. Immediately responding, he was forced to argue, Duncan's announced opinion to the contrary, "I am able to do my work [on the dissertation] quite as comfortably there as here, and I shall be . . . nearer you. . . . So please put up with my behavior." Firmly, "I shall take no notice of [the telegram], and shall leave here . . . on Monday." On Tuesday, 18 August, he was reunited with Duncan. They would be in the Orkneys until 22 October.

Whatever Duncan's reluctances, reunion was sweet. They spent most of their time on Hoy, one of the smaller Orkneys, where their host had an enormous residence, but on their own in an ad hoc farm lodging. Maynard reported to his father doubtless accurately that they had settled into "fixed habits and hours of painting and probability," while he regaled Lytton with images of "exquisite farm lads who flit around and drive us in their gig" and "the loveliest schoolboys in Britain" on holiday there.[43] For his sister Margaret he sketched himself, Duncan, and the view: "I am writing this . . . lying on the ground in Park Rackwick . . . thought the most out of the way and primitive place in the world." It was "certainly one of the most beautiful with its great red cliffs and amphitheatre of copper-colored hills." Duncan had drawn Maynard in ink-and-watercolor and was "now doing a large oil."[44] Maynard had already sent the sketch home and Neville would find it "uncompromising but very clever." The portrait in oil had a romantically handsome and unrecognizable scholar occupied with a writing board on his knee, further documentation of the hours of painting and probability as well as love. "On the whole I like the portrait," Neville pondered and decided. "We shall no doubt buy it."[45] (It was eventually given to King's College.) On Hoy, meanwhile, Maynard "had one of his feverish attacks," Neville recorded on 23 September, but the effect was to enhance rather than spoil the holiday. Invited to their host's residence, the pair could sink into its luxury, which included, besides sofas, a chapel, a museum, a laundry, golf links, and gardens. With Maynard restored after a week and a half, they returned to their still idyllic farm.

Iridiscent with love, the Orkneys episode remained for Maynard a perfect soap bubble of a short season. Its brevity was a necessary condition of its perfection. On 24 October, "Here I am in a whirl of business," Maynard wrote Duncan from King's College. His rooms were "charming" and a temporarily mollified Lytton was coming to stay. "I was miserable to be without you last night, but today I am so happy to be in Cambridge that I am as cheerful as anyone could wish. . . . When I have both you and Cambridge, I shall be the most fortunate creature in the world." Both knew how impossible that was. Maynard's letter the next day only emphasized it: "I live in a breathless condition with work pressing on me from every side and all kinds of social excitement.'' He was busy inspecting ''wits, beauties, and intelligences'' among the embryos: ''How far away the Orkneys seem!''[46]

As Duncan's earlier behavior and his telegraphed doubts about the holiday had indicated, he was not giving himself up totally to his affair with Maynard. During all of his life from adolescence, attracting many others, he periodically found them attractive and, with an infant's lack of inhibition, gratified himself and them. The busy Maynard would have been an unsatisfactory lover to anyone except a perfectly passive, self-abnegating person willing to camp in Cambridge and await occasional audiences. Even today, with so many activities exclusive to university members, like the dining hall privileges, ceremonies, and celebrations, the dons' lawfully wedded spouses must endure frequent separations. (Florence Ada Brown Keynes had known how to function during Neville's absences; Lydia Lopokova Keynes, at a later time in Maynard's life, would have the resources to work out with him a most satisfactory, because extraordinary, solution.) Duncan needed no excuse to continue his established pattern.

London, however, provided another opportunity for Maynard and Duncan to be together. In November 1909, after a brief spell elsewhere, they began cohabitation in a flat at 21 Fitzroy Square, to the west of Tottenham Court Road and contiguous to, but not in, the Bloomsbury district. Duncan took the larger front room as his studio and Maynard contented himself with the back bedroom. Maynard was finding more reason to be in London, and by 1912, with his editorship of the *Economic Journal* impelling him, was spending the middle of the week there, a pattern he would continue, except for the period of his war service, until 1937. Joining other members of the Bloomsbury group, the two moved to 38 Brunswick Square in Bloombury proper before the end of 1911. The lease was taken out in the name of the responsible Maynard while he, more prosperous and more often in London, claimed and paid for more comfortable quarters. When that ménage broke up at the expiration of the lease in late September 1914, Duncan, now attached to another Bloomsbury personage of weight, moved away from Maynard, occasioning, as noted here earlier, another of his depressions. The friendship endured.

From the beginning, as Maynard's letters after the Orkneys holiday make clear, his and Duncan's careers were pulling the lovers apart. Duncan, however, spent three weeks from late November to mid-December 1908 visiting Maynard and finishing his portrait, but Duncan's operative area was ineluctably London. Unfairly ignoring his own separate activities, Maynard was complaining hyperbolically as early as February 1909 that Duncan was ''drifting into all sorts of engagements which make it impossible for us ever to meet again.'' Four days later, pathetically but manipulatively, ''I can't help crying again . . . principally because I'm not going to see you.'' But one had to be philosophical; Maynard was looking forward to dinner that night with intriguing table partners.[47] In April Maynard and Duncan spent a fortnight in Versailles, where Maynard economically finished a university prize essay, but they could not achieve a second idyll. They fell into their first major quarrel, caused by Maynard's tendency to dominate and Duncan's to elude commitment. They resolved it on Duncan's terms, the equivalent of open marriage.

In mid-May, after enjoyably seeing Duncan again, Maynard wrote that he was experiencing the lag effect of more absence: "I've been feeling miserable." He had, however, attempted to relieve that with an attractive undergraduate. He was frank about objective and result: "I've adopted Mr. [Gordon H.] Luce as a possible embryo. I tried to fall in love with him, but couldn't manage it."[48] (Maynard would become fonder of Lucy, as the young man was called, but his amatory record does not list that young man. Lucy went off to Burma as English professor in 1912 and, to Maynard's distress, married a Burmese girl. That friendship endured, with Maynard being gracious to Luce's wife and achieving the publication of a book of Luce's poetry he loyally admired.) Maynard, mean-while, could enjoy his work and investigate the availability of other objects of varying kinds of his affection.

As Duncan's provocations increased, Maynard, too proud to be humbled, drew on his statesmanlike sense of personality and reality to maintain as much of a relationship as possible: an indissoluble friendship. With his yearning to-ward the aesthetic, he always had the artist in Duncan to adore when the lover was absent. He insisted on being happy with what he got and so refused to spoil it, in Lytton's manner, with useless recrimination. At the end of February 1910 Duncan announced he was in love with Adrian Stephen, a Fitzroy Square neigh-bor. Adrian was the younger brother of the Bloomsbury group's more significant Vanessa Bell and Virginia (future wife of Leonard Woolf). "I don't see why we should lose our tempers with one another," Maynard temperately returned. "I wonder what your Adrian affair is like now. When you last wrote it seemed perfect from the point of view of pleasure."[49]

Maynard could not always keep to this level of discourse. In March–April 1911, traveling to Morocco and Sicily, he had his last holiday with Duncan, who, however, went off to join Adrian in Naples. Toward the end, in April, Maynard wrote from Taormina, suggesting they meet in Naples and visit Pom-peii together. He was "melancholy and miss[ing] you very much, but feel I can get on well enough." The meeting was a failure, Maynard sending Duncan away abruptly. Forgetting his usual "Dearest Duncan" salutation, he opened a sore heart with his first words in a pursuing letter: "My nerves and feelings had been too much strained. . . . You tried to hush up the fact that I had any feelings, and I thought that alone I might get well sooner. But it hasn't been so. . . . I feel miserable and lonely." Duncan had withheld the "kind word . . . some open sign of affection" Maynard wanted. "But I regretted that I sent you away from me . . . I was more miserable after you'd gone." Five days later, as if nothing had happened, he wrote Duncan a chatty letter from I Tatti, the villa of Bernard Berenson in Florence (where he had been a guest in 1906 at the end of his Italian tour): "The way this place saps one's moral fibres is beyond belief." He advised Duncan on the cheapest way of returning to England.[50] He resumed his busy Cambridge life. In September he was "depressed" that Duncan had not joined him on a camping holiday in Devon, in southwest England, but recounted one incipient and one consummated sexual adventure. Later that month he joined fifty Liberal Members of Parliament on a tour of Ireland, reporting informatively to Duncan on the awfulness of politicians. At the end of October he wrote, "Tonight I feel extraordinarily happy and very much in love with you and as if whatever you did and whomever you might love didn't matter in the least." Wryly, he allowed, "But I suppose it's a temporary madness."[51]

Maynard, as his letters to Duncan as well as to Lytton conveyed, never restrained a roving eye or disposition. Doubtless, Duncan's affairs with others led him to more adventuring, but his record of sexual contacts suggests too much momentum to be halted merely by a great love. Maynard would show the greatness of that love in other ways besides faithfulness to a lover valuing it so little. Duncan himself appears as sexual partner every year from 1908 through 1915, the last year of record, long after the affair was over and after he had entered into a lifetime, although hardly exclusive, relationship. The photograph taken in 1912 (p. 94) documents the enduring character of their bond: the correctly dressed young don and the younger painter in someone else's jacket too big for him looking directly at each other against a blank wall, lost in each other's eyes.

Keynes provided an extraordinary wealth of information on his sexual experiences, extraordinarily rare in biographical sources. It comprised a tabulation of sexual incidents and two lists of his partners.[52] The biographer would be ungrateful to complain that tabulation and lists covered just ten to fifteen years and left open many questions.

The statistics themselves, the early part of which had rendered James Strachey breathless, comprised a simple—or not so simple—notation of the number of times Maynard did whatever he did per quarter for nine years and a quarter, from 13 May 1906 through 12 August 1915: 683. If the number is specific, the acts are encoded and classified but unspecified, Keynes mysteriously registering 309 incidences of activity c, 266 of a, and 108 of w. The activities were first totaled up per quarter, thus $4+11+4$ for a sum of 19 for the period 13 May to 12 August 1906, $1+8+7=16$ for 13 August to 12 November 1906, $3+12+4=19$ for 13 November 1906 to 12 February 1907. . . . (There is no indication why Keynes began and ended the quarters on the days indicated.) When he completed the fourth quarter he added up the four quarters to give him the yearly reckoning for 13 May 1906 through 12 May 1907: 73. Then, meticulous mathematician that he was, he continued to total up the last four quarters with every successive new quarter. Thus he could see at a glance whenever he had achieved a new personal record, or pr, as athletes now abbreviate it, for the year ending with the given quarter, as well as for the quarter itself compared with previous quarters. The tabulation began:

		c	a	w	total	
1906	May 13–Aug 12	4	11	4	19	
	Aug [13]–Nov [12]	1	8	7	16	
	Nov [13]–Feb [12]	3	12	4	19	
1907	Feb [13]–May [12]	3	12	4	19	= 73
	May [13]–Aug [12]	2	20	3	25	= 79 …

(The figures for the days in square brackets were left off in most cases during the earlier years, but are all filled in from 13 May 1910. Note that one quarter straddles two years; Keynes simply listed the "Feb" of 1907 under the year 1906 and continued similarly with the succeeding years.) The question is vainly begged: what was Keynes doing under c, a, and w?[53]

The two lists of sexual partners contain the initials of known persons or intriguing designations of the nameless, Keynes recording congress with friends, acquaintances, and risky pickups from the streets or public baths. His letters, also revealing, if not explicit, occasionally confirm or detail the circumstances. The lists evidently parallel each other, with some overlap, a few names and initials appearing on both lists. One list is dated by years and dominated by the names or initials of Keynes's friends. It also includes, inter alia, the mysterious "Brush," Salem," and "Cairo," and, beginning in 1909, develops a taxonomy of such creatures as the "Stable Boy of Park Lane," "Auburn haired of Marble Arch," "Lift boy of Vauxhall," and "Jew boy." Statistically speaking, Keynes achieved nine partners in his greatest year, 1913, after eight in 1911 (when the affair with Duncan had ebbed), but a mere four in 1910. The other list is dateless on one side, while the reverse side not too helpfully carries the date 1909 at the top. Although it repeats three sets of initials from the first list, it consists chiefly of designations. Indeed its characters, even more than those of that list, bear meaningful epithets in Homeric style, thus "The Swede of the National Gallery," "The Baron of Mentone [sic]," the pairs "The Young American of Victoria Sta" and "The Young American near the British Museum" and, ominously, "The Blackmailer" and "The Blackmailer of Bordeaux." There was also the trio "The Grand Duke Cyril of the Paris Baths," "The French Youth of the Baths," and "The Soldier of the Baths." This was clearly in a spirit of self-mockery as taught by Lytton, but also spiced with a suggestion of dangers he knew to avoid. The variety extended to "The beautiful young man in the P shed Mr Blaker," "The clergyman," "The chemist's boy of Paris," "Captain Bonniman," "Bobbi Ross's Young man," and "David Erskine, M. P."

The first list had begun selectively with ADK (for Alfred Dillwyn Knox) alone in 1901. For 1902 A DK was accompanied by DM (for Daniel Macmillan, future head of the family publishing firm and elder brother of Harold, the future prime minister). For the three years from 1903 through 1905 Keynes recorded a chaste "nil." For the three years from 1906 through 1908 he noted both Strachey brothers, Lytton reappearing once more, in 1915. The Stracheys monopolized 1907, but Arthur Hobhouse is also listed for 1906, while Duncan, joining them, entered in 1908. At least by 1909 unselective promiscuity begins, with the Park Lane stable boy and another member of his class, but the second list's cryptically dated grouping may have commenced service before then. One can only guess insecurely, the silence in Keynes's letters providing some support, that his dangerous and grimier adventures began a shorter or longer time after the period of "nil"-described restraint. It would seem that they increased during the problematic moments of his affair with Duncan and then intensified after its end. But at first Maynard had sought congress generating or expressing a modicum of a kind of affection.

A few of Keynes's other sexual partners fill out his Post-Impressionist landscape-with-figures. There were his students Chester Purves, listed in 1912 and 1913, and S. Russell Cooke of 1913 through 1915, Cooke becoming a stockbroker and joining him in a flutter on the stock exchange as well.[54] In addition to Duncan and the Strachey brothers, Bloomsbury was represented by Francis Birrell of 1910, 1913, and 1915, and David Garnett of 1915, the two joining forces, with Keynes's counsel and financial help, as Bloomsbury booksellers for a few years after the war. Frankie Birrell, perpetually immature son of the Liberal politician Augustine Birrell, had matriculated at King's College; he would later function modestly as translator and literary journalist. Bunny Garnett, irrelevantly trained at the Royal College of Science in London and presently to be more seriously entangled in Maynard's love life than in his sexual activities, was the son of a book editor and his wife, Constance Garnett, the prolific translator-from-the-Russian. Bunny would become a minor novelist and, more heterosexual than not, twice a benedict and, cumulatively, father of six. Cambridge was also represented by the King's College fellow John Tressider Sheppard (like Garnett, listed for 1915), who came from a nonconformist background like Keynes, and Bimla Karta Sarkar (1912–14), the name indicating the opposite. Sheppard, we may recall, was the classmate who had joined the young Keynes in resisting a college charity revolving around the Church of England. A classicist later to become King's College provost from 1933 to 1954, Sheppard had a long-term friend, Cecil F. Taylor, known in Cambridge as "Madame." The Sheppard episode was probably a minor moment in the history of a monosexual institution. Originating in Cambridge, the story of Sarkar went out of bounds.

Sarkar was seductively exotic at a price. A resourcefully feckless and beggarly Brahmin, he appears first in January 1911 as object of recrimination by a Trinity College adviser: "You wasted much money for nothing—wasting six weeks . . . without working." The don demanded the payment of a debt of £17. Maynard, drawn into the matter possibly through his India Office connections or at least sympathy for Indian students, found himself defending Sarkar to his colleague and to Sarkar's father. All this made Maynard the object of long epistles, such as Sarkar's eighteen-page inconclusive speculation "whether I spent my time in merriment or whether I was really ill." He threatened to seek the "salvation of my soul . . . devote myself entirely to Sanskrit studies . . . renounce the world . . . take monastic vows. . . . Your most obedient, unfortunate (yet fortunate in your kindness) pupil.'' Maynard's intervention required substantial financing because the father was as undependable in providing funds as Sarkar was in restraining his expenditures. Maynard also got his charge into Clare College, another failing investment since Sarkar, devoting his time presumably to merriment, slipped out of its chill discipline. In September 1911, as he wrote Duncan, Maynard returned to King's "depressed" that Duncan had failed to join him on a camping holiday; he went on to report that he had found Sarkar in trouble again. Challenged as problem solver and otherwise aroused, he had spent most of the day straightening out Sarkar's affairs: "He is a strange and charming creature. . . . I have had all today the most violent sexual feelings towards him.'' Nothing sexual evidently occurred then. Instead Maynard "did in the end stroll out . . . and bring a boy back.''

Sarkar presently found refuge in London, but in January 1912 was writing Maynard, "I am seriously concerned about your health,'' Maynard having failed to continue his subvention. Maynard, instead, threatened to cut him off and told him he would help fund his return to India. Sarkar held out in London, Maynard relenting in his threat to stop support. Sarkar later found a position with a society aiding Indian students and acquired a wife and son, but continued to look to Maynard for help. In an undated letter, evidently of 1920, he sought funding for a desperately needed Swiss vacation. In his last known communication, from Zurich in December 1920, he hoped for 500 Swiss francs to finance his now desirable return to India, where he trusted his family, in view of his wife and child, would help him: "It is your past consciousness of your wish for my welfare . . . that gives me hope that you will not leave me in the lurch.''[55]

Francis St. George Nelson (1909 through 1914 with the exception of 1912) was more dependable and less demanding. A seventeen-year-old Cockney when Maynard first met him in 1909, St. George had posed for Duncan and gone on to an extended career in pantomime. "What do you think I'm doing at the Victoria Commercial Hotel, Ramsgate?'' Maynard wrote Duncan on Christmas Eve 1910; Ramsgate is on the coast a few miles north of Dover. "A letter came from St. George yesterday asking me to come here and stay with him. So I came, and spend my evenings . . . chatting with low comedians.'' St. George was resiliently enduring the classical vicissitudes of road-company life and "had the clap, from which he's only just recovered.'' A few weeks later Maynard was sending money to him because his company was out of funds. In September 1913 he fell upon St. George when he went to the Birmingham meeting of the British Association for the Advancement of Science. He wrote Duncan that while attending the association sessions during the day, he was living with St. George and enjoyably spending the evenings with him.[56]

Maynard's Ramsgate letter has the only mention of venereal disease I have found in the Keynes Papers or other souces. One might note his lightheartedness. It is always possible that other references were removed. Given his activities and those of his friends, one can only speculate about the probability of such ills. About another danger that the fate of Oscar Wilde had too clearly warned, Maynard had sagely pronounced to Lytton, "So long as no one has anything to do with the lower classes or people off the streets, there is not a scrap of risk—or hardly a scrap."[57] This was in 1906, three years before his dated list began to note people off the streets. If he could calculate the probabilities, Maynard, compiling a balance of losses in the casinos of the Continent, was a gambler first of all. He may have had better luck with his sexual chancetaking.

After the records stop at the end of 1915, one can only guess insecurely about Maynard's subsequent adventures on the basis of other data. The correspondence indicates a male lover in 1921, but only that one at the time. Of course, given Maynard's pattern, it is possible and even likely that there were occasional passages of affection for old times' sake with old lovers. As for off-the-street experiences, we know that he was exhausting himself in endless work and responsibility from the beginning of 1915, while his health was frequently bad and under threat. Also, as he was acutely aware, his increasingly important position in the Treasury made him increasingly vulnerable to exposure and blackmail. Probably he sought them less but less probably he refused such as sought him.

The war experience had a pervasively heterosexual effect. Lytton's reaction was to knit warm mufflers for the uniform-clad lads and flirt thrillingly with them, but other friends of Maynard, particularly as they grew away from their monosexual school influences, were moved more profoundly than that. In 1914 Adrian Stephen, his affair with Duncan over, married Karin Costelloe, daughter of Mary Berenson and a companion on Maynard's Italian tour of 1906. Gerald Shove, becoming a close friend and junior colleague, had found Maynard's sexual enterprises fascinating. Obviously asking to be introduced to such adventures, "I'm dying to know what your adventure was," Gerald wrote him at one point in 1911. "[D]o let me know when you've escaped or been arrested."[58] Maynard, however, left it to Shove's initiative, which was lacking. When another friend attempted to initiate him, "Gerald from nervousness refused," Maynard reported to Duncan. "How can he help . . . dying a virgin?"[59] In 1915 Shove married Fredegond Maitland, a Newnham graduate and daughter of a distinguished historian. In 1920, after a long courtship, James Strachey married Alix Sargant-Florence, another Newnham graduate and one of Bunny Garnett's girlfriends; she had done most of the courting. Maynard, meanwhile, had given a few indications of a late-developing interest in women.

At the age of twenty-seven, his position philosophically thought through with Lytton, Maynard had expressed virtually no qualifications about his sexual identity. "I had a dreadful conversation on Sunday with my mother and Margaret about marriage," he wrote Duncan in late 1910, "and had practically to admit to them what I was! How much they grasped I don't know."[60] Later Maynard would discover Margaret's "Sapphic" attachment, while she would come upon *what* he was; they would evidently negotiate a pact of mutual silence and support. Actually, Maynard was more naïve than Margaret on the subject. More than two years before the dreadful conversation he reported this interchange, beginning with gossip about a don's marriage to a lower class woman:

My mother: "He will get bored."

I: "Not much duller than most women dons marry!"

Margaret to me: "I expect you know lots of men you wouldn't mind marrying, don't you?"

I (hedging): "Well they wouldn't be dull anyhow."

My mother: "You mean live with."

Margaret: "Anyhow I know several females *I'd* be quite willing to marry. We'd better arrange it that way."

My mother laughs at the absurdity and the conversation veers off.[61]

If Margaret changed course radically, Maynard began to veer ever so slightly.

In the summer of 1911 Maynard found himself on a camping holiday with several young women. He reported cryptically to Duncan: "I even like the women." A year later, on another summer holiday, now at a house he had rented (and from which the landlady, shocked at his guests' games, was expelling him), he provided Duncan with this snapshot: "Out of the window I see Rupert making love to [an attractive young woman], taking her hand, sitting at her feet, gazing at her eyes. Oh these womanizers. How on earth and what for can he do it[?]"[62] Maynard was protesting too much to be quite sincere about this detestation of womanizing (although he picked a poor exemplar in Rupert Brooke, an unhappy homosexual tease) and he was finding himself more frequently in the company of women and liking it.

In 1913, remaining in his established mode, Maynard advised Lytton, who was going on a holiday to Tunis and Sicily, on modalities "[i]f you want to go where the naked boys dance." Responding to his friend's scatalogical taste, he closed with the lines from a poem: "We paid our suit to Janus/ Mistook the one mouth for the other anus." He himself was going to join an old classmate, now a colonial officer there: "I'm leaving for Egypt. . . . I just learned that 'bed and boy' is prepared."[63] A month later, however, he reported to Duncan, perhaps more informatively than teasingly, that he had "had a w-m-n," among other entertainments.[64]

Maynard experienced another, and more relevant, female person toward the end of the war. In 1932 Virginia Woolf, writing to her brother-in-law, the womanizer Clive Bell, mentioned that their immensely successful friend Maynard and his wife had come to dinner: "The old chief and Lydia were here, and the talk was . . . about the past, and how he met Barbara Hiles and did more than meet her."[65] Barbara was one of a group of a half-dozen young women who had attached themselves to Bloomsbury during the war. She married in 1918, but maintained warm relations with Maynard. Since 1916 he was a substantial London householder; at least twice, in 1919 and 1921, coming to town from her provincial home, Barbara asked if she could be his guest, the first time accompanied by baby and nurse, and the second time, "I want to come to see you, and perhaps get drunk and forget . . . the worries and cares of two infants." In 1940 she was asking his advice on selling her house. In 1945, always generous to friends and lovers, Maynard offered her an annual £200 to help out with expenses when her two sons were matriculated at King's College.[66] Vanessa Bell, never a lover, was infinitely more important to Maynard.

The classically beautiful Vanessa, born 30 May 1879, thus four years before Maynard, was the eldest of the four Stephen siblings, who were the nucleus around which the Bloomsbury group formed in 1905. While Virginia, also classically beautiful, if a touch less perfectly so, was a serious writer since adolescence, Vanessa was no less serious a painter. On 7 February 1907 she married Clive Bell, who had been a Trinity College classmate of Lytton, Leonard Woolf, and her beloved brother Thoby. For some time she had been fending off proposals from Clive, a parvenu's son with an intense appreciation of art and some literary competence but ambitious for little more than appreciative enjoyment. Vanessa accepted a reiterated proposal two days after Thoby had died of typhoid fever acquired on a Greek holiday, on 22 November 1906. It was the last of a series of deaths since May 1895, when her mother died, which sorely tried the survivors. The other deaths were those of Stella Duckworth Hills, her recently married half-sister, in 1897, and of Leslie Stephen, her father, on 22 February 1904, after an agonizing struggle with cancer. Strong, responsible, Vanessa had withstood these shocks with monolithic firmness, but Virginia had broken down mentally first after their mother's and then after their father's death. In the fall of 1904, the young Stephens departed from their dark, if fashionable, South Kensington house for a more cheerful residence at 46 Gordon Square, one of the pleasant squares in Bloomsbury, the socially passé area near the British Museum. Another advantage of the move was separation from their bourgeois connections.

The deeper past could not be so easily left behind, and Leslie Stephen, founding editor of the sixty-two volume *Dictionary of National Biography*, intellectual historian, and great Victorian of letters, endowed his children with problems requiring incessant solution—and also the substantial values assisting that solution. Virginia reconceived him in her novel *To the Lighthouse* (1927) as the impossible Professor Ramsay. In a late memoir of their family life, she drew a self-pitying, self-dramatizing, Learlike figure mounting the "horror of Wednesday." After the death of their half-sister, the eighteen-year-old Vanessa had been made responsible for the household disbursements. "On that day the weekly books were shown him. . . . Silence. He was putting on his glasses. . . . Down came his fist on the account book. There was a roar. His vein filled. His face flushed. Then he shouted, 'I am ruined.' Then he beat his breast. . . . He was ruined—dying . . . tortured by the wanton extravangance of Vanessa."[67] Too proud to defend herself, Vanessa stood silent, perhaps goading her father to worse excesses, Frances Spalding, her biographer, thought.[68] In fact the expenses were normal, and Leslie Stephen had a solid, comfortable capital and an adequate, upper middle-class income, but suffered depressive mood swings that were not so extended as to deposit him in certifiable madness. Such scenes relieved his anxieties at a cost to others he did not recognize. Virginia inherited his literary ability, his profile and physique, and, perhaps driven further by such horrors, his madness. Out of such circumstances, reinforced by the clumsy efforts of their two half-brothers to direct them toward fashionable society and marriages, there logically followed Virginia's feminism and Vanessa's determination not to let another man have such power over her. Vanessa had resisted marriage until she was almost twenty-eight. Clive did not pose such a threat.

"Without a doubt Vanessa's marriage was sexually a great success," Frances Spalding wrote. "Clive . . . was not lacking in sexual experience; Vanessa, though previously confined to vague, half-conscious desires, was highly sexual."[69] Visiting the newly married couple, Lytton reported that on his "coming into the room unannounced, there was a most violent scrimmage heard, and they appeared very red & tousled." He recalled, "It was like those charming days at Cambridge, when one had to cough . . . for fear of disturbing Maynard and Hobby. Good Lord!"[70] Clive's experience had its impelling pattern; he soon slipped into his old habits. His first departure from monogamy was both less and worse than simple adultery. Vanessa gave birth to Julian, their first child, on 4 February 1909, three days before their first anniversary, and instantly became a passionate mother as well. Feeling neglected and appalled by the baby's messiness, Clive fled the house and commenced a flirtation with Virginia, and Virginia, resenting the loss of Vanessa to him and the baby, responded provocatively. This analysis of the complex motivations was made by Quentin Bell, the second son, in his *Virginia Woolf: A Biography*.[71] The flirtation never became an affair, Clive having had sense enough not even to attempt a kiss on Virginia's invitation,[72] and Virginia, as her sexual biography suggests, had not been inclined to go beyond the kiss. Surely hurt by the double betrayal, Vanessa was strong enough to refuse to be provoked, her silence smothering it effectively. Frances Spalding reported no sign of Vanessa's being hurt by the time Clive resumed his unqualified womanizing.[73]

Their friends agreed that Clive was not up to Vanessa, a part of Virginia's resentment at the marriage being due to her agreement. Lytton had been eloquent. "I am the bringer of bad news," he wrote Leonard Woolf. "Vanessa and Bell are engaged. I had feared the probability of it, and here it is!" On the day before the wedding, he specified, "She is very intelligent. How long will it be before she sees he isn't."[74] Neither Clive nor Vanessa would gainsay such opinions. Clive himself, half impeccably attired slayer of stags and other sporting wild life, half lover of art, in sum a rounded or balanced dilettante and aware of it, could write to Virginia, "I sometimes . . . could almost cry for the beauty of the world; that is because I am not great . . . I just go fingering the smooth outside."[75] Earlier, when Vanessa was still refusing him, she had bluntly written

Clive that for his sake, "I wish that . . . you would work at something."[76] She had no illusions to lose.

Vanessa developed her ultimate character as woman, wife, lover, and mother through her relationships with Clive, who remained important to her, and three other men, Roger Fry, Duncan Grant, and completing the pentagon, Maynard Keynes. Fry was an art critic and historian, curator, and painter. He became a friend in 1910 after an earlier meeting around 1905–6, when Vanessa had found his eyes "kind, brilliant interested" and his response to her opinions flattering.[77] An expert in the old masters, Fry had discovered and named the Post-Impressionists. Drawing Vanessa, Duncan, and other Bloomsbury people into his enthusiasms and operations, he organized London's two Post-Impressionist exhibitions, from November 1910 through January 1911 and from October through December 1912, to introduce the art revolution to Britain. By 1910, with Roger providing an invidious comparison, Vanessa was reverting to her first view of Clive. On 19 August 1910, still happily maternal although wanting a girl, she gave birth to Quentin. Clive then went off to the county of Wiltshire to visit his parents and, Vanessa knew, his old mistress, whom she had earlier met and rather enjoyed. She wrote Clive tartly and tolerantly, "I hope you'll see your whore soon and get some amusing gossip out of her." In the summer of 1911, completely in command of her feelings and her marriage, she entered into an affair with Roger Fry.

Although it was the redoubtable "Roger who fully unleashed Vanessa's sexual passion,"[78] she was beginning to find his energy and enthusiasms exhausting by early 1912. Furthermore, his own painting remained academic and "gets on one's nerves," as she wrote Maynard later.[79] The major factor was Roger's dominating personality, which threatened her hard-won freedom as Clive's lighter character never did. By 1914, after a gradual process, Vanessa had ended the affair, but valuing his qualities, kept Roger as a cherished friend.

By 1912 Vanessa and Duncan, encouraged in their development by the French moderns and seeing with similar vision, were companionably painting together. At the time Duncan was still the lover of her brother Adrian, but that did not disturb her. His homosexuality per se was the problem—and yet an attraction and a challenge. She knew that other women had found Duncan appealing and that he was not invulnerable to their attractions. She fell insensibly in love with him. Now in her early thirties, she was in the fullest bloom of her beauty. She had shown her power in managing a household, children, a husband, a lover, and a range of friends of both sexes. In 1914, as she was disembarrassing herself of Roger, Duncan found himself bereft of Adrian by his impending marriage. By 1915, unhampered by Clive, who was undertaking his most serious affair, Vanessa was living with Duncan.

Vanessa found homsexuals sympathetic and contact with them liberating, compared with her experiences of conventional Victorian and Edwardian males. She liked to talk dirty—"bawdy," she called it. An expression of her new freedom, it was probably also, given the infrequency of her marital relations and the deterioration of her affair with Roger, a sign of her sexual frustration. She was drawing closer to Maynard as well as to Duncan, but in terms of straightforward friendship, and she expressed to him her half-defined feelings about sex and such specifics as male homosexuality. In the early spring of 1914 he had played host in a country farmhouse, and after a visit Vanessa praised the ambiance: "I felt myself singularly happy and free tongued. . . ."[O]ne can talk of fucking & Sodomy & all without turning a hair." She empathized with him: "Did you have a pleasant afternoon buggering one or more of the young men we left for you? It must have been delicious out on the downs in the afternoon sun—a thing I have often wanted to do." She could laugh as well as empathize, remarking on "all the ecstatic preliminaries of sucking sodomy." She added reflectively, "[I]t sounds like the name of a station."[80] A year later Maynard, incidentally mentioning a dismaying episode of madness in Virginia, reported to his brother that Vanessa had persuaded an "extraordinarily handsome guest from Australia . . . to take all his clothes off and dance an aboriginal dance."[81] Vanessa was then courting Duncan, to whom she had written playfully but seriously of eloping so that they could "potter harmoniously together."[82] Adrian assisted matters by consorting with Karin Costelloe. Before the end of 1914, evidently, Vanessa and Duncan were lovers.

Besides such serious players as Clive, Roger, and Maynard, one other figure, Bunny Garnett, further added to the complexity of Vanessa's hard-won life with Duncan. As Frances Spalding saw it, "Maynard, with cunning percipience, placed Bunny between Vanessa and Duncan at a dinner he gave" in January 1915.[83] Duncan fell in love with the handsome, blond young man, then twenty-two. Bunny, who had flirted with other men unseriously while actively pursuing young women, found Duncan so entrancing that he entered into a four-year affair with him, later reinforced by the fact that they were thrown together as conscientious objectors committed to farm labor. Vanessa knew she could not have Duncan if she did not tolerate Bunny. Making the best of it, she summoned up the strength, not only to win the love, emotional and even sexual, of a profoundly homosexual man, but also to manage that love while it was distracted by a much more sexual love for another person. She succeeded because of her total acceptance of the Duncan–Bunny relationship and because she had made Duncan dependent on her for a way of life fitted to his temperament.

With a significant difference Vanessa belonged to that category of women known today as "fag hags" for their relationships with homosexuals. She was specifically mentioned in an article about the self-destructive, Radcliffe-educated, black Dorothy Dean (1932–86). Ms. Dean, as studied in a *New Yorker* article in 1995, was the classic type, the punishing figure playing into the classic homosexual masochism. Another fag hag mentioned was the famously punishing alcoholic Dorothy Parker. Vanessa, on the contrary, heroically took the punishment on herself.[84]

Part of Vanessa's punishment was to endure Duncan's black moods. Hypersensitive, he would plunge into depression if he thought anyone had looked on him less than benevolently. Bunny, moreover, gave him more objective reasons because he would depart on occasion for amusements that included making love to any one of a number of girlfriends. During these years Vanessa drew on Maynard for a measure of emotional and financial support. For various reasons, Maynard later becoming a paying weekend guest, she had begun living in a series of farmhouses in the country while retaining part of 46 Gordon Square as pied-à-terre. The ultimate reason then was to establish Duncan and Bunny in a farm-labor substitute for military service. The ultimate residence was the farmhouse Charleston, in Sussex, in the area of rolling downs near the south coast, an hour by train from London. Vanessa first rented it in September 1916 and kept it—and Duncan—for the rest of her life.

In a letter in February 1918 Vanessa thanked Maynard for the food he had sent and counsel on her investments. She mentioned that Clive also needed advice on his investments. About the household, she reported that Duncan had been creating "constantly recurring crises." She confided, "He certainly is a Turk. . . . Bunny & I suffer more than he does on the whole. I can't bear his getting so unhappy." A month later she wrote that she could not put up Maynard during the next weekend because the house would be "full with Clive and Mary [Hutchinson]," his *maitresse en titre*. She went on: Duncan did not talk for two days after Bunny returned late from a London visit and "kept us all in a state of misery. At last it cleared off and he was quite happy." She expected another crisis when Bunny went off to see his current girlfriend.[85] Maynard responded sympathetically. Shortly after the second letter Vanessa and Duncan conceived Angelica, her Christmas child.

Worse than the repetitive miseries was the complete cessation of Vanessa's sexual relationship, such as it was, with Duncan. "[E]ither quite soon after or before Angelica's birth, Duncan is said to have told her that he could no longer sleep with her," Frances Spalding wrote, "not because he disliked it but because the psychological strain was too great."[86] Important as it was, she had to sacrifice her sexual need, but, painting together with Duncan as before, she could keep him as a companion in the kind of life she chose to live.

Each of the other men in her life, receiving rich return, contributed his appropriate share to Vanessa. Clive continued to visit and to act the father of Julian and Quentin. He also formally extended his fatherhood to Angelica out of good nature and in the hope that her birth would encourage his rich father to be more generous.[87] Vanessa, schooled by her horrid experience with her father, kept careful household accounts and provided this record of her Charleston finances to Maynard in late 1921: of £200 required annually, Clive gave £30, Duncan £40, Maynard £60 (plus food and other deliveries in kind), and she contributed £70, besides incurring "some small expenses . . . one can't remember."[88] Roger Fry continued his visits. Valued and still loved, he was always laden with new projects and ideas while persisting to paint irritatingly. In a letter he saluted her: "[Y]ou go straight for the things that are worthwhile . . .

kept friends with a pernickety creature like Clive, got quit of me and yet kept me your devoted friend.'' Indeed, as for Clive, she would successfully discourage him from settling with Mary Hutchinson in a Chelsea residence inconveniently distant—some three London miles—from Bloomsbury.[89] She assigned Maynard to his specific niche in her life.

For a period Maynard, while also becoming functionally important, rivaled Roger in Vanessa's affections. At first she saluted him ''My dear Maynard'' in her letters; on 29 August 1916 he became ''My dearest Maynard'' and remained that or ''Dearest Maynard'' thereafter. In late 1921 she signs, ''Good by . . . Your loving VB.'' In May 1922, after an issue troubling their relationship arose, she could nevertheless express her pleasure at the receipt of ''such a charming & affectionate & amusing letter.'' Confidingly and frankly, ''I felt as if I had been given a good petting & several kisses as you know I am always badly in want of . . . Your devoted VB.''[90]

If Vanessa got much from Maynard, he was receiving more than a fair return. As the pressures of his Treasury position intensified, he would flee to Charleston to find succor. ''I'm rather at the end of my tether,'' he wrote her in July 1917. ''So may I turn up?'' Just before he resigned as Treasury representative at the Paris Peace Conference in June 1919, he wrote, ''I shall be back very soon indeed and in great need of Charleston. I still want desperately to spend a good part of the summer with you, if I can, to recover my health and sanity.''[91] He did so, in the process writing his *Economic Consequences of the Peace* there between June and October. Thus Vanessa, giving and receiving affection, made do, not too badly, with pieces of men instead of the integral masculine force she could not endure. Thus Maynard, embodying the last major piece, received his condign reward.

Vastly multiplying the reward, Vanessa could not fail to have another effect on Maynard—to convey to him in her being and acts what a woman could mean to a man. Although totally accepting of his homosexual character, she perversely radiated a sensual femininity on him. Their closeness, evident to Bloomsbury, gave rise to the rumor that they had ''copulated *coram publico* in the middle of a crowded drawing room,'' her son Quentin wrote with inherited sang froid in his biography of her sister. He credibly discounted the story as improbable, nothing in the archives contradicting him.[92] Certainly the Maynard–Vanessa relationship was profounder than expressed in such physical exercises.

Florence Ada Keynes was also taking effect on Maynard. John Neville was beginning to withdraw, as noted here earlier, ceasing to keep up his diary after 1917 and letting Florence become chief correspondent with Maynard. Blocked off earlier by Neville's bulk, she could now draw closer to her son and show a tenderness hitherto hidden in actions. Hearing rumors of his breakdown in June 1919, superbly, she had gone straight to the chancellor of the exchequer. Reassured, she nevertheless wrote Maynard, ''If you cannot come home at once, I wish you would let me come to you.'' In the old manner this was efficient and salutary action and more promised, but she had better to give: ''You know

I always reckon to look after you if there is anything amiss. . . . Very, very much love, Dearest son—from your devoted mother.''[93] Called back to the sources of his being, by mother as well as womanly friend, Maynard rediscovered the still vital aspect of his sexuality he had earlier abandoned.

Maynard's interest in male beauties was subsiding. The last of such lovers was Walter J. H.—''Sebastian''—Sprott, presently an Apostle, who appears in mid-1920. Perhaps Maynard was referring to him in a letter to Lytton of 17 May 1920: ''I have a recommended young gentleman coming to dinner on the 23rd.'' He elucidated, ''Yes, the shallow waters are the attraction—up to the middle, not head over ears, at my age.''[94] He was accurately predicting the mild character his affair with Sebastian would take. That agreeable young man accompanied him on a holiday in North Africa in the spring of 1921 and then joined him on a Christmas visit to Lytton at his country place. Before that Christmas Maynard had fallen head over ears in love with Lydia Lopokova.

Maynard had first experienced Lydia, a principal dancer with the Ballets Russes, in September 1918. He told a friend who took him to a performance in London, ''She is a rotten dancer—she has such a stiff bottom.''[95] He told Duncan, ''The lady, Lupokova [sic: one of a series of eventually corrected misspellings], is poor,'' while her male partner ''has a charm or two.''[96] Perhaps he was again protesting too much. He met her at a party the following month and found her agreeable. After attending another performance with another friend, he felt well enough acquainted, as he wrote Duncan, to go ''round afterwards to Lupokova who was as usual charming.'' Indeed, she invited them to ''pinch her legs to see how strong she was—which we did very shyly; Clive should have been there.'' Probably she was still figuring in his imagination chiefly as a homosexuals' icon, but he now found her partner ''the most ridiculous little creature.''[97] He did not see her again until 1921, Lydia having departed the Ballets Russes mysteriously in July 1919, the company itself presently departing London as well.

Reunited, Lydia and the Ballets Russes delighted London again in the spring of 1921. England, however, had no resident ballet company and experienced the art as an occasional delectation; its attention span was shorter than had been reckoned. The ambitious five-act *Sleeping Princess* (formerly *The Sleeping Beauty*), which opened on 2 November, lost its allure and its audience. Maynard, meanwhile, had reestablished contact with Lydia and took her to lunch on Sunday, 11 December. His intentions crystallized quickly. In the circumstances he ''was provided with a good opportunity to court Lydia by sitting conspicuously in the thinly-occupied stalls.''[98] On Thursday, 22 December, like a fond son sharing his happiness with a supportive mother, he reported on a second Sunday lunch to Vanessa, then engaged in painting in France: ''I again fell in love with her. She seemed to me perfect in every way.'' He invited Vanessa to join in his appreciation of Lydia: ''One of her new charms is the most knowing and judicious use of English words.'' He was going to the ballet tomorrow and ''asking her to supper with me afterwards at the Savoy. Your affectionate JMK.''[99]

Lydia evidently enjoyed herself sufficiently to ask him to tea on Tuesday, 27 December, but he was taking Sebastian Sprott to the country. Lydia promptly renewed the invitation for 30 December.[100] On Wednesay, 28 December, invitation in hand, Maynard reported to Vanessa: "I am back from a quiet and very happy Christmas with Lytton. My other chief news is the progress of my affair with Loppy." At the Savoy after the ballet they had "chattered until 1 A.M.; and now she has asked me to tea." Glorying in his fall, he teased Vanessa, "What is to be done about it? I am getting terrified."

A New Year's Day letter from Vanessa, maternal but possessive, advised, "As for Loppi, *don't* marry her. . . . However charming she may be, she'd be a very expensive wife & would give up dancing & is altogether I am sure to be preferred as a mistress (dancing)."[101] Nothing could have stopped Maynard. Marriage was not a legal possibility at the moment because Lydia had a husband of sorts, but commitment was. "Perhaps the romance . . . exploded into full passion on the afternoon of 30th December 1921."[102] Lured by his two benign Circes, Maynard steered into a calm, safe heterosexual harbor.

NOTES

1. 25 December 1905, KP, PP/45/174.
2. Penelope Fitzgerald, *The Knox Brothers* (London, 1977), 67.
3. Quoted, Skidelsky, *JMK*, 1: 204.
4. Quoted, Holroyd, *LS*, 1: 211.
5. Letter, 8 April 1906, quoted, ibid., 185.
6. According to his brother James, who said he was also 6' 1", ibid., n. 252.
7. Ibid., 244, 300–2, 322, 328–29. See also ch. 8, "Independent and Spectatorial Essays," ibid., 353–94.
8. Quoted, ibid., 213.
9. Letter, 13 December 1904, KP, PP/45/316.
10. Letter, 2 February 1905, ibid.
11. Holroyd, *LS*, 1: 217, 218–19.
12. Letter, 23 April 1905, KP, PP/45/316.
13. Letter, 3 August 1905, ibid.
14. Letter to Leonard Woolf, quoted, Holroyd, *LS*, 1: 262.
15. Letter to JMK, 17 August 1905, KP, PP/45/316.
16. Letter, ibid.
17. Letter, 11 August 1905, ibid.
18. Letter, ibid.
19. Letter, 15 August 1905, ibid.
20. Letter to JMK, 7 September 1905, ibid.
21. Letter interchange, 18, 20 October 1905, ibid.
22. Letters to JMK, 31 December 1905, 9 January 1906, quoted, Holroyd, *LS*, 1: 267–68.
23. Letter, 2 February 1906, Berg Collection, New York Public Library (hereafter Berg).
24. 10 April 1906, quoted, KP, PP/45/316.

25. Letter to JMK, 28 July 1906, Berg.

26. 4 May 1906, ibid.

27. Holroyd, *LS*, 1: 261.

28. Ibid., 338.

29. To James Strachey in 1906, quoted, ibid., 260.

30. 15 July 1908, BL, Add. MSS 57930.

31. Letter, also 15 July 1908, quoted, Skidelsky, *JMK*, 1: 193.

32. Letter, 20 July 1908, quoted, ibid., 194.

33. Letter, 21 July 1908, quoted, Holroyd, *LS*, 1: 339.

34. 22 July 1908, ibid.

35. 24 July 1908, BL, Add. MSS 57930.

36. Letters, 8, 17 September, 9 October 1908, Berg.

37. Letters, quoted, Skidelsky, *JMK*, 1: 202, 203.

38. 5 February 1909, Berg.

39. Letter to James Strachey, 11 March 1909, quoted, Skidelsky, *JMK*, 1: 203.

40. Letter interchange, 17, 21 March 1909, quoted, ibid., 205.

41. Ibid., 236.

42. BL, Add. MSS 57930, as are all the following letters between JMK and Duncan Grant until JMK leaves for the Orkneys.

43. Letters, 4, 13 September 1908, KP, PP/45/168, 316.

44. Letter, 15 September 1908, KP, PP/45/144.

45. JNK Diary, 2 September, 16 December 1908.

46. BL, Add. MSS 57930.

47. Letters, 8, 12 February 1909, ibid.

48. Letter, 17 May 1909, ibid.

49. Letter, 31 March 1910, ibid.

50. Letters, 11, 15, 19 April 1911, ibid.

51. Letters, 7 September, 3, 31 October 1911, ibid.

52. KP, PP/20A, as noted above.

53. In his *MK* Moggridge speculates (p. 40) that *c* meant copulation, *a* "abuse," indicating masturbation, and *w* wet dream. Although *c* for copulation is not unreasonable of itself, because JMK abbreviated "copulation" to "cop" in letters, the second term should be *self-abuse* and not *abuse*, and only a guess leaps from *w* to wet dream. It is doubtful that JMK would try to impress or shock James Strachey with a record of solitary substitutes for sexual athleticism. If copulation were indicated by one or more of the code letters, a sexologist would ask Lenin's question: "Who whom?" Vanessa Bell would inquire about the absence of sucking sodomy.

54. The stock exchange activity, Skidelsky, *JMK*, 1: 266.

55. The Sarkar file: letters, 19 January, 16 March, 11 April, 21 September 1911; 17, 21 January, 26 March 1912; 18 March 1913 (Sarkar thanking JMK for sending him a parcel of books); 10 March 1915 (Sarkar: "again with a trouble"—£150 in debts); undated but probably 1920 (Sarkar needing a vacation); 22, 28 December 1920, KP, PP/45/282. JMK–Duncan Grant letters, 7 September 1911, 9 February 1912, BL, Add. MSS 57930.

56. Letters, JMK to Duncan Grant, 24 December 1910, 3 February 1911, 11 September 1913, BL, Add. MSS 57930, 57931.

57. Letter, 20 June 1906, Berg.

58. Letter, 26 December 1911, KP, PP/45/296.

59. Letter, 24 April 1912, BL, Add. MSS 57931.

60. Letter, 11 October 1910, BL, Add. MSS 57930.

61. Letter, 26 July 1908, ibid.

62. Letters, 31 August 1911, 16 July 1912, ibid.

63. Letter, 6 March 1913, KP, PP/45/316.

64. Letter, 17 April 1913, quoted, Skidelsky, *JMK*, 1: 274.

65. Virginia Woolf, *The Letters of Virginia Woolf* (hereafter *The Letters*; London, 1975–80), 5: 27.

66. Letters, Barbara H. Bagenal to JMK, 31 January 1919, 16 October 1921, 21 January 1940; JMK to her, 28 January 1940, 8 July 1945, KP, PP/45/13.

67. Virginia Woolf, "A Sketch of the Past" (written 1939–40), in *The Virginia Woolf Reader* (New York, 1984), 32.

68. Spalding, *Vanessa Bell*, 30.

69. Ibid., 62.

70. Letter to Leonard Woolf, 2 May 1907, Berg.

71. Quentin Bell, *Virginia Woolf: A Biography* (New York, 1974), 1: 132–34.

72. Letter exchange of Virginia Stephen and Clive Bell, quoted, Spalding, *Vanessa Bell*, 73.

73. Ibid., 72–78.

74. Letters, 26 November 1906, 6 February 1907, Berg.

75. Letter, 3 August 1908, quoted, Spalding. *Vanessa Bell*, 74.

76. Letter, 8 November 1906, quoted, ibid, 60.

77. Memoir, Vanessa Bell, quoted, ibid., 84. On Fry, see Spalding, *Roger Fry: Art and Life* (Berkeley, 1980).

78. Quoted, Spalding, *Vanessa Bell*, 90; ibid., 99.

79. Letter, September 1921, Charleston Papers (photocopies), Modern Archive Centre, King's College Library (hereafter CP).

80. Letter, 16 April 1914, ibid.

81. Letter, 4 April 1915, KP, PP/45/167.

82. Letter, February 1914, quoted, Spalding, *Vanessa Bell*, 128.

83. Ibid., 119, 135.

84. Hilton Als, "Friends of Dorothy," *The New Yorker* 71 (24 April 1995), 88–95; mention of Vanessa Bell and Dorothy Parker, 92.

85. Letters, 8 February, 2 March 1918, CP.

86. Spalding, *Vanessa Bell*, 213. This is confirmed by Angelica Bell Garnett, who got the story from Duncan's later friend, the poet Paul Roche, who dated the cessation in 1918, *Deceived with Kindness* (London, 1984), 164. She experienced her parents as an "asexual" couple, 122.

87. Spalding, *Vanessa Bell*, 176–77.

88. Letter, 26 November 1921, CP.

89. Fry's letter, 16 September 1917, quoted, Spalding, *Vanessa Bell*, 165; Clive's Chelsea plan, ibid., 195.

90. Letters, the first one undated but shortly after VB's arrival in St. Tropez in October 1921, the second, 16 May 1922, CP.

91. Letters, 28 July 1917, 3 June 1919, ibid.

92. Quentin Bell, *Virginia Woolf*, 1: 170.

93. Letter, 2 June 1919, KP, PP/45/168.

94. KP, PP/45/316.

95. According to the friend, Oswald T. Falk, quoted, Skidelsky, *JMK*, 1: n. 352.

96. Letter, 17 September 1918, BL, Add. MS 57931.

97. Letter, 20 October 1918, ibid.

98. Editorial note, John Maynard Keynes and Lydia Lopokova, *Lydia and Maynard: The Letters of John Maynard Keynes and Lydia Lopokova*, ed. Polly Hill and Richard Keynes (New York, 1989), 27. Although I quote the letters directly from the KP, the reader can find the important ones to the summer of 1925 in this collection, which is also helpfully annotated.

99. CP.

100. Lydia Lopokova to JMK, 26, 28 December 1921, KP/45/190.

101. JMK to Vanessa Bell, VB to JMK, CP.

102. Editorial note, Keynes and Lopokova, *Lydia and Maynard*, 28.

CHAPTER 5

Elective Affinities and Responsibilities: Keynes in Bloomsbury

Maynard was—and was not—very much a Bloomsbury person. This meant a permanent state of tension between him and his elective family while generating an analogous tension within him. Thus, however useful he could be to the group, his position in the wartime government had fixed him in opposition to its spirit.

Still, Maynard's affairs of the heart and body, with their odd parabolas and changes of direction, were Bloomsbury in style, whatever his differences with it. If no one else of the group made so radical a change in sexual orientation, others experimented widely, as seen in the case of Mr. and Mrs. Bell and their respective ménages. More examples follow here. Beyond the tight circumscription of bourgeois moeurs lay personal and professional fulfillment and exquisite enjoyment pursued, however, by lovelessness, loneliness, insecurity, depression, and ultimate despair.[1]

Bloomsbury's achievement of liberation from bourgeois captivity had been exhilerating. In about 1922 Virginia Woolf recalled the event or a signal of it, which evidently took place in 1908, in a paper read to other members of the group:

Suddenly the door opened and the long and sinister figure of Mr. Lytton Strachey stood on the threshold. He pointed a finger at a stain on Vanessa's white dress.

"Semen?" he said.

Can one really say it? I thought & we burst out laughing. With that one word all barriers of reticence and reserve went down. A flood of the sacred fluid seemed to overwhelm us. Sex permeated our conversation. The word "bugger" was never far from our lips. We discussed copulation with the same excitement and openness that we had discussed the nature of the good.[2]

Liberation from social constraints had meant obedience to the more powerful commands of Bloomsbury's deeper individual natures. Maynard had followed his work and sexual compulsions in those patterns already seen here. In the case of the latter, however, he could eventually exercise a choice between two competing imperatives. Lytton's liberation had delivered him to the repetitions of defeated desire, but, although always vulnerable to newer defeats, he would learn to achieve substantial satisfactions. For the richly sensual Vanessa Stephen Bell, liberation meant the free choice of a long life's march of frustration. Virginia, celebrating liberation so consciously and humorously, was a sexual cripple. The group could appreciate the irony of it.

To arrive at a properly proportioned sense of Bloomsbury, we should first take a roll call. The founder had vanished, but it was just as well. Thoby Stephen, more hugely monolithic than Vanessa and fondly called the "Goth" by Lytton, handsome, untroubled, neither intellectual nor aesthetic—astonishingly normal—was not a Bloomsbury type. Thoby had come down to London from Trinity College to read for the bar in 1904. Missing his Cambridge companionship, he announced he would be At Home at 46 Gordon Square on Thursday evenings after dinner. He received his first and only guest, Saxon Sydney-Turner, also from Trinity, on 16 February 1905.[3] A middling civil servant in the Treasury, Saxon was a consistently silent person who occasionally uttered a sibylline phrase that might be perfectly to the point, or at least was remembered as such. Quentin Bell, son of Clive and Vanessa, however, chose to note "the almost sadistic tedium of Saxon's conversation."[4] Other more enlivening guests presently appeared at the Thursday evenings, thus Lytton Strachey later in 1905, when the failure of his dissertation drove him back to London. Trinity was also represented by Leonard Woolf, who dropped in once before departing for Ceylon and remained a disembodied presence as kept in being by his correspondent Lytton. Vanessa and Virginia Stephen, spared the first evening with Saxon, began, in a minor deviation from polite custom, to take part in the Thursday evenings. By the time Thoby had died, on 20 November 1906, Vanessa and Virginia had made their brother's friends their friends. "As a result of Thoby's death Bloomsbury was refounded upon the solid base of deep mutual understanding."[5]

We have also already met Clive Bell, Duncan Grant, Bunny Garnett, Roger Fry, Adrian Stephen, James Strachey, Gerald Shove of King's College, Maynard's economist friend, and Frankie Birrell, his occasional lover. There were, additionally, the novelist E. M.—Morgan—Forster and Harry J. Norton, another friend of Maynard's and a King's College mathematician. Norton was being slowly invaded by a psychosis that would destroy his great ability and meanwhile expressed itself in inane cackling and generally silly behavior. Bloomsbury more easily tolerated Harry's madness and Saxon's tedium than strict conventionality.

The most nearly "normal" members of Bloomsbury were Desmond and Molly MacCarthy, parents of three children. A periodical editor and literary and theater critic, Desmond was the group's greatest charmer and conversationalist, characteristics that may explain why he never wrote his always pending great novel. Molly, daughter of an Eton vice-provost and librarian, created a novel-writing club in 1913 to encourage Desmond's creative process. Having slipped out of Trinity without a degree, however, he continued to elude formal order and his own resolutions to become a man of apt journalistic ephemera, forgotten appointments, and abandoned projects. The novel club soon dissolved, but in 1920 Molly founded the Memoir Club, which remained a lively subinstitution of Bloomsbury into the 1960s, and Maynard, among others, contributed valuable remembrances of times past. If Molly failed to move Desmond to more than article collections, she herself published two well-received books, a novel and a memoir. Desmond went on to his not unmeritorious fate as chief literary critic of the (London) *Sunday Times*.

Life within more conventional limits did not spare Desmond and Molly their portion of pain.[6] After producing their children between 1907 and 1911, Molly was terrified of having another; the result was separate bedrooms and further separation. Feeling neglected, Molly, a giving and reasonably demanding personality, reacted in two classic ways. In 1913 she undertook a summer affair with Clive Bell, always obliging to an attractive woman. In character she made scenes and regretted it; in Bloomsbury character she put her feelings in writing. She composed a letter to Desmond in about 1916, specifying, "I daily want to tell you . . . but feel sensitive about saying . . . that I myself have felt almost *daily* for about a year a great wish to go to bed with you but am too proud seriously to ask it." She calculated, "In the last three years I have only twice been to bed with you. This is the most passionate age of my life."[7] Desmond remained a highly gregarious person with too many invitations for himself alone, and Molly resourcefully anesthetized the pain with her writing and other activities. By the mid-1920s, struggling also against deafness, she had developed her own independent social life, a young homosexual friend of Lytton Strachey's serving as an escort, but he died after two years. The marriage persisted; the children grew up; there were grandchildren. Desmond, suffering from asthma, died in June 1952. Toward the end, Molly and Desmond had grown closer together, Molly writing afterward to Leonard Woolf, "I don't see how anyone *can* be *prepared* for the death of anyone loved and so completely a part of one's life."[8] Molly died a year and a half later.

On the subject of heterosexual relationships, if Maynard ended up happily living with a woman, so did Lytton. She was Dora Carrington but answered only to "Carrington" because she hated being female. This suggested an arrangement that only confirmed Lytton in his homosexuality and contributed an exquisite complexity to Bloomsbury's love life. Trained as a painter at the

Slade School of Fine Art in London, Carrington was another of the young women on the fringe of Bloomsbury. Along with Barbara Hiles, Maynard's erstwhile lover, she was invited to spend an autumn weekend of 1915 with the Bells at Asheham, a house in Sussex that preceded Vanessa's eventual country refuge of Charleston. Lytton was also a guest. In the course of a walk Lytton, perhaps aroused by Carrington's bobbed-hair boyishness, surprised her with an unwelcome kiss. A practical joker with a streak of cruelty, she set out to punish him by cutting off his beard. Armed with scissors, she slipped into his room early the next morning but he woke up and his mild brown eyes transfixed her. She fell profoundly in love.[9] Out of their oddly fitting personalities Lytton and Carrington formed a lasting relationship.

It was not the first time Lytton, experimenting wildly with his dominating but often unhappy sexuality, had made a move toward a woman. This came during a lonely moment after the loss of Duncan to Maynard. Imprisoned in the Strachey residence, now moved to North London but as oppressive as ever, he lunged desperately toward marriage. On 17 February 1909, burdened with a heavy cold, he made his way to Virginia Stephen's home and startled her with a proposal. The next month he recounted the denouement to his brother James, now a prime confidant. "In my effort to escape," as he accurately introduced the episode, "I proposed to Virginia, and was accepted." She was herself seeking to evade the always pursing Stephen family horrors. "It was an awkward moment . . . especially as I realized, the very minute it was happening, that the whole thing was repulsive to me." Virginia obviously had the same second thought: "Her sense was amazing. . . . The result was that I was able to manage a fairly honorable retreat."[10] They remained mutually cherishing friends.

After Duncan, Lytton loved Henry Lamb, another painter, and a talented, but overshadowed, follower of Augustus John. Like the late Thoby Stephen, whom Lytton had adored, Henry Lamb was "exclusively heterosexual" and a married womanizer. "In his company Lytton was customarily quiet, docile, serviceable, and of course, chaste."[11] This does not necessarily contradict a report of Maynard to Duncan on a party at which Lytton "grope[d] Henry under the table in view of all the ladies."[12] In April 1910 Lytton, who had known both for some time, suddenly saw Henry Lamb arriving with Ottoline Morrell, the great hostess and a woman of spectacular attractions, as guests at a party given by Bertrand Russell. Lytton reported on his encounter to Duncan: "I never was so astonished, and didn't know which I was in love with most."[13] Draped in a parti-colored gauzy fabric of her own exotic design, Ottoline, then thirty-seven years old, was very tall and further heightened by masses of auburn hair, and, with long nose and chin, exaggeratedly beautiful. The Pan-like Henry was long-haired, dashingly handsome, and devastatingly charming when he was not being sadistically cruel. Lytton would probably have been less astonished to learn that Ottoline and Henry had entered into an affair, Lamb to be relieved a year later by Bertrand Russell.[14] The Lytton–Ottoline–Henry triangle vanished almost as quickly as Lytton had dreamt it.

Trying to give an innocent appearance to her affair with Lamb, Ottoline, meanwhile, brought him together with Lytton in November of 1910. Both amusing, Lytton and Henry charmed each other and between May 1912 and August 1913 spent three holidays together. Only the second one, in August 1912, turned out disagreeable, when bad weather drove Henry into a cruel mood. This delectated Lytton's taste for masochistic groveling: "Won't my papa come and open the door, and take me into his arms again?"[15] Henry did, presumably metaphorically. The war put an end to their intimacy, Lamb engaging in distinguished war service in the Middle East. Their correspondence ended in 1915 and afterward they met only as casual acquaintances.[16]

As compared with his experience of loving Duncan, Lytton, now stronger and less vulnerable, had suffered little at Henry's hands—and that willingly—and gained more dimension as a person. He was learning to manage the more and more intricate cat's cradles of relationships his oddness inevitably wove. Before Carrington he grew fond of Frankie Birrell, homosexual enough, and Bunny Garnett, on balance heterosexual. These were mild friendships livened by homosexual flirtation. And, with his greater confidence, Lytton, like Maynard, indulged in opportunistic spasms of pleasure with lower-class youths. With Carrington he built a nicely balanced life.

Following the stolen kiss of Asheham, Lytton and Carrington began spending more time together. The sexual relationship, or rather, the absence of it, was a binding force. Attracted to women as well as to men, Carrington was first working through a virginity complex and then plunging into bursts of irresponsible, easily satiated physical passion. Tossed about by her emotional violences—and often unsettling her partners more—she found Lytton a haven of stability and secure affection. Neither burdened the other with impossible demands, while each lavishly met the other's needs, except, of course, for the sexual ones. The formula for their adjustment to each other was suggested in a joint letter to Maynard less than a year after Asheham. After vacationing in a North Wales cottage with "a small juvenile party"[17] including Barbara Hiles and her future husband, Nicholas Bagenal, Lytton took Carrington for a holiday extension to Bath and its environs. Carrington, with her unique orthography, introduced their letter, "a very Christian atmosphere prevails. which Lytton is enjoying incredibly. also the miller's lad. . . ." Lytton appended the poem:

> When I'm winding up the toy
> Of a pretty little boy,
> —Thank you, I can manage pretty well;
> But how to set about
> To make a pussy pout,
> —*That* is more than I can tell.[18]

Thirteen years older, Lytton slipped easily into the paternal role that Carrington needed as an addict needs cocaine. She loved and pitied an elderly father she saw oppressed by her mother, a domineering former governess, whom she detested. Lytton could pleasurably act as fatherly instructor to a casually literate painter while, conditioned by his mother's and sisters' lifelong support, he could draw on her for the numerous services his feeble health and practical helplessness demanded. She gratefully complied.

During the North Wales holiday Carrington and Barbara had begun discussing a plan to provide Lytton with the conditions for a career as independent writer. That meant distancing him from the unsympathetic Strachey family residence, but not so far that he could not take advantage of London's research facilities and cultural nourishment. The solution, achieved by December 1917, was the leasing for £52 annually of the Mill House, a cottage in the village of Tidmarsh in Berkshire, west of London by thirty-five minutes on the express train. In that December Lytton completed the *Eminent Victorians*. With its publication, early in 1918, he achieved his financial independence. A number of Lytton's friends, including Maynard, shared in the cottage costs in return for visiting rights. Carrington, who had been spending more time with Lytton, moved into the Mill House, even before he did, as house painter, housekeeper (commanding a maid, at least), cook, gardener (fruits, vegetables, and flowers), baker, practical nurse, valet, and companion.

Before Carrington met Lytton, and continuing into 1921, she variously teased Mark Gertler, a poor, talented Jewish painter from London's East End. The teasing had consisted of the long-delayed and scanty grant of sexual favors combined with a general elusiveness and an unwillingness to break with him. Gertler, who knew and liked Lytton, had, as incompetent Machiavellian, brought them closer together in the hope that it would improve his relationship with Carrington. Making matters worse, Carrington had prevaricated industriously to hide her coexistence with Lytton. The effects of the inevitable discovery were recorded in synoptic letters by Maynard to Vanessa, and Lytton to Clive.

Once again Maynard found himself at a critical point and acted effectively. After a party at the home of Clive's Mary Hutchinson, Lytton, accompanied by Carrington, was set on in the street by Mark, fists flailing. "Anything more melodramatic and absurd I've never seen," Maynard told Vanessa deprecatingly. "It ended only by my leading Mark off in tears crying in a loud voice, 'Oh Maynard, Maynard, I am so lonely. . . . I must make an end of it, I could not bear that they should do it in front of me, let me hold your hand.' "[19] Introducing his account in remarkably similar terms, Lytton gave Maynard more credit than Maynard did himself. "Anything more cinematographic can hardly be imagined," he told Clive. "[I]t wears all the appearance of a bad dream. . . . Poor Mark! The provocation was certainly great, and I was very sorry for him. . . . Maynard came to the rescue . . . and pacified him with amazing aplomb. Monty [Montague Shearman, a Gertler patron] had already tried and completely failed."[20] After this cathartic episode Gertler troubled Carrington and Lytton diminishingly until he disappeared completely from their lives and they lived happily together ever after.

The happy companions, thus intricately bound to each other, required comparably complex arrangements of associated relationships. The first addition was the young Major Reginald Partridge, a wartime friend of one of Carrington's brothers, who appeared at Tidmarsh in the summer of 1918. Renamed by Lytton, Ralph Partridge was a tall, powerfully built monolith of the Thoby Stephen type, and Lytton soon fell in love with him while Ralph fell in love with Carrington. Returning to Oxford at war's end, Ralph rowed and presumably studied law, but frequently bicycled the twenty miles to Tidmarsh. Efficient and ambitionless, Ralph made himself essential to Lytton while gently communicating his nonreceptivity to a physical relationship with him and courting Carrington. As in the case of Henry Lamb, Lytton knew how to enjoy a friendship on such terms. Ralph and Carrington became lovers, but although she was more responsive than she had been with Mark Gertler, Ralph wanted a securer hold on her. In 1921, by threatening to leave if frustrated, he got Lytton to abet him and impelled a reluctant Carrington to marry him. The three of them lived more or less happily ever after.

The three attached others to their primary unit. In 1921, while also moving toward lesbian lovers, Carrington started an affair with Gerald Brenan, Ralph's best friend (and future author of such distinguished works as *The Spanish Labyrinth*). In 1922, Ralph, himself a womanizer, started an affair with a malicious lady, who told him of the Carrington–Brenan affair. Lytton, anxious to keep the triad in being, used his exquisite tact to reconcile the indignant Ralph with Carrington on a functioning, if not an emotional, level. Toward the end of 1923 Ralph, licensed by Carrington's promiscuity, then undertook a more serious affair with Frances Marshall, a lovely Newnham alumna (English and moral sciences) employed in the Garnett–Birrell bookstore. Going to the country on weekends, Ralph and Frances settled in Gordon Square, while the modestly paid Ralph labored for the Woolfs' Hogarth Press as compositor, secretary, and book salesman. Connected also to Bloomsbury through her sister Ray (for Rachel), who married Bunny Garnett in 1921, Frances showed sensitive awareness of the delicate balance of Lytton's household and, the opposite of possessive, cooperated with him in maintaining it.

In 1924 the household, Lytton's health suffering from the Mill House's winter dampness while his financial power was enhanced by another successful book, moved nearby to the more commodious and comfortable Ham Spray in Wiltshire, Clive Bell's home county. It was Carrington who had found the house; Ralph eased Lytton's daily life by managing his practical and business affairs. Exception taken for recurring illnesses and the inevitable arrythmia of matters of the heart, Lytton continued to savor domesticity in his new house, Mozart generally and Beethoven's last quartets on his gramophone, frequent stays in London (where he established a pied-à-terre in Gordon Square), travels on the Continent, his friends—his life. He continued to write profitably.

In 1924 Lytton, happy but physically ungratified with Ralph, found a young lover in Philip Ritchie, the Oxford undergraduate who was also providing escort service to the lonely Molly McCarthy. Presently, Lytton was "blowing hot and cold over Philip Ritchie and alternatively cold and hot over his companion, Roger Senhouse,"[21] a future publisher. By 1926 Lytton had plumped for Roger, who replicated much of Duncan Grant's elusiveness and taste for other adventures, but who fluttered about him for the rest of Lytton's life. Philip's death in 1927, depriving Molly of his innocent company, simplified matters for Lytton. Carrington, meanwhile, fell passionately in love with Henrietta Bingham, daughter of the U.S. ambassador, but Henrietta dropped her after a brief affair. From 1928 to 1931, when he dropped her, Carrington had an affair with a well-to-do sailing man, whose attraction for her was evidently his insensitivity. Lytton objected mildly to the man's dullness.

In the latter part of 1931 Lytton fell ill with cancer of the stomach, which no doctor audibly diagnosed. At Ham Spray Carrington, Ralph, Frances, Bunny Garnett, Gerald Brenan, and James and Pippa Strachey clung to him and to each other; Roger Senhouse found reason to be elsewhere. Lytton died on 21 January 1932. Carrington, who had tried to asphyxiate herself a few hours before he died, eluded a close watch and succeeded with a shotgun on 11 March, lingering, however, for more than three hours in great pain. Ralph and Frances married happily, worked together contentedly for nine years on a multivolume scholarly book project Lytton had initiated, and had a son named Lytton.

Compared with such complexities, the marriage of Virginia and Leonard Woolf was absurdly simple, almost perfectly monogamous, and a perfect expression of loyalty and support. Indeed, Lytton had prophetically conceived of it when Leonard was in Ceylon and, more seriously than he had offered himself to Virginia, had been urging it on his friend. He had written, "[Y]ou could marry Virginia, which would settle nearly every difficulty in the most satisfactory way. Do try it."[22] In June 1911, reviving and widening relations with his Cambridge and Bloomsbury friends, Leonard returned to England on home leave. At the time, having left 46 Gordon Square to the newly wedded Clive and Vanessa, Virginia and Adrian Stephen were sharing a house at 29 Fitzroy Square. This made them neighbors of Duncan and Maynard at Number 21, the propinquity encouraging the Duncan–Adrian affair. The lease at Number 29 approaching an end in 1911, the siblings decided to dilute their cohabitation, which had become too irritating for both, with friends. In October Virginia found 38 Brunswick Square and created the communal establishment that brought Maynard (and Duncan) physically into the Bloomsbury district. Settling into the house in November 1911, the two took the ground floor, Adrian the second, and Virginia the third. That left the top floor, which Leonard began inhabiting on 4 December.[23] Naturally, the propinquity favored the courtship. Before he had Virginia's assent, Leonard resigned from the colonial service and prepared for a new profession and life.

Agreeing on how much they had in common, Virginia married Leonard on 10 August 1912. While they were courting she was slowly, agonizingly completing *The Voyage Out*, her first novel, and Leonard was efficiently progressing through the first of two novels, which would show his limitations as a fiction writer but direct him toward literary activities for which he had more affinity. Talking to each other endlessly, they had a happy honeymoon despite her evident frigidity. They found the problem serious enough to consult with Vanessa, who was sympathetic but knew Virginia well enough not to be surprised.[24] A compelling factor was sexual abuse by one of their older half-brothers that began when Virginia was about six and, evidently after a quiescent period, resumed more thoroughly and degradingly when she was thirteen. The problem was compounded by Virginia's insanity. The death of her mother, we have seen, preceded her first attack, and, compounding the horrid effects, had encouraged the renewed abuse under the guise of comfort.[25] In Leonard, facing and dismissing objections to his Jewishness with Vanessa's encouragement, Virginia chose the ideal life partner. Stoical and perhaps endowed with a saving masochism, an undeviating believer in G. E. Moore's secular "good," he accepted all the sacrifices as his duty, if not his pleasure. But then, besides her great beauty, he could acutely appreciate the exquisite quality and pure genius of his wife.

Only death could threaten the marriage of the Woolves. The threat seriously appeared a little over a year after they were married, when Virginia attempted suicide. Doctor Geoffrey Keynes, who happened to be nearby, helped save the situation with a stomach pump.[26] Henceforth Leonard remained alert to premonitory signs of mental distress, which appeared after Virginia completed a book or fell under the effects of excitement. A general palliation was to settle in the calm of suburban Richmond, where they lived from October 1914 to March 1924. A specific measure was to depart early from a party that tended to stimulate Virginia too much. Nurturing her through periods of raving lunacy, Leonard succeeded until her sixtieth year.

Nor would technical infidelity threaten the marriage. In about 1925 Virginia entered into a three- or four-year love affair with the aristocratic popular novelist Vita Sackville-West, who was frankly lesbian although blessed with a husband—the diplomat-writer Harold Nicolson—and two sons. Virginia, almost as frigid in that direction also, had loved women friends before she found her way to Leonard. Securely aware of their wives' need for them, both husbands made no effort to discourage the relationship. Indeed both were primarily concerned to see that Virginia's mental stability was not disturbed. In September 1925 Leonard and Harold, a homosexual whose amours Vita easily tolerated, permitted Virginia and Vita to enjoy a six-day excursion in France. The women spent much of their time writing home. Not hearing from Leonard after three days in France, Virginia sent a telegram demanding reassurance that all was well.[27] "I told Nessa the story of our passion in a chemist's shop the other day," Virginia, reporting her sister's *echt* Bloomsburian reaction, wrote Vita in 1929. "But do you really like going to bed with a woman she said—taking her change. 'And how do you do it' and so she bought her pills to take abroad, talking as loud as a parrot."[28] Virginia's novel *Orlando*, published a few days after her return from France, was a love letter to Vita and a soft satire of conventional sex roles. Orlando begins as a dashing Elizabethan male and ends in 1928, after magical adventures, as a magnificent lady—Vita to all who knew her. Whatever physical love they may have attempted would have been the least part of the affair. When Virginia began to write fiction in her early twenties, she wrote a woman friend, "[T]his vague and dream like world, without love, or heart, or sex, is the world I really care about."

On 28 March 1941, going mad again and certain she would not recover, Virginia wrote a note telling Leonard, "I don't think two people could have been happier than we have been," and drowned herself.[29] (Leonard lived on for another twenty-eight years. If he had been patient as Job, he was also doubly rewarded, achieving the earthly love of Marjorie Parsons, called Trekkie, an artist and wife of a publishing associate and tolerant friend of Leonard's.)[30] The Vita episode was an entr'acte in the drama of a great marriage defined rather than diminished by asexuality and madness.

If Maynard's companionable unconventionality as expressed in style of loving and intellectual and verbal capacity placed him centrally in Bloomsbury, other elements in him spun him centrifugally outward. His insecure aesthetic sense made his friends suspicious. Of course not all of the group had a feeling for art, but he was aggressively appreciative in a manner seemingly inauthentic. In a letter to Duncan after going to a Matisse exhibition in Paris, he announced himself negatively impressed and wondered if Matisse were not "almost academic."[31] Of itself his doubtful taste was not enough to condemn him, but it irritated when combined with the confidence flowing out of his excellences. To his friends his best often became his worst.

Setting the private against the public Keynes, Maynard's wartime experience produced the purest, most concentrated perplexity for him and Bloomsbury. His humane desire for a negotiated peace, consonant with its position, had resisted Lloyd George's triumphant leadership and even endangered his position in the Treasury. Privately, also in agreement with Bloomsbury, he went much further than that. His friends were less than appreciative.

Parallel with the Treasury's request that he be exempted because of the need for his services, Maynard first made a silent demonstration by avoiding the legal formality of registering for military service. It was an action analogous to that of Americans refusing to register for the draft during the war in Vietnam. Furthermore, he evidently made the additional and more aggressive demonstration of opposing the conscription process on principle. In a written statement, while granting "conceivable circumstances in which I should voluntarily offer myself for military service," he told his conscription tribunal, "I claim complete exemption because I have a conscientious objection to surrendering my liberty of judgment on so vital a question as undertaking military service."[32] This was another example of Maynard's skill in torturing logic to produce practical unreason. He was trying to stay in empathetic contact with his friends while, at the same time, avoiding quite to define himself as a conscientious objector. Yet his logic overshot the mark: he was arguing that the individual could conscientiously object not merely to military service but to any measure he or she chose to define as "vital." He had arrived at absolute anarchy. The tribunal simply avoided the constitutional issue by noting that it had already acceded to the Treasury's exemption request for him. If it ignored Maynard's statement, he himself canceled it out. Later, a new regulation required that individuals personally register, and he formally did so, according to a certificate of registration dated 26 March 1918.[33] More constructively for Bloomsbury, as Maynard impressionistically reported, "I spend half my time on the boring business of testifying to the sincerity, virtue, and truthfulness of my [conscientious objector] friends."[34] He was exaggerating the amount of time spent, but his testimony was dramatically effective.

Among his interventions, Maynard did not have to defend Lytton, who marshalled his numerous siblings and, as character witness, the Member of Parliament Philip Morrell, Lady Ottoline's husband. Asked by a hostile member of the tribunal, " '[W]hat would you do if you saw a German soldier attempting to rape your sister?,' [Lytton] answered with gravity, 'I should try and interpose my own body.' "[35] The tribunal was not amused, but Lytton's health, as a physical examination determined, protected him definitively. Maynard did, however, successfully defend "the genuineness of James's conscientious objection . . . before the wicked leering faces of the Hampstead Tribunal," as he reported to his mother.[36] Lytton, who was present at his brother's hearing, praised Maynard's "startling performance" unreservedly. Maynard had flourished his credentials: " 'I have just arrived from the Treasury,' " as Lytton recounted to Pippa Strachey. "He stated James's point of view with great incisiveness and vigor. . . . At last [the tribunal members] were reduced to silence."[37] Maynard was similarly overwhelming in defending Duncan and Bunny in May 1916. He "took the aggressive line from the first moment," Bunny later recalled. "Carrying a large locked bag with the Royal cipher on it, he demanded that our cases should be heard as expeditiously as possible, as he had left work of national importance."[38] His success with the tribunal led to the establishment of his two friends in farm work at Charleston. In June his testimony also succeeded with his pacifist friend Gerald Shove.

In the eyes of patriots Maynard, loyally supporting his friends, made himself variously guilty by association. Besides his testimony, he contributed £50 to the National Council Against Conscription.[39] In April 1916 he attended the secret convention of another group, the No Conscription Fellowship, as he reported to Vanessa, "to see what they were like," and slipping into the kind of sexual note she enjoyed, found himself "absolutely ravished by a longhaired dark-eyed C. O." Seriously, he found it "rather an impressive gathering." Even more guiltily, "In the evening [his fellow don, John T.] Sheppard and I gave an all-male party in honor of the Convention." In 1917, more than a year later, he informed her, "Tonight I'm giving a pacifist dinner party."[40] He often appeared at the 1917 Club in the Bohemian district of Soho, where radical and antiwar intellectuals met.[41]

More aggressively, Maynard had followed Lytton into attacks on authority. His friend had written a leaflet, published in a half-million copies, which accused:

CONSCRIPTION

Why they want it, and why they say they want it.
THEY SAY THEY WANT IT to punish the slackers
THEY WANT IT to punish the strikers.
THEY SAY THEY WANT IT to crush Germany
THEY WANT IT to crush labour.
THEY SAY THEY WANT IT to free Europe
THEY WANT IT to enslave England. . . . [42]

As the anonymous, but easily identifiable Politicus (ch. 3), Maynard had not only advocated a negotiated peace without victory in his article for *War and Peace*, the pacifist monthly edited by Gerald Shove, but also, in a letter to a newspaper, paraphrased Lytton's arguments from the leaflet. He speculated suggestively that some proponents of conscription might want ''to persecute a minority who differ from them on the moral aspects of war or on the obligations of citizenship,'' and perhaps also might seek ''a new weapon for the subjugation of labour through the will of the governing classes.''[43] Yet, however helpful he had been and however vulnerable he had made himself, Lytton thought he had not done enough and punished him appositely.

It was young Bunny Garnett, recipient of so many of his favors, who first swung around and attacked Maynard. In November 1915, ignoring the war, Duncan and Bunny went to France for private purposes. Angered at the sight of such insouciant noncombatants, English and French officers serially treated them insultingly, the French officer sending Duncan back to England from Dieppe. From Paris Bunny, humiliated but permitted to stay in France, wrote Maynard, ''What are you? Only an intelligence they need in their extremity.'' Maynard was ''a genie taken out of a bottle by savages to serve them faithfully.''[44] He closed, ''Your affectionate Bunny.'' Maynard was gracious and masochistic enough later to admit ''a great deal of truth in what I had said.''[45] Maynard went on to testify for Bunny a few months later and otherwise help him.

On 20 February 1916, reversing the accepted standard for civic conduct, Lytton ''put the conscientious objector's equivalent of the white feather on Maynard's dinner-plate.''[46] The equivalent was a clipping of a jingoistic-militaristic speech by Montagu, still Maynard's patron, with a note, ''Dear Maynard, Why are you still in the Treasury?''[47] So reported Lytton to James: ''He really *was* put out.'' Lytton had thereupon castigated his friend ''with considerable virulence, Nessa, Duncan, and Bunny sitting around in approving silence. . . . The poor fellow seemed very decent about it, and admitted that *part* of his reason for staying was the pleasure he got from his being able to do the work so well.''[48]

Maynard had confessed only to *part* of his reason for staying at the Treasury, indeed the lesser part. In this sense, at least, he was a true artist and took a self-confident artist's satisfaction from doing good work. This, however, was the lesser part of his reason. The greater part was fundamental and not based on an artist's egocentricity. A matter of pure principle, it placed him in total opposition to Bloomsbury's principled philosophy. It was a matter of being responsible. He was absolutely responsible. Bloomsbury, limiting its loyalty to art and friendship essentially, was symmetrically irresponsible. This was the fault line separating Maynard from the rest of the group.

A comedic episode exposed the fault line. His friends eventually pressed Maynard too hard. "Did you hear of Maynard's terrible outburst at Easter?" Virginia wrote Vanessa in 1917, "when he said that [former Prime Minister] Asquith is more intelligent than Lytton? Lytton thinks this a very serious symptom.''[49] Lytton was right about its earnest although he could not imagine Maynard imagining Asquith more intelligent than he. However pained at alienating his friends, Maynard had to grant the superior wisdom and even principles of Asquith and other responsible leaders. Blood on their hands, they had not resigned and neither did he.

The child Maynard had very early accepted his responsibility to understand the world and carry out his work in it (ch. 2, "Training"). In kindergarten he had, we recall, wanted to stay on longer in the day to get more done. The adolescent acted as his father's "private secretary" responsible for the family's mail when Neville and Florence were on holiday. At Eton Maynard began his lifelong committee service. Always extending his area of responsibility, he was becoming a world-historical busybody. As his classmate had it, the freshman had found King's College '' 'pretty inefficient' '' preparatory to going on to "running the world." Keynes's *General Theory* was a scheme to manage the global economy from his King's College rooms. As a responsible leader Maynard had also accepted the need for deadly decisions; this was consistent with the reasoning of the Eton schoolboy who saw the sacrifice of life as a fair price to maintain empire in South Africa. It is true that, as a reasonable Treasury civil servant, he had strained to conceive a way to make war with minimal loss of life. Yet, however much the private man wept over the lives lost of his friends, Lytton was right that Maynard still wanted to win the war or, at least, not lose it, and that this perversely entailed "the maximum slaughter at the minimum expense" (ch. 3).

Maynard recognized murderous reality, as Bloomsbury did not. War was endemic in human society, and the World War was not a radical break in history. It is true that England had escaped general war for ninety-nine years, but during that period the defenders of its empire, including Lytton's father, had fought the innumerable savage wars of peace. In its false security Bloomsbury denied the existence of empire and even nation. Duncan articulated the group's purest expression of irresponsibility and thus rejected Maynard's position absolutely. He put it in a letter to his father, Major Bartle Grant, another imperial defender as career officer in India and Burma. "I had become I suppose in a sense unpatriotic, as most artists must do," he wrote. His enemies were not "vague masses of foreign people," but the "mass of people in ones's own country and . . . in the enemy country," as opposed to "one's friends [who] were people of true ideas . . . in every country."[50] Famously and pathetically, E. M. Forster took the thought as far as it could go in *Two Cheers for Democracy* (1951): "If I had to choose between betraying my country and betraying my friend, I hope I should have the guts to betray my country."[51]

Duncan accepted no responsibility for friends, lovers, or relations. Vanessa might see to his well-being, but he did as he pleased with her. Angelica, who did not learn he was her father until she was eighteen years old, found him "light, easy, and undemanding," but uninterested in her life before then and equally nonpaternal thereafter.[52] Duncan was Bloomsbury's limiting case.

More typically, while refusing to peer beyond, majority Bloomsbury, Vanessa as exemplar, accepted total responsibility for its people and related concerns like the integrity of art. Similarly, Lytton, Maynard following him, had led the battle for sexual freedom, and his *Eminent Victorians* had attacked Victorian inhibitions and hypocrisy. Years after the war Lytton would defend Radcliffe Hall's right to publish her lesbian novel, *The Well of Loneliness*, although he thought little of its merits.[53] But this was an extension of the individual's or the select group's interests. Conscientious objection, combined with pacifism, remained a defining expression of Bloomsbury. The rise of Nazism would give its survivors another view of pacifism, at least.

It was Maynard Keynes's sense of responsibility, an essential part of his character, that was leading him beyond Bloomsbury to his greatness. It should be said here, as one sees him beginning to engage more broadly and deeply in events and ideas that he was well on his way of becoming an unqualifiedly great man; not simply great economist, but great man, great historical figure. This was another reason why his friends resented him. His brilliance as lecturer and don had been acceptable, but his wartime functioning expressed power. They distrusted power and correctly felt it would lead to still more power: the impending greatness. As part of it, the public Keynes had known how to make his peace with his private being.

Compared with Maynard Keynes, only one member of Bloomsbury could claim the adjective "great" in a public sense. Virginia Woolf was a great novelist and, more broadly, a great writer, but one has only to mention her contemporaries Marcel Proust, T. S. Eliot, and James Joyce to suggest her limits. At her best, in *To the Lighthouse*, for example, she communicated a complex of reality and multiple consciousnesses that gave new dimensions to that reality. With Proust and Joyce she created the modern novel. Yet, a whining note of self-pity keeping her pain too much to herself, her work was often mysteriously self-referential. Only someone familiar with her biography would know that her novel *Jacob's Room* was a condensation of mourning for poor dead Thoby Stephen—and herself. E. M. Forster wrote very good novels, most notably, *A Passage to India* (1924), with its agony and bad conscience of empire. Lytton Strachey semi-revolutionized the practice of biography by riddling restraints on frankness, but his three major works,[54] an idiosyncratic rendering of selected facts from secondary sources, deserve to be appreciated more than trusted. Other biographers, his own among them, have more constructively used the freedom he gained for them. Duncan Grant, with his great facility, and Vanessa Bell, in her uncompromising integrity, would establish themselves as leading British painters in the 1920s, but they never got beyond national borders in a world visually dazzled by Van Gogh, Degas, Cézanne, Picasso, Matisse, and Bracque, among others; and Britain later turned away from them. Roger Fry was a great teacher and propagandizer of the new art produced elsewhere. Leonard Woolf was a creative publisher and the author of a score of constructive, forgotten books, including a one-thousand-page, half-million-word trilogy proposing an international order that would develop the conditions for an appropriate "communal psychology" and so prevent war.[55] In the posthumous collection of Desmond MacCarthy's writings, "Bloomsbury: An Unfinished Memoir" (1933) was characteristic.[56] Clive Bell further propagandized Roger Fry's ideas on art,[57] but, more importantly, wove much of the social webbing that held Bloomsbury together. The enduring, powerfully loving and mothering Vanessa was the greatest private person of them all. In this regard Maynard, for all of his personal distinction, had to take second place.

Maynard's increasing power, including his comparably growing money power, made him an often enragingly convenient resource for his friends. Before the war he could find a more agreeable position for Cecil Taylor, John Sheppard's "Madame." Taylor was not too close to Maynard to feel threatened by this "unseen power steadily, regardless of time and trouble, working for [one's] good." Simply "very grateful," he saluted Maynard: "You are awfully like God."[58] For the members of Bloomsbury that was the problem although they continued to let him help them.

Characteristically, Maynard's services were varied, sensitive, and cost-efficient. As all-round economist he functioned on both the micro- and macro-level. Besides his funding of Charleston, he continued to subsidize Duncan, also taking occasion in the summer of 1918 to send him two suits.[59] He tried, but failed, to move Lord Beaverbrook, then minister of information, into giving Duncan a commission to paint, despite his conscientious-objector status, in the ministry's war artists program.[60] He financed Bunny's production of honey at Charleston, taking partial payment in the honey produced, and lent him money additionally, the debt reaching "very near £20" at one point, as Bunny noted.[61] In 1919 he was helping "your ever affectionate Bunny" and Frankie Birrell to start up their bookshop.[62]

Maynard's supportiveness proliferated around Vanessa. In 1917 he sent a

Chinese carpet and a bed to her at Charleston.[63] In 1918, after she had fallen and feared a miscarriage, he solved the problem of getting her safely from 46 Gordon Square to the Ballets Russes and a post-performance party. "Maynard who has the generosity and something of the manner of an Oriental prince, has hired a brougham for Nessa—an infinitely small slow, antiquated carriage drawn by a very liverystables looking quadruped," Virginia recorded in her diary. "Roger, Duncan, Maynard, Nessa and I all crammed in and padded along slowly across London to Chelsea." Virginia lighted up the episode with a brilliant irrelevancy: "Somehow we passed Ottoline, brilliantly painted, as garish as a strumpet, displayed . . . under an arc lamp."[64] After Angelica was born, "I was simply overcome by your magnificence yesterday when £200 fell out of the letter," Vanessa wrote Maynard. "I felt I oughtnt to take it but Duncan says I cant refuse money given to my daughter. . . . [I]t oils the wheels amazingly."[65] In 1921 Maynard, besides advising Vanessa on her investments, had her money exchanged into francs at a better rate when she transferred her household to the French Riviera to paint.[66] In a chatty letter from St. Tropez, remarking, "I wish you were here," she asked him to send a ten-pound tin of jam or marmalade and oatmeal or rolled oats for the children.[67] It was at St. Tropez that Vanessa learned about Lydia.

One action of Maynard's in his public character was a perfection of appropriateness to Bloomsbury's ends. In March 1918 Duncan alerted him that the contents of the studio of Edgar Degas were to be sold. From Chancellor of the Exchequeur Bonar Law, a Philistine but amused at the idea, he got £20,000 for the National Gallery and, accompanied by Sir Charles Holmes, its director, combined Treasury business with attendance at the Paris sale on 26 and 27 March. With the German bombardment making its last threat, the purchases were bargains. Holmes bought thirteen paintings by Corot, Delacroix, Forain, Gaugin, Ingres, Manet, Rousseau, and Ricard plus eight drawings by Delacroix, two by Ingres, and one by David. With Holmes being selective and disliking Cézanne, Keynes could buy Cézanne's *Apples* for himself (paying £327), two Delacroix paintings and an Ingres drawing. It was the start of his serious collecting (often guided by Duncan).[68] Before the sale Vanessa, doubtful about his taste, warned him about possible trickery and suggested he consult Roger Fry. (Of course he was too confident for that.) She blessed his voyage: "We have great hopes for you & consider that your existence at the Treasury is at last justified." She decreed, "[A] feast of pig will be one of your rewards." In a postscript Bunny wrote, "Nessa and Duncan . . . are very proud of you." He emphasized Bloomsbury's verdict: "You have been given complete absolution & future crimes also forgiven."[69]

The absolution endured two months. At the end of May, stopping at 46 Gordon Square, Vanessa joined Harry Norton and John Sheppard in attacking the government for its failure, they thought, to respond properly to Austrian peace overtures. Maynard, entering in the middle of the discussion, put a stop to it, angrily commanding the discussants, "Go to bed. Go to bed." Upon his exit,

the three sat about deploring him. Vanessa "thought . . . that the strain of prolonged overwork might have injured the quality of his brain." She added that
he "might be so far on the downhill path that nothing could save him." Harry
Norton found his table manners "disgusting." The nonconformist Sheppard
blamed Maynard's nonconformist ancestry for producing an evident *folie de
grandeur*. In his own comments Bunny, recognizing the public Keynes, was
more understanding and saw Maynard's "impatience and irritability" as arising
from his "great responsibility" along with the overwork.[70] Exactly. If Maynard
had been absurdly arrogant, his friends had been talking nonsense about state
policy they could not even conceive in their irresponsibility and ignorance. Their
only recourse to his bad manners had been to condemn him weakly behind his
back. Their weakness only emphasized his power in general and over them. As
their continued association with him showed, they had accepted that power, and
would continue to accept it, as integral to the man. Vanessa, furthermore, wanted
her share of Maynard undiminished, however trying she sometimes found him.

On 6 January 1915, when Maynard had achieved his Treasury appointment,
he invited *tout* Bloomsbury, seventeen persons, to bless his elevation at a dinner
party in the Café Royal on Regent Street, a prime London celebratory site.
Guests included the Bells, Woolfs, MacCarthys, John Sheppard and Cecil Taylor, a selection of Stracheys, Frankie Birrell, Duncan Grant, and Bunny Garnett.
(This was when Bunny was fatefully placed between Vanessa and Duncan.) The
Bells appended a private affair at 46 Gordon Square, where an enchanting feminine trio played Mozart and three eight-foot puppets created by Duncan de-
claimed the last scene of Racine's *Bérénice* in Strachey voices.[71] Bloomsbury
talent honored Bloomsbury authority.

His friends, however, simply could not understand the simple nature of Maynard's sense of responsibility and the ordinary facts to which it responded. In
early 1920, Virginia had been puzzling over his *Economic Consequences of the
Peace*. It was, she found, "a book that influences the world without being in
the least a work of art." She speculated: "[A] work of morality, I suppose."[72]
Of course it was a profoundly moral work. But it was shaped by passion and
humanity into a powerful expression of art to which she was blind. Furthermore,
it based itself on a substratum of objective factors Bloomsbury too often ignored.
It had not occurred to Virginia that Maynard, predicting such consequences as
starvation, disorder, and more war, was trying to describe and ameliorate *reality*.

Seduced nevertheless by his efficiency and *responsibility*, Bloomsbury invited
Maynard to become a central power in it. An expression of that power was the
group's residential arrangements. Thus the lease of the communal Brunswick
Square establishment, created in 1911, had been taken in his name, although
Virginia was in charge of meals. When that ended, in the fall of 1914, he took
rooms alone in 10 Great Ormond Street nearby; it was a depressing moment of
loneliness, as Vanessa had reported, but temporary. He was not lonely for long,
the exuberant activity there leading to efforts at blackmail by the landlady, and
he rented another Bloomsbury house at 3 Gower Street in February 1915. Here

he was landlord to Gerald Shove and John Sheppard, the latter fixing himself in London as a War Office translator, and also, in the top floor attic, the writer-editor Middleton Murry and his future wife, the short story writer Katherine Mansfield. The Bells then brought Maynard into Bloomsbury's great house.[73]

By 1916 both Vanessa and Clive were out of Gordon Square and London. In the summer of that year Clive, also a conscientious objector, became a (theoretically) working boarder at Garsington Manor, the country estate of the pacifist Morrells near Oxford and a refuge for several of his ilk. Trying to reduce expenses while retaining a pied-à-terre at No. 46 for himself and Mary Hutchinson, Clive proposed that Maynard occupy part of the house and share expenses. A hard-headed negotiator for himself as well as for the Treasury, Maynard could see the impressive advantages of the offer but also the complications. Writing to Vanessa on 21 August 1916 from 3 Gower Street, he swathed his misgivings in humor. Of the various proposals, "The latest plan sounds very good, but my brain is so weak that I barely take it in. The theory is . . . that in the break-up of No. 46, Duncan takes you, Mary takes Clive, and I take the children." He was bound by the lease at Gower Street; what to do about it? Could that house become a "boarding establishment for Sheppard, Clive, and Harry?" In that period of warming friendship with Vanessa he went off into chatty notes. He had won £25 from Margot Asquith, "which was rather scandalous"; G. E. Moore had played Brahms at a party in the country; "Please ask Duncan to give Ottoline a kiss from me." Four days later, writing from Garsington itself, he shifted definitively from "My dear Nessa" to "My dearest Nessa." Now he became more serious. Dismissing that problem, he saw a way of arranging for Gower Street. He got to the point: Clive "may be rather a difficulty," because he wanted "to be an inhabitant of Gordon Square, and there isn't really any room for him." Maynard felt "a little in danger of becoming . . . instead of a householder the rather insecure tenant of two rooms." It was hardly possible for the house to accomodate the "Bell family plus Mary on occasion, and for Sheppard and me to be superimposed on it." Clive evidently wanted Maynard and John Sheppard as lodgers while "the house shd. remain yours." He put it to her as supreme authority for the Bells: "What do you think about all this?"[74]

Maynard got what he wanted although he was right about the difficulties and could not displace Clive from No. 46. Rightly, he decided he could manage them and gain substantially on balance. He shared the costs with the Bells: he paid the taxes and the wages of the two servants while they paid the rent and retained four rooms for themselves. He had become approximately half a householder. (3 Gower Street was passed on to Carrington, Barbara Hiles, and another young woman.) Maynard and Sheppard moved into 46 Gordon Square before the end of September 1916, Harry Norton following them a few months later. Left in physical possession by the arrangement, Maynard formally became a full householder in September 1918, when he took over more space and the lease was renewed in his name.[75] Master of its master mansion, future host of its most splendid parties, he controlled the commanding heights of Bloomsbury.

Before this ultimate assertion of his command Maynard, incautiously arrogant, had to engage with Clive in a passage at arms. Clive, still at Garsington, had hospitably offered his rooms to an amorous couple, who mistakenly used Sheppard's room instead. Terribly upset, Sheppard was afraid to go to bed until 3:30 P.M., after the lovers had disappeared. Maynard remonstrated with Clive, who exploded in a letter to Vanessa; their friend "took it on himself to write me the sort of letter an ill-bred millionaire might write to a defaulting office boy. . . . [E]verything is organized for Maynard's convenience so that I am made to feel more like an unwelcome guest than a tenant. . . . The house is ours . . . I say—denounce the treaty."[76] To Maynard Clive wrote firmly but without the threat to break the agreement: "[Y]ou have chosen to write me such a damned high & mighty censorious letter that I am bound to say something in reply." He granted Maynard's right "to be vexed," but, recognizing superior power, ended almost pleadingly: "[A]re we not . . . all tenants standing on an equal footing as regards 46?"[77] In another letter, evidently responding to a more tactful communication from Maynard, Clive averred that he was "only sorry if a slightly irritating letter provoked an irritable reply." Clive inquired, "If Mary should precede or overstay me by a day on a visit to London . . . I presume she would count as a member of Bloomsbury—or a relation?" Another disagreement occurred after the new lease was signed.

At issue were beds. Evidently in November 1918, as the war was ending and Clive was preparing to leave his Garsington refuge, he wrote Maynard, "I am weary of trying to snatch an hour or two's sleep on that . . . bed of mine . . . that's more like the seat of a third-class railway carriage." He wanted the return of his original bed, which Maynard had requisitioned, and he had asked a Mr. Shaw to switch the beds under Vanessa's supervision.[78] Unsupervised, however, Mr. Shaw had removed the bed from Maynard's bedroom without leaving a replacement. Upon Maynard's remonstration, Clive wrote, "I had no intention of leaving you to sleep on the floor." Keynes was supposed to get the railway seat: "As you appear to fuck less than I do it may serve well enough."[79] Clive's next letter expressed empathy and promised a solution: "I gather that Shaw's men are already getting to work." He was "afraid that for a few days . . . you will be in a state of discomfort. This was an inevitable horror of peace." Clive expected to be settled in London before Christmas.[80]

On 10 January 1919 Maynard went to Paris as Treasury representative at the peace conference. From Gordon Square on 16 January and 2 February Clive wrote him long, gossipy, friendly letters. Every bed at 46 was occupied: "Surely this is quite out of order?" Clive was appalled by the prospect of being for a month "nose to nose" with Alix Sargant-Florence, James Strachey's future wife. At one point he had found the couple "lying fucking on the hearth rug." Lytton himself and Aldous Huxley had also appeared, and Clive had caught Bunny "slinking into your bedroom. How long O Lord! How long." He pleaded, "Do please make some protest. They will be impressed by you."[81] Once again, dealing with him, Bloomsbury showed its weakness. From Paris Maynard was in command.

On 8 February 1919, intriguingly, Clive announced to Maynard, "Lopokova has invited me to dinner her next night off—one day next week.'' In July Clive wrote that Lydia's husband was devastated and leaving the country because she had left him and disappeared.[82] It is unclear where she was much of the time, but she was evidently in the United States before being reunited with the Ballets Russes in 1921. Bloomsbury would find it difficult to assimilate Lydia. With her and his expanding activities, having just conquered Bloomsbury, Maynard would begin to break out beyond. But, public and private Keynes perfectly integrated, he would command it as much as he chose.

NOTES

1. For this study, the most useful general works on Bloomsbury include: Noel Annan, *Leslie Stephen: The Godless Victorian* (New York, 1984); Quentin Bell, *Bloomsbury* (London, 1968) and his *Virginia Woolf*; Leon Edel, *Bloomsbury: A House of Lions* (Philadelphia, 1979); S. P. Rosenbaum, *The Bloomsbury Group* (Toronto, 1975); Richard Shone, *Bloomsbury Portraits* (Oxford, 1976); and Spalding, *Vanessa Bell*. Michael Holroyd's *Lytton Strachey* (New York, 1968), besides its general relevance, has an illuminating chapter, ''Bloomsbury: The Legend and the Myth,'' 1: 395–424, and Skidelsky, *JMK*, has the section, ''Bloomsbury,'' 1: 242–51.

2. Paper read to the Memoir Club (see below), quoted, Quentin Bell, *Virginia Woolf*, 1: 124.

3. Ibid., 97.

4. Quentin Bell, introduction, Virginia Woolf, *The Diary of Virginia Woolf* (hereafter *The Diary*; London, 1977), 1: xxvii.

5. Quentin Bell, *Virginia Woolf*, 1: 113.

6. Details from Hugh and Mirabel Cecil, *Clever Hearts: Desmond and Molly MacCarthy: A Biography* (London, 1990).

7. Quoted, ibid., 159.

8. Letter, 11 August 1952, quoted, ibid., 301.

9. The Asheham episode, Holroyd, *Lytton Strachey*, 2: 182–84; the rest of their story from this point in ibid.; also, Gretchen Gerzina, *Carrington* (London, 1989), and Frances Partridge, *Love in Bloomsbury: Memories* (Boston, 1981).

10. The proposal, Holroyd, *Lytton Strachey*, 1: 430–33; letter, quoted, ibid., 432. GLS had been nurturing the idea for some weeks, writing to Leonard Woolf, ''Don't be surprised . . . if you hear one day . . . that I've married Virginia,'' section dated 19 November in letter begun 29 October 1908, Berg.

11. Holroyd, *Lytton Strachey*, 2: 10, 47.

12. Letter, 5 January 1912, BL, Add. MSS 57931.

13. Letter, 4 April 1911, quoted, Holroyd, *Lytton Strachey*, 2: 8. GLS had met Lamb as early as 1906 at an At Home at 46 Gordon Square, but Lamb ''talked the whole time with Vanessa . . . whom I should fall in love with if I could,'' GLS to Leonard Woolf, 21 June 1906, Berg.

14. Miranda Seymour, *Ottoline Morrell: Life on the Grand Scale* (New York, 1993), 96–107.

15. Letter, quoted, Holroyd, *Lytton Strachey*, 2: 59.

16. Ibid., 138.

17. Letter to Virginia Woolf, 28 July 1916, quoted, Holroyd, ibid., 206.

18. Letter from the George Hotel, Glastonbury, 29 August 1916, KP, PP/45/316.

19. Letter, 21 February 1918, CP.

20. Letter, 18 February 1918, quoted, Holroyd, *Lytton Strachey*, 2: 254.

21. Ibid., 517.

22. 27 May 1909, Berg. Leonard Woolf replied on 1 February 1909, "Do you think Virginia would have me? Wire me if she accepts, I'll take the next boat home." Quoted, Bell, *Virginia Woolf*, 1: n. 142.

23. Bell, *Virginia Woolf*, 1: 175.

24. Letter, Vanessa to Clive Bell, quoted, ibid., 2: 6.

25. Ibid., 1: 42–43, n. 43, 44, 61, 95–96, n. 96.

26. Ibid., 1: 15–17.

27. Ibid., 115–20, 139; Victoria Glendinning, *Vita* (New York, 1983), 129–311 passim; Nigel Nicolson in Alen MacWeeney and Sue Allison, *Bloomsbury Reflections* (New York, 1990), commentary accompanying plate 45.

28. 5 April 1929, Virginia Woolf, *The Letters*, 4: 36.

29. Quoted, Bell, *Virginia Woolf*, 1: 126, 2: 226.

30. See Woolf's letters to her, Leonard Woolf, *The Letters of Leonard Woolf*, ed. Frederic Spotts (New York, 1989), e.g., letter of 30 October 1943: "Dearest (I suppose I musn't say & most beautiful) of creatures. . . . If ever anyone was worth a passion, dearest, it's you" (483). Mrs. Parsons' husband, Ian, was chairman of Chatto & Windus, which had bought an interest in the Hogarth Press; he was a close friend and colleague of LW's for the rest of LW's life. Obituary of Mrs. Parsons, who died 24 July 1995, aged 93, *New York Times*, 2 August 1995.

31. 14 May 1919, BL, Add. MS 57931.

32. Draft statement, 28 February 1916, *CW*, 16: 178. Although it is not clear that this statement was submitted, JMK did request exemption in some manner because the tribunal mentioned his request in its reply, editorial note, ibid., 179.

33. Editorial note, ibid., 179.

34. Letter to D. H. Robertson, 18 June 1916, quoted, Skidelsky, *JMK*, 1: 327.

35. Holroyd, *Lytton Strachey*, 2: 179, from GLS's letter to his sister Pippa, 17 March 1916.

36. Letter, 26 March 1916, KP, PP/45/168.

37. Letter to Pippa Strachey, 25 March 1916, quoted, Moggridge, *MK*, 256.

38. David Garnett, *The Flowers of the Forest* (London, 1955), 121–22.

39. Moggridge, *MK*, 256.

40. Letters, 11 April 1916, 28 July 1917, CP.

41. Skidelsky, *JMK*, 1: 348.

42. Quoted, Holroyd, *Lytton Strachey*, 2: 167.

43. *CW*, 16: 158.

44. Letter, 15 November 1915, KP, PP/45/116.

45. Garnett, *The Flowers of the Forest*, 97.

46. Paul Levy, "The Bloomsbury Group," in Milo Keynes, ed., *Essays on John Maynard Keynes* (Cambridge, 1975), 68.

47. Note, 20 February 1916, and clipping attached from the *Observer*, also 20 February, KP, PP/45/316.

48. Letter, 22 February 1916, quoted, Skidelsky, *JMK*, 1: 324.

49. 24 April 1917, Virginia Woolf, *The Letters*, 2: 150.

50. Quoted, Skidelsky, *JMK*, 1: 326.

51. E. M. Forster, "What I Believe," in *Two Cheers for Democracy* (New York, 1951), 68.

52. Angelica Garnett, *Deceived with Kindness*, 2 (quotation), 4, 134.

53. Holroyd, *Lytton Strachey*, 2: 641.

54. *Eminent Victorians* (1918), *Queen Victoria* (1921), *Elizabeth and Essex* (1928).

55. Leonard Woolf, *Downhill All the Way* (London, 1967), 200. The first two volumes were gloomily entitled *After the Deluge*, 1 and 2 (1931, 1939). The third volume, after G. E. Moore's *Principia Ethica*, was entitled *Principia Politica* (1953) on JMK's suggestion: "To all intents and purposes they have been a complete failure"(196). Woolf abandoned plans to write a fourth and fifth volume (205).

56. Desmond MacCarthy, *Memories* (London, 1953), 172–75.

57. In Clive Bell, *Art* (London, 1915). Bell referred to "conversations and discussions . . . with Mr. Roger Fry, to whom I owe a debt that defies exact computation" (viii).

58. Letter, 20 December 1911, KP, PP/45/324.

59. Letter, JMK to Vanessa Bell, 25 August 1918, CP.

60. Letters, JMK to Duncan Grant, 16, 26 June 1918, BL, Add. MSS 57931.

61. Letter (above), JMK to Duncan Grant, 16 June 1918, ibid.; letters, David Garnett to JMK, 6 October 1916 and n.d., KP, PP/45/116.

62. E.g., letter, David Garnett to JMK, 15 August 1919, KP, PP/45/116.

63. JMK to Vanessa Bell, 20 January 1917, CP.

64. Virginia Woolf, *The Diary*, 12 October 1918, 1: 201; Spalding, *Vanessa Bell*, 176.

65. Vanessa Bell to JMK, 19 March 1919, CP.

66. Vanessa Bell to JMK, 8, 25 February 1918 and 26 November 1921, ibid.

67. Vanessa Bell to JMK, ?October 1921, ibid.

68. Details of the purchase, JMK to Vanessa Bell, 23 March 1919, CP; editorial note, *CW*, 16: 286; Harrod, *The Life*, 223–26, n. 225; Skidelsky, *JMK*, 1: 349–50; Moggridge, *MK*, 282–83.

69. Letter, Vanessa Bell to JMK, 22 March 1918, CP.

70. From Vanessa Bell's account to him, Garnett, *The Flowers of the Forest*, 148–49.

71. Ibid., 21–23.

72. Virginia Woolf, *The Diary*, 24 September 1920, 2: 33.

73. Spalding, *Vanessa Bell*, 161–62.

74. CP.

75. Skidelsky, *JMK*, 1: 331, 351.

76. Quoted, Skidelsky, *JMK*, 1: 351.

77. Letter, n.d., but related to another letter in an envelope dated 18 June 1918, KP, PP/45/25.

78. Letters, n.d., ibid.

79. Letters, Clive Bell to Mr. Shaw and JMK, n.d., ibid.

80. Letter to JMK, n.d., ibid.

81. Ibid.

82. Letters, ibid.

CHAPTER 6

Retraining

After the war Maynard Keynes began to retrain himself to address the radically changed economic world. He found himself dealing with a great variety of new private and public problems—and opportunities. Again and again he was experiencing how different the world had become and how differently from established opinion he viewed it. He was still functioning as an applied economist in terms of neoclassical economic theory. Yet, throughout the 1920s, he would find himself demolishing the foundations of his proper Marshallian beliefs from one ad hoc instance to the next. Entering a field of increasing tension, he would only slowly begin to realize what he was doing. His tactical responses would have to be unified within the frame of new thinking.

One of the fortunate consequences of the peace was to deposit Keynes at a great remove from power and policymaking. Events, as he saw them, had swerved wildly from the straight line of rational action that he had pursued, and he had no intention of accomodating himself to them mindlessly. As a great technician in the war effort he had enjoyed the luxury of freely imposing his principles on the financial management of Britain's allies; he had been able, minor politic compromises granted, to function in terms of his own interpretation of right reason and rational economic science. But, however important his role, it had not been on the level of statesmanship. At the peace conference, as he had wryly informed his mother, his position "sound[ed] rather grander than it is."[1] Yet circumstances teased him excruciatingly, Lloyd George having for a moment expressly invited him to rise to the high statesmanship of peacemaking.

Indulging his best hopes, he had permitted himself to believe further than he could think. It did not take him long to collect his harder thoughts and get out. Now he was finding his way to another, more elevated critical point, his distance from power being expressed in vertical as well as horizontal terms. However thin the air at that altitude, the private Keynes was unerringly directing the public man.

Keynes was extraordinarily well equipped for his new role. He was an economist, and the great new issues, as he powerfully and dramatically argued in his *Economic Consequences of the Peace*, revolved around economics—pure and applied. Yet a competent economist limited essentially to his professional wisdom would have been helpless. It was the wide range of Keynes's capabilities as administrator, political thinker, general logician, financial manager, and Bloomsbury culturemonger that permitted him to contend with all the perversities of the situation. He had to address rage, nonsensical thinking, and pervasive ignorance as well as the objective problems thrown up by the war and the peace. In that sense one perspicacious critic, reviewing his *Economic Consequences*, found it was "two or possibly three [books]—a mordant political pamphlet, a masterly technical discussion of the economic provisions of the Treaty, and interwoven with both an impressive and largely philosophical critique of the economic relations of nations and classes."[2] Furthermore other problems, the effects of time and progress, were burgeoning under cover of the more spectacular issues while further complicated by them. Of course all this was too much for any person to grasp, but Keynes would do better than anyone else.

Although the contemporary sufferers would disagree, the subjective dominated the objective concerns. The absolute victims were the dead but they were no longer problems. The destruction of values and their bookkeeping mirror images of debts were indeed enormous, but the material losses seemed greater than they were. No one, Keynes included, gave enough weight to the increases in productivity generated by the war effort combined with the forced advances in technology. The world could replace and add to those lost values much faster than believed. This is a faint suggestion of a general failure in thinking. A related and derivative error was the sense in the minds of the financial professionals, as enforced by business experience and formal economic thought, that the great debts should be expeditiously paid off. One result was a powerful deflationary thrust that overcame the expansive effects of reconstruction. The experts, Keynes presently to become more and more of an exception, were virtuously and urgently recommending financial and general economic self-maiming.

Yet, in regard to the objective elements, the European economic base had in fact shrunk drastically. Just three nations, Great Britain, France, and Germany, remained as major economic units, the first two as impoverished victors and the last impoverished and subject to their exactions. The rich and nicely balanced economy of the Austro-Hungarian Empire of some fifty million inhabitants was shattered into beggared fragments. With the liberation of the Baltic states and

Finland, Europe had nine new more or less miserable successor states, all of them, impelled by a sauve-qui-peut necessity as well as a fervent nationalism, blocking intra-European trade with tariffs and other negative policies. Russia, lurching from war to civil war, had been ripped away from the European comity by bolshevism, Lenin's victory securing its wretched isolation by 1921. Rather, the new Russia had become a source of revolutionary infection and the negative inspiration of a counterthreat in the form of exacerbated nationalism extending from authoritarianism to fascism and nazism. Together with Germany, Great Britain and France had been relativized, the war accelerating the process, into economic near mediocrity by the industrial and financial magnitude of the United States, commanding more than two-fifths of the world's industrial production, compared with roughly one-tenth for each of them.[3] To this invidious humiliation (which Keynes had rudely experienced in Westminster, Washington, and Paris), one must add the early movement toward imperial dissolution. The European allies were vanquished more than victorious.

The Paris Peace Conference, such leading players as the United States in the process of departing Europe and a bolshevized Russia simply absent, was a quarrel over half loaves and crumbs. Seeing this better than most of his contemporaries, Keynes had nevertheless been forced to work within the perspectives of the decision makers until he gave up, thus his evanescent "grand scheme" of April 1919. Had anyone else suggested it, he could easily have pointed out that the old enemy Germany and the new enemy Russia could not be fitted into it, while allied reparation and U.S. war debt claims were sure to annihilate it anyway. These negations confirmed, he could take refuge with Vanessa in Charleston and write *The Economic Consequences* to attack what he saw as criminal folly and to seek the beginning of a way out of it.

In making Germany responsible for all the war costs, the Versailles Treaty gave it an impossible task, thus grievously laming the international political economy and continuing the war's destructive work. Ignoring the economic realities, the allies had made reparations a matter of morality and German guilt. In his book Keynes could only call attention to the economics and hope that its irrefutable sense would eventually penetrate the public consciousness. With an exquisite feeling for the workings of the European economic machine, he provided tables organizing such vital materials as "[b]ooks, maps, and music . . . [p]ianos, organs, and parts . . . [c]ereals, etc. (wheat, barley, bran, rice, maize, oats, rye, clover)."[4] He succeeded with British public opinion in less than three years, affected American understanding after a long decade with the help of time and the Depression, and failed sempiternally with France.

In 1919 the dominant factors had been war hatred and German reparations, as *The Economic Consequences* had to recognize. Later, England became more realistic and France began to weary of its frustrations without, however, losing its sense of having been raped and cheated. Henceforth the innocent American assumption that the war debt claims of $11 billion had to be paid like any other bills kept the allied reparation demands in force as a necessary defense. The figures expressed the logic. To pay $11 billion to the United States the straitened allies demanded some $12.5 billion from Germany, thus the equivalent plus a margin of error or profit. (A much greater figure of $32 billion was flourished in the headlines to appease allied public opinion, but the small print reduced it, although not to the point of making payment possible.) Desperately, Keynes could only prophesy, should the errors of the peace not be repaired, a "final civil war between the forces of Reaction and the despairing convulsions of Revolution."[5]

The Economic Consequences was essentially a conservative statement accepting the economic order of things according to the neoclassical verities, although, like others of Keynes's writings, it sounded a few populist notes that reverberated more loudly. He began by emphasizing the "intensely unusual, unstable, complicated, unreliable, temporary nature of [Europe's] economic organization," which he saw based on "the *inequality* of the distribution of wealth." It was a "remarkable system depend[ing] . . . on a double bluff or deception," persuading the "capitalist classes" to accept a situation in which they could "call the best part of the cake theirs . . . on the tacit underlying condition that they consumed very little of it is practice," the remainder providing the savings for reinvestment. "The war has disclosed the possibility of consumption to all and the vanity of abstinence to many," Keynes concluded. "Thus the bluff is discovered; the laboring classes may be no longer willing to forego so largely and the capitalist classes," discovering the joy of consumption, might "thus precipitate the hour of their confiscation." If this might sound like a radical's hyperbole, Keynes was pleading for a sensible defense of free enterprise, and in another strophe he warned against the danger of inflation. He mysteriously attributed to Lenin the thesis, undiscoverable in Lenin's collected writings, that "the best way to destroy the capitalist system was to debauch the currency." Keynes agreed, "Lenin was certainly right. There is no subtler, no surer means of overturning the existing basis of society."[6] He would spend the rest of his life trying to save capitalism from itself as well as from such secondary dangers as Leninism.

The obstinate wrongheadedness of the Versailles Treaty's economic clauses and the efforts to implement them, as Keynes had predicted, were hollowing out the foundations of the advanced world's economy. As time went on, and as he concentrated on the immediacy of the succeeding problems, he may have been somewhat distracted from appreciating the deep truth of his warnings. He soon became aware also of a convergence of terrific deflationary pressures, with reparations to intensify the economic strains, and began to develop ideas of dealing with them as well. Beyond deflation itself he would soon glimpse the great thesis of his ultimate economic thinking, the new economic responsibility of government.

Reparation, a direly threatening issue in 1919, became an acute one in 1921. Germany was then ordered to pay some $750 million annually, amounting to one tenth of its gross national product. Although this was a huge sum, it was, of itself, not necessarily an impossible burden, but on the assumption that the country could earn the money by foreign trade. At this point the impossibility imposed itself. Germany could have paid only by building up great trade surpluses with its major trading partners, thus with the United States, Britain, and France. Of course they were not going to permit that to happen because the result would have been to drive their economies into slump and unemployment. Indeed, during 1922 both Great Britain and the United States increased their tariffs. The United States, a high-tariff country since the days of Alexander Hamilton, established a new and higher tariff level of 30 percent ad valorem (and the Hawley-Smoot tariff of 1930, crucially worsening the Great Depression, would exceed that substantially). The allies had given Germany an impossible problem and driven the nation crazy trying to solve it, Hitler and his Nazis incorporating the madness.

The point of the reparation problem extended well beyond German hardship to the worldwide Depression itself, the self-destructive United States as a prime victim. When the Hoover Moratorium of June 1931 and the Lausanne Conference of June–July 1932 effectively ended reparations (and war debts), Germany had paid somewhat less than $6 billion although, with its trade in deficit, it never had the money. Foreign speculators and investors (although not the canny Keynes) provided it to the sum of $6.5 billion, first betting and losing on the inflationary German currency and then buying German bonds that proved similarly, if more slowly, worthless.[7] (These sums were substantial, although they seem small compared with the inflated national income and debt figures of recent years.) Desperate for funds, Germany paid up to 9 percent, twice the interest rates of its creditor countries.[8] The system worked on the principle of the classic pyramidal swindle by offering returns greater than those of sound businesses, paying earlier investors with the money poured in by the later ones—until doubts lead to a sellout and collapse. The grander swindle led to political as well as financial breakdown.

The international economy was strung between a debt-ridden Germany and a cash-bloated United States. Protected by its high tariffs and running a trade surplus of more than $2 billion annually, the United States was filling up with too much gold. This left too little to the other major nations, Germany struggling with more debt, Britain, with 10 percent unemployment, undergoing its depression from 1922, and France keeping solvent only by devaluing its currency and cheating its war bond rentiers. The result was general deflationary pressure affecting all nations. The excess gold was a problem to the United States, the Federal Reserve System palliating matters temporarily by burying it and restricting the money supply. It prevented a moderate monetary inflation, which might have relieved the nation's European debtors by altering the terms of trade in their favor. Yet the relief would have been modest at best. In the United States the excess liquidity concentrated its inflationary effect on the stock market. These factors led not only to the Wall Street Crash of October 1929, when too many investors realized that stocks were overpriced, but also, breaking through the nation's economic weaknesses, to the terrific Depression of the 1930s. The weaknesses included an agricultural depression since the early 1920s and the absence of a social welfare safety net and effective banking and stock exchange regulations. The monstrous U.S. economy plunged steeply and dragged down with it the other nations, who had been enfeebled by all the consequences of the peace.

In the fall of 1931, having resisted the policies creating this situation, Keynes gathered and published the testimony in his *Essays in Persuasion*, commenting deprecatingly for all, "Here are collected the croakings of twelve years—the croakings of a Cassandra who could never influence the course of events in time."[9] He was not losing heart. The essays seethed with suggestions to correct the thinking and policies that generated those errors and promised more. No longer a Marshallian, Keynes was challenging all authority.

By the mid-1920s the immediate and specific postwar insanity of reparations and war debts had merged into the generalized insanity of a virtuous deflation, its essence expressed in Britain's return to the gold standard in 1925. Keynes croaked his warnings in superb isolation. Germany, its hyperinflation of 1923 exhausted, was graciously permitted to enter into a more neighborly deflation by the agency of the Dawes Plan. It got temporary relief from reparations and could then contract for the loans that would pay the installments when they were resumed later in the decade. By 1928–29, however, these reached a level of renewed impossibility at more than $600 million annually. At the time Hitler, who had gotten his start protesting the Versailles Treaty, rose out of the obscurity that followed the failure of his Beer Hall Putsch and won renewed publicity and support denouncing the Young Plan, which trivially softened the Dawes Plan's provisions. Heinrich Brüning, chancellor of the Weimar Republic from 30 March 1930 to 30 May 1932, tried to maintain financial balance and pay reparations by three savage wage-and-price reductions, another and a greater example of deflationary action than the British return to the gold standard. Keynes, who had spoken with Brüning in Berlin on 11 January 1932, published an article telling the world five days later, "Germany today is in the grip of the most terrible deflation that any nation had experienced. . . . We need to have an imaginative apprehension of all this." Few possessed it. Unemployment in the United States was rising to one quarter, and in Germany, to one third of the workforce. Brüning was no fool. He was trapped between the need to pay the reparation debt and the international financial community's application of sound economic practices combined with its threat to call in its loans. He saw no alternative, as he told Keynes. In three years Brüning cut Germany's imports to one third of the 1929 level.[10] This was the moment of the Hawley–Smoot tariff bill, passed on 17 June 1930. Other nations retaliated, Britain itself with its Import Duties Act of February 1932 and greater emphasis on its policy of imperial preference. A hard nationalism, political as well as economic, became increasingly dominant in international relations. Every national economy acted as a falling domino to every other economy. Thus the Depression. The Weimar Republic disintegrated.

Keynes had found the situation from 1919 ideal for indulging his compulsions. The monumental self-destructiveness of official wrong-headedness challenged him profoundly, thrillingly. All the great decisions were wrong. He must put them right. He was now free to do his public service—his duty—as he chose, untrammeled by bureaucrats and bureaucracy. He could also engage in lucrative private enterprise, the private gains assisting his public purposes. With politicians and government departments compromised in perpetrating the nonsense, he was the singular incorporation of His Majesty's Loyal Opposition.

When Keynes published *The Economic Consequences*, Roy Harrod had him "incurr[ing] great odium in official circles" and located him "in the wilderness." A dozen pages further, Harrod had him dining with Bonar Law, lord privy seal at the time and future prime minister, in January 1920, and, the next month, advising Austen Chamberlain, chancellor of the exchequer, on dealing with Britain's postwar inflation.[11] The chancellor had been chairman of the prewar Indian Finance and Currency Commission and knew how to value his advice. Although, as he had written Keynes frankly in December 1919, the book was making matters difficult for British policy, he was nevertheless "full of admiration for a brilliant piece of work." Distinguishing between the private and public Keynes, he cheerily congratulated, "In the end I relapse into the attitude of a private individual and I hope, I may say, personal friend, and confess that I chortled with joy over the conference chapter!"[12] Keynes's counsel on the peace, as Chamberlain suggested, was simply too good to be followed in the political circumstances. The explosive success of the book, translated into a dozen languages and selling 100,000 copies in six months, established Keynes as an independent power, albeit notorious and temporarily lacking much immediate influence. He accepted patriotic recriminations as confirming the justice of his position, firmly telling a French economist, "I will be no party to a continuation of a European blood-feud."[13] An exacting critic, Lytton Strachey gave Bloomsbury's verdict: "Dearest Maynard, Your book arrived yesterday and I swallowed it at a gulp." It was "entirely impressive," its "argument . . . most crushing, most terrible. . . . I admire the style very much." Lytton predicted precisely, "What the wretches will try to do will be to turn their backs on it."[14] This was a grander absolution than that pronounced on Maynard's capture of the Degas-studio paintings for the National Gallery.

Keynes's wilderness was extraordinarily fertile, permitting him to establish in it his numerous, interlocking activities and, exercise by exercise, retrain himself. While he was writing *The Economic Consequences*, in August 1919, he reported to his mother from Charleston on a "very feverish ten days," which included a weekend at the country place of former Prime Minister Asquith, where he won £22 from "world celebrities" at bridge, and a party he himself gave with Clive Bell at 46 Gordon Square: "We sat down thirty-three to supper." That was followed by a ballet evening, "all of my various worlds being there." In September, besides boasting that he was writing "1,000 words a day fit for the printer," he added, "My diversion, to avoid the possibility of tedium in a country life, is speculation on the foreign exchanges, which will shock father but out of which I hope to do very well."[15]

Maynard Keynes, King's College student, had begun speculating modestly on the stock exchange in 1905, and, economics don and civil servant, more ambitiously during the next decade; he continued these operations and soon would enter hugely into commodity as well as currency trading.[16] In November 1919, also, he acceded to his bursarship at King's, a function to which he would give as much attention as he did his private undertakings. The college profited immensely while he gained in investment experience as well as satisfaction.

Keynes had already established another operational base in the City, London's financial district. On good advice from both parents, among others, he had refused a tempting offer from a Scandinavian bank, which would have paid lavishly for little work, but might have spoiled relations with the Treasury and other government departments.[17] Among other offers, including that of a possible directorship of the London School of Economics, he found a much better situation. His Treasury experience had given him wide City contacts, many by way of the Tuesday Club, composed of practical men and academics meeting in the Café Royal for dinner discussions once a month. One of its founders (in 1917) was the broker Oswald T. Falk, who had given a talk Keynes found sufficiently impressive to enroll him in his A Division. Strong-minded, brilliant, and passionate about art, Falk had much, indeed too much, in common with Keynes, and they became friends as well as sometimes contentious associates. In a perfect turnabout Falk (and another Tuesday Club member) got Keynes into the substantial National Mutual Life Assurance Society as a board member in September 1919.[18] Keynes became its chairman, as had been agreed at the beginning, in May 1921. In December 1923 he also became a board member and Finance Committee president of the smaller Provincial Insurance Company. At both firms he left the actuarial side to the experts and took charge of the security portfolios. A pioneer in this regard, he significantly increased their revenues from investments as compared with premiums. His annual speeches as National Mutual chairman became major City events and influenced the financial community in his sense, albeit against the current. He was exercising power, or rather persuasions, to a modest degree, he knew. He trusted that the economic truth would win out in due time and increase that power to the requisite strength. In this way he began to position himself at a series of critical points in the British political economy.

Keynes's first major financial operation of the postwar period, the currency speculation, paralleled his public position on the Paris peace agreements. Once again he failed because he was right and the majority wrong. With his great confidence he bet heavily on the healthy economies of the United States, Norway, Denmark, and India, and sold short the problematic currencies of France,

Italy, and Germany. But financial opinion, disbelieving, for example, his evaluation of the reparation–war debt situation, was slow to see the weaknesses so clear to him. Emboldened, however, by early success, Keynes organized the Syndicate, the first of four speculation groups, bringing in family and friends. One of the friends was Oswald Falk, who, often disagreeing vigorously, joined his other speculative ventures as well. The Syndicate had a profit of £7,000 (about $300,000, present value) by 14 May 1920. But then virtually all the currencies moving counter to sense, it fell into deficit in a week, with due effects on the private economies of the associates. Virginia's diary recorded Vanessa's worries about "money difficulties which threaten Maynard and through him, her."[19] His confidence in his monetary judgment unshaken, Keynes continued his speculations, investing the early profits from sales of *The Economic Consequences* and borrowing £5,000 from the great financier Sir Ernest Cassel, who had, however, not unreasonably refused to risk a colossal £190,000 in a joint venture.[20] After the Syndicate fell into a new deficit of £8,587 by 1 August 1920, its currencies began to agree with Keynes's predictions and it achieved assets of £21,000 by the end of 1922. By the mid-1920s he had become a modestly rich man. He would have to wait longer for events to confirm his views on political economy generally.

After 1922 Keynes shifted his major speculative emphasis to securities and commodities. Besides illustrating his style as man and thinker, these operations provided most of the funds for his political and policymaking activities as he broadened his counsel from the consequences of the peace to the general deflation and the economic responsibilities of government. In 1924 his net assets rose to £63,797 and remained above £40,000 for the next three years. Reporting Bloomsbury's combined hyperbole and calculations, Lytton Strachey wrote Carrington in 1925, "The Charlestonians declare that il gran Pozzo is now immensely rich—probably £10,000 [*income*, that is] a year."[21]

Keynes's portrait as financial man requires a wider, darker, more Rembrandtian palette. His marvelous confidence, although generating splendid results, also subsumed the pure arrogance of a person who cannot quite believe he might be mistaken and makes grand mistakes. Keynes did possess, as he often claimed, a remarkably true intuition, but for unremarkable reasons: he internalized the examples set by both parents, who were functioning efficiently on a great range of reality from finance to charity, from administration to politics, as mediated by their sensitive responses to living persons. Negatively, however, the ultracautious John Neville impelled John Maynard also to reverse his model of action. The younger Keynes *would* gamble, would break out beyond the limits set by the laws of logic and economics as interpreted by his father. His *Treatise on Probability* provided the rationale by overwhelming mathematical frequency with his intuitively registered probabilty-as-belief. Maynard Keynes was a self-indulgent, sensually delectated gambler all his life.

The young man who on holiday had gambled away his funds in the casinos of the Riviera became a City financier doing the same on the commodity markets. Yet Keynes had made himself as much of an expert as the professionals specializing only in commodities. Between April 1923 and September 1930 he wrote seven "Special Memoranda" of nearly four hundred pages, accompanied by numerous statistical tables, for the London and Cambridge Economic Service, of which he was an executive-committee member. He was on intimate terms with jute, cotton, wool (merino and crossbred), copper, tin, lead, spelter (zinc ingots), rubber, sugar, coffee, tea, oil and its derivatives, nitrates, and wheat, which "is a very baffling commodity—because it is a seasonal crop, coming from many different sources, and harvested at many different times of the year."[22] In fact, as he always refused to accept, the unpredictability of commodity values, which are subject to so many influences, many of them hidden or disguised, tended to remove them from obedience to rational calculations. In any case he was engaged in too many disparate speculations to know enough to anticipate the value changes. In the later 1920s he lost hugely in rubber, corn, cotton, and tin. He had begun with net assets of £16,315 in 1919. In 1929 he was down to £7,815 and threatened with a new bankruptcy.

Keynes stopped the gambling. Sensibly, he turned away from commodities and, developing a new investment strategy based on manageable knowledge, found and courageously exploited a great opportunity in the Depression stock market of the United States. His finances recovered fast enough to continue to support his comfortable living standard and his public activities. A central factor causing his great losses *and* gains was his heavy borrowing (leverage in modern idiom), another expression of his spring-steel confidence as well as his gambler's instincts, controlled or not. In 1936, with the world still deep in depression and his gloomy *General Theory* achieving publication, his assets had mounted magically to £506,522, say $25 million in present value. The gambler could not, however, resist another blind throw over the next two years, betting on lard and cotton, and reducing those assets to £181,547 in 1938. Moderating and then eliminating his commodity gambles, he coolly returned in force to the more calculable stock market and brought his fortune up to £411,238 in 1945, the last full year of his life. On balance, the scientific economist had won over the compulsively losing gambler.

In his scintillating arrogance Keynes always made his own rules, whatever authority, parental, intellectual, governmental, or institutional, commanded. At the end of 1914 he had securities worth £4,617 and four years later, six months before resigning from the Treasury, had doubled their value to £9,428.[23] Surely he was deep in conflict of interest. He doubtless assumed that he was not letting his inside knowledge influence his investing. Certainly he consciously made decisions against his own interest. Thus, attempting to determine Treasury policy in this regard, he had vainly recommended against the government's guarantee of premoratorium bills. That guarantee saved him and John Neville, his fellow investor, "several hundred pounds at the expense of the general taxpayer" on loans to discount houses, as he wrote his father.[24] Similarly, when he gave the Treasury advice on the modalities of quitting the gold standard in 1931, he patriotically resisted the effort of his associate Oswald Falk to shift their investment group out of sterling; the result was a substantial loss of £40,000.[25] This was at a time when his own portfolio had minimally recovered from near bankruptcy. His principles, whatever pain they caused Falk, who ceased being an associate while remaining a friend, and whatever a supreme court might adjudicate, remained intact.

Again, it should be emphasized, the importance of these financial operations was not the personal money, at least not beyond the rather modest standard of comfort Keynes required. At the end of 1929 Virginia wrote Vanessa that the Keyneses had arrived at her country house in a "seedy grey Rolls-Royce," which he had bought second-hand.[26] Keynes was concerned essentially with financing his activities as politician and policymaker. Much more than wealth, his ego demanded power. Like Luther and Loyola, Voltaire and Rousseau, Marx and Freud, he was a revolutionary and conqueror. If, like them, he never managed his power directly, his sense of proportion told him how he and his companions-in-theorizing compared with the commanding Charles V, Louis XIV, Napoleon, and Lenin in changing the world. The theorists, Keynes consciously as a follower of G. E. Moore, all accompanied their demand for power with the requirement that it do good. We have seen Keynes's general program of the good from 1919. The specifics followed.

With his bravely gotten gains Keynes captured another intellectual strong point besides his *Economic Journal*, the weekly journal of opinion *The Nation & Athenaeum*. He had joined with William H. Beveridge, future Lord of the Beveridge Plan, and other well-intentioned intellectuals of the Liberal Party, who proposed to revive it with new ideas. To that end the associates, known as the Grasmere group from their Lake Country meeting place in the summer of 1921, had acquired control of *The Nation*, the control thus devolving on Keynes and his money power. As the journal's chairman Keynes made difficulties for a Grasmere member who expected the position, and established his Cambridge economist friend Hubert Henderson as editor, with Leonard Woolf as literary editor. Cambridge and Bloomsbury in place, Keynes's first issue, on 5 May 1923, carried articles by Virginia Woolf and Lytton Strachey, the latter to write eighteen of them. Keynes had brought outstanding talents to his new enterprise but failed to repair one outstanding deficiency.

The Nation began with a programmatic statement that demanded "radical social change" but lapsed into the confession, "[T]he ideas of all of us are so confused and incomplete." Although it would have its "center well to the left," it tried to keep a clear distance from the alleged "nakedness of Labour policy."[27] Here Keynes exposed his group's dilemma doubled. He was correctly criticizing the Labour Party's poverty in ideas, but he could only offer his own group's unique confusion as alternative. Furthermore it was jostling Labour for a place on the left and risked being identified too closely with it, as *The Nation* itself had already become under its departed editor. The confusion confession, while disarming, made matters worse. Although Keynes was a triumphant pol-

itician within an elite of dons, economists, and establishment people, his negative instincts for democratic politics betrayed him. No Asquith or Lloyd George
would inaugurate a great new campaign by proclaiming he did not know what
to do.

Keynes expanded on these unpolitic thoughts in two other programmatic statements to his fellow Liberals. Beginning in 1922 the Grasmere group held Liberal
Summer Schools of instruction and presumably inspiration alternately at Oxford
and Cambridge, the locations emphasizing their elitist character. At a session in
Cambridge on 1 August 1925 Keynes began and ended a wry, witty talk, published later that month in *The Nation*, with the sincere question, "Am I a Liberal?" Again he offered discouragement: "The *positive* argument for being a
Liberal is, at present, very weak." Faithful to his revolutionary pact with Lytton,
meanwhile, Maynard advocated birth control, free use of contraceptives, marriage law reform, and tolerant "treatment of sexual offenses and abnormalities."
He insisted, "I cannot doubt that Sex Questions are about to enter the political
arena."[28] He was being prophetic more than political; his timing was off by
more than a generation. The next February he told the Manchester Reform Club
that the Liberal Party would never again be "a great party machine" like the
two other parties, but placed his trust in its immaterial power to "play ... a
predominant part in molding the future."[29] He did not elucidate.

Keynes was consciously using *The Nation* and his position in the Liberal
Party defensively—against the negative thrust of events. At least he had evaluated that correctly.

Internationally, also operating as journalist, Keynes built on the logic of *The
Economic Consequences*. In the late summer of 1921, defensively also, he had
published five articles in the London *Sunday Times* arguing a cause-and-effect
relationship between the reparations (and war debt) burden and the depression
beginning to invade England.[30] He assembled the articles and related writings
into *A Revision of the Treaty*, published in January 1922 as a sequel to the first
book.[31] In 1922 he expanded his journalistic activities in two projects for the
Manchester *Guardian*. The first was coverage as special correspondent of the
Genoa Conference, meeting from 10 April to 19 May 1922. Lloyd George was
using the conference to resolve the reparations issue within a general economic
settlement and failing with both.[32] (That was the great man's last throw as
coalition prime minister; in October the Conservatives would revolt and take
power alone under Bonar Law, Lloyd George joining Keynes in the wilderness.)
Certainly the best paid journalist at the conference, Keynes could, at least, use
his reporting as another argument for right reason on all the economic questions
so stirred up. Beginning at the time of the conference and extending to January
1923, he also mounted a great positive effort, which consisted of the twelve
Reconstruction Supplements of the Manchester *Guardian Commercial*. Covering
810 huge pages, the supplements surveyed and tried themselves to assist the
solution of the European economic problems. Keynes wrote a number of the

articles while persuading some two hundred distinguished experts and leaders from Arthur Pigou and Basil Blackett to H. H. Asquith and the Queen of Rumania to write the others. Most of the collaborators provided the expected technical suggestions or political pap, and no one, Keynes included, offered acceptable plans of any significance.

Keynes's concluding article, "The Underlying Principles," matched his programmatic statements for British Liberalism with both discouragement and utopian proposals. He found "[e]very one of our religious and political constructions . . . moth-eaten." He went on to advocate disarmament and a symmetrical British renunciation of force to maintain the empire.[33] More functionally, Keynes was offering expert advice, beginning at Genoa, to address a new series of reparation crises, his efforts culminating, with his supplements, in January 1923. His conception, conciliatory to Germany, was the essence of the official British proposal that his old chief Bonar Law made to a reluctant France at a failed conference on 2–4 January 1923.[34] Instead, on 11 January, the French and Belgians invaded the Ruhr to seize reparations in kind in place of the unforthcoming cash. There followed the German passive resistance, violence, chaos, hyperinflation, Hitler's Beer Hall Putsch of 8–9 November, and economic losses for all. Later, a final initiative of Keynes, who was in Berlin from 1 to 4 June 1924 and collaborated more or less secretly on a German note to Britain, also failed.[35] Afterward came the catharsis that produced the Dawes Plan, which temporarily palliated the reparations and related problems. Keynes turned back to the problems at home, although he engaged in a reparations reprise five years later.

In the March 1929 issue of the *Economic Journal*, during the efforts to shift from Dawes to Young Plan, Keynes argued that payment of reparations remained impossible. His basic thesis was that Germany's competitors, as in the past, would not let the country increase its exports to earn the necessary income. The "economic structures" of the countries involved, he wrote, "permit[ted] . . . a certain 'natural' level of exports and . . . arbitrarily to effect a material alteration of this level . . . is extremely difficult." It followed that the effects on German economy and society would be disastrous. He indulged himself, however, by adding the technically correct but redundant consideration that a forced export increase would require discounting German export prices, thus falsifying initial projections of expected returns and making matters even worse. This licensed his opponents to restrict themselves to hypothetical technical questions. Keynes found himself publishing rebuttals in the June and September issues by the Swedish economist Bertil Ohlin and a French expert, both of whom advanced recondite economic theses avoiding the real problem and the internal situation of Germany. After an elegant demonstration Ohlin admitted, however, that his "theoretical solution" of deliveries in kind was "outside the range of practical possibilities."[36] At the time the German Nationalist Party gave the Nazis the respectability they had hitherto lacked by joining with them in a campaign denouncing reparations and the Young Plan. Hitler was one step away from power. Keynes did not need so much confirmation of his *Economic Consequences*.

Beginning in 1921 the great problem at home, to which Keynes's advice may indeed have contributed, was deflation-and-depression. Reparation together with war debts constituted a simple-minded problem in bookkeeping, but the newer one opened up an illimitable range of economic issues. Although Keynes had begun as a theorist in logic, he was not a natural economic theorist. Indeed, until the 1920s he had little regard for economic science, which he found too easy, as a field for the exercise of pure intellection, and remained content to apply Marshallian analysis as received. As an applied economist he responded to the economic situation with his command of the ad hoc and his inexhaustible talent for improvisation. Despite his irreducible elitism, as his *Economic Consequences* brilliantly demonstrated, his multiple sensitive antennae reached into the major neuralgic centers of society and reported back accurately to his synthesizing intelligence. For this he required little additional theory until the long-enduring British depression of the 1920s began to force it out of him, the world Depression of the next decade completing the process. When he achieved his *General Theory*, he confessed how hard this change in thinking, as revolutionary to himself as to the world, had been. "The composition of this book has been for the author a long struggle of escape . . . a struggle of escape from habitual modes of thought and expression," he wrote in the preface. "The difficulty lies, not in the new ideas, but in escaping from the old ones, which ramify, for those brought up as most of us have been, into every corner of our minds."[37] *The General Theory* itself, later expressions of Keynes concurring, betrays how powerful these "habitual modes" remained in his thought.

As suggested by *The Economic Consequences* despite its radical asides, Keynes had begun the postwar era classically. The wartime defender of the gold standard wasted no regret when Britain was forced to leave it in 1919, but anticipated its restoration in due time. A return would, as he accepted, require monitoring the outflow of gold and raising bank rate, the Bank of England lending rate and determinant of all interest rates, when the gold reserve fell too low. Of course this would have meant deflation. Actually Keynes began the decade strongly urging immediate deflationary action to break the postwar inflation-and-boom when he met with Austen Chamberlain in February 1920. Warning of the pathological effects on British business and the capitalistic system, he advised the chancellor to increase bank rate from 6 to 10 percent.[38] His counsel was too Draconian for the government, which raised it just one point in April. In July Keynes criticized the Treasury as inexcusably faint-hearted in a talk at the Tuesday Club. He said unrepentantly, "I am still a dear money man" and demanded a "drastic and unpleasant cure. And I would do it though I knew I risked a depression and possibly a crisis."[39] The one point was more than sufficient. Unemployment rose from 2.4 percent in 1920 to 14.8 percent in

1921.[40] Keynes expeditiously changed his view about the comparative threats of inflation and deflation. At the time a gold standard return remained an academic question because of Britain's general impoverishment, but the academic Keynes gave his attention to it as well in the university lectures he resumed in the fall of 1920. Although he still thought national existence on the gold standard to be right and inevitable, he insisted that excessive deflation had to be avoided by devaluing the pound.[41] In that projection he was disagreeing with established professional opinion, which refused to conceive of any figure except the old value of $4.86. Contemplating the new unemployment figures, he would change his thinking about the gold standard almost as quickly as about salutary deflation. His self-retraining was beginning.

By the fall of 1921 Keynes had turned against deflation. To cure "The Depression in Trade," as he entitled the third of his *Sunday Times* series (mentioned previously) on reparations and depression, he proposed a countercyclical application of bank rate, thus a reduction. He was optimistic enough to expect recovery and continued even-handedly, "As soon as a boom appears to be in progress, rates for money should be raised at once."[42] A few months later he was more concerned about the deflationary danger. In a long article of 20 April 1922 on the Genoa Conference, although still favoring a return to the "gold standard, in as many countries as possible," he emphasized the need to adjust for depreciated currencies to prevent disastrous deflation.[43] By December, uncannily anticipating Britain's experience, he deplored the action of Czechoslovakia, which had increased the gold value of its currency at the cost of an industrial crisis and unemployment: "To what purpose? I do not know."[44] Proleptically, in reference to his own country, he was protesting the Czech goverment's mindlessness, more dangerous to good policy than simple self-interest or malevolence.

Keynes reacted more quickly and sensitively to the problems of labor, a victim of deflation, than any other major British economist. In a series of four lectures to Britain's Institute of Bankers in November and December 1922 he granted that unemployment was largely due to the comparatively high British wages. Although the cost of living was up 60 percent above the previous level, wages were 80 percent higher, the high wages "compelling us to ask double for our exports." Aware of the humanity of the workers *and* the power of their unions, rejecting his profession's solution of lower wages, he boldly proposed heresy: "The only way [wages] will get into gear will be by an increase in the level of prices."[45] Another condition had to be fulfilled before exports could improve, but Keynes was perhaps too politic to mention it. The pound would have to lose value compared with other currencies, thus devaluation. In a talk to Liberal candidates for Parliament four years later, Keynes articulated his principled and expedient—Burkean—attitude toward the British working man as related to these issues. While noting the "immense destructive force of organized labor," he argued that it behooved the Liberal Party to "treat the gradual betterment of the economic welfare of the workers as the first charge on the national wealth.''[46] Betterment and economic welfare could not permit a 10 percent unemployment rate.

Before the end of 1923 Keynes had publicly given up on the gold standard. In November he published his brief *Tract on Monetary Reform*,[47] which advocated a managed currency. Making no gestures toward recondite theorizing, he borrowed the idea from Irving Fisher, the American monetary economist. Fisher would change the amount of gold returned on presentation of treasury notes or certificates, paper money in any form, in order to counterbalance the rise and fall in price of a commodity index. If it worked, this would mean money of constant value, eliminating both inflation and the greater distress, as Keynes now saw it, of deflation. The *Tract* led to bolder ideas in 1924, which ranged from socialism back to the refinement of neoclassical monetary theory.

Keynes put his broader and more radical views into the title of a lecture he gave at Oxford University on 6 November 1924, "The End of Laissez-Faire." (He repeated the lecture in Berlin in June 1926 and the Hogarth Press published it as a book the next month.)[48] The title expressed the sense which he considered developing in two books he never wrote entitled "Prolegomena to a New Socialism" and, also suggesting a socialist outcome, "An Examination of Capitalism," this latter including the section, "The Decay of Capitalism."[49] He did not get much further than the idea of the demise of laissez-faire and its replacement by a vaguely defined social control of the economy. Publicly, Keynes was not loath to use the word *socialism*. In a letter to *The Times* of 25 March 1925 he attributed to the Bank of England, surely to the surprise of its officers, its character as an example of the "socialism of the future."[50] His letter was part of a debate about the pending return of the nation to the gold standard, the great practical issue of the moment. Keynes was much more concerned about the gold standard at the time, although the notion of socialism, along with his earlier radical speculations, pointed toward an ultimate and revolutionary expression in *The General Theory*. Meanwhile, beginning in July 1924, he had begun his six years of labor on *A Treatise on Money*. In a practical way this ultimate exercise led beyond neoclassical economics to *The General Theory*. The retraining was proceeding steadily.

In 1925, reminiscent of his experience of the Paris Peace Conference six years previously, Keynes could see a consensus irresistibly arriving at a damagingly wrong-headed decision. In February 1920 the British pound had declined to $3.40 from its gold standard level of $4.86, but then it rose to $4.63 by the end of 1922. Although it failed to stay there but fell to $4.28 in January 1924, it gathered itself and began confidently to rise. The perverse nature of the problem is suggested by the fact that an important cause was the belief of the international financial community that it would do so.[51] Combined variously with the subjective, a number of more or less objective factors were lifting sterling very nearly to parity at $4.86 in the free market place. These included England's standing as a financial center, a measure of financial backing by the United

States, England's economic stability despite a deep undertow of unemployment, and the more spectacular weaknesses of most of Europe's economies and currencies. Money tended to flow toward the City as a traditional safe haven. All of this, Keynes argued correctly and unavailingly, falsified the market valuation of sterling. He would not have fought so desperately if the pound were to be devalued, as he had earlier proposed, but that question was excluded because, obedient to the mystique radiating around gold, a devalued gold pound would have been too shocking to contemporary thinking. A return to the gold standard meant parity.

Once again the postwar Keynes was arriving at a critical point promising failure for him. He fought the coalescing decision almost single-handedly. His only significant supporter was Reginald McKenna, his old chief at the Treasury, who was now chairman of one of the five major joint stock banks. With his background in politics and affairs McKenna escaped the dogmas of the financial community but suffered from a politic tendency to flinch under pressure. Against Keynes were arrayed the City, the Treasury, the Bank of England, and even the Labour Party. In power for the first time, albeit only from January to November 1924, Labour was trying to demonstrate its sense of financial responsibility. Crippled by the fact that its socialism said nothing about free-market economics, it was submitting to neoclassical theory until the day its utopia would transform matters. In May 1924 Philip Snowden, chancellor of the exchequer and a grimly obedient student of the old economics, named a committee under his Conservative predecessor, Austen Chamberlain, to plan the return. The Conservative victory in the election that fall generated the financial confidence to float the pound higher—to $4.74, only a 2.5 percent gap, by January 1925. Arguing that the real gap, as still falsified by misguided opinion, was 10 percent, Keynes countered the consensus with a series of articles in *The Nation*.

Together with McKenna, however, Keynes faltered in a crucial battle for the mind of Winston Churchill, Conservative chancellor of the exchequer from 1924 to 1929. Churchill was trying to live down his Liberal past, but had a fine sensitivity to the situation—and the politics—of the working class, and demanded hard argument, if not proof. On 17 March 1925 he gave a dinner to the disputants, who included, besides Keynes and McKenna, Otto Niemeyer of the Treasury (who had beaten Keynes for the Treasury position in the civil service examination of 1906) and John Bradbury (a former Treasury permanent secretary, from 1920 to 1925 occupied with demanding reparations from Germany as principal British representative on the Reparations Commission). Against the experts and the political ambiance McKenna had to admit that Churchill had no alternative but the old gold standard, and Keynes, according to a reliable witness, said nothing to this.[52] Probably he refused to waste his spirit on one more hopeless effort; it would be unkind to suggest that he had flinched. With the official return on 28 April 1925 Britain had locked itself into a state of deflation and unemployment, which would be relieved only after more than a decade. If Keynes had been defeated at this critical point, he located others and acted with his more characteristic confidence to ameliorate the succession of horrid results.

Keynes now found himself in substantial agreement with Lloyd George, after his passionate disagreement on the peace the prime minister had made. On 8 May 1925 he wrote, "My dearest tender Lydochka . . . I had a terrible flirtation with Ll. G. yesterday, and have been feeling ashamed of myself ever since!" He explained, "[W]e had a tête-à-tête lunch . . . in which . . . he declared himself to be against gold and in favor of birth control. . . . He was slightly pathetic and forlorn, without a friend or intimate in the world . . . and that helped to melt my heart." The great man had also volunteered the opinion that their "Liberal Party was in quite a hopeless position," an acute judgment that could dampen their best hopes.[53] But both men had resilient optimism. The flirtation, which would become an affair of convenience into 1929, had actually begun more than one year earlier, when Lloyd George and Keynes had joined in trying to do something about unemployment. In his own wilderness since his government fell in 1922, Lloyd George had resumed his radical character and held a conference on 25–27 March 1924 to develop an unemployment policy. Keynes, using the occasion to expatiate on his new ideas, contributed a speech urging a bank rate reduction and a money-supply expansion.[54] Entering his *Nation* in his service, he opened its columns on 12 April to an article by Lloyd George calling for large-scale public works. Keynes himself pursued the thought the next month with his *Nation* article, "Does Unemployment Need a Drastic Remedy?" His answer, demanding more inflationary action, was enthusiastically affirmative.[55] The deflationary current, however, swept these complicit politicians backward.

Dashing another old relationship, Keynes flaunted his affair with Lloyd George on the occasion of the General Strike of 1926. Soon after the gold standard return, in July 1925, Keynes had predicted such dire effects in a series of newspaper articles immediately expanded and published as the pamphlet *The Economic Consequences of Mr. Churchill*. He characterized Churchill's statements as "feather-brained" and asked, "Why did he do such a silly thing?" The government was "intensifying unemployment deliberately in order to reduce wages," thus to compensate for the overvalued pound. He emphasized the situation of the miners.[56] When the workers took action, Keynes was sympathetic, if not quite supportive.

On 1 May 1926 the miners, militant and their wages under particular threat by the economy action, went on strike. With the support of the Trades Union Congress, the transport, iron and steel, building, and printing workers made it general two days later. But the government, backed by middle-class volunteers, called it illegal and broke the general strike in nine days, the miners staying out for seven months before drifting back on their employers' terms. Keynes saw the conflict as a defeat for all—workers, employers, and the public. Miners lost jobs as uneconomic mines closed. The strike, however, intimidated the employers of other workers and prevented them from reducing wages generally, thus leaving Britain's export prices too high, and business continued bad and unemployment high.

The issues raised by the strike caused great strains in the Liberal Party and severely tested Keynes's position in it. Disagreement on policy toward the strike ended the uneasy reconciliation between Lloyd George and Herbert Asquith, the old radical refusing to condemn the action and the legally minded Asquith upholding law and constitution against the strikers. Mediating among the various tensions, Keynes had to decide between an old chief he had found a crook and one who had been his patron and host for many years. As an honest Machiavellian politician, he had no difficulty in affirming his association with the crook. In a letter in *The Nation* Keynes easily saw Lloyd George as a "bad colleague . . . responsible in the past for wrong and disastrous policies" but still supported him against Asquith, and an unsigned item had found him "triumphantly and unmistakably in the right."[57] The aging Asquith, who suffered a slight stroke on 12 June 1926, never again spoke to Keynes. He died in early 1928.

Lloyd George could give Keynes new opportunities for action against deflation and Britain's other ills. A related problem was the Liberal Party's impotence. The election of October 1924, which had ended the Labour Party's brief first administration, had nearly annihilated the Liberals, who went from 159 (in December 1923) to 40 seats. When it came to general politics, Keynes's instinct for critical points was lacking or even negative. Yet he would be able to eke out his kind of victory from alien defeat, although slowly, and tortuously. In 1926, at one with him, Lloyd George proposed economic reform and Liberal revival. Using funds from an old election campaign, he financed the Liberal Industrial Inquiry, which mobilized Grasmere group members, among others, to produce the book-and-program, *Britain's Industrial Future*, by January 1928. Of course Keynes contributed energetically, writing a substantial part of it and influencing its vague suggestion of countercyclical public works.[58] He contributed even more energetically in the election campaign of May 1929.

The ad hoc politics of the election enriching his thought, Keynes produced the first element of his new theory. Lloyd George promising to reduce the unemployment figure by more than a half million in a year, Keynes backed him with a primitive form of *The General Theory*'s famous multiplier.[59] The idea was that the employment arising from a public works increase would generate successive waves of additional income and demand, which would generate additional employment. Britain's voters treated the Liberals unfairly for being the only party with ideas, which the Conservatives disdained as bad economics and Labour would steal along with the election victory. The Liberals increased their representation from forty to fifty-nine, that is to say, they remained moribund. Perversely, the defeat freed Keynes to discard his party politics and, gradually, *The Nation* itself, which he folded into the further left *New Statesman* in February 1931 and let slip away in the next years. Thus he could concentrate his mind wonderfully on the materials for his ultimate achievement. Tortuously he would make his way back from the wilderness.

Keynes's relationship with the reformed and reforming Lloyd George, left to wander out his life in *his* wilderness, dimmed. In 1933 he returned to his unhappy memories of the peace conference and the other Lloyd George. Another element in his *Economic Consequences* had been the ad hominem, a form of argument that reflected his tendency to take differences personally and play the advocate. Ignoring the period's war hatred and most of the world and its history, he had seen the conference leaders "in a manner never before paralleled . . . in the first months of 1919 [as] the microcosm of mankind." Woodrow Wilson was a "blind and deaf Don Quixote." Keynes asked, "What chance could such a man have against Mr. Lloyd George's unerring, almost medium-like sensibility?" To them and Georges Clemenceau he attributed an amount of power that surely surprised those powerful personages. He said more about Lloyd George, which Asquith, among others, advised him was too true to be published. In 1919 he took that advice. In 1933, compiling his *Essays in Biography*, he could not forbear folding into it his repressed comments, which drew Lloyd George as a *"femme fatale* . . . goat-footed bard, this half-human visitor to our age from the hag-ridden magic . . . of Celtic antiquity," an incorporation of "final purposelessness, inner irresponsibility, existence outside . . . our Saxon good and evil."[60] Taking the newly published comments personally, Lloyd George lustily returned the blows in his presently published *War Memoirs* and denounced Keynes for expertly supporting Reginald McKenna's defeatism and fears about financing the war expenditures. In a letter to *The Times* Keynes granted that "these polite exchanges [were] perhaps as inexcusable on the one side as on the other." He tried to retreat from the ad hominem, on the war if not explicitly on the peace, to remark that a more objective "history and criticism of our financial policy during the war . . . still remains to be written."[61]

In November 1929, just after the Wall Street crash, the Labour government appointed Keynes to a function more appropriate to his genius—policymaker, indeed, policymaker doubled. Philip Snowden, back as chancellor of the exchequer, named him a member of the fifteen-man Committee on Finance and Industry (called the Macmillan Committee after its chairman, a barrister unrelated to the publishing family). Keynes had more than earned the appointment, the committee's mission being to pursue economic improvement essentially along the lines suggested by the Liberal Industrial Inquiry. In the same month Prime Minister J. Ramsay MacDonald also invited Keynes with other experts to advise him on improving his office's economic advice. Maynard and Lydia agreed on the new turn of events in his life, Maynard writing her about the first appointment, "As you said, I am becoming more fashionable again."[62] He had put it precisely. He was not unqualifiedly fashionable, simply less unfashionable, and being fashionable was not his aim anyway. He was not yet, he knew, out of the wilderness. The tensions rising, he would have much more hard fighting against entrenched thought and policy.

The extensively, if incompletely, retrained Keynes ran as hard as he could with the new set of opportunities. Probably no other economist showed so swift and sure a sense of the developing magnitude of the economic disaster. He acted with his characteristic expeditiousness, much as he had done in the war crisis of 1914. In early December he fired two memoranda at MacDonald, the first proposing emergency action attacking unemployment that comprehended co-operative and self-sacrificing efforts by employers, unions, and banks, and the second, a kind of economic general staff to guide the government guiding the economy, this latter with a view toward possible redistribution of income, among other objectives.[63] The sum, except for the sacrifices openly demanded, was a British New Deal, more than three years before the American. In the event none of the interest groups would agree to such sacrifices as easier credit or a wage freeze for a year, while the political forces would not grant an economic general staff the authority Keynes wanted for it. Although his emergency program vanished, the economic body became the Economic Advisory Council (EAC), holding its first formal meeting on 17 February 1930. It became a modest advisory group with a small permanent staff and experts like Keynes who met with the prime minister once a month. Keynes had to see Britain muddling through the great Depression as it had muddled through everything else. Impressing, if not necessarily persuading MacDonald, Keynes worked intensely on the EAC for a year. He had to overcome the effects of occasional tactlessnesses, once hurting MacDonald's feelings by remarking, more accurately than not, that he was "the only socialist present."[64] He nevertheless was able to place Hubert Henderson, departing the sinking *Nation*, as the EAC's senior economist, and Richard F. Kahn, a brilliant student of his and collaborating theorist, as a joint secretary, and led a committee to recommend tariffs as a prime recovery measure. In this, completing a long journey away from free trade, he had selected the more politically possible over the economically desirable, which, for him, was public works and departure from the gold standard. But Lionel Robbins, a younger economist at the beginning of a distinguished career, clung enragingly to free-trade principle and frustrated Keynes's desire for a unanimous committee recommendation. Keynes attempted to bully Robbins with his famous, in this case, purposeful rudeness, but Robbins was resolute and documented his dissent.[65] It made no difference. Snowden was a classical free-trader, and the cabinet did not even consider the Keynes committee's (less-than-unanimous) plan, submitted in October 1930, until December and abruptly dismissed it as unworthy of serious thought. (The EAC itself faded away although it led to successor bodies, eventually the contemporary Economic Section of the Cabinet Office.) Keynes went on trying with the Macmillan Committee.

One other person had similar ideas for aggressive action. He was Oswald Mosley, then a noncabinet member of the Labour government, who wanted a £200-million public works program and won Keynes's cautious encouragement. In May 1930, when his plan got no more support than Keynes's proposals, Mosley resigned, presently founding the transitional New Party, and, by 1932, a fascist movement. By then he represented one more danger to Keynes, who told Mosley he was doing his best to save the country from him.[66]

One other omnicompetent economist had reformist ideas approximating Keynes's, although he carefully distanced himself from the spectacular theses of *The General Theory*. He was Walter Layton, whose career uncannily paralleled Keynes's. Conceived about the time Keynes was born, Layton studied economics under Arthur Pigou and, although failing to join the Apostles by mutual agreement, won first-class honors in the Cambridge economics tripos in 1904. In 1908 he was the other supernumerary economics lecturer installed along with Keynes on Pigou's charity. "But Keynes usually outshone him." Layton's intellectual ambitions were limited to a study of prices, but as a variously applied economist like Keynes he engaged in valuable government service in both World Wars. Unlike Keynes he established himself in a series of solid institutional positions (after a period as an appreciated personal assistant to Lloyd George) and never had to wander a wilderness of disregard. He was editor of the influential *Economist* from 1922 to 1938 and also editorial director and then chairman in the 1930s of the *News Chronicle*, a major newspaper. Layton had been a member of the Grasmere group and later tactfully chaired the Liberal Industrial Inquiry, where Keynes had less tactfully and more humbly served. In the 1930s, leaving the theorizing to Keynes, Layton was advocating the same economic policies, namely "moderate inflation coupled with government intervention," as his biographer put it.[67] Less adventurous privately, Layton married young and contentedly, and fathered three sons and four daughters, but like Maynard Keynes, was a compulsive worker and, like Geoffrey Keynes, neglected his children. Professionally cooperative and unrivalrous, the two economists had little personal in common; the Keynes Papers contain a few official communications between them but not one personal letter. Living two decades longer than Keynes, serving responsibly to the end of his life, Layton was one of the stalwarts bearing Britain on their shoulders. His importance, so precisely fitted to his era, disappeared with it while Keynes's aggressive genius was expanding exponentially beyond his own time and place.

The Macmillan Committee required longer labors than did the EAC, with more than one hundred meetings, forty-nine of them spent boringly taking repetitive, interested evidence from representatives of the economic groups affected. Keynes balanced adeptly between theory and improvisation. Correcting the final proofs of his *Treatise on Money* at the time, he was using them to lecture to his committee colleagues and attempting to develop policy with its basic conception. But that conception, constructed around the relation of investment to saving, was both sterile and inapplicable usefully to the Depression, as he would presently admit by abandoning the book and writing *The General Theory*. The committee members, anticipating Keynes and the general consensus, were not persuaded.[68] A Treasury man even gave Keynes a lesson in the exposition of theory.

Sir Richard Hopkins, the department's controller of finance, resisted Keynes's call for public works with the famous "crowding-out" argument. This was the thesis that such increased expenditures would increase the demand for funds, raise the interest rates, and thus crowd the weaker private enterprises out of the money market, canceling any apparent initial advantages. In pure theory this cannot be refuted, certainly not with Keynes's marvelous multiplier, although, as he would later demonstrate, inflation could outflank the problem. But, given the general fear of it, the German hyperinflation as grotesque example, he had to avoid the issue. It would have defeated his own purposes to blurt out the fact that public works would resolve the crowding-out problem precisely because they were inflationary and might thus reverse a slump situation. Rather, he found it politic to deny that effect. At the Macmillan Committee session Hopkins could hold his ground easily on crowding-out and double the negative, furthermore, by pointing out the pragmatics. Big projects required so much time for planning, preparation, and satisfying all kinds of restrictive laws that they could not reduce unemployment in time. At the end Chairman H. P. Macmillan judicially called the encounter a draw, hence a defeat for Keynes.[69]

Nevertheless, Keynes could fluently demonstrate his greatness as applied economist. Over three sessions in late February and early March 1930 he discoursed on seven remedies with a profound and delicate sense of British society as it then functioned and felt. The possibilities were slipping off the gold standard, wage reductions, subsidies to employers to maintain wages, industrial rationalization, protection, public works, and international banking cooperation.[70] He had to grant the political impossibility of departing from gold, labor's obstinacy on reducing wages, the long lags in achieving results from efficiency or banking improvements and even the difficulties in his favored public works and protection. He gave a superb series of lectures, but he knew only too well that the question was not academic, that the world's worsening economic situation meant a piling up of disasters as correctives failed to work.

As Keynes wrote to Montagu Norman, the powerful and enduring governor of the Bank of England, "I twist and turn about trying to find some aid to the situation, even if only temporary." This introduced a long letter in late May 1930 recommending to bank and banker an intricate set of actions orchestrating an increase in the supply of Treasury bills with the purchase of long-dated securities. Of course Keynes's objective with these subtleties, consistent with his long-term policy since he stopped being a dear-money man, was the simple one of forcing interest rates down as low as possible to enliven enterprise. He achieved an interview with the busy and reluctant governor one month later, and Norman unsurprisingly proved impervious to his twistings and turnings.[71] Indeed they sometimes strained logic beyond comprehension to bankers as well as ordinary mortals. One year earlier Keynes had visited the Treasury to propose to Richard Hopkins and a colleague that bank rate, thus interest rates generally, should be raised! His reasoning was that higher rates would attract funds from abroad and so increase investment money available to British business.[72] Of course more money would have flowed into the country, but Keynes was refusing to see for the moment that, as he knew only too well, the higher interest rates would have *discouraged* investment and business. In the dark night of a confused time he had reversed direction so abruptly that he crashed full tilt into himself.

Keynes's desperate improvisations deserve forgiveness. With his command of the economic factors he could see too clearly that government and financial community had preempted the great policy questions with the huge and totally wrong answers of reparations (and war debt) policy and deflation. In 1926, in *The Nation*, one of his many croakings on the subject noted the presence of "the worm of deflation" in Germany under the pressure of the Dawes Plan. " 'Sound finance' has Germany by the throat, just as it has England."[73] He was forced to settle not for second or third best, but sixth or tenth best. Thus bad policy led to the drain of funds out of England, and he gave himself the problem of devising means of holding them back. In a Liberal Summer School talk in 1924 he had been led to question the value of the traditional free-trade policy of foreign investment. He went so far as to "see no special virtue in exports." But the corrective he suggested was a desperate triviality. He would repeal the Trustee Acts, which permitted trustees managing British funds to buy colonial securities. Besides angering the colonies, repeal would have retained in England an absurdly small sum that he disdained to calculate.[74] That year—the year when he had joined Lloyd George in addressing unemployment—he made a much more ambitious, if naïvely Machiavellian, suggestion. He would use the Treasury's sinking fund not for its classically deflationary function of debt retirement, but to finance public works at the magnitude of £100 million, so achieving a fine inflationary effect. Accused of inflationary designs, he airily defended himself, "My heresy consists in proposing not to abolish (or raid) the sinking fund, but to use it."[75] Of course it meant inflation, which he had been urging tirelessly, the means usually in the form of lower interest rates, from 1922 until armament expenditures later in the 1930s made such advice unnecessary. (His momentary reversal on his Treasury visit to Richard Hopkins is not to be taken so tragically.) Inflation was a simple solution to the simple, government-generated problem of deflation. In the desperate summer of 1930 an M. P. parodied the faith of those few who agreed: "I believe in one J. M. Keynes, the Lord & Giver of Inflation, who with Lloyd George & Sir Oswald together is worshipped & glorified, who spake through *The Nation*."[76]

On 13 July 1931, having labored too long, the Macmillan Committee produced a report saying too much too inconclusively.[77] Keynes himself had engaged in thirty drafting sessions. Radically discontent with it, he tried to save something by writing an addendum, signed by a sympathetic six of the fifteen members, demanding more acutely defined and positive action, but he could think of nothing more than protection and public works as politically possible, while he had to soften his ideas to gain his subgroup's assent. Another committee member, John Bradbury of reparations and the gold standard return and the most purely negative personage in Keynes's professional life, wrote a "memorandum of dissent" opposing all economic intervention as delaying a natural recovery. None of it mattered.

Dead old ideas and wretched events annihilated the Macmillan Committee's work. During its last months, in February 1931, Parliament created a new committee specifically instructed to bring forward an economy program, thus pile deflation on deflation. Its alarmist report, published on 31 July and emphasizing the threats to Britain's economic situation, eliminated any lingering attention to the Macmillan report. At the same time the country was beginning to feel the tremors from the continental banking crisis, which had begun on 11 May with the collapse of Austria's leading bank, the Creditanstalt, and was spreading through Germany. The only answer the international financial community knew was economy to reduce the British government's deficit, still more deflation. On 4 August, the majority of the Labour Party at last rebelling, MacDonald found himself at the head of a "national government" chiefly staffed by Conservatives grimly pursuing economy.

The situation was too much for economy. On 5 August Keynes had grimly responded to a query from MacDonald on his opinion of the economy committee's recommendation: "[M]y views are not fit for publication."[78] With gold draining from Britain, the new government's promises of financial virtue won it puny, fearful loans of £85 million in New York and Paris. On 21 September it was forced off the gold standard, Keynes later commenting on the "lucky way" it had at last happened.[79] The consequent devaluation helped the country more than any other action, however elegant, could have done. Unemployment halted at 22.5 percent in 1932, receding to 17.7 percent in 1934, 14.3 percent in 1936, and 11.3 percent in 1937, rearmament and war ending the problem. The urgency over, his experience immensely enriched and his retraining complete, Keynes was developing his grand systemic cure: the ultimate critical point, this one of his own creation. His wilderness wandering was over.

NOTES

1. Letter, 16 March 1919, KP, PP/45/168.

2. Dennis H. Robertson, former student returned from the war to become a junior colleague, review, *The Economic Consequences, Economic Journal* 30 (March 1920): 77–84; quotation, 77.

3. League of Nations, Secretariat: Economic, Financial and Transit Department, *Industrialization and Foreign Trade* (New York, 1945), 12.

4. *CW*, 2: 120–21.

5. Ibid., 169.

6. Ibid., 1, 11–13, 148–49. A researcher could not find the statement in Lenin's writings: Frank W. Fetter, "Lenin, Keynes and Inflation," *Economica* 44 (February 1977): 77–80.

7. Both estimates, given as loose approximations because of the many statistical problems, Étienne Weill-Raynal, *Les réparations allemandes* (Paris, 1947): 3: 769–71.

8. Karl Erich Born, *Die deutsche Bankenkrise* (Munich, 1967), 16.

9. *CW*, 9: xvii.

10. "An End to Reparations?" *New Statesman*, 16 January 1932, *CW*, 18 (*Activities 1922–1932: The End of Reparations*), 366–69; quotation, 366–67. Brüning–Keynes talk, editorial note, ibid., 364. Walther G. Hoffmann, *Das Wachstum der deutschen Wirtschaft seit der Mitte des 19. Jahrhunderts* (Berlin, 1965), 520–21 (table).

11. Harrod, *The Life*, 283, 294. Chamberlain's notes and JMK's memorandum on his oral counsel, *CW* 17 (*Activities 1920–1922: Treaty Revision and Reconstruction*), 180–84.

12. Letter, 22 December 1917, *CW*, 17: 11, 12.

13. Letter, 25 February 1921, ibid., 219.

14. Letter, 16 December 1919, KP, PP/45/316.

15. Letters, 6 August, 3 September 1919, KP, PP/45/168.

16. Account drawing on *CW*, 12 (*Economic Articles and Correspondence: Investment and Editorial*), 1–647, which has detailed studies of Keynes as investor, his investment policy and insurance work, and his experiences with commodities. Relevant aspects summarized in Felix, *Biography of an Idea* (New Brunswick, NJ, 1995), 44–48. See also analysis in Moggridge, *MK*, 348–52, 407–11, 585–86.

17. Separate letters, FAK and JNK to JMK, 27 June 1919, KP, PP/45/168.

18. Harrod, *The Life*, 220, 289.

19. Virginia Woolf, *The Diary*, 2: 40, 20 May 1920.

20. Letter, JMK to Cassel, 26 May 1920. Other details on subsequent developments, *CW*, 12: 6–8, and editorial note, ibid., 8–17, including tables of JMK's assets and investment income, 1919–45, among other data.

21. Letter, 29 September 1925, quoted Holroyd, *Lytton Strachey*, 2: 517.

22. JMK's memoranda, *CW*, 12: 267–647; quotation (from his first memorandum), 311.

23. Tables, JMK's assets, 1919–45, 1905–13, ibid., 4, 11.

24. Letter, 28 August 1914, KP, PP/45/168.

25. Letter, JMK to O. T. Falk, 18 September 1931, and editorial note, *CW*, 20: 611–12.

26. Virginia Woolf, *The Letters*, 4: 118, 30 December 1929. JMK bought the car from the wealthy manufacturer Samuel Courtauld (see later), who acquired a new model.

27. Editorial Forward, *CW*, 18: 125–26.

28. "Am I a Liberal?," 8, 15 August 1925, *The Nation, CW*, 9: 298, 302–3.

29. "Liberalism and Labour," also published in *The Nation*, 20 February 1926, ibid., 311.

30. The sum entitled "Europe's Economic Outlook," ibid., 17: 242–78 (including related material).

31. Reprinted as vol. 3 of the *CW*.

32. See Carole Fink, *The Genoa Conference* (Chapel Hill, N.C., 1984), and Felix, *Walther Rathenau*, 127–46.

33. Published 4 January 1923, *CW*, 17: 448–54; quotation, 449.

34. JMK's plan (23 December 1922), ibid., 18: 97–99.

35. Editorial notes, ibid., 158–61, 165; JMK's article, 16 June 1923, praising his own handiwork in the German note, ibid., 165–66; Chancellor Wilhelm Cuno's message thanking JMK, also 16 June, ibid., 171.

36. Keynes, "The German Transfer Problem," *Economic Journal*, March 1929, *CW*, 11 (*Economic Articles and Correspondence: Academic*), 451–59; quotation, 457–58; his rejoinder, *Economic Journal*, June 1929, ibid., 468–72; "A Reply by Mr. Keynes," *Economic Journal*, September 1929, ibid., 475–80. Ohlin, "The Reparation Problem: A Discussion," *Economic Journal* 39 (June 1929): 172–82; quotation, 178; and "A Rejoinder from Prof. Ohlin," *Economic Journal* 39 (September 1929): 400–404. Jacques Rueff, "A Criticism by Mr. Jacques Rueff," *Economic Journal* 39 (September 1939): 388–99.

37. *CW*, 7: viii.

38. Ibid., 17: 180–84 (as noted in n. 11).

39. Talk of 8 July 1920, ibid., 184–85. See also Susan Howson, " 'A Dear Money Man': Keynes on Monetary Policy, 1920" and D. E. Moggridge and Susan Howson, "Keynes on Monetary Policy, 1910–1946," *JMK: Critical Assessments*, John Cunningham Wood, ed. (London and Canberra, 1983), 1: 442–71.

40. B. R. Mitchell, *European Historical Statistics 1750–1970* (New York, 1978: abridged), tables, 66, 69.

41. KP, University Affairs (hereafter UA)/6/24.

42. "The Depression in Trade," *CW*, 17: 259–65; quotation, 264.

43. Subtitled "A Plan for Genoa," ibid., 355–69; quotation, 356.

44. "The Stabilization of the European Exchanges, II," 7 December 1922, ibid., 18: 70–84; quotation, 78.

45. Ibid., 19 (*Activities 1922–1929: The Return to Gold and Industrial Policy*), part 1: 6–76; quotations, 67, 66.

46. "Liberalism and Industry," 5 January 1927, ibid., pt. 2: 638–48; quotations, 639, 646.

47. Reprinted as vol. 4 of the *CW*.

48. Reprinted, ibid., 9: 272–94.

49. R. M. O'Donnell, "The Unwritten Books and Papers of J. M. Keynes," *History of Political Economy* 24 (Winter 1992): 807–10.

50. *CW*, 19, pt. 1: 348.

51. On the whole process see D. E. Moggridge, *British Monetary Policy 1924–1931: The Norman Conquest of $4.86* (Cambridge, 1972).

52. P. J. Grigg (Churchill's principal private secretary), *Prejudice and Judgment* (London, 1948), 182–95.

53. KP, PP/190.

54. *CW*, 19, pt. 1: 82–93.

55. 24 May 1924, ibid., 219–23.

56. Ibid., 9: 207–30; quotations, 210, 212, 213.

57. JMK's letter on Lloyd George as a "bad colleague," 12 June 1926, ibid., 19, pt. 2: 538–41; quotation, 541. Item in "Events of the Week," *The Nation* 39 (29 May 1926): 195.

58. Liberal Industrial Inquiry, *Britain's Industrial Future* (London, 1928).

59. In JMK's pamphlet, *Can Lloyd George Do It?*, *CW*, 9: 86–125; the multiplier (not yet named), 102–10.

60. Ibid., 2: 17, 25–26. "Mr. Lloyd George, A Fragment," ibid., 10: 20–26; quotations, 22–23.

61. Quoted from *The Times*, 18 November 1933, Harrod, *The Life*, 440–41.

62. 25 November 1929, KP, PP/190.

63. "The Industrial Situation" (undated) and "Economic General Staff," 10 December 1929, *CW*, 20 (*Activities 1929–1931: Rethinking Employment and Unemployment Policies*): 18–22, 22–27.

64. Quoted from the diary of Hugh Dalton, Clarke, *The Keynesian Revolution* (Oxford, 1988), 160.

65. Lionel Robbins, *Autobiography of an Economist* (London, 1971), 150–53.

66. Sir Oswald Mosley, *My Life* (London, 1968), 178–83; Robert Skidelsky, *Oswald Mosley* (London, 1975), 171, n. 305–6.

67. David Hubback, *No Ordinary Press Baron: The Life of Walter Layton* (London, 1985), 22, 93.

68. Committee discussions, 20 February–7 March 1931, *CW*, 20: 38–157. JMK admitted that his remedy of lower interest rates would not work "if there are no . . . borrowers ready to come forward" (149).

69. Hopkins testimony, 16, 22 May 1930, *CW*, 20: 166–79.

70. Sessions of 28 February and 6, 7 March 1930, ibid., 94–117, 119–57.

71. Letter, 22 May 1930, ibid., 350–56; related material and correspondence, 345–49, 357.

72. According to a communication by Hopkins' colleague, F. W. Leith-Ross, to Churchill, 12 March 1929, quoted, Clarke, *The Keynesian Revolution*, 91. Clarke reports JMK's recommendation without remarking on the reversal of his usual advice. Similarly, Skidelsky simply notes the Treasury's baffled reaction to JMK's "endless ingenuity," *JMK*, 2: 302.

73. "Germany's Coming Problem," *The Nation*, 6 February 1926, *CW*, 18: 271–76; quotations, 274, 275.

74. "Foreign Investment and National Advantage," talk published in *The Nation*, 9 August 1924, ibid., 19, pt. 1: 275–84; quotation, 283.

75. "Does Unemployment Need a Drastic Remedy?" (cited above) *The Nation*, 24 May 1924, ibid., 219–23; and ". . . Reply to Critics," *The Nation*, 7 June 1924, ibid., 225–31, quotation, 225.

76. From the diary of Hugh Dalton, quoted, Clarke, *The Keynesian Revolution*, 158–59.

77. Committee on Finance and Industry, *Report*, Cmd. 3897 (London, 1931; reprint, 1969).

78. Letter, *CW*, 20: 590.

79. JMK's notes for a talk at the (London) Political Economy Club, 11 November 1931, ibid., 21: 12.

CHAPTER 7

Life with Lydia:
An Affair of State

The profound change in Keynes's private life effected by and with Lydia immediately thereafter provided a totally secure base for his public activities. Until then Bloomsbury had been his strength, a substantial one but, as has been seen, shaken by its competitive personalities and differences in life philosophy. However powerful a public man and (forcing doubt into his subterranean chambers) certain in belief, Maynard was at his most vulnerable and weakest in dealing with Lytton Strachey's mocking criticism, Duncan's uncaptureability in the face of his incompletely exhausted yearning, the claims on him and rigorous judgment of Vanessa, who was even more powerful than he privately, and Virginia and Leonard's half-damped dislike and disapproval. With Lydia he became complete, his private and public characters a unity.

Maynard's capture of Lydia, or rather, their capture of each other, required profound, long-resented readjustments in Bloomsbury. As Vanessa's immediate reaction showed, she would not give up her honestly earned share of Maynard without a war. She called on her virtuosity in human relationships to resist Lydia's intrusion. As great managers of feelings and life's realities, Vanessa and Maynard had spun numerous bonds between each other in their feelings as well as in material arrangements. When Lydia appeared they were sharing, inter alia, Duncan, Gordon Square, Charleston, and, besides long membership in Bloomsbury, participation in the Syndicate, one of Maynard's speculation groups. Indeed, together with Duncan of course and buoyed by the Syndicate's early gains, they journeyed to Italy for a six-week excursion from March into May 1920, a kind of belated honeymoon for their ménage à trois.

Maynard Keynes and Lydia Lopokova, c. 1922. Photo courtesy of Milo Keynes.

In Rome the painters painted and the economist wrote. He dined eloquently as well, Maynard being, as he boasted to his mother from Rome, "inconveniently famous and have had to lunch and dine out almost every day." He also profitably arranged for an Italian edition of his *Economic Consequences*. Insouciantly, he reported that his speculative profits in francs made up for his losses in dollars. He was buying vastly with the cheap lira, which had fallen from eighty to one hundred to the pound in two weeks, Maynard writing his father that they had bought nearly a ton of furniture and other weighty objects for 46 Gordon Square in an "orgy of shopping" at "amazingly cheap" prices. Given the bargains, the economist informed his companions, spending was a duty and not gratification of luxurious proclivities. Vanessa bought seventeen pairs of gloves.[1]

The three then descended on Bernard Berenson's villa I Tatti, where a neighboring expatriate also entertained them. At the neighbor's estate Maynard and Duncan exchanged identities to substantiate the host's error, Maynard discoursing on the qualities of the man's Cézannes and Duncan on the devaluation of the lira to the governor of the Bank of Italy. Berenson was not amused when he learned of the doubled deception, his hospitality to Keynes and friends evidently being thenceforth withdrawn for all time.[2] That possibility did not disturb Vanessa, who, knowing that Berenson and Roger Fry had quarreled, wrote Fry, "I'm sure that he has no more notion of what it is that's important in a painting than a flea."[3] Going on to Paris, they saw Picasso and Braque, and Vanessa and Duncan sketched on the quais.

In the second week of May, returned home, the friends found their Syndicate overwhelmed with losses. Florence Keynes comforted her son about "this trouble-some affair. You must not worry too much," and Neville provided substanital comfort in the form of a grant of £2,000 to reduce Maynard's debts.[4] Maynard coolly wrote Vanessa that the financial situation had been "so bad . . . that I thought it better to tell you nothing. . . . For a short time the Syndicate and I had lost every penny we possessed. Now we may . . . have turned the corner." Ominously, he added, "Forgive me if I do in the end (as I may) lose your money." He qualified, "But there is no need to feel the least anxiety for the next days."[5] *But*, according to Virginia's diary (ch. 6), Vanessa had beeen apprised of the losses before she got Maynard's letter. Anyway, at the very least, she could expect the responsible Maynard to make up her losses, and at the anticipated best, that, with his genius for success, he and the Syndicate would emerge with a profit at the end. Vanessa more easily excused him for this wrenching, if temporary, loss of her money than her loss of the man himself to Lydia.

Vanessa's New Year's Day letter of 1922 signaled the opening of the battle. With Duncan and her sons she was then in St. Tropez, in the south of France, and from there worked up negative arguments against Maynard's announced intentions. In his second letter about "my affair with Lydia," on 28 December 1921, he had also written, "Aren't you getting at all homesick[?] I at any rate would like to see you all again.'' Maynard was not letting her go in order to concentrate on Lydia, although he was specifying ''you *all*'' and not just the singular Vanessa. Clearly, he had long accepted Vanessa and Duncan as a unit and simply wanted to enlarge his relations, not change them. For her part Vanessa, in her New Year's response, had surrounded her resistance to Lydia with chatty details keeping Maynard involved in her problems of managing the children, Duncan and Clive, and finding a cure for neck and shoulder pains. At the time Maynard was planning to go to India as vice-chairman of the Tariff Commission of the Government of India, a nomination he owed evidently to his patrons Edwin Montagu, then secretary of state for India, and Lord Reading, now viceroy there. In that letter Vanessa also wrote, ''Flight to India may save you.'' She wanted Maynard and not ''you all.''

In his next letter, dated 6 January 1922, Maynard was delighted that Vanessa was indeed returning to England ''and will certainly pay your return charges. Not least because I am in great need of advice from you.'' But he specified the kind of advice he wanted to hear: ''You needn't be afraid of marriage, but the affair is very serious, and I don't in the least know what to do about it.'' He granted that going to India might be a ''good thing. . . . However she's very adorable.'' He had bought carpets and, including Angelica's nursery, was rearranging their Gordon Square residences.[6] Three days later, on Monday, 9 January, he wrote her that he was going to Amsterdam on Friday, but expected to see her before he left, if she kept to her return schedule. Celebrating the new heights of his relationship with Lydia, he teased further, ''I'm in a terribly bad plight, almost beyond reason. Clive simply grins with delight at seeing me so humbled. However I long to have a gossip with you.'' Sebastian was arriving on Wednesday, but ominously, ''it doesn't interest me!''[7] Vanessa's presence in London did not change matters.

Wanting to develop her painting further in France's encouraging ambiance, Vanessa remained in London only long enough to deposit her sons in boarding schools and find a nurse for Angelica. After a few days she rejoined Duncan, now in Paris, and resumed painting industriously. On 4 February, from a Left Bank hotel, she continued to oppose Lydia and began to deploy Bloomsbury's masculine forces in her cause. There was Duncan: ''But he remains Sphinxlike. He says he cannot write or say anything until he sees for himself but will only remark academically that (as you ought to know) he disapproves of marriage. . . . Give Lydia my love.''[8] In another letter she added the opinion of Clive, who ''says that he thinks it impossible for any one of us, you, he, I or Duncan, to introduce a new wife or husband into the existing circle for more than a week at the time.'' After having mobilized Duncan and Clive, Vanessa went over to the attack on her own: ''Don't think however that what I say is any kind of criticism of Lydia for it isn't. We feel that *no one* can come into the sort of intimate society we have without altering it. . . . That is inevitable, isn't it?'' She referred to the Charleston arrangements for the summer. With not enough room for her, "I'm afraid you may be forced to choose between us and Lydia." While discussing vacation plans only, Vanessa's sense, spilling beyond Charleston, implied a choice for life. Having marvelously complicated matters, she closed, "It all seems horribly complicated and I wish it weren't. Your VB."[9]

Maynard understood Vanessa better than she understood herself. More than eight years later, retailing the latest Bloomsbury gossip to Lydia, he mentioned that Vanessa had spoken "bitterly" about her son Julian's current girlfriend. "I am sure it is partly her deep complex about any of her men attaching themselves to another female—Mary [Hutchinson, by then Clive's ex-mistress], you, Helen Anrep [Roger Fry's ultimate mistress]; it is always the same."[10] Vanessa's daughter Angelica agreed. In her memoir, *Deceived with Kindness: A Bloomsbury Childhood*, she recounted discovering how, as she thought, Vanessa's possessiveness had blocked her own development; "Vanessa clung to Roger, Duncan, myself, and Julian, and perhaps to a lesser degree to Quentin . . . like a limpet."[11] Angelica did not mention Maynard, but her acquaintance with him began only after he was safely Lydia's and Vanessa's claim on him had faded.

Imperturbably, remaining unbreakably, if flexibly, bonded to Vanessa and all of Bloomsbury, Maynard undertook a range of actions around Lydia as his fixed point. On 4 February 1922 *The Sleeping Princess* closed, a few days after Sergei Diaghilev had fled its huge debts; Lydia became a member of the unemployed for the rest of her life except for an occasional free-lance engagement. Maynard took over her finances and installed her in Vanessa's flat at 50 Gordon Square while she was in France. This situation was hardly pleasing to Vanessa, but she was too wise to admit it. On 14 February, Maynard, recovering but weak from an attack of influenza, informed her that Lydia "seems satisfied with the flat and gave an enormous tea party there." One may enjoyably imagine Vanessa's feelings. Ten days later he suggested that Vanessa stay away for another week. Wisely, strategically, Vanessa was gracious and Maynard wrote her on 3 March, "Lydia is very grateful . . . but she feels very apologetic about not moving out."[12] When Vanessa returned, Lydia, finding other rooms there, however, remained at 50 Gordon Square, and, for a period, Vanessa, contrecoeur, rather enjoyed her company. But much remained to be settled.

Another question had been resolved earlier. On 27 January 1922 Maynard wrote Lytton, "I'm not going to India." He explained romantically, "Indeed I'm entangled—a dreadful business—and barely fit to speak to. . . . Ever your affectionate JMK."[13] If Lydia was a sufficient cause for giving up the Indian project, it was not the only one. In the previous fall Maynard had agreed to produce the Manchester *Guardian* Supplements, a sufficient cause in itself. Certainly Lydia was the more important reason, but Maynard had a perfect sense of comparative professional values, and distant work in a colony would have removed him from too many essential and more promising projects in England. The Genoa Conference, which he would cover for the *Guardian*, would further validate his decision. Lord Reading announced himself "intensely disappointed as I regarded Keynes as the pilot to steer the craft into safe waters.''[14] Romantically, pragmatically, Maynard stayed home. The expert on Indian finance never got to India.

Many more readjustments at Gordon Square, correlative with the emotional changes, had to be effected. Maynard had responded to Vanessa's more negative proposals firmly enough to impel her to cohabit with Lydia at 50 Gordon Square, but all agreed that the arrangement was temporary, particularly because Lydia's conversational flow tended to drown Vanessa's painting. On 5 May 1922, writing to Vanessa, he continued the discussion, beginning with a false proposition, as it turned out: ''[W]e must take Clive's leaving No. 46 as a fixed point.'' He continued: Vanessa and her household would remain at No. 50, with Duncan and Maynard at No. 46; Lydia might move to No. 41, residence of James and Alix Strachey, who inhabited the top floors and let out rooms below. Maynard then returned to the placement of Clive, which became a question rather than a proposition as he discussed it: ''[A] great deal depends on whether you can face Clive's leaving the Square. We all want both to have and not to have husbands and wives!''[15] Clive had been thinking of establishing himself with Mary Hutchinson in the Chelsea district, some three London miles away, but Vanessa, as she soon made evident, could not face it and prevailed. The solution was for her and Clive to exchange her No. 50 and his No. 46. One part of Maynard's proposal, Lydia's move to No. 41, did at least come to pass in mid-October. In this Vanessa prevailed as well. James Strachey later remembered his tenant: ''Lydia was on the ground floor and shook the whole house when she practiced her entrechats.''[16] Vanessa, meanwhile, variously continued her campaign against the Maynard–Lydia connection while enjoying Lydia's company more often than not during the rest of 1922. The Bells and the (de facto) Keyneses were still taking meals together at No. 46, but in the fall of 1923 Vanessa, continuing her campaign, set up a separate dining room there for the Bells. She was succeeding in fending off Lydia, but at the cost of losing much of Maynard.

During 1922 both Maynard and Lydia, engaged in their respective concerns, traveled frequently and wrote each other passionately. On 8 April 1922, their relationship firmly established, Maynard left her at 50 Gordon Square and spent three weeks as special correspondent at the Genoa Conference. Lydia had begun a brief dancing engagement with the choreographer-dancer Leonide Massine in Covent Garden, reporting to Maynard on 10 April that Vanessa, Duncan, Clive, and Mary Hutchinson were coming that evening to attend her performance.[17] She was seeing the Bells and Duncan frequently that spring, later in April inviting them to dinner and the cinema and in June enduring a tea party of Clive's with ''as usual great many boring persons.''[18] In June she was dancing in the Colosseum, another entertainment locale in London, and, as she wrote Maynard, a joint group of his and her friends ''all came in.'' Vanessa, who was still being gracious, as Lydia thought, ''said I was 'extraordinary.' I came home with her, we spoke a little.''[19] One could interpret Vanessa's comment less charitably, while Lydia, as her comment on Clive's guests suggested, had a limited taste for Bloomsbury's company and no inhibitions about communicating it.

Charleston remained a problem, although not quite as Vanessa had seen it. On 22 August 1922 she wrote Maynard that she was disappointed at his not having arrived yet. Hardly hospitably, she added, "Please give my love to Lydia and tell her I hope very much she'll come here and not put us off at the last moment. English households cannot be treated like that."[20] Reacting to the complications Vanessa was making, Lydia generated complications of her own and did put Vanessa off. She had been dancing in the north of England and went directly to stay at the country house of her close friends, Vera and Harold Bowen (about whom more follows), in Bedfordshire, not far from Cambridge. Maynard, who had gone to Germany to give a talk to Hamburg bankers, went from there to Charleston alone on 30 August, but remained only until 5 September. So he did find himself making a choice between Lydia and Charleston, but it was Lydia and not Vanessa who managed it. In September the lovers were reunited for three happy weeks in Wiltshire (Clive's home county), some sixty miles west of London, in a house that Maynard had rented from a former associate. So much for Charleston.

The course of alienation did not run smoothly and often reversed itself, Maynard remaining essential to Bloomsbury, and Lydia, however disturbing, too much of an artist and personality to be denied. A week after her move to No. 41 Maynard, temporarily elsewhere, got a letter beginning in Vanessa's hand, "Dearest Maynard," continuing in Duncan's, "We are all absolutely crazy drunk," and concluding more soberly in Lydia's, "We are slightly tipsy. Duncan invited Vanessa and me to a big jug of beer at Gatti's [a well-known café on the Strand, in central London]. We all drank your health and we kiss you, and I too more than anybody."[21] Lydia even got to stay at Charleston, but on a weekend in the spring of 1924 when Vanessa and Duncan were away. Maynard thanked them: "I leave you the bequest of a ham (if the servants don't eat it). I find my love for this place not less. . . . Lydia too is overcome by its beauties." He wanted Vanessa to find out if the neighboring farmhouse called Tilton, a few hundred yards from Charleston, was available: "There's no other county like this."[22] The ham (if it survived) was poor recompense for the threat to plant Lydia nearby. In fact Maynard succeeded that summer in renting Tilton, making him and Lydia as happy as he anticipated. After failing to keep it for the 1925 summer he leased it from 1926 for the rest of his life. Vanessa could never get away from Maynard and Lydia, but then she never quite wanted to let them go.

Virginia's letters and diary refracted her own and Bloomsbury's varying views of Lydia like an eccentric kaleidoscope. She tried out a number of images on Jacques Raverat, an English-educated and -married (to Gwen Darwin, sister of Geoffrey Keynes's Margaret) French painter. Jacques could appreciate them and, crippled with multiple sclerosis, needed entertainment. He could understand that

Virginia, spurning reportorial accuracy, was experimenting with perception and expression in her letters (as she did in her diary) preparatory to further refinement in her novels. In the summer of 1922 she had introduced Lydia to him by way of Maynard's burgeoning success. "Maynard of course scarcely belongs to private life save that he has fallen in love with Lydia Lopokhova, which is, to me, endearing"[23] She changed her mind about Lydia's attractions soon enough and in December wrote Vanessa half-seriously, "Seriously, I think you ought to prevent Maynard before it is too late," when it was far too late. "I can foresee only too well Lydia stout, charming, exacting, Maynard in the Cabinet; 46 the resort of dukes and prime ministers. Maynard being a simple man, not analytic as we are, would sink beyond recall. . . . Then he would awaken, to find three children, and his life entirely and forever controlled."[24] To Bloomsbury such a bourgeois success with aristocratic decor was truly appalling.

Laughing at everybody, Virginia returned to the same theme in two letters to Jacques Raverat two years later. In the first she found Maynard "passionately and even pathetically in love, because he sees very well that he is dished if he marries her, and she has him by the snout." But Bloomsbury was a similarly pitiable spectacle: "You can't argue solidly when Lydia's there, and as we set to the decline, and prefer reason to any amount of high spirits, Lydia's pranks put us all on edge; and Bloomsbury steals off to its dens, leaving Maynard with Lydia on his knee, a sublime but heartrending spectacle."[25] Jacques wanted to know why Maynard was "dished" and Virginia repeated Bloomsbury's majority opinion on Lydia's intelligence: "Because she has the nicest nature in the world and a very limited headpiece. . . . Her contribution [at tea] is one shriek, two dances . . . then silence, like a submissive child, with her hands crossed. . . . And they say you can only talk to Maynard now with words of one syllable."[26]

Earlier, Virginia had complained of Lydia's lack of intelligence, as Bloomsbury defined it, to Vanessa, "Oh dear . . . why must she beg me to believe that she thinks seriously, every day of her life, as she says? When her brain is a cage of canaries?"[27] This last view approximated Lytton Strachey's, who called Lydia more simply a "half-witted canary."[28] When Lytton lay dying, in December 1931, Virginia's diary recorded Maynard as saying that their relationship had become "very thin. . . . They did not go to Ham Spray because Lydia disapproves of the immorality of Carrington."[29] For the tolerant Lydia of the ballet and theater worlds that seemed an odd reason. More likely, although Lytton was always, she remembered, "very kindly and aimiable,"[30] Lydia was surely aware of his opinion of her intelligence; in any case, either found it impossible to talk to the other. But many persons, like Maynard and even Virginia and Vanessa, the latter two complaining the while, found Lydia intelligent, if not intellectual, and enjoyed her shrieks, dances, acute observations, and improvements on English. Another Bloomsbury opinion supported Maynard's, E. M. Forster later saying, "How we all used to underrate her!" H. G. Wells, representing general opinion, said, "She is not only clever for a dancer, but clever for anyone—and

Keynes's brain is the best in the country."[31] Besides her natural, untutored intelligence, what did Maynard see in her?

Lydia was short, the top of her head barely level with Maynard's shoulders, a disparity that disturbed neither. She had a rounded figure and a bird-beaked nose that did not prevent her from being pretty at her infrequent best. Although she usually disdained make-up, and when tired could appear washed-out, her sparkling spirit made her an attractive woman and personality. Her sense of humor, which her letters richly document, expressed itself in enormously effective comic roles on stage and lighted up her many friendships. For the man who could unlock it, she offered a wealth of happy feeling along with immense love.

Lydia was the third of five children of an usher in St. Petersburg's Imperial Alexandrinsky Theater (25 rubles monthly plus tips) of part-Mongolian ancestry and a German-speaking, part-Scotch housekeeper from Estonia.[32] Four of the children, after qualifying for entry, were educated free, another perquisite their father enjoyed, at the Imperial Ballet School, the exception becoming an engineer. One dancing brother, Fyodor V. Lopukhov (1886–1973; Lydia had simplified the family name to Anglo-Saxon taste), became a prominent Soviet choreographer in the 1920s. A conservative in the aesthetics of the ballet, Fyodor could prudently balance his *Ice Maiden*, "a fascinating extension of traditional classicism with *The Red Whirlwind*, an exercise in the agitprop manner."[33] In 1910, when she was 17 or perhaps a year or two older, Lydia threw up her position with the corps de ballet at the Maryinsky Theater and joined Sergei Diaghilev's Ballets Russes for a summer tour of Western Europe.[34] She was, Diaghilev said on further experience of her, "a bit of a bolter,"[35] but meanwhile she displayed the talent that excused her much, and Diaghilev presided over her "remarkable leap" as her brother Fyodor reminisced, from the corps de ballet to the status of principal dancer, frequently partnered by the great Vaslav Nijinsky, as soon as she reached Paris. Fyodor added, "Diaghilev already began to base his box office calculations on her appearances."[36]

As her association with Nijinsky suggested, Lydia was, simply put, a great dancer. Her brother was expressing himself professionally and not fraternally when he evaluated her Paris performances: "Her cheerful nature, the optimistic, youthful joie de vivre of her interpretations, infected audiences; any number she danced ended with thunderous applause." She was not superior in everything by any means: "Her pirouette technique was unremarkable, but her running on points was infectiously gay and light, as if she were tripping on air."[37] In London, eight years later, Osbert Sitwell was enraptured: "[I]t was the grace, pathos, entrancing cleverness, the true comic genius and liveliness of a dancer new to this country, Lydia Lopokova, which made the chief impression. . . . Her wit entered into every gesture."[38] During most of the interval between her triumphs in Paris and London, however, she had been avoiding them. As her dancer-friend Lydia Sokolova, agreeing with Diaghilev, recalled, "[S]he always seemed to be hopping off somewhere, and obviously valued her private life as much as her life in ballet.''[39] It was her talent for *living* that made her such a great life's companion for Maynard.

Still in 1910 Lydia forsook the Ballets Russes to continue westward to the United States in the company of Fyodor and her eldest sister, Eugenia. They had a contract with a vaudeville producer, and Lydia went on to dance in ad hoc ballet companies. Brother and sister presently returned to Russia, but the adventurous Lydia stayed behind and also, earnest enough to take drama lessons, essayed acting, for which she had a serious talent. Without, however, completely dominating English, she was in the United States for seven years, until 1917, except for a brief ballet excursion to Spain in 1916.[40] Also adventurously she had become engaged to the famously mountainous Heywood Broun, a New York newspaperman, later to become a widely syndicated columnist and head of the New York Newspaper Guild. Acting as drama critic, he had fallen in love while reviewing her as actress. At that moment, in January 1916, the Diaghilev company arrived in New York and invited her to rejoin. She not only did so, but broke her engagement to Broun. Still in 1916, furthermore, she entered into an odd marriage, as it turned out, with Randolfo Barocchi, the Ballets Russes business manager, who was suitably small but otherwise unsatisfactory in the long run. It was in 1918, the ballet company having returned to London, that Maynard had his first experience of Lydia (ch. 4) and got over his initially negative view of her bottom. His change of mind is documented in the first known letter exchanged between them, Lydia writing almost correctly on 28 December 1918, ''Dear J. M. Keynes, The book was most welcomed. . . . I wish you a most happy New-Year in which my husband joins me heartely.''[41] By then she was beginning to rue her marriage and in July 1919, adventurously and mysteriously, she bolted again, leaving husband and Ballets Russes.

Perhaps accompanied by a Russian general—a mysterious general is mentioned later in her correspondence with Maynard—Lydia disappeared from public view but may have, at first, gone no further than the North London district of St. John's Wood. Later in 1919, she was granted permission to travel to Batum in Russia on the Black Sea. At the time Batum was still held by White Russian forces and would have been a not unreasonable port of entry for someone unreasonably entering a country in civil war. It is not known if she ever got to Batum. She was evidently in France in the summer of 1920 and assuredly in New York in early 1921, dancing in an entertainment called *The Rose Girl*. In March 1921, out of training and unhappy with her dancing, she asked Diaghilev if she might return and, on his assent, borrowed the passage money to join the company in Madrid. Opening in London in May 1921, the company and Lydia enjoyed a successful two months during which she danced splendidly in a dozen ballets. In June, ''ovations such as greeted her at the end of the can-can in *La Boutique Fantasque* can surely seldom have been equalled.''[42] In November, after a summer break, she was a sensation as the Lilac Fairy in *The Sleeping Princess*, but London thereafter lost interest, Maynard Keynes once again going against majority opinion.[43]

Maynard and Lydia began their affair in a burst of passion that almost immediately solidified into the steady state of a union for life. The realism of both had matched and so perpetuated their romanticism. In a letter early during the affair, on Thursday, 9 February 1922, Maynard incidentally reported to Vanessa on his attack of influenza that month, his health remaining a continuing problem. He added, "I still love Lydia very much. We had a good deal of *éclaircissement* on Sunday, which was painful for a moment, but seems to have made no real difference to us at all. Indeed we are extremely happy."[44] Doubtless Maynard spoke of his old love for Duncan, entirely unsurprising for anyone in the world of ballet. Certainly Lydia mentioned the general, as their letters document. When she went on to perform in Paris in the spring of 1924, Maynard, held in Cambridge during the summer term, wrote on 7 May a chatty letter proposing that he come over for a weekend on the 24th. In a postscript he added, "I sent letters from your mother, the general etc in another envelope." On 8 May Lydia responded to a number of his remarks, said that her mother's letter reported her ill for two weeks, and: "The lettre from general, he thanks me also for papers [Lydia's idiom for banknotes] and hopes to depart to America not to be lonely; and he needs capital but he does not ask me, the lettre is quite nice in spirit and a little mad."[45] Clearly the general was no surprise to Maynard; clearly their explanations had anticipated any such possible surprises. Indeed the character of their letters at the time and all other expressions show that the lovers had quickly got down to the bedrock of truth and built their joint life securely upon it.

When, on 9 February, Maynard had written to the Paris-situated Vanessa about both influenza and explanations, she wondered about the last: "Why was it painful?" The Keynes and Charleston Papers record no response to the question: there was a limit to Maynard's confidences. About the influenza, coolly and punishingly withholding sympathy and more profoundly right than she knew: "But I don't pity you very much as no doubt Lydia dances attendance on you very nicely and I remember her saying she likes people when they were ill." He had no need of Vanessa's pity: "So I daresay you come in for plenty of extra affection."[46] This quality was crucial for a person of his vulnerable health; "in sickness and in health" had precise meaning for Maynard and Lydia before and after they married. Her letters are rich in admonitions to be careful, to avoid chilling himself, to wear the proper clothers, to rest. . . . This concern would be all the more important after he suffered his massive heart attack in 1937. For their love sickness was a bond, and not a burden.

Virginia had uncannily preceded Vanessa—and even the affair itself—in identifying another bond for the Maynard-Lydia union. In May 1921 she "sat in Gordon Square . . . for a hour and a half talking to Maynard. . . . Maynard said he liked praise and always wanted to boast." She returned, "It's odd that you, of all people, should want praise—you and Lytton are passed beyond boasting." Even more revealingly he explained, "I want it for the things I'm doubtful about."[47] This is an astonishing admission by someone who always avoided publicly or privately admitting he might be wrong. Maynard was saying that under his thick, smooth crust of arrogance a hot lava of uncertainty roiled and bubbled. Indeed he would find a major role for uncertainty in the great economic conception he would develop. This could help expain why he never found a feminine love in critical Bloomsbury. Lydia, prepared to support her man totally, instantly understanding Maynard's need for reassurance against all terrors, needed no briefing from Virginia.

The lovers had to solve one fiendishly perverse problem. Quite early in the affair it was agreed that they would get married as soon as possible, but they could not. Barocchi himself, back in Italy and unhappy but unvengeful over Lydia's bolting, presented no active difficulty. He was agreeable to any solution, but had, in fact, caused the problem. He and Lydia had undergone a marriage ceremony after he had received his decree *nisi*, but not the decree *absolute* that would definitively dissolve his marriage to an American woman. Thus Lydia was, in fact, not married to him, but the cautious guardians of the law demanded proof that his wife was still alive in order to establish a nullity suit.[48] The wife in question was elusive. During 1923 Lydia began to feel insecure, an odd initiative of Maynard's giving her cause. He was evidently thinking of an Easter holiday in North Africa with Sebastian Sprott.[49] In any case letters of Lydia allude to a moment of acute distress about a putative holiday of Maynard's, certainly without her. On 25 January 1923 she wrote him vaguely but unhappily enough, ''I can't put myself yet to that state of wisdom when all is over happiness and unhappiness. I am ashamed it came out. Forgive me.'' A month later, enormously relieved, she wrote, ''I see your strength is regained. 'Holiday' was only a whim. Your life balances without it (except in summer).'' She closed caressingly, ''Balancing touches on and into your eyes.'' Three days after that she reemphasized, ''[A]s for holiday it only comes once a year—summer time,''[50] that is, with her. Few letters of Maynard's to her before Sepember 1923 survive, none referring to the matter. Plentiful from September, they express a deep and settled love. But Lydia's insecurity remained.

Both Lydia and Maynard were individually very busy the rest of 1923 although they were together much of the time. Charleston becoming unavailable to them, they spent three weeks from the latter part of August into early September in Dorset, on the south coast to the west of Sussex, in a rather grand seaside house rented from a duke. Maynard invited a number of friends from the university and, representing Bloomsbury, the Woolves, Virginia finding Maynard ''very gross and stout,'' with a ''queer swollen eel like look,''[51] and Lydia making a disgrace of herself. The disgrace consisted of tossing her used sanitary pads into the fireplace. The ducal staff reacted dramatically: ''such a scene as shook the rafters—rages, tears, despair, outrage, horror, retribution, reconciliation.''[52] Despite the reconciliation—no one could stay angry with Lydia long—the scene may have further shaken her sense of security about her relation to Maynard. As it happened his bachelor pattern resumed for a few days, and after their Dorset stay he joined the vice provost of King's College to undertake stag-hunting in Devon, west of Dorset. Lydia, first intercalating a weekend with other friends, descended on Vera and Harold Bowen at their Bedfordshire country place on 19 September. She brought her insecurity with her.

Lydia's arrival was a dramatic surprise to her hosts because she and Maynard had quarreled with them. According to Harold Bowen's diary, she had a desperate need to confide in Vera "as if no cloud had darkened the horizon." Aware of its attitude to Lydia, Vera encouragingly "ventured on the most outspoken criticism of Bloomsbury and its ways." The invitation to unburden herself worked. "Loppie looks on the end of her Maynard attachment as inevitable and not even out of sight." Two months later, at the Bowens' London residence, Lydia exhausted Vera by remaining almost until midnight "discussing interminably the problem of whether Maynard is to marry her or no." Yet, during this period, their letters to each other express seamless affection and commitment on both sides. Maynard had given no indication of discontent, yet Lydia could indeed agitate herself over his North African holiday plan, even if given up, for what it might signify, most particularly in the context of Bloombury's moeurs and negative reactions to her. Surely Lydia was also talking out her unreasoned impulse, which she half-recognized, to extend a deeply fixed pattern and bolt once again. Four years later, on 31 December 1927, she would send her friend a photograph of herself and Maynard, inscribing on it, "Second thoughts are best. To Vera from Lydia."[53]

The Lydia–Maynard relationship is documented in masses of letters, Lydia writing more than 200,000, Maynard, 150,000 words.[54] During the teaching half of the year (except for years skipped because of public service) Maynard normally spent five days of the week as a Cambridge bachelor, cohabiting with Lydia in London only two full days, Wednesday and Thursday. From 1922 to 1937, when his heart attack transformed Lydia into a full-time spouse and nurse, they wrote to each other nearly every day they were apart, Maynard particularly enjoying Monday mornings, when he got two letters, writing (e.g., on Monday, 3 December 1928) "Two very nice letters from you this morning," and, with ever fresh appreciation on Monday, 6 February 1933, "Your two letters received this morning were delightful—my greatest pleasure today."[55] (During the non-teaching half of the year they were, of course, together nearly all of the time.) The correspondence is marvelously good-humored, one of the very few exceptions being the references to that aborted holiday of 1923. All the other sources similarly suggest a remarkably easy union and an absence of conflict. One other exception emphasizes the rule. As recollected by Roy Harrod, "stormy conflicts of will" erupted when Maynard played naughty cardiac invalid and broke beyond the bounds set for him by his doctor and enforced by Lydia.[56] The conflicts were a game, albeit a life-and-death one, between two loving persons, one enslaved to his compulsions, and the other understanding it. Maynard nevertheless was as tractable as his compulsions permitted, while Lydia was reciprocally as yielding through the exercise of "consummate tact."[57] The rest is only a love story.

The extraordinary four- to five-day separation, particularly in an era when most women had no careers except as wives, turned out to be extraordinarily suitable for both Maynard and Lydia. It permitted them to immerse themselves slowly in a union providing each with the maximum strength and the minimum confinement. The bolter Lydia was no canary to be caged, but a free-flying, talking—Maynard appreciatively called her "Lady Talky," among other pet names—and initiative-taking, exotic parakeet, however sparrowlike she sometimes appeared, and he was perpetually enchanted with his prize. Most of his life remained rooted in Cambridge, although town and university remained irrelevant to her professional life (with one exception Maynard would later masterfuly achieve) and the personal life connected with them. Although she had no established ballet company as a base, her occasional engagements maintained her presence in the ballet world, and Maynard, besides removing her need to support herself, could be helpful here with his connections and money. In July–August 1923, for example, providing the finances, he arranged for her to dance in a London ballet revival, an affair of three weeks. If this was brief and temporary, and led to the quarrel, also temporary, with the Bowens, it was a promise of more help toward more engagements in both ballet and theater—and more, toward Lydia's leadership in establishing a permanent ballet company in Britain. So secured and secure, Lydia could enjoyably serve all-day, Russian-style lunches on Sunday to her many friends in London, while Maynard, in Cambridge, worked through *Economic Journal* contributions during the morning and then went off to 6 Harvey Road, where Neville carved the roast. It all meant being together more than not while apart.

The Bowens, cultivated and conveniently wealthy, were one of three couples providing Lydia with consistent company in the 1920s. Vera, her closest friend, had gravitated to London from an Ukrainian estate by way of Switzerland and a discarded Swiss husband. An enterprising and talented choreographer, she created and produced a series of successful ballets beginning in 1917. It was her *Masquerade* of 1922 which Maynard revived for Lydia the next year. Harold Bowen, a linguist, student of Islamic history, and future lecturer in Turkish history,[58] kept a sensitive, indeed prissy, diary recording choice moments in Lydia's biography, thus the contention and her uninhibited sillinesses. Vera, despite a generous nature, was famously quarrelsome, while Maynard was Maynard, thus, inevitably, the quarrel. After he had begun preparations as de facto producer for the *Masquerade* revival, Vera suddenly suggested that she should take control, act as producer, and pay Lydia a salary as her employee. Maynard, after making a possibly diplomatic counterproposal, then wrote the Bowens a letter which Harold found "amazingly rude." Cooperatively, loyally, Lydia "treated [Vera] as a stranger" when Vera visited her in her dressing room after Lydia began the engagement.[59] The dispute was simply abandoned when Lydia descended on the Bowens with her doubts about marrying Maynard. Reconciled with Lydia, her friends never learned to like Maynard, although, unlike many other outstandingly rude persons, he did not try to validate his brusqueries by disliking his victims. Indeed, from his stag hunt he wrote Lydia that if she did indeed visit Vera, as she had mentioned, "Do your best to compose the quarrel with her so far as I am concerned, I don't want to quarrel. . . . It is no good."[60] Other help Maynard gave Lydia's career did not have such tortuous consequences.

Of the two other couples, the "tall Florrie [Florence Grenfell] prances through Lydia's letters" accompanied by her husband, a banker and Conservative M. P. A balletomane friend of Diaghilev, Florrie entertained splendidly in her Cavendish Square residence.[61] If Lydia was more befriended with Florrie than with the less interesting Teddy Grenfell, she was closer to Samuel than to Elizabeth— Sam and Lil—Courtauld, art and music patrons, respectively. Sam, "the only man to arouse Maynard's jealousy,"[62] dumbly, awkwardly, openly adored Lydia, but she managed both adorers so tactfully that Maynard never felt impelled to move beyond well-contained feelings and became a friendly associate of Sams's, enrolling him in one of his benefactions. The masterful chairman of the vast Courtaulds Ltd., a rayon producer, Sam collected impressionist paintings, gave £50,000 to the Tate Gallery to buy more of the same, and founded the Courtauld Institute of Art. Lil Courtauld (who would die of cancer in 1931) subsidized Covent Garden performances and otherwise supported music in Britain. It was with Lydia's help, as well as through his City and other activities, that Maynard enriched his life beyond Bloomsbury, although he never left it, just as he never left 6 Harvey Road or King's College.

In June 1924 Maynard wrote Lydia that he had learned Sam Courtauld was coming to Cambridge for a university art event: "I dare say I should arrange to sit next to Sam and so hear some news of you." He rather took pity on Courtauld, the object, as he knew, of a new appeal by the university for money: "Sam will soon be the most famous milking-cow in England! . . . I think that his udders must be sore with so much pulling by strange hands."[63] But then he had Sam tucked away in his mind for milking himself. Perhaps Lydia calmed Maynard's jealousy on another occasion, when she reported, "Sam telephoned, Lil is not well, would I first visit Tate gallery with him and then comfort Lil. I did both." Lydia and Sam enjoyed the French paintings: "Cézanne that intoxicates Sam with it's serenity and subtlety. . . . Sam wishes me to tell you that he is jealous over your Cézanne." Perhaps reading Maynard's mind, she added, "I alwayes feel a pact of friendship to Sam (without going to bed, and that is why it is so nice)."[64]

When Lydia had a brief but successful engagement outside the country in the spring of 1924, Maynard wrote, "I consider how all your circle follows you and cannot be content without you—Veras, Sams, Florries all in Paris. If you had an engagement in Pekin they would all be in Pekin. You are their elixir, and without you they are not fully alive. I should like some elixir too."[65] He was saying that he, too, needed her to be fully alive. It was still term time and he had to wait two weeks to get to Paris.[66]

During all this time Lydia's marital situation remained unresolved as incompetent investigators dimly sought Barocchi's wife. It was while Lydia was dancing in Paris that Maynard could exuberantly report, "Mary Hargreaves as been captured,—run to earth! So the case is complete." It had taken, he said, more than one hundred inquiries to find the lady.[67] The law could still delay. The court hearing formally to take cognizance of Barocchi's bigamous and hence invalid marriage to Lydia was postponed until January 1925. On 15 January Lydia was at last awarded a decree *nisi* of *nullity* of her nonmarriage to Barocchi. On that day, expressing for the first time the chronic distress she had felt, Lydia wrote Maynard, "How fortunate I am, after these swift dramatic developments, my mental state no more bedraggling, 'Gods divine' have been benevolent to me. . . . I bow into your knees and kiss your feet."[68] Another half-year of delay followed. On 27 July 1925 Maynard wrote his mother, "The decree was made absolute just after lunch today, and in the afternoon we went to the St. Pancras [the legal district in which Bloomsbury is located] Registry Office to give notice that we would be married there tomorrow week (4 August)."[69]

NOTES

1. JMK to FAK, 3 April, JMK to JNK, 16 April 1920, KP, PP/45/168.
2. The trio's adventures in general, Spalding, *Vanessa Bell*, 185–87; Skidelsky, *JMK*, 2: 42–43; Moggridge, *MK*, 360–61.
3. Quoted, Spalding, *Vanessa Bell*, 187.
4. Letters, 25 May, 4 June 1920, KP, PP/45/168.
5. 2 May 1920, CP.
6. Ibid.
7. Ibid.
8. Letter, ibid.
9. Undated letter, but written, as the context indicates, in 1922, well before the summer vacation, ibid.
10. Letter, 24 November 1930, KP, PP/45/190.
11. Angelica Garnett, *Deceived with Kindness: A Bloomsbury Childhood* (London, 1984), 33.
12. CP.
13. KP, PP/45/316.
14. Letter to Edwin S. Montagu, 4 February 1922, *CW*, 17: 332.
15. CP.
16. Quoted, Holroyd, *LS*, 2: n. 372.
17. Letter, LL to JMK, KP, PP/45/190.
18. Letters to JMK, 10 April, 12 June 1922, ibid., 34, 44.
19. Letter to JMK, 23 June 1922, ibid., 45.
20. CP.
21. 27 October 1922, KP, PP/45/190.

22. Note dated 24 April 1924, CP.

23. Letter, 25 August 1922, Virginia Woolf, *The Letters*, 2: 554.

24. 22 December 1922, ibid., 594.

25. 8 June 1924, ibid., 3: 115.

26. 4 September 1924, ibid., 129.

27. Early May 1923, ibid., 3: 24.

28. Quoted, Holroyd, *LS*, 2: 516.

29. Entry, 27 December 1931, Virginia Woolf, *The Diary*, 4: 56.

30. As LL told Holroyd, *LS*, 2: 516.

31. Quoted, Milo Keynes, "Lydia Lopokova," in Milo Keynes, ed., *Lydia Lopokova* (London, 1983), 15, 13.

32. Milo Keynes, "The Lopukhov Family," ibid., 39–49.

33. Clement Crisp, "Revolution Afoot," review of Elizabeth Souritz, *Soviet Choreography in the 1920s* (Durham, N. C., 1990), *New York Times Book Review*, 23 September 1990, 40.

34. Milo Keynes gave her birth date as 21 October 1892, but added, "[T]he year has long been doubted as each of her three passports differed on this point." "Lydia Lopokova," 2. Other details, ibid., passim.

35. Quoted, Hession, *JMK*, 181.

36. Quoted, introduction (by Polly Hill), Keynes and Lopokova, *Lydia and Maynard*, 19–20.

37. Quoted, ibid., 20.

38. Quoted, ibid., 23.

39. Quoted, ibid.

40. See Frank W. Ries, "Lydia Lopokova in America," in Milo Keynes, ed., *Lydia Lopokova*, 54–70.

41. KP, PP/45/190.

42. Milo Keynes, "Lydia Lopokova," 3.

43. Lydia's adventures, ibid., 4–10; editorial note, Keynes and Lopokova, *Lydia and Maynard*, 26–27. See below on the general mentioned in the letters.

44. CP.

45. KP, PP/45/190.

46. 12 February 1922, CP.

47. Entry, 26 May 1921, *The Diary*, 2: 120–21.

48. Editorial note, Keynes and Lopokova, *Lydia and Maynard*, 25, n. 200.

49. Skidelsky, *JMK*, 2, 142.

50. KP, PP/45/190. Second and third letters, 23, 26 February 1923.

51. Virginia Woolf, *The Diary*, 2: 266.

52. Virginia Woolf to Jacques Raverat, 4 November 1923, *The Letters*, 3: 76.

53. Diary of Harold Bowen, quoted, editorial note, Keynes and Lopokova, *Lydia and Maynard*, 100–101.

54. Introduction (Polly Hill), Editors' Preface, ibid., 9.

55. KP, PP/45/190.

56. Harrod, *The Life*, 480.

57. Milo Keynes, "Lydia Lopokova," 16.

58. On the Bowens see Dramatis Personae, Keynes and Lopokova, *Lydia and Maynard*, 342–43.

59. Quoted, editorial note, ibid., 97.

60. Letter, 19 September 1923, KP, PP/45/190.
61. Dramatis Personae, Keynes and Lopokova, *Lydia and Maynard*, 346.
62. Ibid., 344.
63. Letter, 13 June 1924, KP, PP/45/190.
64. Letter, 22 November 1924, ibid.
65. 9 May 1924, ibid.
66. Letter, LL to JMK, 22 May 1924, ibid.
67. Letter, 21 May 1924, ibid.
68. 15 January 1924, ibid.
69. KP, PP/45/168.

CHAPTER 8

Married Life with Lydia: A British Institution

Attracting many news cameras and bystanders, the Keynes–Lopokova wedding was a major media event. One newspaper expressed the relative importance of the principals: "FAMOUS DANCER'S MARRIAGE SURPRISE."[1] The wedding party was modest: Maynard's mother, maternal grandmother, and sister, but, inexplicably, not his father, and, as witnesses, a supportive Vera Bowen and a reluctant Duncan Grant. For the Gordon Square tea party that followed, Florrie Grenfell had provided a delicious wedding cake.[2] Unable to rent Tilton for 1925, Maynard found a nearby house and he and Lydia could have their Sussex idyll. Then the couple, leaving on 3 September, went off to Soviet Russia to meet Lydia's family in Leningrad and to go on to Moscow, where Maynard, as Cambridge University's official representative, spoke at the bicentennial celebration of the Russian Academy of Sciences. Lydia and Florence Keynes, each unpossessive and appreciative of the other, had already met well before the wedding and established easy cooperation in support and adoration of Maynard, and now Maynard could close the circle by meeting Lydia's mother and family, the trip thus strengthening the union of two persons who held to their families. In Moscow Maynard airily recommended a modicum of capitalism while seeing Leninism as "a persecuting religion and an experimental technique."[3] The couple's private and public objectives had been economically achieved.

Earlier in 1925, with marriage definitely pending, Maynard had announced he needed all of No. 46 Gordon Square for himself and spouse. Vanessa, unable to resist his logic and money power, moved with Duncan Grant to No. 37. More

Mr. and Mrs. Keynes at home at 46 Gordon Square, 1929. Photo courtesy of Milo Keynes.

and more Bloomsbury connections were settling in Gordon Square. Lady Stra-chey, with resident daughters, had left North London to move to No. 51 in 1919. This provided Lytton with a pied-à-terre for his London visits, although, pros-pering, he later took the ground floor of No. 41. Other residents of No. 41, at various times, were Ralph Partridge, Carrington, and Frances Marshall, the prime tenants of the house remaining James and Alix Strachey, who, appropri-ately enough, practiced psychoanalysis there. Oliver Strachey, a brother of Lyt-ton's, occupied No. 42 with his daughter, Julia. Clive Bell held out on the top two floors of No. 50, which became the home and operations center for Adrian and Karin Stephen, also psychoanalysts, and, eventually, their two daughters, Ann and Judith. "Very soon I foresee that the whole square will be a sort of college," Lytton wrote to Virginia Woolf on 28 September 1919. "And the rencontres in the garden I shudder to think of."[4] Virginia herself found that "Gordon Square is like nothing so much as the lion's house at the Zoo," as she wrote a year later to Barbara Hiles Bagenal. "All the animals are dangerous, rather suspicious of each other, and full of fascination and mystery."[5] None was more dangerous than malicious, mad Virginia. Maynard, making himself useful to his friends, was the masterful lion tamer.

Partnered perfectly by Lydia, Maynard enforced his dominating position by giving the square's grandest parties, in the expert estimation of Bunny Garnett. "Sometimes Lydia danced . . . partnered by Duncan, who acquitted himself with character and originality," he recalled. "But at one party Maynard danced a delightful pas-de-deux with Lydia in which she showed an exquisitely graceful solicitude in supporting him and making his part easier for him."[6] This was the famous Keynes–Keynes, performed in 1926 and 1927, and perhaps more often than that, as parody of the more famous can-can that Lydia had danced in *La Boutique Fantasque* of the Ballets Russes. The Maynard–Lydia act was the climax of an elaborate Bloomsbury–Cambridge entertainment, written by May-nard's imaginative economist-protégé Dennis Robertson and based on a contem-porary scandal. The cast included the painters Walter Sickert, Roger Fry, and Duncan Grant "disguised as dogs" (who had played a role in the affair) and, in transvestite style, a Beauty Chorus composed of three six-foot Cambridge men in long skirts and pearl necklaces partnered by three small young women as gentlemen in white tie and tails. Vanessa, expressing herself precisely, painted a cartoon of the Keynes–Keynes, with Lydia plumped out to dumpling shape and Maynard as lecherous and wistful satyr.[7]

No. 46, like its neighbors, was a roomy, five-story Georgian residence for prosperous, appropriately served occupants. It had a basement, with its kitchen, pantry, and servants' sitting room. The ground floor held the communal dining room until Vanessa, in 1923, had hived off a more exclusive dining area for her family and left Maynard and Lydia in contented privacy. The huge drawing room dominated the second floor. Maynard established his and her bedrooom and his study on the third floor. He also took over the two upper floors, which had been the Bells' quarters. And, of course, the servants' bedrooms occupied the attic. Maynard and Lydia began putting their stamp on No. 46 when Lydia moved in as legal chatelaine. For his book collection Maynard built a library, and for bourgeois comfort, more bathrooms *garnis* with bidets. Vanessa and Duncan, as in their other habitats and Maynard's King's College rooms, had earlier applied their talents here and decorated the drawing-room ceiling with murals. This is where Lydia held her Sunday lunch salon; she announced her taste by having the ceiling whitewashed. One can imagine Vanessa's feelings. Later the prospering Maynard, finding No. 46 cramped, leased No. 47. Letting out the rest, he took over its drawing room; the Woolfs, as Virginia recorded, proceeded from No. 46's drawing room "two steps up into the great new room" and took lunch there in early 1938.[8] Maynard had two other residences, and, eventually, Lydia had another herself.

As Bloomsbury chose to ignore but exploited, Maynard meant business at No. 46. From the square, never leaving his economics behind, he moved into his City, Westminster, and other activities. In June 1922 Roy Harrod, an Oxford humanities graduate destined to teach economics there a year later, came to consult with the Cambridge authority about learning his subject and was immediately, kindly, and imperiously taken up and over. He found himself in No. 46's drawing room:

The room itself . . . seemed empty, devoid of the usual ornaments . . . strange to me. On the walls were two pictures only . . . perhaps by Matisse and Picasso. . . . There were two others at lunch, one of whom was a young French economist. . . . Keynes was discussing with the Frenchman the latest gossip about Continental statesmen, their mistresses, their neuroses as well as their political maneuvers. . . . I supposed they must be real. There was financial talk of the latest movements of the exchanges, budgetary positions, the international movement of money. . . . [T]he three of them seemed able to relate their items of financial intelligence to theoretical doctrine, the quantity theory of money, foreign exchange equilibrium. . . . I was in the presence of something quite unusual—this mixture of expertise in the latest theories with wide knowledge of day-to-day events. . . . The excitement was almost unbearable.[9]

Maynard's King's College rooms, modest and monastic in part, remained the fulcrum of his exercise of power. These were not the rooms he had inhabited when he wrote his early love letters to Duncan in the summer of 1908 as he looked out at "the best view in the world . . . the river and the backs beyond" (ch. 4). As a beginning lecturer he had been shifted around in temporary quarters until he got his own rooms the next summer. There he no longer had much of a view, one side facing the flank of the main range of college buildings across a space called Webb's Court and the other side looking out at the (usually) quiet corner of King's and Queens' Lanes, the latter fronting Queens' College. With the addition of another room (at his own expense) a few years later, he could, however, enjoy agreeable quarters. His suite of rooms was on the third floor above the side-street gatehouse opening into Webb's Court. The suite was composed around a generously large sitting room with big windows where he received his Political Economy Club, students, and guests. After a visit in 1923 Virginia Woolf found it "the pleasantest sitting room I have ever been in."[10] Duncan had originally decorated it with murals of vestigially clothed grape pickers and dancers, but he and Vanessa began a more ambitious project in 1920.[11] This comprehended eight eight-feet-tall panels expressive of decorative rather than unqualified art, with figures representing disciplines or arts as muses (although the Greeks had nine). The figures were not always identifiable, a lady with a violin evidently connoting music, but the muse with a sheaf of grain was open to various significations. However interpreted, their visible aesthetics softened the intellectual rigors the room's occupants represented. A somewhat smaller room served as a study where Maynard could write or, bringing in a secretary, dictate his articles, memoranda, and correspondence. A narrow cell held a monastic bed; the bathroom was primitive.

Of course Maynard had no cooking facilities, but the dining hall was a few steps away, across Webb's Court, and college servants could bring food from the kitchens. In sum his rooms were perfectly fitted to the needs and velleities of a bachelor don. This suggests part, at least, of the problems of a don's wife. But even the spouse in her own house, Florence Ada Keynes, Cambridge councilwoman and mayor, was excluded from many university functions and festivities. One need not wonder that Lydia came to Cambridge reluctantly, and that Maynard never considered placing her in a replica of 6 Harvey Road. Cambridge was a male don's world.

In the circumstances Lydia's visits required premeditation and careful management. Once trying to distract her after a new delay in her annulment proceedings, Maynard urged her to come that weekend "and I can console you with kisses." Lydia returned, "I can't come to Cambridge, it would disturb too much my mode of life." She would instead accept posted kisses.[12] She had an excuse then because they were not married, but she had to do her duty thereafter. Until 1937, when she did come, she would stay at 6 Harvey Road or in a "good room" in a Cambridge hotel, as Maynard offered her the choice on one occasion.[13] College and university reminded her too insistently that she was an outsider both as woman and nonmember. In February 1935 Maynard invited her for the weekend when King's College would have a "feast," a celebratory dinner at which the choicest delicacies would emerge from its pantry and cellars for the fellows. The occasion was the performance of "theatricals" put on by George "Dadie" Rylands, a young friend of Maynard's and a don in English, who was the university's leading actor-director. As Maynard put it less tactfully than he realized, to entertain the women of her acquaintance in Cambridge, "the plan is that during the feast you have a 'hen party' in my rooms." Ineligible for the feast, the ladies could later go on to Dadie's show: "Isn't it a good idea?"[14]

Toward the end of 1934 Lydia found herself invited to a similar experience on the occasion of the Founder's Feast, an annual event and the most important of the feasts. Two years earlier Maynard had invited Felix Frankfurter, then a visiting professor at Oxford, as his Founder's Feast guest and wove with him a plot to influence President Franklin Delano Roosevelt first by open letter and then, in May 1934, by interview, the sum constituting actions of historical significance.[15] Lydia was not treated like Frankfurter.

On 17 November 1935 Maynard wrote Lydia the plan for the last week of the Michaelmas (fall) term. He would not go to London. Instead, she would come to Cambridge on Wednesday, 4 December, attend a play given by the university's Amateur Dramatic Club that evening, join Maynard at a party given by a new friend of his on Thursday, the fifth; Founder's Feast would be on Friday the sixth, and Lydia and Maynard would return to London on Saturday "for good." Eight days later he filled in the blanks. For the sixth, the day of the Founder's Feast, she would not, this time, be obliged to work her way. She would simply be a guest. The wife of John H. Clapham, the economic historian, would function as hostess of the "hen party" in Clapham's rooms. The ladies would, moreover, dine on the same food "that the cocks will be eating." Given Maynard's (hence Lydia's) duty to college and the mitigating factors, "I don't see how you can get out of it. Will you say yes?"

On Tuesday, 3 December, transforming the imperatives of the situation, Maynard wrote Lydia that he had a cold. He had remained in his rooms, lunch and dinner being brought to him. He would not meet her tomorrow; she should go straight to 6 Harvey Road for lunch, and then come "here." On the same day she returned, "I am sad that you are not well, do not go out, stay in, will you? . . . I will see you tomorrow and hug you on your neck." She was bringing mouthwash and promised to "hold your vertebrae."[16]

If Lydia could not fit into the rooms above the Webb's Court gatehouse, she understood the sense of their stripped-down character as Maynard's power base. She might feel homeless herself in Cambridge, but she was too wise to resent it. Defending his health, cooperating in the social maneuvers of the university community, she supported him in all conceivable ways. In his innocence, as his letters inviting her to Cambridge show, Maynard never quite realized how absolutely the university excluded nonmembers, but he had been born into it and could not imagine how one felt out of it. But then he had also earned his place. Virginia Woolf's diary recorded Maynard's words "on becoming a fellow of King's. The moving nature of the service." Maynard recalled how the provost "reads a statement about preserving the laws and traditions, and then they all shake hands and he is admitted to the brotherhood. . . . I said did this society, this coming together move him, and Maynard said very much."[17] His labors for King's testify to it. His will stated that he be cremated and his ashes deposited in the crypt in King's. His brother Geoffrey, however, forgot that clause and no less appropriately scattered them over the downs above Tilton.[18] Lydia could not share Maynard's connection to Cambridge, as she could not fully share his membership in Bloomsbury. Receiving her friends and giving them Sunday lunch, she had her power center in Gordon Square.

Lydia managed, gracious compliance to Maynard's more urgent wishes excepted, to be rarely in Cambridge, as their letters document and her nephew Milo Keynes noted.[19] In the end, only in 1936, perhaps after achieving some awareness of her feelings, Maynard purchased and commenced rebuilding a flat for her a few paces away from the grand (front) gatehouse of King's College. This was at 17A St. Edward's Passage, a tiny street on the other side of King's Parade. Other factors encouraging him were the nearby theater for Cambridge (and her) his initiative had brought into being earlier in 1936 and his grand gains on the U.S. stock market since 1934. It was to be very much her, and not their, flat, as Maynard described it to her in October 1936: "Today I've been planning your flat. I think you can have a spare bedroom as well as [a servant's] room, and *two* bathrooms."[20] As it happened she occupied it only in May 1937, just before his heart attack, which changed everything.[21] From then on they were almost inseparable, the war further tightening their union and distancing Maynard from Cambridge for extended periods. Yet the flat, in theory at least, nicely balanced off Maynard's King's College rooms.

Tilton, like Gordon Square, was as much hers as his. It was "a plain but surprisingly roomy two-story farmhouse, beautifully situated, in its several acres of lawn, orchard, and woodland, on the north edge of the South Downs," in the words of an equally contented recent occupant.[22] Maynard captured it, beginning in 1926, on a twenty-year lease that gave him the security to make improvements and play master builder there as in Cambridge. The first change was a library at the end of a courtyard south of the house, from which Maynard could look out on an orchard and see the downs rising up beyond. From the top of the downs he could see the British Channel. On the day before he died he rode to the summit in his seedy Rolls-Royce and walked back down to Tilton.

Both Maynard and Lydia loved Tilton despite burst pipes, a frequently chilly boiler, and sooty fireplaces. (Guests like the Courtaulds were less happy.) There, Maynard got a great deal of work done in a two-and-a-half month summer stay, *The General Theory*, particularly, flowing out of his busy contentment, the process assisted by Richard Kahn, his ultimate protégé, as working guest. Maynard and Lydia also came to Tilton for the Christmas and Easter holidays; he died there on the Easter morning of 1946. At Tilton during the Easter holiday of 1933, as he reported to his mother, Lydia, who did it often, was "able to sunbathe naked in the garden from 10 o'clock in the morning."[23] Or, as Lydia herself wrote, "I am surrounded by broad beans, green peas, weeds, my skin rattles from the sun, so rewarding and sudorous. . . . I circulate . . . like a plant with two arms. . . . I am shelling broad beans like a Tibetan monk with his beads. . . . I find life a melody, away from Oxford Street."[24] After Maynard died she lived on in Tilton for more than thirty years, until four years before her death in a nursing home on 8 June 1981, three days after his birthday. In the home she was "happy and contented, though muddled and forgetful."[25]

And so Maynard, evicted from Charleston, found another Eden a few hundred yards away. Vanessa, cherishing her resentment, was unable to eradicate her affection for him and his persistent usefulness to her. She spent long periods in Cassis, another sympathetic locale for her painting, in the south of France, but always came back to Charleston and to Gordon Square (or, later, to a nearby street within walking distance of the square), and to her friendship, however distanced, with Maynard. Tilton was the third leg of the secure tripod of his working residences.

When it was over the professor of music at Cambridge, one of the many persons they brushed against, wrote Lydia, "It was the most wonderful union, you two. I believe it was the most wonderful I have ever known between two humans."[26] The widow of Alfred Marshall, speaking of the marriage and knowing them better, said to Roy Harrod, "The best thing that Maynard ever did."[27] All the interior evidence supports these external opinions: the letters, the things unsaid, the suggestions in their behavior, her dancing and cheery nonsense, his work and sense of satisfaction. Duncan had been Maynard's deepest love, but it had been a fundamentally unhappy one, meeting him on his level of "natural sadness" and deepening it further. Duncan's perfect selfishness could give too little back to a being who had everything except love. Maynard had been fortunate that he had removed himself as lover and wisely made him a lifelong friend still to be helped, an adviser in art, and an enjoyable companion of the road. Lydia gave and asked to give more. She spied out all possible ways to help, protect, amuse, love, and adore. Lifted by her spirit, Maynard could plane above his old sadness. She made him absurdly happy. Geoffrey Keynes, ballet-omanic adorer of Lydia—"I loved her at sight and she loved me"—summed it: "She brought joy to us all, especially to Maynard."[28]

Of all the critical points in his life which Maynard had identified, addressed, and dominated, the encounter with Lydia was the most important. Surely Mary Marshall was suggesting that the marriage was as essential in making him a great man as it was in making him a happy one. Because so intimate, it gave him the strength and solidity necessary for his ultimate public persona. In a mediocre sense of course, it made him marvelously acceptable, indeed more so than if he had married an English lady. With the Russian dancer he was more interesting while the legality of marriage, confounding the whispers about his homosexuality, itself established him as unassailable. But the public face of it would not have succeeded if it had not been built on unqualified love, its aura visible to all. The loving marriage of Maynard and Lydia became a British institution immediately.

Given Maynard's two decades of homosexual promiscuity, one is obliged to ask if his extraordinary change was complete. In one sense it was not. He never left his homoerotic home when he became a seriously practising heterosexual. He kept many of his old lovers as friends, Duncan particularly. At King's he lived in a male society and could continue to enjoy the gossip about old and new amours, old style. He assiduously attended Apostle meetings, especially in the 1920s, and recruited new members. The King's fellows (and fellows of the closely allied Trinity) included a great proportion of apparent homosexuals or men detached from women except, possibly, their mothers: his colleagues Arthur Pigou and Dennis Robertson, both subject to a tragic love for a succession of undergraduates; Dadie Rylands, with whom he worked closely on theater projects for the university; another protégé, the subtle Marxian theorist Piero Sraffa of Trinity, with whom he might undertake "a short totter . . . in the afternoon, when I bought a new tie at Bodgers" (a Cambridge haberdasher) or play patience[29]; John Sheppard, his classmate and King's provost from 1933, attended by Cecil Taylor—"Madame"; Goldsworthy Lowes Dickenson, Apostle and political philosopher, lover of men and, more passionately or less shyly, shoes; Maynard's good but difficult friend, the great philosopher Ludwig Wittgenstein, intermittently at Trinity; the Etonian Dil Knox, although usually off in a government office; and Sebastian Sprott, no longer a traveling companion but a Cambridge-area riding one until he went off to the University of Nottingham as psychology professor in 1925. Maynard had had carnal knowledge of Duncan at least as long as his amatory record continued, into 1915, thus long after their affair was over and Duncan was established for life with Vanessa. Is it possible that Maynard resumed such exercises for old times' sake at odd moments? The available documents do not say, but if anything physical happened, it would have been insignificant.

Incidents related by the biographer of his (and Lydia's) ballet friend Frederick Ashton (1904–88), Britain's greatest choreographer and a homosexual, suggest the extent—and limits—of Maynard's retention of his old erotic behavior. Entering into Lydia's world, Maynard found it an "added attraction . . . that it brought him into proximity to a new circle of attractive youths to whom he was clearly still susceptible." He would invite Ashton and his lover, the dancer William Chappell, to King's College, as they recounted, "where he made the habit of wandering into the room when they were taking a bath." Chappell also recalled a dinner invitation for the two of them at No. 46 Gordon Square, where Maynard took them onto the balcony, "ostensibly to explain which Bloomsbury figure lived where, but then pounced, giving them both 'terrible great smacking kisses.' " Chappell may have improved on the story: " 'And there was Madame, twiddling her thumbs inside. When we appeared, she made a typically wonderful remark, "Have some more *Bols*," she said to Maynard.' " More to the point, however, Maynard cultivated Ashton, Chappell continued, because he " 'wanted to further Lydia's career and Fred was quite clearly the one to do it.' "[30] All the sources support the thesis of a great, steady, and ever fresh love for Lydia even if Maynard submitted to momentary seductive distractions and if its sexual expression, affected more substantially by his health, declined after a period. All other thoughts are idle.

The Maynard–Lydia union began with a burst of fluent physical affection, with Lydia responding with exuberance, if not taking the lead. Very few of his letters before September 1923 survive, but those that do and those thereafter indicate an equality of frankness, if not a matching of Lydia's natural lack of inhibition. The regular correspondence begins in April 1922, when Maynard left for the Genoa Conference, and just one known letter, evidently written in March 1922 (in the archivist's opinion), precedes the series. Lydia mentions Leonide Massine, with whom she was dancing in ballet numbers in Covent Garden. She ends, "Oh I go to bed I am so sleepy. Shall I see you with gobbling greetings tomorrow?" Writing from 50 Gordon Square on the day of his departure, 8 April, she sounds a number of characteristic notes: his great presence in her life already, naturalness and odd daily details, Russian superstitious belief, nice things happening to her, concern about his health (reflecting his own), and sensitivity to his professional excellence and ambition:

> It is very empty Maynard, without your walk of life in 46 or 50.
> I have just arrived after the theatre, I expect to drink tea, now Grace [Vanessa's housekeeper] comes in—stop—
> I had tulips this afternoon, besides other things I also received 100 pounds. Very nice!
> You shall not have a cold I put my vows. I send you my very best, and I know you will achieve splendidly wondrous results with the Genoa Conference.
>   L.[31]

In the rest of April nearly all her letters sound graceful, carnal notes of affection, usually in closing, although the next letter, on 10 April, begins and ends: "I gobble you dear Maynard . . . I re-gobble you." Other phrasings from 13 April to 1 May follow:

Your expressions in the end give me nice tremblings. I kiss . . . I am inexhaustibly fond of you, Maynard. . . . You are *very nice* dear Maynard I kiss you . . . I want to wrap up around you and give the abundance ["abundance" set off in Egyptian-style cartouche] of my feeling. For this specially designed word I had to look into the dictionary . . . I blend my mouth and heart to yours . . . I kiss your eyes. I see they look at me just now . . . I gobble you from head to foot . . . I embrace you, and so add one more comfort if you can bear it. . . . My boundless caresses to you . . . I detain infinitely your warm wet kisses . . . I cover you with kisses full of flame. . . . With caresses large as sea I stretch out to you . . . I warm my lips to yours, they feel very red. . . . Very tender at same time exotic kisses . . . I place melodious strokes all over you Maynard, you are very nice . . . [and, veering out of control of English] Feeling dry in general toward you—liquid.[32]

A few more Lydian notes of the spring and summer of 1922: "I lick you tenderly . . . I taste your buttons . . . I contemplate you . . . I have so much intensity for you . . . I kiss especially the head, and lick your hands. Your dog . . . I kiss you outside inside."[33]

Maynard's one known letter of April is awkwardly responsive: "I want to be foxed and gobbled abundantly. It is only half a life here, says the fountain pen to the metronome." When his flow of letters begins, it conscientiously echoes the physical note: "I am very fond of you. I kiss you and touch you."[34]

At least Maynard could draw on his scholarship to express his (physical) love. In research for an essay on Babylonian and Greek weights, he had found a love

em and quotes it to Lydia: "Come to me my Ishtavar and show your virile
ength/ Push out your member and touch with it my little place." Lydia's
reply returns more than fair value: "From intelect to the Babylonian poem, what
openness of mind, I smiled from head to foot." Her next sentence strains English
but is clear enough: "When I tell to you 'thrillings' she sais 'touch with it my
little place,' a 'positive' woman no doubt she was."[35] An earlier expression is
an improvement on English: "Mucuous membrances to you."[36] In 1924 Maynard began working on his *Treatise on Money* and rose to the occasion: "You
and the new book are mixed up in my dozing imagination. I stand over you
and touch you with fertilizing drops and water you like a plant. He is big as I
write and smells of incense and holds his moisture like a cloud."[37] One might
unkindly guess, since they cohabited only two nights a week for half the year,
that this fine physical passion was more verbalized than acted out.

For Lydia love naturally meant children, as she initially communicated to
Maynard. How he felt is mysterious. Although he showed deep family spirit,
his busyness and his mission to correct the world probably damaged a similar
instinct in him, but he respected Lydia's. Furthermore he was always willing,
indeed too willing, to accept extra chores. In 1923, to a reference of hers, he
responded with a cooperative, institutional note: "Shall you and I begin our
works on population together and at the same time?" In his next letter he
continued the thought, beginning parenthetically, "(I am sure that when you
make your contribution to the population, it will be a poet that comes out.)"[38]
Because they were not yet married, the issue was doubtless remanded to the
future. Cryptic remarks in his letters to her suggest that she had miscarriages
once or twice in 1927.[39] That was as far as their joint movement carried. A
gynecological examination determined that Lydia could not have children, according to the oral history of the Keynes family.[40]

Perhaps related to the loss of hope for children and Maynard's flickering
health, the happy sexual intimacy of these earlier letters expresses itself less
frequently as time goes on. Maynard writes of many other things. Lydia's references become wistful, more reminiscent than actual. A month after his heart
attack, when he was a helpless invalid in a sanitorium, Lydia wrote, "Water is
hot at 46, I had a bath. With touches all over you."[41] Before then, toward the
end of 1935, she mentions Freud sagely, perhaps suggestively, "[E]very good
pupil he had revolted . . . but still he was the discoverer and so will remain
great." She reported on an engagement with Sam Courtauld, now a widower,
"Now I will go and dress for Sam, probably tête-à-tête." Is she trying to light
a tiny flame of jealousy? The decline in sexual expression had come much
sooner, certainly enforced by the first evidences, in 1931, of Maynard's cardiac
condition, when his health turned suddenly much worse. With her sympathetic
feelings toward the ill, Lydia seems to have begun substituting concern about
his physical condition for the attenuating sexual bond. Her letters are as affectionate as ever and now deal exhaustively with the details of his condition and
every change when it comes. A fortnight before the heart attack, when he was

beginning to complain of ominous new distresses, Lydia wrote more than presciently, "Try to forget shares, markets, fortune, because it must crumple the
muscle of your heart, and you must not decrease your strength, because I am
so fond of you. The world shakes and we must shake as well and be philosophical."[42]

In Quentin Bell's ultimate reminiscence, providing an equilibrating note to
the Ashton episodes, he recounted a qualification, or rather an enhancement, of
the story of a perfect union. A letter of Leonard Woolf's confirms and enhances
the enhancement. With his genius for enlisting apt ability, Maynard had brought
Logan Thompson, a middle-aged bachelor Yorkshireman (along with his parents, with whom he lived) from the King's College estates to manage the farm
being developed at Tilton. For an agricultural person Thompson was a surprisingly late riser, but he spent long evenings reading good books. A year after
Maynard's heart attack, as Bell remembered, Lydia and the well-read farm manager "used to drive around the farm together and seemed, all through the summer of 1938, to be inseparable." It was an "affair," as Bell defined it, which
he thought Thompson's elderly mother—and not Maynard—broke up in the
end. Surely Maynard could see what was going on. Surely he tolerantly and
generously granted Lydia's need for the kind of loving a cardiac invalid was
incapable of giving, and continued to love her as deeply as ever in all other
ways, as indeed she continued to love him. After Maynard died in 1946, Logan
was always with Lydia, Bell resumed: "[I]t seemed that a ménage of a kind
had been established."

In 1966, twenty years later, the 86-year-old Leonard Woolf, in a continuation
of the Keynes–Woolf custom despite deaths on both sides, reported having the
traditional Christmas dinner with Lydia—and now Logan. Lacking servants,
Lydia invited Leonard to the local inn: "She was all tied up in a multiplicity
of shawls out of which looked her bright red face. The White Hart was packed
and the other guests looked at us and each other in a wild surmise." Like
Leonard, Lydia had found an appropriate successor to a great love. Indeed, as
Leonard recounted, he had a second Christmas dinner that day—with Trekkie
Parsons and her exquisitely tolerant husband Ian.[43] Certainly Maynard and Vir-
ginia would have approved.

Both Maynard and Lydia had worked incessantly, naturally, and fluently, to
ramify the bonds of their union. When she was dancing in Paris and separated
from him, she found a thought uniting their work in the sense of art: "I see
how a composition creeps out into a forme out of your lectures; in a different
and lesser degree it is when I make exercises and then compose dance. . . ."
With due distaff modesty she continued, "of course your head is infinitely more
elastic than my legs."[44] But Maynard would not let her set him on a higher
level. He discussed his work and ideas with her as with an equal and accurately
calibrated her intelligence, thus in 1923, "Everything you say about what is in
The Nation is true. . . . How are you so wise? (*No* I don't mock.) I kiss you and
your big bump of wisdom."[45] A dozen years later, reacting to "a most dreadful

review'' of *The General Theory* by Arthur Pigou, he wonders whether he should respond: "I will think over what you say about corresponding any more about my book. I expect you are right—you always are.'' For good reason, however, he was preparing to make an exception, or a partial one, as he apologetically implied: "But I have such a dreadfully controversial temperament that it is difficult to keep away from it."[46] He did not attempt to rebut Pigou's review directly, although his followers did, yet he was operating on the general principle that his revolution in theory did require controversy that compounded aggressive defense. Perhaps Lydia did influence him in the case of Pigou himself, while Maynard lustily returned other blows. Whether he accepted her advice or not, he always paid serious regard to her natural bump of wisdom. During her Paris stay he evaluated her intelligence and grouped around it the qualities that confirmed their joint wisdom in brushing past Bloomsbury's intellectual-ghetto standards. "In my bath today I considered your virtues—how great they were.'' Lydia was a great apple eater: "You must have spent much time eating apples and talking to the serpent! But I also thought that you combined all ages—a very old woman, a matron, a debutante, a girl, a child, an infant, so that you are universal."[47] Well put: her life and letters express all these personae.

Either involved the other in all concerns so that neither was excluded from anything important—or vitally trivial. Thus Maynard had inevitably discussed *The Nation* and *The General Theory* seriously, if not wearyingly, with Lydia. She read many of his accessible writings and attempted the technically difficult at times—and praised. In late 1923 she writes that she is reading his *Tract on Monetary Reform*: "I arrive to capital levy. . . . I like to read financial literature with taste.'' Perhaps she is joking. She refuses to take his advice and avoid the discussion of the quantity theory of money: "I feel that if I escape this chapter I am not an advanced person."[48] It does not matter if she understood or not. Her readings, comprehending or not, were exquisitely flattering—and Maynard, she understood without Virginia's advice, needed flattery. Certainly she was showing that she wanted to know him as well as possible, including his character as great man. Furthermore, Lydia had a peasant's shrewdness raised to the level of unqualified intelligence by the pursuit of her art and intercourse with intelligent and cultivated people. Most of Bloomsbury had not paused to listen to her, but Sam and Lil Courtauld, Vera and Harold Bowen, the Grenfells, and Maynard, among many others, appreciatively collected her lapidary utterances. She also knew to agree with Maynard on the questions that were important to him. Thus she moved with him when his thinking swung away from deflation. She had been reading "innumerable speeches in the press, a good deal of high polluting or high falluting nonsense. Even I, a noneconomic person, see that deflation in the extreme is just as bad as inflation in the extreme, also no real solution for the unemployed."[49] She listened well.

On her own subjects Lydia filled her letters with the ordinary details of daily living illuminated by intelligence and humor. Savoring her humor, Maynard accepted her ordinary preoccupations as essential, indeed existential, and usually more interesting than his great issues. He responded always seriously—and re-paid in kind. His letters, carefully rationing mention of his professional works, are filled with personalities and their quiddities, his daily chores, his walks with Piero Sraffa, his visits to 6 Harvey Road, his moments of fatigue, his colds and other ills. Together, Maynard and Lydia humanized the great issues and dignified the minor.

Lydia's sense of humor easily dominated. Although Maynard had the wit accompanying a razorlike intelligence, he was rather deficient in humor; indeed his best sallies were responses to her. Lydia was aware of her professional proficiency, reporting thoughtfully to Maynard, "Sam wants me to play tragic parts. I disagree. I say I have comic elements in me."[50] (With Maynard's en-couragement she would, however, prove that she could play Ibsen roles.) The comic elements pervaded her private being and, assisted by her Russianate Eng-lish, led Maynard and her true friends into serial smiles and laughter. More than a decade after their relationship had begun she reports as freshly and phenom-enologically as ever that she had been to the dentist and, afflicted with swollen lips, could not "articulate," writing the word in different ink to suggest that she had plucked it out of her assiduously used dictionary. She went on to recount how she had then vainly sought a green hat at Harrod's department store. "I ended the day in a taxi with a bunch of tomatoes in my lap." Always watchful about his health, she prescribes: "Don't do too much, use the . . . scarfe. Your fond Loo-Poo." The next day she shares her pleasure: "Dearest Lank [another pet name], I felt very well this morning, with a good lesson [in acting]. I sailed on the street at 11 o'clock with the sun pouring at me from above." Her good friend, the choreographer Ninette de Valois, who "stayed for three hours . . . cannot forgive me [for] describing her dancers as 'puddings,' says it was 'prickly.' " (One should guess that it was all in good fun and accepted as such, with a lacing of acute professional judgment for the future Dame de Valois, founder of the Royal Ballet, to consider.) Two days later—it was mid-October—"It is too hot for your scarfe, you can wear it as a sash."[51]

The story of the green hat continued. "I was in disturbance, my green hat to order arrived in absolute controversy with my green suit." She was unhappy with "a sort of peacock green" instead of the desired "bottle olive green, the manageresse herself . . . coincid[ing] with me sighing 'Quel damage.' " In com-pensation, "I managed to buy two pairs of pantalettes, as they always wear out, most unreliable . . . between the legs." The following day she "bought more shoes (last day of sale) for you." They were for golf and shooting, "so that when you walk on the downs you'll gallop ahead of me, as the soles are in-cubated with small bullets." She took a shoe of his to get the right size: "I was so afraid to lose your shoe, so I tucked it over my bosom and felt a phisical responsibility."[52] Naturally Maynard supported her on the green hat: "I am shocked to hear of the greens in controversy.' " He reinforced her policy with his own: "But you must be ruthless and get it right."[53]

The next spring Lydia appreciated a fine day: "Oh, the sweetness of the soft air makes me feel how nice it is to breath on this earth. I walked, I took taxis and I guzzled through the sun." A few days later, "I had a bumble bee pay me a visit and how she whizzed saying to me, oh buzz!" One Monday, occupied from morning to evening, Maynard had written, "I am so tired." Instead of working, he had read her letters "two or three times. [This] refreshed and delighted me and was much the best preparation for the lecture."[54]

Lydia's intelligence and professional judgment kept breaking in. She reports seeing the great John Gielgud and Edith Evans in *Romeo and Juliet*, which, she thought, should be called *"Mercutio and Nurse*. Gielgud was like a [Saint] Bernard and Edith Evans so important that the whole production was upside down out of balance . . . slick, like Hamlet in very good bad taste." A few days later she saw Ibsen's *John Gabriel Borkman*. "Remarkable play . . . the three characters are possibly not human, but like with the Greeks, they are the mouth pieces of the inevitable." On matters of high policy she was equally just. She saw the Bolsheviks trying to implement Pavlov's conditioned reflex, "forgetting that mice is mice, and human kind is filled to the utmost with discriminations . . . and I shall not accept things collectively at all (except pantalettes and chemises it is delightful to have a collection of those), nor could you, being so humanistically human."[55] In her comments on the *Romeo and Juliet* performance she added an admonition about his health: "Do not write to me tomorrow, you will have your lecture and the [Political Economy] Club and a few congregations [formal college meetings] in between. Lots of kisses all over. Loo-Poo."

In another expression of solidarity with Lydia, Maynard attuned the swings of his own psyche and body to the progress of her period, her "cycle," as the student of credit and trade cycle termed it. In the building of union, she was, for her part, reciprocally putting herself in accord with his range of ills. Compared with his experience of frequently recurring ills, she enjoyed excellent, indeed serene health, but she reacted rather dramatically to the onset of her "bleedings," as she reported them unabashedly, or "guests," when she played at the pretence of ladylike euphemism. Probably she was not seeking sympathy, but rather the drama of it, while taking account of a phenomenon that affected her body as a professional instrument. Maynard, however, wanted sympathy as well as coordination. In his letter to her when she was in Paris attended by her friends, he had begun, "I am rather depressed and a little tired (I expect it's the cycle—I always have one the same time as yours) and want to be comforted." He goes on less unhappily, "However I've just got a very nice letter from you and that comforts me a good deal."[56] But then, always the professional economist, he remarks in mock complaint to her report in another letter, "[Y]ou have gained two days again [in her period] and put all my calculations out!"[57]

If Lydia is dramatic, she takes care not to go so far as to cause Maynard distress. In a chatty letter she incidentally remarks, "I feel better at present, but my last night was disturbed by coming bleedings."[58] More poignantly on another occasion, "*Oah* Maynardochka, nothing prevents the pain of my 'bleedings,' I am so suffering." But she does not dwell on the pain and goes on to retail various gossipy items, then remarking flatteringly, "I have read again 'the return towards gold,' " his published forebodings on that imminent error, "and again was impressed with it's truthful mastery."[59]

Two years later Maynard still wants comforting for his companionable distress. Lydia had left him behind to join his sister's family and his parents on a Swiss holiday, and he writes, "Dear Lydochka, I am a little melancholy today. Perhaps it is being a bachelor for a whole week; perhaps it is a touch of cycle." Once again, bringing her into his labors, he cheers up, "However I did a very good morning's work at my book [*A Treatise on Money*]."[60] So went their joint work of union, fluently, continually.

One of Freud's great commonplaces is that happiness builds on love and work. Maynard's life illustrates it precisely. Lydia and love were a necessary cause of his happiness from December 1921, but not a sufficient one. He continued to need the work that had heretofore given substance to his life, although the love she brought meant a fine balance to it. When one surveys all his Herculean labors, one can see that it must have been a very great love to have maintained that equilibrium.

Chapter 6 recounted Maynard's many activities centered on his two days in London, from Tuesday to Thursday evening, thus his speculations on the various exchanges, his work with his two insurance companies, his management of the *Economic Journal* and *The Nation*, his efforts to revitalize the Liberal Party, the government conferences at home and abroad, and the ad hoc operations from covering the Genoa Conference to work on the Macmilllan Committee and the Economic Advisory Council. That was not enough. In 1926–27 he descended to the regional level and attempted to save the Lancashire cotton mills from deep depression, but his plan required that the weaker firms commit suicide for the general good and they defeated it.[61] He often took the 3:15 P.M. train from Cambridge on Tuesday, going directly to a meeting in London before arriving at 46 Gordon Square. A typical Wednesday schedule included meetings of the National Mutual and Provincial insurance societies followed by an editorial talk with Hubert Henderson at *The Nation* from 5:30 P.M. Once a month, on Wednesday, he attended the perversely scheduled Tuesday Club meetings.[62] This was much more than enough for two or three energetic persons. Then there was the rest of the week in Cambridge.

In 1919, after resigning from the Treasury, Maynard had first reduced his Cambridge labors. He condensed his lecture obligation to one set of eight annually, other demands on his time eliminating the academic years 1921–22, and 1930–31 and 1931–32 before his heart attack and the war ended his lecturing career close to completion of the 1936–37 series. In 1920 he had also resigned his Girdlers' Lectureship. But these reductions simply made room for his other work. After *The Economic Consequences of the Peace* (1919), he completed his long-pending *Treatise on Probability* in 1921 and went on to *A Revision of Treaty* (January 1922), *A Tract on Monetary Reform* (December 1923), *A Treatise on Money* from July 1924 (published, October 1930), and *The General*

Theory from 1930 (published, February 1936). There were the articles or invitational lectures that became short books, *The Economic Consequences of Mr Churchill* (1925) and *The End of Laissez-Faire* (1926), and important articles like a long memorial to Alfred Marshall (*Economic Journal*, September 1924) and similar appreciations of Thomas Malthus and Stanley Jevons, among other economists. He also assembled his more trenchant articles in his *Essays in Persuasion* (1931) and *Essays in Biography* (1933). He also researched and wrote at length but inconclusively on ancient coinage, but this was hobby, he apologetically explained to Lydia.[63] Prolific academic people can achieve similar word and page totals of significant contributions to knowledge, but Keynes was still taking pupils (usually three or four at a time, however, on Friday or Saturday from 6:30 P.M.) and holding his Political Economy Club meetings Monday evenings *and*, as indefatigable administrator, spending endless hours in committee meetings.

The postwar Keynes intervened everywhere, it seemed, into university and college administration. In 1920 he was elected to the university's Council of the Senate, where his father had prospered in his rise to the registraryship. Here the committee work, taking the whole university under its purview and granting the individual member too little power, defeated the younger Keynes; worn down to discouragement, he resigned, but not until 1927. He functioned more naturally in King's College, where he could get his will done. He was a member of the King's College Council, which met on Saturdays and also sometimes on Mondays for four to five hours with a break for lunch. But the college council was only a starting point. His hard administrative work and prominence as economist (his public prominence, however, remaining a negative factor in a dons' world) made him a natural candidate for provost of King's when the incumbent resigned in 1926. Although he was aware he had too many other commitments, as he wrote Lydia, he agonized intensely before deciding against it: "I hope I have done right. I feel sad about it in some ways." His father loved the idea, but his mother, who like Lydia, was always right, was negative, as were most of his good college friends.[64] In the end, he swung his support, powerful enough to be effective, to a mediocre, moderate candidate against the conservative economic historian John Clapham. The new provost wrote him humbly, "I know it is you who have done this. You must support and teach me what I have to do."[65] Maynard won such power by overwork.

Maynard's lifeline was a double braid of compulsive overwork making his life bearable and the related ailments jeopardizing it. He would be driving himself to excessive labors to the very end of his life, as his letters to Lydia and his engagement diary, chockablock with appointments, some of them extending three months beyond, document.[66] In June 1924 he reports to her: "This has been one of my dreadful wasted days—I have spent more than eight hours in college and university meetings and am much too tired to do anything sensible." On a Monday in November: "A terrible day of meetings. In 12 hours I have less than an hour to myself—which is at this moment as I write. Tomorrow we have our great college meeting—the Annual Congregation which lasts all day.''[67] On a Monday three years later: "This again will not be a proper letter— I haven't the strength left to have a single idea or thought. I have been working at top speed (including a very difficult lecture) ever since breakfast; and after dinner the [Political Economy] Club comes which means two or three hours more. I am exhausted. . . .'' Maynard catches himself, "but really very well.''[68] But he knew that his exhaustion did not conduce to the best of health. *But* he could not escape his duties on the three key college committees, the Estates, Building, and Fellowship Committees.

Through the Estates Committee, as bursar (second bursar from 1919, first from 1924) Keynes managed the college's investments. In the 1920s, quickly selling off one third of its estates, he shifted its investments substantially from medieval land holdings to higher paying securities. In 1925, he could boast to Lydia that he had made King's College richer by £235,000.[69] Later in the decade, in one of his characteristic reversals, he intuitively found reason to shift back to land and himself engaged in active farm management of the college's three thousand acres. (World War II's effect on the demand for food may have retroactively, if temporarily, justified his action.) At Tilton, in the same spirit, he leased contiguous farm land and, raising pigs, inter alia, became a farmer (assisted by Logan Thompson) on his own account as well. On a Friday in late 1927 he wrote Lydia that he had been in ''my office on bursarial affairs all day. . . . My cold sits heavily on me and dulls the brain, but not so much that I can't do college business!'' After a college feast he had had ''conversations with tenants [of the college's land] all last night and all this morning [which] I rather enjoyed.'' He also gave a party for the tenants in his rooms and successfully mollified an irascible farmer who had been ''in a state of violent quarrel with the college for seven years.''[70] More important than his decisions between land and securities was the radical change he effected in the character of the college's security investments themselves. In 1920, while moving it to more profitable, if more risky, general investments, he got King's to create the ''Chest,'' a special fund of £30,000 which he could manage on his own. By 1944–45 he had multiplied the Chest's value by eleven, more than three times better than the value increase in the college's regular investments, into which that fund was averaged.[71]

In the Fellowship Committee, as fellowship elector and loyal friend, Maynard was subject to spasms of intense activity to support his numerous protégés. These included Richard Braithwaite (named a fellow in 1924), who, as the university's Knightbridge Professor of Moral Philosophy, could repay him by writing the introduction, glossing over its logical problems, of the *Collected Writings* volume of his *Treatise on Probability*. Another fellow of the same year was Frank P. Ramsey, a brilliant straddler of mathematics and philosophy, who distressed him by pointing out those flaws; Maynard had to grant that he could not repair them, although he did not quite admit they weakened the book's sense.[72] His old friend Gerald Shove, now not so close but forever attached, presented another problem. Shove won his gratitude by doing most of the hard economics teaching at King's, but he was publishing shy, a great handicap in a fellowship election. Masterful, indefatigable, Maynard achieved a fellowship for the embarrassingly mature Gerald in 1926. Another successful protégé (in 1930) was Richard Kahn, who wrote a rigorously and beautifully argued dissertation.[73]

Also, operating from the Building Committee, Maynard became a modest master builder and left monuments in stone behind. He was a leader in the college's postwar construction program, which, including a new provost's lodge, extended its buildings to the Cam, among other changes. In 1923 he was resisting designs that the committee had commissioned and got it to invite other architects to submit theirs.[74] He had his own candidate, George Kennedy, a friend and Etonian, who had the skill to adapt his imagination to the given coutours of centuries of the college's architectural history. With his talent for combinations, Maynard soon had Kennedy working for himself at Tilton, beginning in 1926, constructing his library and relating house and library by a kind of loggia. This led Kennedy back to King's and Keynes's finest monument, the Cambridge Arts Theatre, which would be a stage for Lydia as distinguished actress and memorial for Mr. and Mrs. John Neville Keynes as distinguished servants of university and town. The Keynesian combination included Dadie Rylands as theater expert.

Always supportive of Lydia, Maynard was trying to find her a worthy occupation as her ballet career declined. She appeared again in a Diaghilev production in 1927, but the great man died later that year and she was indubitably getting older. In November 1928 Maynard arranged for her to dance and act in the Cambridge Amateur Dramatic Club, the acting bringing her to Shakespeare, in his *A Lover's Complaint*. She was charitably praised despite her undomesticated accent, but a more ambitious effort five years later, in October–November 1933, as Olivia in an Old Vic production of *Twelfth Night*, was a failure, with less charitable comments about the accent. Encouraged by Dadie Rylands, Maynard directed Lydia toward Ibsen and brought her into his building program.

Late in November 1933, on a Monday, Maynard, master builder, wrote Lydia that he had given a "good lecture this morning. Since then I have been amusing myself thinking out a plan to build a small, very smart, modern theatre for the college. Will you agree to appear in the first performance if it comes off?" He explained that the theater of the Amateur Dramatic Club (ADC) had burned down. The college owned a small site on the other side of King's Parade close to St. Edward's Passage, where he would build a flat for her presently. The plot thickens: "The project fascinates me and I already begin to draw up plans of my own for it."[75] Maynard spent the whole of 1934 negotiating the creation of The Arts Theatre, as it was formally named, and all of 1935 building it. In the construction he was assisted by the wisely selected team of architect George Kennedy, theater man Dadie Rylands, and a Cambridge cinema manager brought in as a practical-minded theater manager. Maynard tried to get the ADC to join in the project and failed; he tried to get formal sponsorship by King's College and got only toleration. He tried to get broad financial support by selling shares to well-wishers; he sold 2,350 "preference" shares at £1 per share for a theater costing £36,000. In the end he provided more than £22,500 of the costs, if not more.[76] This was, however, the period of his greatest speculative profits, Maynard happily boasting to his mother at the end of 1935, "[T]he results for the year are horribly prosperous. . . . At present it all seems very easy, indeed indecently so." He also reported having just completed his *General Theory*.[77]

Maynard vaguely imagined the theater, seating an audience of five to six hundred, as providing a stage for undergraduate drama and performances of visiting companies. But the real point was Lydia (and his parents). Given his prosperity, the financing did not trouble him. As he rationalized it to Lydia, "The greatest comfort of all . . . from having some money is that one does not need to badger other people for it."[78] To this day it remains a question whether Cambridge, an hour from London by train and possessing other entertainment facilities, needed still another theater. Although it was the frame for some successful productions, it has remained closed for long periods and could never be defined as a financial success. For Maynard that was irrelevant.

Busying himself about all the details, Maynard decided that the theater needed a restaurant, a *good* one in the French manner. He essayed humor in a letter to Lydia: "I will leave the theatre to you, if I can be allowed to manage the restaurant." The result was a British–French farce. One early problem was the incompetence of the first chef and an administrative inhibition that prevented dismissing him in May 1936. In less than one month, however, Maynard could triumphantly report that the chef and most of the staff were being forthwith sacked. Recognizing, however, that the British cuisine might defeat his best efforts, he achieved a classic administrator's resolution; he delegated the responsibility to another person. In the early fall he lunched at the restaurant and reported to Lydia that the food was a bad as ever; "However, this is Mr. Samet's project." Two days later, unable quite to disclaim responsibility, he complained, "[N]ot a vestige of French cooking from the alleged elderly French chef; it all seems without a doubt British."[79] Britain has defeated greater restauranteurs.

Lydia, meanwhile, was working her way. While giving up dancing, except for special appearances into 1933, she joined her friend Ninette de Valois on the managing committee of the Camargo Ballet Society, founded in 1930, and became an energetic patron of the art. By January 1931 she had discovered that cash was more important than expert committee and signaled Maynard for help.[80] He took the critical post of treasurer, and the Camargo achieved two ballet seasons before succumbing to the Depression in 1933.

Geoffrey Keynes, the true aesthete of the family, created the Camargo's greatest triumph by conceiving of a ballet adaptation of William Blake's *Illustrations of the Book of Job* in the form of *Job: A Masque for Dancing*, music by Ralph Vaughan Williams and choreography by Ninette de Valois. Its successful initial performances, on 5 and 6 July 1931, were followed by a run of more than three score in Covent Garden. Geoffrey cites ballet historians for the

theory that his and the Camargo's masque saved British ballet.[81] (Later, Maynard, his talent for combinations always operative, got the Camargo, before it
vanished, to give a gala performance for the delegates to the World Economic
Conference of 1933 before the conference vanished without a trace.) So buoyed
by Geoffrey Keynes's masque, the Camargo led to the founding of the English
National Ballet.

Although she did not, as Maynard had projected, perform at its inauguration,
The Arts Theatre of Cambridge was constructed around Lydia's acting. On 4
March 1934, after her mixed notices in Shakespearean efforts, she had gone on
to achieve a fine success as Nora Helmer in a London production of Ibsen's *A
Doll's House*, leading to a run of eighty days. Even Virginia Woolf had to soften
her critical focus and find Lydia just right. On 3 February 1936 The Arts Theatre
opened with a gala program by the Vic-Wells Ballet, Maynard and Lydia in
their box, and the senior Keyneses and the senior heads of the colleges and their
wives in the first row of the dress circle. *The General Theory*, was published
the next day. (Maynard's health had begun to give off threatening signals again,
chest pains in May 1935, and then influenza keeping him in bed more than a
week in January; he had arisen just in time for the opening.) On 17 February,
two weeks less a day after it opened, the theater presented an Ibsen cycle, with
Lydia as Nora again and as Hilda Wangel in *The Master Builder*, appropriately
enough. (Another actress, the fine professional Jean Forbes-Robertson, appeared
in *Hedda Gabler* and *Rosmersholm*.) Certainly Lydia again deserved Virginia's
report on her Nora of 1934. It had been "a triumphant success, much to our
surprise. Dear old Maynard was—this is exactly true, streaming tears; and I
kissed him in the stalls between the acts; really she was a marvel, not only a
light leaf in the wind, but edged, profound, and her English was exactly like
what Ibsen meant—it gave the right aroma."[82] Now, in 1936, Clive Bell agreed
with Virginia, commending Lydia for Nora's speech of self-liberation as being
effectively personal rather than falling into the trap of suffragette utterance.[83]
To Maynard's overflowing happiness Lydia and the Ibsen program transferred
to London in March for more than a month of performances.

Of course Maynard, driven by loyalty, even love, and his lust for ascendancy,
continued to exert himself for all of his friends as well, sometimes whether they
wanted or needed it or not. After Lytton Strachey's great success with his *Eminent Victorians* in 1918, Maynard decided that Harcourt Brace, his own American publisher, could do better for Lytton's *Queen Victoria* in the United States
than G. P. Putnam's, which had paid a generous 20 percent in royalties on the
earlier book. Audacious for himself, Maynard properly was more cautious for
Lytton and elicited a Harcourt Brace offer of a fixed sum of $7,000. In Novem-
ber 1920 he wrote Lytton, "I hardly know what to advise." He proceeded to
advise: "But for you there seems a good deal of virtue in certainty." Giving
up the hope of royalties, Lytton got the offer raised to $10,000 in return for his
giving up serial and Canadian book rights.[84] For diametrically opposed reasons
this was a financial error in a class with Maynard's personal disasters on the

commodity exchanges. *Queen Victoria* was Lytton's most successful book. In August 1921 he wrote Maynard piteously, but not quite recriminatingly, that he had got a correct but wretched installment of $3,000 from Alfred Harcourt: "The wicked man says he has printed 30,000 copies . . . and I spend my time calculating the immeasurable sums I've lost by not going in for royalties." Reluctant as ever to admit error, Maynard returned, "Harcourt prints wildly . . . and you must console yourself . . . that he hasn't sold nearly all." He shuffled figures about to minimize the loss and, in the end, half-admitting his poor counsel, suggested, "Your best revenge will be to write a very bad book and sell it to him for $20,000."[85] Maynard went on to proffer advice to Lytton on investing his $10,000.[86]

Maynard did much better for Vanessa and Duncan. Indeed, adoring both, he continued to indulge his masochism with Duncan, who continued to accept his largesse and support Vanessa's long-seething resentment. Maynard simply added Vanessa to Duncan as another beloved exploiter and asked only for more of the same treatment. In 1927, when Maynard was well launched in new service to both, Virginia, after enjoying his hospitality, reported to Vanessa, "[H]e almost brought tears to my eyes . . . by his doglike affection for you . . . but I'm convinced he feels at his heart your malicious ways, and yet can't overcome his superstition that you and Duncan are the soul and salt of the world. Vanessa says this—and Vanessa used to do that."[87] In the fall of 1925, on his return from honeymoon and Sussex vacation, plunging into overwork as usual, Maynard set about to organize the London Artists' Association (LAA). He built it around Vanessa, Duncan, Roger Fry, and four other painters. Having recognized Sam Courtauld as vulnerable to this type of benefaction, Maynard brought him in, along with two other wealthy men, as co-sponsors with himself.

Maynard's objective was to guarantee the artists an annual income of £150 and so remove their money worries. Covertly, the whole structure was his way of providing for Duncan, whom he had accepted forever as his responsibility. (Lydia, refusing to be jealous and understanding his grand generosity, gave no evidence of distress at this expenditure elsewhere of money, energy, and feeling.) Maynard had also identified a critical point in Duncan's and Vanessa's careers and acted to make the most of it. (Roger, independently wealthy, did not need or take the money, but was most helpfully contributing his great prestige to the LAA.) In 1920 and 1922, respectively, Duncan and Vanessa had started off the decade auspiciously with successful one-man/woman shows and were reaching their highest plateau of painting and popularity. Nevertheless, the LAA provided a saving security within the general insecurity of the art world's economy. Vanessa's biographer thought the association "successfully steered Vanessa and Duncan into the limelight. Duncan, especially, soon found himself fashionable and famous."[88] Later, in February 1930, Vanessa had her greatest triumph with another show, a critic saluting the "subtle delicacy of her painting . . . united to a hard-won but inevitable solidity of objects." Although she always humbly accorded Duncan primacy, her biographer found in her work "more feeling and integrity than discernible beneath the flourish and animation of Duncan's bravura."[89] Others, including Roger Fry, agreed that Duncan could be misled by his facility. In any case both painters had resoundingly arrived.

Vanessa and Duncan condignly rewarded Maynard by quarreling with him and frustrating his best plans for the LAA. At one point she coolly advised Roger "not to listen to a word he says" and continue to do what they chose.[90] These senior painters frustrated Maynard's efforts to bring along younger artists and so keep abreast of change. Giving up, Maynard ironically but humbly wrote Vanessa, "I don't know why, with my low ideas, I mix myself up with these high matters!—it is very foolish." Surrendering in fact, he held to principle: "[T]here should be the *appearance* as well as the reality of . . . no sort of discrimination."[91] This was not enough for the malcontents. The next year Duncan and Vanessa resigned from the association after soliciting better financial terms from a private gallery. At last "Maynard was furious and argued (rightly) that their departure would bring an end of the LAA." He pointed out to Duncan that the organization had sold £10,587 worth of his paintings in six years, but Duncan had no organ of gratitude.[92] He got his, and Vanessa got her, condign punishment. They had picked a critically bad point in British painting and their own professional lives. The Depression was crushing the art market, while Duncan was slipping out of fashion and Vanessa, never so much in fashion, was losing her more modest popularity. In 1933 Maynard dissolved the much diminished LAA. He was not done helping his beloved friends.

Duncan and Vanessa, their reputations still lingering, were later commissioned to paint panels and plan color schemes for the great ship the *Queen Mary*. In the summer of 1935, just after they had completed their panels, the Cunard Shipping Company suddenly canceled Vanessa's contract for a panel in the sitting room next to the Catholic ship's chapel and told Duncan to reduce the size of his large panels, meant for the main lounge. One reason was the objection of Roman Catholic authorities, who found Vanessa's designs offensive. The Cunard people had been brought to realize that Bloomsbury taste, never broadly acceptable, was now passé. Naturally, "Vanessa went straight to Maynard for advice"[93]—and help. Maynard, who knew Sir Percy Bates, the Cunard chairman, suggested that her work be used in another room, and emphasized that the "cancellation of her contract not only takes away advantages she has been relying on, but is actually bad for her reputation." Bates accepted his logic totally, Cunard paying her £200 for the rejected panel and advancing her £150 for a new one. Maynard was able to write him that "Mrs. Bell . . . is not only completely happy, but feels she has been handsomely treated."[94] It was nevertheless a setback. Maynard could not stop time and alter fashion.

Maynard went on caring for and taking care of Duncan. In 1937, while feeling poorly from his (not yet diagnosed) cardiac condition and while suffering large financial losses (on the commodity exchanges), he settled a permanent income on Duncan, recently become quinquagenarian. "Dearest Maynard," Duncan wrote, "I do not know how to thank you for what you are doing for me. . . .

But honestly it is the greatest blessing that I need no longer worry about old age and decrepitude . . . quite apart from all the pleasure it will give me to have a little extra money now . . . Much love, Duncan.''[95] In the present Duncan could accept gifts gracefully.

And, as he showed again for Vanessa, Maynard gave more than money, he gave of himself, his best thought and energy. On 18 July 1937 Julian Bell, who had gone to Spain as an ambulance driver (after Vanessa persuaded him not to volunteer for combat duty), was killed by a piece of shrapnel. Julian was a big, blubbery, unfocused young man of twenty-nine, who had been a poetry-writing Cambridge undergraduate, Apostle, and, like his father, womanizer (after a brief affair with the future spy, Anthony Blunt). He had been Vanessa's perfect, most nearly total love; indeed, he had gone to China as an English professor to seek a liberating distance from her, but a disastrous affair and idealism had combined to shift him to the Spanish Civil War. When Roger Fry had died in 1934, Vanessa fainted and her daughter Angelica remembered, ''[T]he following day, on going near her bedroom, I heard her howling in anguish.''[96] Vanessa had then suffered a brief physical breakdown. Julian's death nearly killed her. Only her sister Virginia, with ''infinite love and persistence,'' was able to call her back to life.[97] In his way, in his enduring friendship, Maynard addressed Vanessa's anguish as appositely.

On 22 July, two months after his heart attack and still weak and gravely ill, Maynard wrote Vanessa from his sanitorium: ''A line of sympathy and love from us both on the loss of your dear and beautiful boy with his pure and honorable feelings. It was fated that he should make his protest, as he was entitled to do, with his life, and one can say nothing. With love and affection, Maynard.''[98] In an undated, penciled letter Vanessa wrote back: ''Dearest Maynard I want to tell you that your words are almost the only ones I want to keep. I tried to write to you the other day to thank you for what you wrote in the *Nation* [*sic: New Statesman*] but I could not—I felt too much. . . . It is the message of our generation to the young. Please get well. You are very dear to me and you must help us all Vanessa.''[99]

Maynard did more than write a sympathy note. Following his notice in the *New Statesman* he composed an obituary of Julian for the King's College Annual Report, another meed of comfort for Vanessa. As she said, he was there to help them all, and the next year she was asking him and Lydia to get Angelica started as an actress. Maynard responded with a detailed, thoughtful letter and included a letter of recommendation to a theater manager obligated to him.[100] Here, however, his best efforts, Angelica possessing other talents, could not succeed.

Maynard's generosity, accompanied as it was by his voluptuous exercise of power and instinctive movement toward ascendancy, inevitably called up negative reactions from those he helped. The life of the LAA had produced fine examples. Another marvelously contradictory characteristic accompanied his generous spirit—and provided justification for ingratitude and mockery: miserliness. Magnanimous in large matters, he could be mean in the minuscule, which he sometimes promoted to issues of economic principle. Thus he refused to pay more than what his "inner consciousness" told him to pay a North African boy to polish his shoes. The boy expressed his disagreement by throwing stones, and when Sebastian Sprott, Keynes's companion on that trip in early 1921, suggested additional payment for the sake of peace, "Keynes was firm: 'I will not be a party to debasing the currency.' "[101] (This was before he shifted from deflationary to inflationary policy.) In 1931, managing the LAA, he tactlessly, if responsibly, rejected Duncan's request for an advance of £100 on a one-man show because its funds were low. At that moment, ignoring Maynard's benefactor role in his life as well as the association, Duncan used his power as one of its leading painters and impelled him to produce the money. He was too successful in the mind of Frances Spalding, Vanessa's biographer: "Vanessa . . . was disappointed of [a] row." Frances Spalding was percipient on Maynard's motive: Vanessa had "failed to see that to him money was . . . the medium for his creativity: he handled it with a passionate fastidiousness."[102] But this was doubtless another excuse for Duncan and Vanessa to depart the LAA that year.

Maynard's friends often felt like the shoeshine boy when, for example, he neglected to break into his excellent wine cellar for dinner. In 1925, reporting to Carrington on his visit to Tilton, Lytton recounted, "Would you believe it? Not one drop of alcohol appeared." This was when he made his extravagant estimate of Maynard's wealth—"and water, water everywhere! Such is the reward of wealth."[103] On occasion Maynard provided as poorly in nourishing solids as in liquids. In 1927 Virginia could match Lytton's story in a letter to Lytton himself. The Woolfs and Vanessa had been at Tilton and "picked the bones of Maynard's grouse of which there were three for eleven people. This stinginess is a constant source of delight to Nessa—her eyes gleamed when the bones went round."[104]

During the 1920s, absent life-threatening crises, Maynard's health was rather better than it had ever been, but he was still vulnerable to lesser ailments. One brushes swiftly past anodyne excuses calling up affection, thus, "Since yesterday I have had rheumatism in my shoulder and want your rubbing for it very much." His mother, however, had given him "a very long rub," but then, "I have pain from a small pile (do you know what it is?). Put crosses on it."[105] More seriously, in January 1925, "I need your delicate touches—because I don't feel very well today. The 'stomach cough' has become more stomach and also more cough. It might almost be a slight influenza." Lydia immediately returned, " 'More stomach and more cough'? *Oah* biedny [dear] Maynardochka, how unsympathetic. . . . Please, take good comfort around you, don't stand in the drafts."[106]

It was indeed influenza and held on for weeks. In February, "Influenza is a strange thing—I still feel collapsed most days between 5 and 7; for instance today—not fully myself." In late April, "I feel a little nervous today and would like to be touched by Lady T [for Talky]; also a slight earache." The next day, "The earache has turned out to be the symptom of a slight cold. So I am a little devitalized today." At this point, upsetting him considerably, Maynard discovered that he had made an embarrassing technical error in an article on Britain's return to the gold standard. Recovering his morale, he wrote a week later, "My spirits are much better today but my physical condition is still very weak and queer—a bad head and strange feelings. I must have had influenza and am now suffering from not having noticed it." In October, diagnosing "very slight stomach influenza," Maynard reported, "I am better today but not yet 'right.' I am easily tired, slightly low vitality and sometimes feel a little 'strange.' "[107] In the next four years, until 1931, the influenza relented and the ailments were minor. Maynard did suffer mildly from an occasional cold, a touch of diarrhea, moments of being "weak and seedy," a general nervous fatigue, and a knee that "slipt out again."[108] On a Sunday in late October 1931 he scrawled a more serious message to Lydia in pencil.

"I am after all having my day in bed and in horrid circumstances," Maynard reported. He did not try to mitigate the import of it: "I woke up yesterday with the most dreadful pain in my chest so that I telephoned at once for a doctor." He was assured that what he was experiencing was not dangerous, but it was nevertheless, he said, "horribly painful." Precisely at this time Lytton was dying of undiagnosed stomach cancer, and Maynard's doctor provided him with a fine, sophisticated sounding, anodyne interpretation of his condition, which any medical student today would immediately recognize as angina pectoris: "a sort of rheumatism, an inflammation of the sheaths of the small muscles which encircle the lungs (intercostal)." Ringing various changes on it as his symptoms waxed and waned, Maynard would live with that interpretation into 1937. The doctor had assured him, after another night of "severe pain all over again," that it was common and "he would get well by mid-week."[109]

It took Maynard a year to "get well," that is to say, for the symptoms to become slight enough for him to ignore or try to ignore. For a year, however, his letters report on a range of distresses. In mid-November 1931 he was experiencing an occasional "rheumatic twinge," "tender" teeth, and eyes "not so strong." In February 1932, "I am bunged up with a genuine cold." In April, "My body is terribly full of rheumatism and lumbago, especially in the mornings, when I cannot manage to sit comfortably." The next day his "rheumatics [were] flying about the body and I am a little nervous about them settling in my chest." On 23 October 1932, "I feel somewhat of a rheumatism in my chest ... and am nervous about my intercostals—it is just a year since I was afflicted." He was off by two days. In January 1933 he was at last unequivocal about feeling better: "I am still in excellent health—not even rheumatics." But the next month he was reporting fatigue and lack of energy.[110] Thereafter, however, the complaints subside, but do not at all disappear. Always he was suffering colds, working too hard, and exhausting himself. At one point in November 1936, he softened his compulsiveness. Arranging a table of figures for the college accounts, as he wrote his mother, he could not find a mistake; he was "so exhausted that I cooked it to make it come right by cheating."[111] Before then he had half-recognized an ominous signal.

Maynard had got over the influenza that attacked him just before The Art Theatre opened and his *General Theory* was published, in February 1936— perhaps. In May 1936, two days after a "most sharp attack of lumbago," he felt "very well today except that I have rheumatics flying about—which is seasonal, I suppose."[112] And so he warded off the thought and let the signal flicker out. Yet he was not feeling too well that summer, although, with his great book completed, it was otherwise a period of deep content and relaxation at Tilton. In late September he took Lydia for a visit to her family in Leningrad. He was trying to ignore "attacks of breathlessness and discomfort in starting a walk," which had begun to afflict him before summer's end. They relented but he had a mild case of influenza in the fall and seemed to recover. Afterward, however, he could not walk more than fifty yards without "great distress in the chest." Before he consulted with a physician, he prescribed his own cure by taking Lydia to Cannes on 13 March 1937, but the breathlessness and pain got worse. On his return, on 25 March, he detailed the history of these and other symptoms to his uncle, Walter Langdon-Brown, Regius Professor of Physic at Cambridge University.[113] The thought was now addressed.

The next month, as Virginia Woolf noted in her diary, "L[eonard] went to Tilton and had a long quiet cronies talk. Maynard not well; cramp in the muscle of his heart. His toes curl up. Lydia anxious."[114] On 31 March his uncle examined Maynard and, as Maynard reported to his mother, "found nothing *prima facie* wrong—heart, lungs, blood pressure, etc., all good and sound." He added, however, "But I am to go up tomorrow to be x-rayed."[115] Dr. Langdon-Brown then rather vaguely and less reassuringly determined that the heart muscles had, after all, been damaged. He thereupon prescribed medicines that Maynard found unpleasant, but he carried on while suffering spasms and other distresses. He collapsed of a coronary thrombosis—a classic and massive heart attack—at his parents' home on 16 May 1937.

A truly distinguished physician, Langdon-Brown was limited to his generation's knowledge of cardiac conditions. Lydia had met him in 1925 and found him a "nice woolly creature! I understand the children that climbed on him all over."[116] With all due conscientiousness Langdon-Brown had incompetently diagnosed his nephew's condition. Even after the collapse and recognizing the gravity of Maynard's condition, Langdon-Brown missed important pathological evidences and euphemized the cardiac event as a "pseudo-angina." That was the heading of analysis attached to his report, dated 20 May 1937. The report, made in association with a Dr. Ryle, did take Maynard's condition seriously enough to recommend more testing and a rest of six months. It also quoted and appeared to agree with Dr. Ryle that Maynard's " 'terrifically exacting life' is having its effect." The diagnosis of the "pseudo-angina" defined it as closely resembling the true angina while being, however, "independent of structural disease of the heart and coronary arteries.'' The pseudo-angina, it went on to specify, was ''often associated with mental anxiety and overwork.''[117] This comment of Langdon-Brown's showed more insight than he had in Maynard's sheerly physical condition. An expert in many fields, according to a nephew who wrote a family memoir, Langdon-Brown, besides mastering physiology, pathology, and endocrinology, was a pioneer in psychosomatic medicine and freely (and indiscriminately) quoted Freud, Jung, and Adler.[118] That psychosomatic interest might explain the acute emphasis on ''anxiety and overwork'' and the rest of the analysis: ''The treatment is that of the underlying neurosis . . .'' Langdon-Brown had recognized Maynard's pathological compulsiveness. The analysis concluded with threatening optimism: ''and the prognosis is a good one, sudden death not occurring.''

Miraculously, Maynard could recover—partially—from the terrific cardiac damage. Lydia would further display that sensitivity to sickness that Vanessa had spied sixteen years earlier and even more intensely and passionately protect Maynard against himself as much as possible. He would rise again and, indulging his compulsions and further endangering his vulnerable defenses, enter a new phase of distinguished and richly honored service to his country even as he could observe his *General Theory* conquering opinion. He would enjoy nearly nine years more of life with Lydia.

NOTES

1. *The Evening Standard*, Keynes and Lopokova, *Lydia and Maynard*, plate 45.
2. Skidelsky, *JMK*, 2: 208.
3. JMK's two talks, 14, 15 September 1925, *CW*, 19: 434–42; quotation, 441.
4. Quoted, Holroyd, *LS*, 2: 372.
5. 23 December 1920, Virginia Woolf, *The Letters*, 2: 451.
6. David Garnett, *The Familiar Faces* (London, 1962), 64–65.
7. Cover, *Maynard Keynes Collection of Pictures, Books and Manuscripts*, David Scrase and Peter Croft, eds. (catalogue of exhibition, Fitzwilliam Museum, 5 July–29 August 1983; Cambridge, 1983). Details in *Maynard Keynes Collection*, 45–46, which notes a first performance of the Keynes–Keynes in 1926, another in 1927, and possible repetitions; and Frances Partridge, *Love in Bloomsbury: Memories*, 92.
8. Note and entry, 28 February 1938, Virginia Woolf, *The Diary*, 5: n. 129; on the arrangements, Harrod, *The Life*, n. 317.
9. Harrod, *The Life*, 317–18.
10. Quoted, Skidelsky, *JMK*, 2: 5.
11. Letter, JMK to FAK, 13 September 1920, KP, PP/45/168. Photograph of detail of Grant's grape-pickers, Richard Shone, *Bloomsbury Portraits* (London, 1976), 67.
12. JMK to LL, 23 October; LL to JMK, 24 October 1924, KP, PP/45/190.
13. Letter, 22 January 1937, ibid.
14. Letter, 11 February 1935, ibid.
15. Editorial note, *CW*, 21: 289; related details, Felix, *Biography of an Idea*, 226–30.

16. KP, PP/45/190.

17. Entry, 19 April 1945, Virginia Woolf, *The Diary*, 4: 209.

18. Moggridge, *MK*, 836, n. 836. LL's will would have her ashes placed beside JMK's; the solution was to scatter them also on the Downs.

19. Milo Keynes, "Lydia Lopokova," 13–24.

20. Letter, 9 October 1936, KP, PP/45/190.

21. Milo Keynes, "Lydia Lopokova," 14.

22. Skidelsky, *JMK*, 2: 215.

23. Letter, 23 April 1933, KP, PP/45/168.

24. Quoted, Milo Keynes, "Lydia Lopokova," 35.

25. Milo Keynes, ibid., 37.

26. Patrick Hadley, quoted, Milo Keynes, "Lydia Lopokova," ibid., 1.

27. Quoted, Harrod, *The Life*, 365.

28. Geoffrey Keynes, *The Gates of Memory*, 198.

29. Letters, JMK to LL, 10 February 1933, 27 January 1935, KP, PP/45/190.

30. Julie Kavanagh, *Secret Muses: The Life of Frederick Ashton* (London, 1996), 116.

31. KP, PP/45/190.

32. Ibid.

33. 11, 23, 25, 27 June, 2 July, 17 August 1922, ibid.

34. 24 April 1922, 14 September 1923, ibid.

35. 20, 21 January 1924, ibid.

36. LL to JMK, 20 January 1923.

37. 2 May 1924, ibid.

38. 28 October, 2 November 1923, ibid.

39. JMK to LL, 6 May, 10 October 1927, ibid.

40. Milo Keynes, "Lydia Lopokova," 13.

41. 25 June 1937, KP, PP/45/190.

42. 15, 30 November 1935, 29 April 1937, ibid.

43. Quentin Bell, *Elders and Betters* (London, 1995), 102, 104; letter, Leonard Woolf to Dame Peggy Ashcroft, 27 December 1966, *Letters of LW*, 550–51.

44. 4 May 1924, KP, PP/45/190.

45. 22 October 1923, ibid.

46. 17 May 1936, ibid.

47. 8 June 1924, ibid.

48. Letters, 25 November, 8 December 1923, ibid.

49. 26 October 1923, ibid.

50. 12 April 1922, ibid.

51. 10, 11, 14 October 1935, ibid.

52. 18, 19 October 1935, ibid.

53. 20 October 1935, ibid.

54. LL to JMK, 27 April, 4 May 1936, ibid; JMK to LL, 14 October 1935, ibid. The letters he mentions must have been those of 10 and 11 October (above).

55. 20, 26 October 1935, 7 February 1924, ibid.

56. 9 May 1924, ibid.

57. 23 February 1925, ibid.

58. 13 October 1924, ibid.

59. 22 February 1925, ibid.

60. 9 June 1927, ibid.

61. Felix, *Biography of an Idea*, 185–86; *CW*, 19: 578–637.

62. JMK's engagement diary, KP, PP/41.

63. 18 January 1924, KP, PP/45/190.

64. 2 May 1926, ibid.

65. Quoted by JMK to LL, 30 May 1926, ibid.

66. Concluding items for 1946, the engagement diary, KP, PP/41.

67. 9 June, 17 November 1924, KP, PP/45/190.

68. 14 November 1927, ibid.

69. 12 November 1925, ibid.

70. 18 November 1927, ibid.

71. Editorial note, "Keynes and King's," *CW*, 12: 88–92; table, 91.

72. JMK, *CW*, 10: (*Essays in Biography*): 338–39. See also Harrod, *The Life*, 141, 652–56. Ramsey, mysteriously afflicted with jaundice, died in 1930, aged 27.

73. Published only in 1989: *The Economics of the Short Period* (London).

74. JMK to LL, 10 February 1924, KP, KP/45/190.

75. 20 November 1933, ibid.

76. Details, Harrod, *The Life*, 473–77; Moggridge, *MK*, 586–90.; Skidelsky, *JMK*, 2: 8–9, 502–3, 528–31. Precise figures on JMK's total contribution are unclear because of mortgage arrangements and a later gift he made.

77. 26 December 1935, KP, PP/45/168.

78. 26 May 1935, KP, PP/45/190.

79. JMK to LL, 2 December 1934, 15, 31 May, 11 October 1936, ibid.

80. LL to JMK, 29 January 1931, ibid.

81. Geoffrey Keynes, *The Gates of Memory*, 204–8.

82. Letter to Quentin Bell, 18 March 1934, Virginia Woolf, *The Letters*, 5: 282.

83. Letter, Clive Bell to LL, quoted, Skidelsky, *JMK*, 2: 625.

84. JMK to GLS, 3 November 1920, followed by letters and cables in a three-cornered correspondence, including Harcourt Brace, to 20 January 1921, when Keynes advised it to correspond directly with GLS, KP, PP/45/316.

85. GLS to JMK, 25 August, JMK to GLS, 28 August 1921, ibid.

86. GLS-JMK interchange, 13, 19, 30 October 1921, ibid.

87. 15 May 1927, Virginia Woolf, *The Letters*, 3: 376.

88. Frances Spalding, *Vanessa Bell*, 211.

89. The young artist John Piper, quoted, ibid., 211–12; and ibid, 212.

90. Letter, 8 September 1926, quoted, Skidelsky, *JMK*, 2: 244.

91. JMK to VB, 2 June 1930, CP.

92. Frances Spalding, *Vanessa Bell*, 261.

93. Ibid., 275. Account of the Cunard contract, ibid., 271–76.

94. Letter interchange, JMK and Percy Bates, 25 September, 7, 9 October 1935, CP.

95. Quoted, Hession, *John Maynard Keynes*, 311.

96. Angelica Garnett, *Deceived with Kindness*, 104.

97. Spalding, *Vanessa Bell*, 298.

98. CP.

99. KP, PP/45/27.

100. Letter interchange, 18, 25 May 1938, ibid.

101. Harrod, *The Life*, 304.

102. Spalding, *Vanessa Bell*, 247.

103. Letter (quoted above), 29 September 1925, Holroyd, *Lytton Strachey*, 2: 517.

104. 3 September 1927, Virginia Woolf, *The Letters*, 3: 418.

105. JMK to LL, 25 November 1923, 22 February 1924, KP, PP, PP/45/190.

106. Interchange, 23, 24 January 1925, ibid.

107. JMK to LL, 20 February, 26, 27 April, 4 May, 16 October 1925, ibid.

108. JMK to LL, 18, 25 January, 28 February, 17 October 1926, 18, 20 November 1927, 25 November 1928, 24 July 1931, ibid.

109. JMK to LL, 25 October 1931, ibid.

110. JMK to LL, 15 November 1931, 19 February, 24 April, 25 May, 23 October 1932, 22 January, 5 February 1933, ibid.

111. JMK to FAK, 2 November 1936, KP, PP/45/168.

112. JMK to LL, 24, 25 May 1936, KP, PP/45/190.

113. JMK to Walter Langdon-Brown, 25 March 1937, KP, PP/45/179. Langdon-Brown had legally attached his middle name to the family name.

114. Entry, 4 April 1937, Virginia Woolf, *The Diary*, 5: 77.

115. JMK to FAK, 1 April 1937, KP, PP/45/168.

116. LL to JMK, 26 April 1925, KP, PP/45/190.

117. Report (typescript) by Walter Langdon-Brown and ''Pseudo-Angina'' analysis (carbon copy of typescript), 20 May 1937, KP, PP/45/168.

118. Neville Brown, *Dissenting Forbears: The Maternal Ancestors of J. M. Keynes* (Chichester, Sussex, 1988), 123–28.

CHAPTER 9

A Life in Theory

From his Eton years Keynes had functioned as a fertile theorist. He had speculated on aspects of religion and, more appositely, had thought through raison d'État from the ruthlessness of Cromwell to the expenditure of lives in the Boer War. At King's College he had plunged into the philosophical promiscuity of Cambridge's discussion groups from the Parrhesiasts to the Apostles. His probability dissertation, rising on his intellectual concerns, kept him theorizing in general even as he sharpened his mental and scholarly capacities into those of an economist. Perhaps he was being vainglorious when, approaching the life of a don, the twenty-four-year old wrote a friend, "Really the most substantial joys I get are from the perception of logical arguments."[1] Perhaps those joys were more substantial than those of the flesh. Surely he spent the rest of his life thinking fluently and energetically. But then his thinking, the essay on Edmund Burke showing his precise balance, was always associated with the practicalities of action, and he was always *acting*, often in advance of his logicizing, if always in accord with his intuition.

Yet Keynes was, as his *Treatise on Probability* demonstrated in professional detail, a passionate and determined logician and theorist. If, as a committed economist, he could focus his thinking down to pure economic theory, he could as easily widen its band to take in everything from probability and frequency, and the richly humane heterogeneity of his many other noneconomic interests. Dennis Robertson, his protégé of the 1920s, had written the *Economic Journal* review of *The Economic Consequences of the Peace*, which accurately saw it

Maynard Keynes in the library of his London house in 1940. Photo courtesy of Milo Keynes.

as two or three books, only one economic. Keynes was always living two, three, and more books simultaneously. In the 1920s he kept them separate, if bonded variously amongst each other. His great achievement, in the 1930s, would be to fuse them into the unity of *The General Theory* while maintaining the appearance of pure economic theory. The movement toward that end would be tortuous.

Like all the social sciences, economics must work incessantly to remove the impurities in which reality submerges it. Economy, polity, society, and psychology pervasively interpenetrate each other as they all move through time, historiography attempting desperately to keep up and give them meaningful continuity. The economist cannot isolate economic laws as the chemist separates out sodium or radium in a laboratory or isolation chamber. Only pure thought can keep economic laws pure, their study becoming a mental tour de force impervious to testing. One can easily imagine supply and demand determining the price in a free market, for example, but no market is completely free, and all kinds of noneconomic influences, religious belief, a wave of fear, the passage of a restrictive or relaxing law, a war, a dictator's ego, can impose themselves on it. The economist is obliged constantly to shift his or her vision from the pure economy to the whole mess. It is almost a necessary professional deformation to be blind to these other factors in order to command the economics. Indeed, all social scientists tend toward interpretive imperialism, the economist translating too much into economics, the political scientist into politics, the sociologist into sociology, and so on. If Keynes was similarly guilty, he was less so than most because of his varied interests and activities. It was this range that made him a great economist while most of his fellows remained pure or purer—and lesser.

Significantly and positively related to the essential character of the new book, Keynes's theorizing, like his earlier sexual life and penetrating as far, was adventurously promiscuous. Sometimes, floating on his general and intellectual arrogance, its excesses became as harmless as they were extravagant. Thus he enraged Bunny Garnett, trained in the Royal College of Science in London, when he rejected Bunny's explanation of bombardment sounds carried across the Channel and assured him, on the basis of archaic Cambridge science, " 'Sound waves travel through the ether.' " Clinging to the Newtonian ether, Maynard easily dismissed the suggestion that " 'Cambridge physicists [were] wrong about the diffusion of sound.' " Garnett concluded, "Such an incident was not unique. Maynard picked up knowledge with lightning rapidity and occasionally got it wrong and would bluff through if possible."[2] Keynes was more complicatedly and oddly theoretical about Jews.

The sympathetic Robert Skidelsky quoted Keynes on " 'the race which . . . has . . . done most for the principle of compound interest and particularly loves this most purposive of human institutions.' " He granted the existence of "a few other references in Keynes's writings which would now be construed as anti-semitic." It is easy to find many more than a few such references, augmented by others in his letters that could be so construed at any time past or present. Skidelsky does not make note of another reference, this one to a trip in Ireland in 1911 with fifty Liberal M. P.'s whom Keynes found *"awful"* and among whom he recorded a "Jewish barrister, who seemed such a cad that I spent most of my time cutting him."[3] Skidelsky goes on to locate "Keynes's ... stereotyping ... on the philosophical, not vulgar, plane."[4] Does the one exclude the other?

It should be emphasized, however, that Keynes's anti-semitism was, in part, a very ordinary phenomenon among the English (and French, Germans, other Europeans, and Americans) of his time. Indeed all people in any group, Jews as human as the rest, tend to attribute a negative sense to any group aspects that appear different. Of course the unique history of the Jews, perambulating so far in time and space as a minority, brought on them vast amounts of negative feelings. Eleanor Roosevelt, writing to her mother-in-law, thus expressed herself in regard to Felix Frankfurter, one of Keynes's Jewish friends or friendly acquaintances, when her husband brought Frankfurter to lunch: "An interesting little man but very jew." Quoting her was Joseph P. Lash, a Jewish protégé of hers, who apologized for her possession of a prejudice that "was part of her social and cultural inheritance."[5] Many of Keynes's friends and associates gave vent to such expressions. Virginia Stephen, even as she moved to accept the name "Woolf," had to overcome that pervasive prejudice in herself, and could never endure most of the Woolf family as too Jewish as well as stuffy-bourgeois. In a letter to an old friend she wrote, "My Violet, I've a confession to make. I'm going to marry Leonard Woolf. He's a penniless Jew." Later she later wrote even handedly, "Work and love and Jews in Putney [home of her mother-in-law] take it out of me." On one occasion, when the Woolfs were visiting at Charleston, a question was asked and Virginia volunteered for Leonard: "Let the Jew answer." Leonard returned firmly, "I won't answer until you ask me properly." Yet, compromising with her attitude, he had invited none of his family to their wedding, hurting his mother (and sisters) deeply.[6] Among Keynes's intimates Skidelsky quotes the mild, sensitive Dennis Robertson writing him apropos of meeting persons of suspiciously Jewish appearance: "How hard it seems not to murder Jews."[7] Lytton Strachey, identifying strongly with minorities, seemed impervious to anti-semitism, certainly with regard to Leonard Woolf and the painter Mark Gertler, even when Gertler assaulted him. In the end Keynes had to be a special case.

As Skidelsky discovered in the Keynes Papers, Keynes, wildly indulging his taste for logical arguments, further developed his theory of a usurious Jewry on second thought. Debating with an American professor who challenged him on the subject in 1933, a half-year after Hitler took power, he insisted, "I still think that the race has shown itself, not merely for accidental reasons, more than normally interested in the accumulation of usury." On this Skidelsky shifts his logic of exculpation from philosophy to theology: "Keynes's anti-semitism, if such it was, was little more than a theological fancy."[8] Does a philosophical or theological gloss make his anti-semitism, for such it was, any sweeter? But it was more complicated, and, moreover, mixed with comparable magnitudes of philo-semitism. Keynes indulged in both revulsion and lust, as well as more moderate expressions of either, vis-à-vis the Jews.

In an account read to Bloomsbury's Memoir Club in February 1921, adding a soupçon of the sexual, Keynes expressed the extremes of his ambivalences toward Jews. He was discussing his efforts at the Paris Peace Conference two years earlier to get food into a starving Germany over the resistance of the French, who first wanted assurances on reparations. Keynes had met with German financial experts, one of whom, the Hamburg banker Dr. Carl Melchior, impressed him particularly, "his eyes gleaming straight at us, with extraordinary sorrow in them. . . . This was he with whom in the ensuing months I was to have one of the most curious intimacies in the world. . . . This Jew, for such, though not by appearance," thus the stereotype again, "I afterwards learnt him to be, and he only upheld the dignity of defeat." At a later meeting, taking a risky initiative, Keynes negotiated with Melchior. He was "terrified out my wits at what I was doing, for the barriers of permitted intercourse had not then begun to crumble." To his friends Maynard added a Bloomsbury note: "In a sort of way I was in love with him."[9] Virginia Woolf remembered, "I think he meant it seriously, though we laughed."[10] Maynard maintained relations with Melchior over the years, Lydia joining him at least on one occasion, as both men tried to reduce the reparation burden. Keynes's story of the French-Jewish finance minister, Louis-Lucien Klotz, achieved a fine equilibrium with his account of Carl Melchior.

At a meeting of the Supreme Economic Council, "A short, plump, heavy-mustached Jew, well-groomed, well kept, but with an unsteady, roving eye, and his shoulders a little bent with instinctive deprecation," as Keynes saw him in his memoir, Klotz continued to make difficulties. Lloyd George thereupon staged a scene by flourishing a report from the British commanding officer on the Rhine. "Never have I seen the equal of the onslaught with which that poor man was overwhelmed," Keynes recounted. "Women and children were starving, he cried, and here was M. Klotz prating and prating of his 'goold.' He leaned foward and with a gesture of his hands indicated . . . the image of a hideous Jew clutching his money bag." Innocently, Keynes concluded, Lloyd George "can be amazing when one agrees with him. Never have I more admired his extraordinary powers."[11]

Matching Bolshevik Jews against Jewish usurers and capitalists, Keynes created another variant of equilibrium, this one negative on both sides of the equation. In his first Manchester *Guardian* article from the Genoa Conference he remarked upon "Bolshevism . . . [a] delerium bred by besotted idealism and intellectual error out of the sufferings and peculiar temperaments of Slavs and Jews." For the *Guardian Commercial* he reworked the thought, "The genius of the Russians and Slavs showed itself ill-adapted to the modern business and the management of the complicated economy of the industrial world . . . and more than any other Europeans they were at the mercy of their Jews.''[12] Similarly, Keynes pitied the Germans because he saw the Jews victimizing them as well. In June 1926, after a visit to Berlin with Lydia to give his lecture, "The End of Laissez-Faire," he wrote a memoir imagining Jews as "serving devils, with small horns, pitchforks, and oily tails." If he had "lived there, I felt I might turn anti-semite. For the poor Prussian is too slow and heavy in his legs for [this] kind of Jews.'' He saw a society "under the impure thumbs of its impure Jews, who have all the money and the power and the brains." But then he balanced off this image as well.

Keynes's memoir contrasted the devilish Jews with the "sweet tender imps who have not sublimated immortality into compound interest." Among them he included Carl Melchior and Albert Einstein, the latter actually the subject of his reminiscence. Keynes had just met Einstein at the official dinner after the lecture, and Einstein, like Melchior, had now in 1926, despite the companionship of Lydia, also aroused his erotic interest. As in a remarkably revealing dream he had earlier recounted to her, Maynard identified himself with a Jew. In a similarly revealing fantasy combining sexual with masochistic feelings, and again identifying himself with a Jew, he saw Einstein as " 'a naughty boy,' a naughty Jew boy, covered with ink, pulling a long nose as the world kicks his bottom; a sweet imp, pure and giggling." The fantasy expanded: "It is obvious that literally he has had his bottom many times kicked, that he expects it, that he finds it compatible with truth and independence . . . and that it has not soured him." Keynes wrote that he had sought out Einstein himself, although Einstein was one of the few guests to whom he had not been personally introduced: "After dinner . . . I got from him before he left a sympathetic look and a little compliment (*sehr schön und fein*) for my speech. I had indeed had a little flirt with him." Keynes did not leave well enough alone. He ended the memoir: "But I'm not sure that I wouldn't even rather be mixed up with Lloyd George than with the German political Jews.''[13]

Few anti-semites could more truly than Keynes say, "Some of my best friends are Jews." Recall the Jews in his life already met: his patrons Edwin Montagu and Lord Reading, his fellow Apostle and (somewhat uncomfortable) employee Leonard Woolf, the painter Mark Gertler, who wanted him to hold his hand in his distress over Carrington, and Richard Kahn as deputy in theorizing and bursarial practice. (Kahn was very much a family friend, incidentally dubbed "Alexander" by Lydia because another friend, the young philosopher Richard Braithwaite, had priority on "Richard.") The foreigners for whom Maynard felt an affinity very often turned out to be Jews, thus the Germans Melchior and Einstein (and two others mentioned in the Einstein memoir), and, warm acquaintances of the Paris Peace Conference, the Americans Walter Lippmann (who was notoriously anti-semitic himself) and Felix Frankfurter. Then there were the Italian Piero Sraffa, who was half-Jewish, and the difficult Ludwig Wittgenstein of Austria, baptized a Catholic but three-quarters Jewish, whom Maynard variously excused, sponsored (into the Apostles, but Ludwig could not endure them), and helped. Of course Maynard's variously contradictory nature meant ambiguities and ambivalences in these and other relationships.

In the case of Leonard Woolf the ambivalences were mutual. Lytton's denunciations of Maynard-the-satyr and Leonard's puritanical nature combined to infuse his judgment of Maynard with disapproval. The couples Keynes and Woolf, however, later got into their rhythm of a "traditional reunion" at Christmas.[14] Years before, in 1917, Maynard wrote Vanessa that he had taken Clive to visit Virginia, reporting, "No Jew, nor did he appear at all, which gives great pleasure."[15] Yet this was an isolated extreme. Thus Maynard and Leonard had their "cronies' " talk, assuredly resting upon a secure base of friendship, when Maynard felt so ill that he had accurately anticipated his heart attack. In 1938 Virginia recorded, "The Keyneses to tea. . . . Maynard and Lydia very congenial—dear old Maynard, so sanguine, so powerful, somehow lovable too and Lord how brilliant. I kissed him. Hope all is forgotten and forgiven."[16]

With the Nazi accession to power in Germany, Jewish refugees began turning up in Cambridge and Keynes expended his energy to help them. With deadly wit he consciously expressed his perfect ambivalence in a letter to Lydia in 1934: "I had some nice refujews to lunch." Earlier that year he had been put off by the bitten fingernails of a young refugee Jew, as he wrote Lydia. Kahn was trying to persuade him to do something for the young man: "I suppose I shall give way, but I shall be wrong." Already in 1933 he had begun occupying himself in this manner. In one letter he reported, after taking him to lunch with Sraffa, Kahn, and Austin Robinson, that a "very nice little Jew Rosenbaum from Hamburg has arrived for a visit." In 1933, also, he became positively enthusiastic over Victor Rothchild, the opposite of a needy person as scion of a great family. Apostle from Trinity College, a future scientist, Trinity fellow, baron, and corporate director, Rothchild was "a very handsome Jew, full, dominating, and victorious, should be clothed in nothing but rich furs," as Maynard described him to Lydia, "sane and attractive too, but not at all a rabbi like Leonard or Alexander, nothing Talmudical, but possessive and Jewish." Maynard was hoping Lydia would come to Cambridge the next weekend, when he would have Victor and his wife, a daughter of Clive's former mistress, Mary Hutchinson, as guests.[17] He would see the Rothchilds enjoyably and frequently for some time. The extremes in his attitude toward Jews proliferated endlessly.

The dream Maynard had recounted to Lydia emphasized his identification of himself with Jews for good and evil. A tiger appeared in a garden with "many glass houses" into which people hurried to save themselves. One man, however, "took no notice. . . . When I asked him, how this was, he replied, 'oh! I am not at all tasty—look at my hands,' and then I saw that he was a Jew."[18] Maynard of the deformed finger and the old sense of being ugly and unlovable—the whipped child and the caned Etonian—was obsessed by hands, which he thought showed character.[19] Like the dream Jew he was not "tasty." Like a real Jew, he was threateningly competent and had lived as the member of a threatened minority, which, as he saw Einstein, was always having its bottom kicked. The contradictions plunged to the depths of his being. He evaded them with a joke, writing Lydia in November 1931 about a chat with Richard Kahn: "We came to the conclusion that everyone we knew is a Jew except [former Prime Minister] Baldwin (for certain) and you (perhaps)!"[20] If it was oddly theoretical, Keynes's anti-semitism was also oddly humane compared with that famously possessing those eminent contemporary poets Ezra Pound and T. S. Eliot, the first kind psychotic and deadly and the second, sneaky and poisonous, if sanely neurotic and housebroken.[21]

As his inexpert and anti-expert thinking indicates, Keynes loved to theorize after hours and he found a sympathetic pen pal in a French financial journalist. Marcel Labordère, fourteen years older, was an acutely thinking piece of human flotsam left behind by the shipwreck of the American stock market in the Panic of 1907. A prematurely aged bachelor, he supported himself exiguously, living on bread and water much of the time in a forty-franc-a-month furnished room, by literary-financial writing for the *Revue de Paris*, a general-interest publication that wanted culture along with a minimal expertise. One example was his survey of "Les migrations de l'or en 1910," which imagined the gold movements in the manner of a Homeric epic.[22] Keynes genuinely enjoyed such exercises and wanted Labordère to contribute to his *Economic Journal*, but Labordère, who could write excellent English, demurred with fearful modesty. The two corresponded for the pure pleasure of it for a third of a century.

This essentially epistolary relationship, except for a rare meeting of a half-hour or so, is somewhat similar in character to the friendship, beginning in 1877, of Sigmund Freud with Wilhelm Fliess, a Berlin eye, nose, and throat specialist. Wreaking considerable damage on that organ, Fliess theorized that the nose was the dominant organ and operated on it accordingly. Also, taken with numerology, he thought that males and females, respectively, were subject to biorhythmic cycles of twenty-three and twenty-eight days, a theory that Maynard and Lydia would surely have approved. Freud, an outsider at the beginning of his great career and encountering the famous resistance, found Fliess, a well-established physician despite his tangential ideas, a valuable source of theoretical and emotional support. Freud was human enough to attribute scientific wisdom to his friend. The great man's historic self-analysis, however, made him aware of his dependence on Fliess and he went on to find him in egregious scientific error. After more than a score of years, in 1900, they quarreled violently and the friendship foundered.[23] The mutually supportive and unbroken Keynes–Labordère friendship was also notably dissimilar on second view.

Neither of the friends, however sympathetic, exaggerated the excellences of the other. Suggesting certain limits in his evaluation of Labordère's judgment, Keynes addressed him affectionately as "My dear Alchemist." Perhaps he also recognized how close he was to his unfortunate friend in financial theory and fate. At the end of the 1920s, after his near disaster earlier on the currency market, Keynes had nearly bankrupted himself in commodities. Then, after his great stock market gains in the mid-1930s, he returned to the commodity market for renewed heavy losses before repressing his gambler's lust. Back in the 1920s, also, Keynes had worked out a method on the stock market he called "credit cycling," which required him to keep one step ahead of the market's cycle, as he explained to Richard Kahn.[24] Stripped of its technical name, the method simply required him to predict the future. He was not so perfectly prophetic, as he had sense enough to realize in time. More banally, after admitting the failure of credit-cycling, the realistic and knowledgeable applied economist Keynes applied his scientific attention to the richer U.S. economy, studied and selected a few promising utility corporations, decided that they were undervalued in the Depression stock market, and invested in them to splendid effect. This is where he diverged from his sympathetic French friend.

Keynes and Labordère remained admiring of each other's financial philosophy and imagination. As Labordère put it in 1928: "I highly revere your moral qualities and so many graceful shades of your sensibility." But, after a graceful salutation, he had begun: "I have practically always adhered to a technical standpoint exactly opposite to yours."[25] Actually, although the near-indigent Labordère was functionally a failure as applied economist, he remained a sensible, theoretical neoclassical economist in the style of Dennis Robertson (who appreciated that side of him). Nine years later Labordère produced an exquisitely apposite but respectfully critical, eleven-page typewritten analysis of Keynes's *General Theory* while prophetically celebrating it as "an equatorial jungle of fecundity . . . providing a program of research [for a] century's time." He found it retroactively justifying his refusal to study economics at the Ecole de sciences politiques: "Only a week ago did I learn that such men as Ricardo, Alfred Marshall, [Francis Y.] Edgeworth, [and] Professor Pigou had talked nonsense, and what nonsense! I suspected it by instinct." But he feared *The General Theory*'s encouragement of inflation as leading to the "gradual debasement of the currency with all the attendant evils," noted that Keynes's famous multiplier unrealistically assumed no consequent "fluctuations of banking credit," and limited the notorious Keynesian "liquidity trap" to being "[i]nteresting as a theoretically 'limiting case.'" He also defended the saver-rentier against Keynes's populist attack as an "invisible social asset [supporting] benevolent, humanitarian, scientific, [and] literary institutions."[26] Gently he had suggested that Keynes could be a crank.

Although such arguments, as used by Dennis Robertson, had further alienated Keynes, Labordère was so tactful and had been such an old, enjoyable, and inessential friend, that he accepted the criticism in good part and even, in his submerged but undissolved neoclassical character, granted its justice. On the rentiers, "I fully agree with this, and I wish I had emphasized it in your words. The older I get the more convinced I am that what you say here is true and important." He caught himself: "But I must not allow you to make me too conservative."[27] He excused himself for the delay in writing; he was not feeling well. Indeed it was just a fews days before his heart attack. After the wartime interruption the two terminally ill men enjoyed a final letter interchange in 1945.[28]

With his incomparable facility the economist Keynes had taught and applied economics according to Marshall until the war and the peace ground their grit into his face—his life. Before then he had been one of the golden children in an age of ease and solved problems, as it falsely seemed to Bloomsbury. With the publication of his *Treatise on Probability* in 1921, Keynes could freely release his logical powers on the economic problems, now obviously matters of terrific import. There followed *A Revision of the Treaty*, *A Tract on Monetary Reform*, and his various published and unpublished speculations on the failings of free enterprise and the possibilities of socialism. As a disciplined son of John Neville and as protégé of Marshall, however, he put his rebellious speculations aside and concentrated his best mental energy on producing a neoclassical solution to the economic problems of the day. In principle he could believe that all the errors were violations of the Marshallian system. He began and finished— from July 1924 to October 1930—his *Treatise on Money* as a neoclassical exercise. True to himself, he intercalated scintillating exceptions into it.

Neoclassical economics had been established nearly simultaneously and independently by three great theorists in the 1870s: William Stanley Jevons (beginning with a paper in 1862 as the building block of marginal utility, developed in his *Theory of Political Economy*, 1871), the Austrian Carl Menger (*Principles of Economics*, 1871), and the Frenchman established in Switzerland Léon Walras (*Elements of Pure Economics*, 1874–77). Although widely different in style of thought and exposition, all three agreed on the simple but elegant conception of supply and demand, the subjective character of value as determined by sellers and buyers in the free market, value being nothing other than a measure expressed as price and satisfying both groups, and equilibrium, as that point where supply and demand met, fixing price and quantity exchanged to mutual satisfaction. If, for example, sellers or buyers became more or less eager, the meeting point would shift, producing a new price and quantity. These marvelous simplicities had not, as the younger Keynes had thought, reduced economics to unproblematic application.

The difficulties began with communicating economic sense to the layman. The idea that labor and other costs did not determine value and price seemed unjust—a denial of the centuries-old conception of the ''just price''—and was simply hard to believe. The result was a communications gap between the profession and the society it served, the economists caught between talking among themselves and inventing baby talk for politicians and public.

In the course of writing and defending his *Treatise on Money*, Keynes found himself intensely and variously engaged with three other neoclassical economists, Dennis Robertson from beginning to end, and, at the end, Ralph G. Hawtrey and Friedrich von Hayek.[29] The engagement was a slim but significant chapter in the history of economic thought.

A laggard as original thinker, Keynes was actually pursuing his junior follower Robertson in a conceptualization of the contemporary economic problem.
They saw it as revolving around the relation of saving and investment, this
related to the relation of the profit level to the interest rate (cost of loanable/
investible funds). Robertson had seized on this double relation in the work of
Knut Wicksell (1851–1926), the great Swedish economist and a major link to
Carl Menger, thus to the first generation of neoclassical theorists. A properly
prosperous business or economy had to have the profit level elevated comfortably over the cost of funds as expressed in the interest rate. The idea was simple
enough; implementation was not simple at all as recorded in the history of
bankruptcies and depressions. Addressing the problem, Robertson was writing
his modest and tentative, 103-page *Banking Policy and the Price Level: An
Essay in the Theory of the Trade Cycle* (1926), while Keynes was developing
his expansive 689-page, two-volume treatise on essentially the same subject.
Either affected the other profoundly and indeed painfully, however different
their books and theories ultimately became.[30]

Keynes and his three contemporaries were attempting to identify and trace
the effects of money and credit on production and the real economy generally.
This meant launching out beyond the static approach, which compared one state
of the economy with a later state, and plunging into "dynamic" economics,
which attempted to track the changes as they occurred. To this day, however,
dynamic economics has failed to establish itself as a secure discipline with
generally accepted conceptions. Keynes's own experience is instructive; following the (attempted) dynamics of *A Treatise on Money*, his *General Theory* retreated to the security of the static. One can trace the line of retreat in the
Treatise itself.

Robertson's language in his *Banking Policy* suggested the agonizing difficulties experienced by all four economists in advancing beyond their great predecessors. He invented new words for such basic economic terms as saving, which
became "lacking" and broke down into *spontaneous, automatic,* and *induced*
lacking. Robertson conceded that this "last distinction is . . . a troublesome
one,"[31] but they were all troublesome, terms as well as distinctions. We need
not exercise these thoughts further; economic science shook them off as doubt-
fully meaningful, incoherent, and sterile. If Robertson's language was odd, he
also fell off into plain nonsense. Thus he imagined that inflation would cause
forced saving (never mind "lacking") because money would lose some of its
value and people would have less to spend. This is a good example of an
economist (or social scientist) concentrating too much on a fractional detail and
remaining blind to the larger reality. Overwhelming the effect of the reduction
in the value of saving, inflation drives the average person or business into forced
spending, because they seek to transform their value-losing money into consum-
ables before more value is lost.[32] In a similar manner other economists, Keynes
in the lead, would perpetrate their own distinctive nonsense.

Robertson must not be abandoned in such a wretched posture. A fine economist, he was straining toward usable sense. On another, larger issue, he saw the dilemma of economic managers: a boom had to be restrained before it got out of control, but one faced the danger that a salutary dampening could lead to an intensification of recessive factors and a slump redoubled. His statesman-like solution was a permanent and sensitively watchful countercyclical policy, nowadays axiomatic. This hopeful note did not blank out his harsher thought, for which history could provide considerable support, that "the explosive forces of industrial progress," granting the inevitable distress, required a measure of "industrial instability."[33] Keynes of *The General Theory* would agree more easily with the first than with the second proposition.

A Treatise on Money, Keynes's largest work and ambitious enough in its effort to define a large subject, was an exercise in redoubled ambition. It would also provide the solution to the problem of economic stability and well-being that Robertson, Wicksell, and all their predecessors had posed and left open. During these half-dozen years of intensely creative theorizing, as recounted here, Keynes was engaged in his parallel and reciprocally related speculative and business activities, his interventions in politics and policy, his intellectual lead-ership of the Liberals, his electioneering, his committee work for the various organizations in which he found himself, the memorandum-drafting of the Lib-eral Industrial Inquiry, and more.

The new book grew well beyond the original intentions of its creator, who had thought he was writing a one-volume work until late in the process. Like his earlier treatise it combined the intuitive element with its claim to apprehend the deeper truth, and expert, fluent mathematics. It grew in various directions as Keynes's imagination warmed up, as his varied interests from mathematical logic to his stock and commodity speculations contributed their expertise, and as the real problems of the 1920s demanded attention. Keynes tried to discipline his intuition and imagination by writing more than a dozen successive tables of contents as guides.[34] The result, although he started and ended with simple formulations, was creative, but hardly coherent.

Following Wicksell and Robertson, Keynes had begun by studying the econ-omy's saving and investment as affected by profit level and interest rate, and the resulting swings of the credit (or trade) cycle into boom and slump. He tried to impart movement to his system, thus to "treat the problem dynamically . . . exhibit the causal process by which the price level is determined and the method of transition from one position of equilibrium to another."[35] At one point he conceived an algebraic notation measuring greater or lesser than normal mon-etary velocity, the speed with which money passed from hand to hand. This was a teasing promise of dynamics, but he did nothing with it. Indeed he had already speculated earlier in the treatise on "The Problems of Transition," as the section was entitled, and fallen into a mathematical problem he admitted he could not solve.[36] So much for the dynamics of transition.

Keynes also proposed to transcend the quantity theory of money, a dominating conception in monetary economics. By this one may (simplistically) see the determination of the price of commodities and services as affected by the sheer quantity of money and its velocity in the economy. As symbolized by a quantity *equation*, the quantity *theory* of money should show whether an economy is experiencing inflation, deflation, or an approximation of monetary stability. This was too simple for Keynes, who proposed a "qualitative investigation." He would replace the quantity theory with the mathematical conceptualization of his ten fundamental equations, developed eventually over 11 chapters and 181 pages. The final equation, however, translated into the statement that price equals cost plus profit, even simpler than a quantity equation, useless in exposition, and consorting awkwardly with supply–demand price determination. Indeed, in his marvelously disarming manner, Keynes went on to concede, "[A]ll these equations are purely formal . . . mere identities, truisms which tell us nothing in themselves. In this respect they resemble all other versions of the quantity theory of money."[37] Before the reader asked why not drop them and proceed with the established theory, Keynes had moved on to add other complications.

We need not pursue the complications much further. We might note that Keynes conceived of four different types of inflation, two types of profits, and three varieties of money, income and business and savings deposits. The latter went on to be divided themselves into demand and time deposits, while the total quantity of money, cutting across these divisions, could also be categorized as industrial and financial circulation.[38] Blurring Keynes's sense, the varieties of each group tended to run into each other like ink blobs from a leaky pen. One simply cannot give a clear interpretation of such a sophisticated complex of muddles. While defending himself furiously and artfully, Keynes also admitted he was not satisfied. His *General Theory* became the ultimate expression of his self-criticism.

Hawtrey, Robertson, and Hayek, in ascending degrees of the negative, all objected to aspects of the treatise noted here and many others. Hawtrey, the mildest, was beginning a dialogue that would continue unwearyingly with *The General Theory*. A slightly senior Apostle and personally friendly to Keynes, he was director of financial enquiries at the Treasury, a post isolated from its power structure, and had the time to write more than a score of books on monetary matters that had little effect on the Treasury's policy. Although he found himself in significant agreement with Keynes about the importance of money and credit on productive activity, he rather surprisingly wondered whether his fellow monetary economist was not trying "to derive a nonmonetary theory of money."[39] His critique baffled rather than distressed Keynes, who reacted with real pain to the comments of the other two.

In a long review article for the *Economic Journal* Dennis Robertson, seeing the disunity of the whole and the fundamental equations as contradictory in conception, arrived hesitantly but definitively at the sense that the *Treatise* was a failure.[40] Maynard reacted so intensely that their friendship began to deteriorate into distant, prickly collegiality. He was finding more comfortable protégés. On the galley proofs of his formal rejoinder he scribbled the opinion that the review was "sadistic" and proposed psychoanalysis, then being practiced in Gordon Square, as a cure.[41] The distance would be widened as Maynard moved on to *The General Theory*

The young Hayek, recently arrived at the London School of Economics from Vienna and early in his long and distinguished career, entered into a protracted debate with Keynes. In a two-part review he first insisted, with Viennese courtesy, that it "would be decidedly unfair to regard [the *Treatise*] as anything else but experimental," while making a point of saluting Keynes's "astonishing qualities of learning and erudition, and realistic knowledge." But he suggested that Keynes had ignorantly incorporated Wicksell's ideas into his system. These had built on the capital theory of Eugen von Böhm-Bawerk, a great follower of Carl Menger, whom the insular Keynes had evidently never studied. Despite the author's talents the *Treatise* was incoherent and incredible.[42] Keynes reacted personally and unfairly. On his copy of the review he complained, among thirty-four penciled notes, that Hayek had lacked "that measure of 'good will' " owed to any author.[43] His long rejoinder, following a cursory defense of a few points, was essentially an attack on Hayek's recent book, *Prices and Production*. He found it possessing "scarcely a sound proposition" in the last two-thirds of the exposition and otherwise so mad that it arrived at Bedlam.[44] Hayek could easily respond that Keynes was trying to change the subject with an "unproved condemnation of my views in general."[45] (It says much about both men that they later became quite friendly, if not quite friends.) For good measure Keynes then loosed his young friend Piero Sraffa on Hayek in his *Economic Journal*. Sraffa wrote a review of *Prices and Production* that called it a model of modern "unintelligibility . . . only add[ing] to the prevailing confusion of thought." Indeed, in "running away" from his confusions Hayek "had landed himself right in the middle of Mr. Keynes's theory. And here the review must stop."[46] The deftness of the replique did not save it from a similar objection.

In fact all four neoclassical economists—Robertson, Hawtrey, Hayek, and Keynes—were right in their reciprocal criticisms. The three others agreed that the *Treatise*, with all its complexities, reduced itself ultimately to simple failure. For his part Keynes had been right to find Robertson's *Banking Policy* mistaken in such significant details as forced saving, while falling into general inconclusiveness. If Hawtrey, as purer monetary economist, found the *Treatise*'s monetary theory excessively "real," Keynes could adjudge Hawtrey too pure for the financial and economic world as found. Indeed Hawtrey, in all his writings, ignored most of reality and concentrated narrowly on the effects of banking policy on commerce. His *Art of Central Banking* revolved around the importance of bank credit in relation to consumers' income, the price level, and, in the end, but vaguely, exchange and production.[47] His *Capital and Employment* limited itself essentially to the pursuit of the psychology of "traders" as affected by interest rates in the various sectors of the trade cycle.[48] As for Hayek, if Keynes had paid too little regard to Böhm-Bawerk's capital theory, Hayek seemed to be imprisoned in it. His book concentrated on his Austrian predecessor's conception of "roundabout" production as characterizing a modern economy. Although the idea was not unfruitful, it led away from the market, where the ultimate economic determinations were made, Hayek going on to speculate darkly about the connection between the length of the production process and the onset of depression. As he saw it, the leading cause was forced saving, but acting differently from the pattern as seen by Robertson. The effect, Hayek theorized, was first to bring about an increase in consumer demand resulting from the greater savings, but this "inevitably brings about a shortening of the process of production, and so causes depression."[49] Increased demand led to depression! In any case Hayek did not convincingly show that a *shortening* of the production process eo ipso, another positive phenomenon, meant depression. Keynes was not the only reader who found Hayek's reasoning mad.

All four neoclassical economists had driven their neoclassical theory further than it could go. In the first place, as purists they had ignored the inevitable economic effects of noneconomic factors such as the social element in general and institutions in particular. Within their pure economic models, moreover, they had presumed to see the dynamic movement through the real economy of their selected economic variables—investment, saving, interest rates, employment, production runs, foreign trade, traders' stocks, inflation or inflations, varieties of money and credit, among innumerable others—and correctly evaluate their effects on, and their reactions to, each other. Imagine boys on a barn roof trying to catch a skyful of swallows with their bare hands.

Keynes, author of the grandest neoclassical confusion, would be the only one of the four to emerge with a new vision in economics. Hayek, retaining his fossilized neoclassical faith, would move on into psychology, political philosophy, the philosophy of the law, and the history of ideas—and achieve his transforming vision as well. Hawtrey and Robertson would remain fine technicians, right or wrong. Failure served the greater pair well.

Keynes's greatest error, he realized, had been to keep his theorizing pure. In *A Treatise on Money*, while addressing the insecurity of the economic system and living through a period of unemployment, he had innocently used the pristine neoclassical economic model, which assumed constant maximum output and full employment. Increasingly uncomfortable at the contradiction between theory and reality, he had ripped open its structure, to the extent that it had one, to insert ill-fitting matter. A fifty-four-page chapter reviewed economic history to find inflation more beneficial than deflation, although he had to admit that the collapse of the Roman Empire was accompanied by inflation.[50] More theoretically, he conceived of a community producing bananas befallen by a thrift campaign.[51] The result was a continuing decline ending with total unemployment and general starvation. It was an impressionistic theoretical correlative of the Great Depression, which broke in on the writing of the *Treatise* in the last stages, but it could fit neither book nor economic theory. While denying the book's assumption of constant output, it failed as an economic model because the banana community, producing only one product, was not an economy, with exchange as a central element, but simply a production unit or aggregate. More baldly, Keynes inserted the brief section, "The Slump of 1930,"[52] into his second volume to address the reality of the moment, but this only emphasized the irrelevancy of the *Treatise*, published on 31 October 1930. In the book he was continuing to demand, as in his policy advice, the encouragement of investment by low interest rates and a general attack on the contemporary deflation, but he lacked the theory persuasively to justify such action. It behooved Keynes to conceive a new formulation that would fuse thought with the brute fact of the Great Depression, hence *The General Theory*.

Keynes has been nurturing a natural culture of theorizing much as his grandfathers Brown and Keynes had, respectively, led a congregation in matters of the spirit and maintained nurseries for roses and dahlias. Since he had begun lecturing and leading his Political Economy Club in 1909, he developed a living, continually renewed followership in Cambridge. Out of this the "Circus," a group of intimates among students and former students become junior staff, created itself in January 1931 and functioned until May. Joining in discontent with the *Treatise* and creation of the work to transcend it, the Circus included Richard Kahn, who was replacing the regretfully recalcitrant Robertson as protégé-in-chief; Joan Robinson, becoming a first-rate theorist independently and publishing her important *Economics of Imperfect Competition* in 1933; her husband Austin, economics lecturer and later to become assistant editor, and still later, joint editor of the *Economic Journal*; Piero Sraffa, actually a Marxian theorist but shyly reserved about it; and the future Nobel Laureate for his studies in international trade James E. Meade, then a young Oxford don temporarily at Cambridge (to return later). Mentioning discarded ideas still "littering these pages," Keynes had given the signal in the preface of the *Treatise* itself.[53] After such public defenses as Piero's (and another by Joan Robinson),[54] loyalty demanded the most rigorous criticism to anticipate the expected attacks on the new work, but, at the same time, secure in his intuition, Keynes was indicating the theses he regarded as inviolable. The demand for both correction and acceptance can be called Keynes's Law of Criticism, Keynes exercising subtle control of the Circus by staying out of its sessions, instead receiving Kahn's reports and charging him with relaying his reactions back to it. After the Circus ceased meeting, Keynes continued to discuss his developing theory individually with some of its members, particularly with Kahn and Joan Robinson. He also continued the discussions, begun during the writing of the *Treatise*, with Robertson, but intermittently and unhappily for both, indeed only to confirm their estrangement, and with Hawtrey, who also persisted in disagreeing with him, but usefully and more tactfully. Later he brought in as correspondent Roy Harrod, teaching back at Oxford, a most helpful, if sometimes trying, auxiliary. Keynes's theorizing and writing moved forward fluently.[55]

Besides Harrod's communications, the criticism of both Kahn and Joan Robinson was particularly helpful. More positively also, Kahn further developed Keynes's multiplier of the election campaign of 1929 in his famous article with the understated title, "The Relation of Home Investment to Unemployment," in the *Economic Journal* of June 1931.[56] While testing Keynes's theoretical points exhaustively, Joan Robinson provided comfort when Keynes found Hawtrey's objections discouraging, however well meant, and responded supportively when Keynes dispatched her packets of his prepublication and postpublication letters.[57] Life beyond theory was proceeding variously, even romantically. Falling on them twice in flagrante delicto, Keynes discovered that Joan, in a slow process of estrangement from Austin, had taken Kahn as her lover.[58] Keynes was also intensely engaged, although quite unromantically, in his other activities in the City and in the corridors of goverment in the United States as well as Britain, but then Lydia provided him all the necessary romance—and pure joy.

In contented ease at Tilton, Keynes happily proceeded there with his theorizing, the Easter and summer of 1934 being particularly productive. At Easter he reported to his mother: "The weather is fine, water plentiful and pigs fat. Kahn is with us and we are discussing the ms. of my next book, now nearing completion." At summer's end, again to his mother: "Kahn has just left after a longish visit—as usual he was extraordinarily helpful and a very pleasant visitor. Now he has to occupy himself with a series of Jewish festivals!"[59]

Kahn, particularly, supported Keynes in the manner demanded. Further developing the multiplier for publication in a newspaper article, Keynes wrote him, then at conferences in the United States, in early 1933: "I hope I don't make any bloomers—I wish you were here to look over my shoulder." Kahn was reassuring: "[T]he exposition of 'secondary employment' is beautiful." In 1935, correcting *The General Theory*'s galley proofs in meticulous detail, Kahn first commented, "I find all this reads most beautifully. It carries with it an air of finality and inevitability which I find most convincing."[60] Keynes could confidently approach publication.

Roy Harrod, another recipient of the galley proofs, began with resistances articulated in a series of letters with detailed comments between 31 July and 10 October 1935.[61] At first Harrod defended neoclassical interest theory against Keynes's criticism. This called into question the replacement for it, Keynes's General Theory of the Rate of Interest, which was effectively, if not theoretically, the most important part of *The General Theory*. (Consumption theory was as important logically, but received less attention from Keynes and his interpreters.) Unlike Dennis Robertson, who had found his new theory "almost complete mumbo-jumbo,"[62] Harrod was appalled at Keynes's sense that "I had not understood."[63] He responded with a reflection back to Keynes of his critique of neoclassical interest theory and included a diagram illustrating it. Keynes forgave him, invited him to Tilton, and appropriated the diagram for use in the book, the only one in it.[64] *The General Theory*, although denying the major premises of established economic theory, was marvelously well armored against rebuttal. But then its best defense was provided by its creator, perceiver and master of logical arguments.

One personal critic and helper was no longer in action: John Neville Keynes.

The younger Keynes's celebration of his father in 1942, we recall, would accurately note "his withdrawal . . . to his dear wife and the bosom of his family."
In 1914 John Neville had been reading, correcting, and commenting on the
proofs of *A Treatise on Probability* just before Maynard abandoned the project
for the war's duration. Neville had praised the discussion on "what I always
felt to be the vital induction problem." Modestly as usual, he granted that his
own treatment was "essentially incomplete." He was afraid he would not be
able to grasp another section of the proofs, which he was then beginning to
read.[65] (He was probably right; the family was beginning to note a weakening
in his mental powers.) And so Neville blessed his son's first attack on him, that
treatise putting intuition above the objective laws of logic as laid down in his
Studies and Exercises in Formal Logic. When, in 1920, Maynard returned to it
for revision and completion, he evidently no longer consulted with his father,
although at one point he showed a proof to Clive Bell and, puzzled, asked,
"[C]an you remember what I meant by that?"[66] By the middle 1920s Neville's
mind had dimmed, and Florence, functioning in a parallel manner as civic leader
and compiling a scrapbook of clippings marking Maynard's national and international progress, became the pair's exclusive correspondent with him. In the
1930s, as Maynard constructed his *General Theory*, his father could remain
unaware that the new book was assaulting the essence of his *Scope and Method
of Political Economy*—himself again. Also unaware, Maynard let the whipped
boy in him take his last revenge.

Spinning out the filaments of his pure theory, the passionately engaged applied economist Keynes was, at the same time, looping them around personalities and circumstances in the descending depths of the Great Depression and,
later, the hesitant recovery. Precisely at the moment when the Circus was criticizing it, he was using *A Treatise on Money* as a theoretical basis for his
suggested policy with his fellow members of the Macmillan Committee. Its
weaknesses, as we have seen, limited his persuasions and provided a more pressing argument for the newer work. Just then the United States began to present
itself as a vaster field on which to apply *The General Theory*-in-becoming. On
30 May 1931, after completing his drafting work for the committee, directing
himself with instinctive accuracy toward a great new critical point, he sailed for
the United States to attend a Chicago conference on unemployment. There he
moved on ideationally to develop such conceptions, which would be central in
The General Theory, as the false equilibrium of an economy with unemployment
and the curative value of deficits.[67] Given the near-absolute dominance and
rigidity of neoclassical theory, the Chicago conference was more important as
a record of a new stage in Keynes's thinking than as a generator of action.

Keynes himself pressed on with both theory and action. In March 1933 he
published four articles in the London *Times* about the general problem and an
article in the *New Statesman* of 1 April entitled "The Multiplier," this latter
providing the recovery mechanism he and Kahn had invented. The sum was
then published as the pamphlet *The Means to Prosperity.* Keynes identified the

situation as "an economic problem or, to express it better, as suggesting a blend of economic theory with the art of statesmanship, a problem of political economy."[68] He was also defining the character of *The General Theory*: although he would present it as pure economic theory, he meant it to be profoundly political—to act upon the situation and not merely describe it. This would be the new work's great achievement—and the essence of its problematic aspect. Robertson, Hawtrey, and Harrod variously tripped over that aspect while Kahn and Robinson, delicately attuned to Keynes's intentions, moved gracefully with him.

In Britain and the United States Keynes was continually thrusting his developing ideas on other economists, politicians, and the public. As early as 19 February 1930 he had broadcast on "The Problem of Unemployment" over the BBC. A second talk, on 12 January 1931, emphasized the seriousness more acutely than any other economist: "The slump in trade and employment and the business losses . . . are as bad as the worst which ever occurred in the modern history of the world."

At the time Keynes's advice was ruthlessly simple: spend, don't save! To the government he prescribed public works: "[P]ull down the whole of South London from Winchester to Greenwich" and reconstruct it. To private individuals, particularly the female managers of family budgets, his talk pleaded, "[W]henever you save . . . you put a man out of work. . . . Therefore, oh patriotic housewives, sally out tomorrow early into the streets and go to the wonderful sales."[69] With its multiplier, *The Means to Prosperity* of 1933 had marked a great advance in Keynes's theorizing. Later, in July 1933, he published a newspaper article praising President Roosevelt for effectively annihilating the World Economic Conference, which had been meant to establish international financial stability, an old Keynesian objective. Instead, Roosevelt was carrying out, as he now saw, an aggressive, necessarily nationalisic recovery program of an ad hoc Keynesian character.[70] With his instinct for critical points, Keynes had recognized another one and changed his policy accordingly. He was renewing his relations with the influential Walter Lippmann and Felix Frankfurter, and through them established contact with the president, first by way of an open letter (preceded by a private copy delivered by Frankfurter) published in *The New York Times* of 31 December 1933. Then, on 28 May 1934, he had an hour's interview in the White House. Although the fastidious theorizer and the practical politician baffled and disappointed each other, they nevertheless worked out an alliance helping either. Keynes's ideas were providing a post hoc logic for Roosevelt's New Deal and, reciprocally, its recovery action supplied a pragmatic argument for Keynes's theory as it emerged. Although Roosevelt found Keynes mysteriously numerate, Keynes thought the president insufficiently literate in economics. Also, Keynes's obsession with hands asserting itself, he found Roosevelt's too much like those of a businessman,[71] for him a despised stereotype. On his U.S. visit Keynes also spoke to many personages in economics and business as well as government, but to ambiguous effect at the time.[72] On 25 May he reported to Lydia that he "began the day with Mrs. Frances Perkins," the Labor secretary, lunched with the brain truster Rexford Tugwell, met with an assistant secretary of state, took tea with Supreme Court Justice Louis Dembitz Brandeis, and was honored at a dinner given for him by a State Department economic adviser: "Awful hard work to be at the top of one's form, to put oneself over the blighters, all day."[73] Putting himself over the blighters was his life method. Despite the ambiguities, based on an idea shaped for the circumstances, his distant alliance with the U.S. leadership prospered.

Later in 1934, in the November BBC broadcast, "Poverty in Plenty: Is the Economic System Self-Adjusting?", Keynes hurled the challenge of *The General Theory* at his fellow economists and economic conservatives generally. The economy was not self-adjusting, he answered his question, opposing "almost the whole body of organized economic thinking and doctrine of the last hundred years." Boldly, "Now I range myself with the heretics. I believe their flair and their instinct moves them towards the right conclusion." Agreeing with them, he proposed that consumption was endemically weak and saving similarly excessive, the result being low production, unemployment, and the all too evident general poverty.

Along with faltering consumption and increasing unemployment, Keynes had integrated the thinking of the "isolated groups of cranks,"[74] as he baldly identified them, the underconsumptionists and the monetary cranks, into his new theory. The first, including Thomas Malthus, Karl Marx, and the contemporary John A. Hobson, argued that capitalistic enterprises poured out a stream of goods the underpaid workers lacked the income to buy. The monetary cranks, like the well-forgotten Silvio Gesell (1862–1930), theorist of a money that would progressively lose its value, accused the banks and moneyed persons of demanding usurious rates for investment funds. On 1 January 1935 Keynes wrote George Bernard Shaw, then approaching Marxism and the Soviet Union in oddly experimental sympathy, that he was challenging Marx with his own theory, which would more effectively revolutionize economic thought and action as well.[75] This meant overthrowing the edifice of neoclassical economics as completed by Léon Walras and Keynes's professional father, Alfred Marshall. He knew he would need all his powers of persuasion. His confidence blazed.

Although *A Treatise on Money* had assumed that the normal economy tended toward maximum consumption, production, and employment, *The General Theory*, supporting itself on the present reality, assumed the contrary, namely laggard consumption, failing production, and substantial unemployment. The conclusion was clear: governmental action to substitute for the absent self-adjustment. In his BBC talk, Keynes, however, had specified, "For me . . . it is impossible to rest satisfied until I can put my finger on the flaw in . . . the orthodox reasoning." He did not quite claim to have found it, although, "I believe that I am on my way to do so."[76] In his letter to Shaw, five weeks later, he seemed to think he had arrived. In any case the book had been almost completely drafted when he made his broadcast, the remaining work being minor revisions. As it stands *The General Theory* is the culmination of Keynes's career as economist. It did carry out its revolution. Again, with his genius for locating and conquering critical points, Keynes had identified the greatest economic disaster of the twentieth century and, by way of precisely reasoned theory, laid down the policy to overcome it. That theory has dominated economic thought and policy since the 1950s, but more and more cavils have been articulated since the inflation of the 1970s. On second thought had Keynes found the flaw? Had he repaired it? Or had he achieved a theoretical tour de force like his marriage?

At this point, I must advance toward the reader from behind the paper shelter of this text. There is no great problem about Keynes's earlier work because I agree approximately with the professional consensus, but I disagree with it absolutely on *The General Theory* as a canonical work. To an extent I am basing the foregoing analysis on my previous Keynes volume, which analyzed it in four detailed chapters.[77] I cannot repeat them here, but I must communicate their sense, even if this chapter is about a *life* in theory and not directly about the theory. Yet, rejecting all argument from authority, I claim none for myself. Accordingly, in order to make sense of Keynes's life, I charge myself to make that theory clear to the lay reader. The general impression is that it is impossible. Thus I once tried to discuss the interest theory with the author of an economics textbook, who excused himself: "Oh, it's too difficult, too difficult!" Nonsense!! He was unwilling to reexamine the shaky basis of his teachings. The theory, as can be forthwith demonstrated, is essentially, excruciatingly simple when one has translated its economist's idiom into bare English and cut through Keynes's marvelous contradictions and confusions. The General Theory of the work *The General Theory* is a model of the modern economy assumed to possess the fundamental elements to illustrate its character and operation. That model can be seen as an upended double pyramid resting on its two points: consumption and interest theory.

In proceeding from the *Treatise on Money*, Keynes added a new argument on consumption that, he said, was too weak in a modern economy. His interest theory was a further development of his emphasis on the interest rate in the *Treatise*. The significance of the rate, Keynes's simplified way of expressing the cost of funds financing production, was that it was too high and hence discouraged business investment. Thus consumers and producers reinforced each other in failing to employ enough of the workforce, unemployment becoming the most poignant aspect of the malfunctioning modern economy.

Consumption was a problem in its failure to fulfill itself. Keynes argued that an income-earner, with increasing income, would tend "towards accumulation"—saving—"when the margin of comfort has been attained." Keynes concluded that "as a rule . . . a greater *proportion* of income" would then be saved. In his next sentence, however, he flinched: "But whether or not a greater proportion is saved . . ."[78]—and let his logic lose itself in another proposition. With that tacit admission—that he was not claiming a proportional saving increase—

he had let his argument die. For if one saved proportionately only as much as the income increase (or possibly less), consumption would not begin to lag. If, for example, income doubled, and the income-earner saved 50 percent more, the proportion of savings would be proportionately less. Hence Keynes could not claim an endemic tendency toward insufficient consumption. And that is all there is to his essential argument on consumption. One could say much more, but his reasoning aborts itself on its own terms: the argument of failing consumption is simply nonexistent. We can begin to appreciate his persuasive powers when we take into account that he had promised the consumption lag beforehand and, following this passage, wrote as if he had proven his point. The interest rate argument exists, at least.

Keynes's interest rate thesis was simple, but mystifyingly argued. Simply put, the persons controlling the money, the *liquidity* Keynes liked to call it, demanded too high a price—the interest rate—for the use of it. They could do so because, as the monetary cranks had always theorized, they had too much power over it as compared with the entrepreneurs who needed it for their business enterprises. Indeed, Keynes argued that behind the veil of credit operations the masters of liquidity had absolute power over the interest rate and the entrepreneurs none at all. Of course this is an astonishing claim. How does Keynes support it?

The mystification begins. While promising to discuss neoclassical interest theory in the next chapter, Keynes first erected his General Theory of the Rate of Interest. This gave him the advantage of beginning his rebuttal of neoclassical theory advantageously and threateningly with his theory preestablished in the chapter order. He began his argument with a favorite strategy of his, the use of a deft petitio principii, a logical fallacy in which what is to be proved is implicitly taken for granted. Preparing to bring forward liquidity preference as sole interest rate determinant, he told the reader, "[T]he rate of interest is the reward for parting with liquidity [cash] for a specified period." One eminent critic has commented on the "breakneck speed" of Keynes's argumentation.[79] We must bring Keynes to a halt here. His apparently straightforward definition of liquidity preference is crooked.

Keynes has correctly enough said that the interest rate is the reward for parting with liquidity. But it is more than that as well. Like a surgeon—one thinks of Geoffrey Keynes—he has neatly amputated half of a true proposition and made it grotesquely false. His statement has eliminated the entrepreneurial "borrower," who must agree to the rate of interest in a free (money) market before the transaction of lending–borrowing takes place. The rate of interest, Keynes to the contrary, is both the saver's reward for overcoming his liquidity preference to part with his cash and the borrower's sacrifice for the advantage of having cash to invest, the reward–sacrifice being a compromise price received and paid and satisfying both transactors. But Keynes's petitio principii permits him to assert negatively, "The rate of interest is not the 'price' which brings into equilibrium the demand for resources to invest [by an entrepreneur who 'borrows' the money for investment in productive capital] with the readiness to abstain from present consumption [by the saver–lender]." With this he denies the reality of the lending–borrowing operation as carried out in the money market between income-earning saver and entrepreneurial borrower and instead proposes his liquidity preference.

Keynes now defines the interest rate affirmatively as "the 'price' which equilibrates the desire to hold wealth in the form of cash with the available quantity of cash."[80] In this way the saver's liquidity preference claims and achieves its price. But this is a pure solipsistic proposition, with only the saver–lender in sight. Keynes permits him alone to determine the interest rate to his own satisfaction. A master logician, in this case, paralogician, Keynes misleadingly substitutes for the missing borrower another actor, the monetary authority, which regulates the supply of money in the economy and thus affects the lender's demand for a satisfactory interest rate. Yet the authority does not transact directly with the lender, but with the whole public in a different sense, regulating money to buy all goods and services, not just debts paid by the interest rate as negotiated in the money market. Keynes has conflated money market and monetary system to produce absolute confusion. Under cover of this confusion the purely passive borrower–entrepreneur reappears—to pay whatever interest rate satisfies the saver–lender in his solipsistic absolute power. And that is all there is to Keynes's General Theory of the Rate of Interest, as based on (the saver's) liquidity preference.

Keynes's "liquidity preference" is a perfect example of his ability to use reversals of reality to advantage. The phrase itself asserts that the rational person prefers cash to the commodities and services it can buy. But who, other than a mad miser, actually does so? The rational saver, when he lends his money to the entrepreneur, simply choses a greater stream of those real values in the future (perhaps when he is retired) above the lesser amount available for instant gratification. Moreover, he receives the added benefit of a greater sense of security. Of course people do cling to their cash in a depression as long as possible to take advantage of falling prices, among other reasons, and Keynes was able to magnify this grain of reality to deny the sense of liquidity as a source of (possibly delayed) material benefits. But to his followers, the magician's sleight of hand proved his command of forces beyond the ken of ordinary, unconverted mortals.

The Shylockian passion for liquidity suggests another reason for Keynes's clinging to his view of the Jews as a usurious race. One might compare his attitude to that of the self-hating Jewish anti-semite Karl Marx. Defining the Jew as the quintessential spirit of capitalism in his early essay "On the Jewish Question," Marx went on to indulge his private anti-semitism for the rest of his life. But the machinery of his ultimate statement in *Capital*, except for one gratuitous wisecrack, is innocent of anti-semitism.[81] Marx was too serious a revolutionary and rigorous a social scientist to build upon such a slender ad hominem. Keynes is not quite so professional. His theorizing undergoing metastasis, he has his Jew clinging to his "goold" and burying himself at the bottom of The General Theory of the Rate of Interest, thus at the bottom of *The General Theory*. If the Jew is not absolutely necessary in the theoretical machinery, Keynes, perhaps signaling the weakness of his case, nevertheless finds him useful as an auxiliary in representing an excessive demand for liquidity and its depressive effects. This is not articulated in the book itself, but the reader of Keynes's other writings can too easily make the connection.

The General Theory of the Rate of Interest is as mad as it seems. Of course this begs the question: how could Keynes *persuade* with it? Having already experienced his reasoning, we can guess, but meanwhile let us suspend attempting a definitive answer before we see how he challenges the sense of the neoclassical rate of interest, which he taught for many years.

One influence on Keynes's thinking, as noted here previously, provided advance support to his General Theory of the Rate of Interest. By the 1930s he had begun looking with favor on the monetary cranks, who attributed excessive power over money to such suspects as the rich, the bankers, and the obviously incriminated usurers. But the cranks may not have been respectable enough for him. A better authority could have been Stanley Jevons, whom Keynes had read with great pleasure and admiration. In his classic *Theory of Political Economy* Jevons proposed the famous "catena," a chain of reasoning defining value or price (by way of "marginal utility," a technical formulation we need not explore): "Cost of production determines supply"—leading to: "Final degree of utility determines value." (Shortly after he published *The General Theory*, Keynes gave a talk on Jevons in which he quoted the complete catena.) In this exposition only the seller-supplier (thus lender in the money market) is visible. It might appear that Jevons was advancing a solipsistic value theory, thus providing an example to Keynes. But this is false. The catena comes toward the end of the chapter, "Theory of Exchange," which explicitly discussed supply-demand price determination between supplier-seller and demander-buyer in the free market. Indeed Jevons also provided a brilliantly conceived diagram showing how *two* commodities (one of which could be money and the other a debt or bond) were related to each other by two transactors in order to establish the conditions of a free exchange by two equals.[82] But Keynes, as we have seen, had the genius to make off with just that fraction of an argument or piece of reality needed to win his point—and abandon the rest. Or perhaps he based himself ultimately on his steely will and his compulsion to rationalize a policy he knew would work.

Keynes then attacked neoclassical interest theory by way of the diagram Harrod had conceived to prove his loyal comprehension.[83] The diagram purported to illustrate neoclassical interest theory, but actually falsified it with a cat's cradle of six curves instead of the simple pair of supply and demand curves that economic science, as instructed by Jevons, inter alia, found sufficient. We need not waste our spirit puzzling out Harrod's creation. (To my knowledge, I am the only interpreter who has attempted it, but I do not inflict the necessarily complex explanation on the reader here.)[84] As in the case of any good or service, the neoclassicals determined the interest rate by way of supply and demand for loanable/investible funds. One argument of Keynes, using the Harrod diagram, put it that neoclassical theory could not work because the funds saved varied with income, resulting in continual changes in the supply of money going to the money market. He concluded that the interest rate thus could not be "determinate."[85] But supply and demand, thus their curves, are always changing, a normal situation, as sellers and buyers change their minds or enter or leave the market. This does not prevent price determination. Keynes's objection of "indeterminate" is blankly factitious. He then asserted arbitrarily that only his liquidity preference could achieve the determination and replaced the neoclassical supply–demand interest rate theory with his General Theory of the Rate of Interest as laid down in the preceding chapter. Based on an evanescent consumption theory and a cranks' crazy interest theory, the *theory* of *The General Theory* is not partly wrong; it is totally wrong—total nonsense.

The General Theory contains a great deal more and we might take quick notice of a few other significant elements before returning to Keynes's person and life. He began the book with his conception of *effective* demand, which was less than the full demand capable of consuming all that a modern economy produced.[86] This was a denial of the generally accepted Say's Law of the early nineteenth century, which said that any value produced, a caught fish, a bushel of wheat, provided equal buying power: the fisherman's and the farmer's incomes had to balance out globally. But the idea of a global leakage of buying power seemed confirmed by the weak consumption and business investment of the Depression period, an important factor in the book's persuasions. Typically, however, in the midst of his tortuous argumentation along these lines, the intermittently recidivist neoclassical economist Keynes effectively contradicted his effective demand logic by admitting the "indubitable . . . proposition . . . that the income derived . . . by all the elements in the community . . . necessarily has a *value* equal to the value of the output."[87] Hence everything produced could be bought and consumed: Keynes had simply restated Say's Law. Furthermore, although some followers have made much of effective demand,[88] it provides only a redundant argument in the book. Keynes had only to prove the existence of weak consumption or weak investment (as caused by excessive liquidity preference). His failure with the logic of consumption and interest rate determination redundantly disposed of the redundant effective demand argument. Again, one had arrived at nonsense.

The question is begged: did Keynes know that he was perpetrating nonsense, or rather, considering his marvelously operative brain, how could he not know? It is not a difficult question. We know that he was a debater and a partisan, and a partisan debater does not give away any point. Since boyhood, confident that he was intuitively right whatever the superficial appearances, he had refused to concede any argument and seems to have won every one. Bertrand Russell, philosopher and great *logical* controversialist, said of Keynes, "When I argued with him I felt that I took my life in my hands, and I seldom emerged without feeling something of a fool."[89] Economics, mixed, furthermore, with all manner of impurities, functions with partial realities, and its practitioners must shut out secondary and noneconomic factors to get on with it. After Keynes's *Treatise on Money*, as Harrod put it, "He was in search of simplification. . . . Once more he went into a great tunnel, from which he was to emerge with *The General Theory*."[90] In the *Treatise* Keynes had *seen* constant maximum employment and changing prices; in his tunnel, approaching *The General Theory*, he switched the attributes and *saw* constant prices and variable, declining employment. The will to see was more important than passively seeing.

In the case of interest rate determination, more specifically, Keynes rejected the idea of an equilibrium between lender and borrower as setting that rate in the money market. Instead, he shifted the process to the lender himself, who would intuitively *equilibrate* his desire to hold wealth in the form of cash with the available quantity of cash (in the economy). If one narrowed one's eyes appropriately, one could make the blind leap from the market to the solipsistic perfection of the regnant lender, a dominating figure like Keynes himself. A neoclassical economist would say that Keynes was simply equilibrating one point in the supply curve of loanable/investible funds, but Keynes, unheeding, was off and away on his next argument. He sincerely deceived himself and his followers.

An important part of Keynes's argumentation was his "Book II" (of six "books"), with its four chapters of definitions. As master of the art, Keynes devoted so much space to the definitions because he could phrase them as a series of petitio principii proving his points by assuming his conclusions. Thus he helped himself hugely by assuming constant prices (including wages) in his model and so finessed the problem of inflation. In this way he could attribute magical power to his model's multiplier, which *multiplied* the effect of increased investment because new income provided by new investment became additional purchasing power by multiplying itself a number of times before being exhausted. In the real world, however, more investment would have an inflationary (*and* a "crowding out") effect, thus canceling the multiplier's promised results. Yet in a practical sense Keynes's theoretical elimination of inflation was a brilliant stroke.

On second thought Keynes's assumption of constant prices goes even further in its denial of reality than in denying inflation. Price changes, occurring uninterruptedly in a free-market society and calling up all manner of decisions in buying and selling, producing and consuming, are an integral element of its economy. Communist societies formally determined prices, but their pervasive black markets, registering changes in precisely the same way, gave the lie to these nominal prices. An economy with constant prices is no economy known to man or woman or theory. Like the banana community of *A Treatise on Money*, *The General Theory*'s model of an economy is no model. It simply does not represent economic reality and provides no guide to thinking about it. We might have spared ourselves much mental agony if we had begun—and stopped—here. There was no logical need to enter into the subtleties of effective demand, liquidity preference, the propensity to consume, the multiplier, and the other Keynesian constructions. But then Keynes has much to instruct us in his wrongheadedness—as combined with his being greatly right in other ways.

In a practical sense *The General Theory*, integrating so much of Keynes's genius and experience of reality, was a colossal achievement. That genius subsumed perversities of theory. We must grant Keynes the right to be judged by the standard of his intentions, and they did not aim for the creation of impeccable theory, but the attainment of real objectives: end the Depression, inject (Keynesian) economic science into government, and empower it to maintain a properly equilibrated economy. In the immediacy of the 1930s the ensemble of the book's conceptions, contradictions included, made a perfect fit with the *political* economy of the advanced nations. In combating the Great Depression the most important instrument was inflation, as Keynes recognized and as most other economists refused to see. The Depression was the greatest critical point of the many Keynes had addressed. Indeed his entire personal and professional life was preparation for this ultimate service.

An extraordinary concentration of negative factors had produced the Depression out of deflation doubled, a deflationary reality upon which a rigid neoclassical thought and policy were superimposed. Keynes himself, seeing beyond the immediate war and postwar inflation, predicted much of it in his *Economic Consequences of the Peace*. Burdened with huge debts, the war victors as well as the losers, as we have seen, set about, according to orthodox teachings, to reduce them as expeditiously as possible. In this developing deflationary situation the international debt carousel kept all the major nations in protracted disequilibrium. By way of its favorable balance of trade the United States was collecting too much of the world's gold. Equilibrium might have been partially righted, at least, if that gold had passed into the American economy; the result classically would have been inflation there, the high prices reducing U.S. exports and increasing those of the other nations. But the United States sterilized the gold effectively by restricting its money supply and holding prices stable. This maximized the burden on Germany, which was paying increasingly more reparations in the latter part of the 1920s, and old allies like England who were making some effort to pay their war debts or, at least, lived and made policy under an overhanging debt burden. Neoclassical doctrine, enforced by banks and governments, ultimately the American, continued to press for a general debt payment and reduction policy, hence a self-replicating deflation. A major episode in this was England's return to the gold standard in 1925 as dictated by ill-fitting theory and urged by the United States.

When the Depression struck, the neoclassical economists knew nothing better than to prescribe still more economy—more deflation. Keynes desperately struggled against this madness. No one, however, could openly call for inflation, or, in a phrase used by Robertson, *re*flation. This was because of the bad experience of the postwar inflation, spectacularly represented by Germany's reparation-induced hyperinflation of 1922–23. *The General Theory* had the correct formula. Its model failing to register it, Keynes could rationalize public works and deficit spending—inflation camouflaged. The solution was that simple.

And so Keynes inserted into his General Theory model the theoretically non-sensical underconsumptionist and monetary crank ideas to temporarily positive effect. In the circumstances the cranks had been right to urge inflationary policy, but their general wrongheadedness frightened sensible people. Exquisitely trained in neoclassical theorizing, Keynes could create an anti-theory in neoclassical idiom. Although he deceived none of his professional contemporaries, the younger economists, desperate to do *something*, could be morally converted with the support of the man in the street.

The General Theory had its great long-term value as well. This is where the neoclassicals, rigidly obeying abstract doctrine, had failed to recognize a truth that Keynes himself felt and acted on without quite consciously formulating. Implicitly, the book recognized the much greater economic character of government (and, requiring and facilitating that growth, the creation of the great business corporations—"trusts"—in Keynes's day). In the first decade of the century British governmental costs were about 7 percent of national income; in the 1920s, the great war having accelerated the process, they had risen to close to 20 percent.[91] Today, they are at 50 percent, with similar European economies at about the same level, although Sweden is notorious for its 60 percent and the United States seems Spartan at less than 40 percent. Government was becoming the biggest business concern in the economy; with its terrific daily effects, it had to shape its policies accordingly. Keynes was wrong to say the economy suffered from endemic depressive factors; these were external, "exogenous," the economist calls them, but no less powerful. For the wrong reasons Keynes urged governmental intervention, but it was no less necessary. In *The General Theory* he envisioned essentially reactive governmental economic action, thus public works and deficit spending, but, following on his old demand for an economic general staff, his thinking led naturally to the idea of governmental initiative in setting economic goals beforehand—Keynesian socialism. This continues to be the long-enduring value of *The General Theory*.

Perhaps Keynes was alluding to his intuitive leap from practice to theory in a letter to his old City friend Oswald Falk, who had written to congratulate him on publication of *The General Theory*: "I have needed your letter about my book . . . how much pleasure it has given me.

"The extent to which one sees one's destination before one discovers the route is one of the most obscure problems of all in the psychology of original work. In a sense it is the destination which one sees first." Had he seen correctly? He continued, "But then a good many of the destinations so seen turn out to be mirages."[92]

Creation of *The General Theory* was not quite enough to ensure its success. Keynes had to defend it and lead its assault on orthodoxy personally. We can see that its content of nonsense, however effective psychologically and politically, was a difficult handicap. We have also seen that his charismatic personality had consciously worked to *persuade*, indeed to indoctrinate, from his earliest days as don—as lecturer and leader of the Political Economy Club. Austin Robinson, who had decamped to India to escape Keynes's influence for a period in the 1920s, described it in his obituary article. Keynes was not content to elucidate; he wanted to convert. Over the years he had familiarized the students with his ideas, "subsequent discussion [being] conducted very much in the atmosphere of the revivalist meeting: 'Brother, are you saved?' " The point was not to understand but obediently to believe, even, as Tertullian had it, *because* it was absurd. Robinson's article suggested that, unlike his wife, he had never been totally converted.[93] This did not prevent his becoming a prime agent of the conversion program as influential member of the Royal Economic Society, joint editor of the *Economic Journal*, and senior managing editor of the Keynes *Collected Writings*. The process was not dissimilar from indoctrination in Marxism, assisted by three editions of Marx's works, another theoretical absurdity but a powerful, practical force.

Indeed, his continual denigration of Marx betraying it, Keynes correctly saw himself as *the* rival of that old revolutionary mole. After one stipulates their great differences in style, one can see that their functional similarities were great and deep: both men political synthesizers of thought and action, both turning to theory after their initial action had failed, Keynes as Liberal politician and policymaker, Marx as a leader in the German Revolution of 1848. Both were using crazy theory undershored by powerful realism and mounting revolutionary movements taking massive effect on the world. Against his will Marx created an evolutionary and democratic socialist movement in central and western Europe around the industrial proletariat he had identified and, more according to his taste but in a backward region he had casually spurned, a ruthless, socialist-revolutionary dictatorship that compressed time and led that region in a forced march to economic progress crudely approximating that of Western capitalism. Keynes, for his part, provided the revolutionary rationale within a frame of democratic socialism to correct the failings of the twentieth-century free-enterprise economy. Less absolutistic, he did not have to go beyond an elite sect of specialists in economics who could make sufficient impress on their society by adapting his persuasions and deceptions.

Keynes's eventual defense of his doctrine was carried out in the November 1936 and February 1937 issues of the *Quarterly Journal of Economics (QJE)* of Harvard and his *Economic Journal* from March 1937 to June 1938. In the *QJE* against Robertson and three distinguished American economists he essentially used one shocking argument: uncertainty vitiated all the conclusions of orthodox economics.[94] Of course this could be used against *The General Theory*. In the *Economic Journal*, against Robertson again as well as Hawtrey and the Swede Bertil Ohlin, he dominated the debate, which revolved around his interest theory.[95] He also introduced new ideas and argued mysteriously that the banks had the power to wield liquidity to good or, following their reactionary instincts, evil effect. Although Robertson and Ohlin did mention the role of the entrepreneurial borrower in determining the interest rate,[96] they did so diffidently and let Keynes divert them into other questions. The triumphant debater since his Cambridge Union days easily won again.

It was during the debate, on 16 May 1937, that Keynes suffered his heart attack. One would not guess it from the pages of the *Economic Journal*, where his articles continued apparently uninterrupted, but except for a few weeks, he could write in bed and, of course, dictate when necessary.

Triumphantly, Keynes moved on simultaneously from defense to conquest. The conversion process spread to the United States, a greater field of operations than Britain, which was soon to be superseded theoretically as well as economically. Impatient American students ordered copies of *The General Theory* directly from England.[97] Yet it was too difficult a work even for economists to read comfortably, and few have actually ever read it through. Its very difficulty, like that of Marx's *Capital*, helped it win converts because interpreters offered simplified formulae to communicate what they claimed was its essential meaning. In the process they made the digestive process much easier and elided or blurred the great contradictions. The three main interpreters were the English don, John R. Hicks, who invented a diagram translating a fair amount of the theory's (claimed) sense, Alvin H. Hansen, the Harvard professor who popularized the diagram (known as the Hicks–Hansen or IS–LM diagram), and Paul A. Samuelson of the Massachusetts Institute of Technology, who wrote *Economics*, (lately in its sixteenth edition),[98] the textbook (and model for many others) introducing *The General Theory*'s ideas in a form that indoctrinated as it taught. Students are imprinted with Keynes's theory while their brains are still soft. Rushed past the point where they could think about what they were learning, they are set quickly to calculating with the formulae as given and producing mindless answers denying reality. Thus, because the *General Theory* as model could not produce inflation, economists trained with it generated inflation precisely because they had no fear of the theoretically nonexistent. And so Keynes conquered the economic science of the non-Communist world.

Keynes's victory is an exorbitantly apt demonstration of Thomas S. Kuhn's famous thesis about the change of paradigm, now a commonplace. Paradigms he defined as "universally recognized scientific achievements that for a time provided model problems and solutions to a community of practitioners," a formulation, like Keynes's definitions, which encapsulates a petitio principii and elides at least one central area of reality. Although Kuhn contrasted the near unanimity characteristic of the natural scientists with the many unresolved disagreements among the social scientists, he nevertheless said that for the former, despite the more convincing proofs available to them, "neither proof nor error is at issue. The transfer of allegiance from paradigm to paradigm is a *conversion* [italics added] experience that cannot be forced."[99] Thus the "community of practitioners" had to be convinced before the new theory was accepted, and the change was as much due to human subjectivity as to the reality being described. The heliocentric theory of our planetary system advanced by Aristarchus in the third century B.C., for example, had to wait for more than a millenium and a half to be accepted. Kuhn, who had to defend himself against the charge that he had made science subject to mob rule, had at least attenuated the perceived relation between science and truth, and was impelled, without succeeding in stilling the criticism, to make substantial revisions in his original study. If the demonstrable truth can be so blankly rejected in the natural sciences it is not surprising that the social sciences, with their vaguer standards and, necessarily, proofs, are so much more influenced by nonrational factors. In the circumstances, Keynes's sheer charisma and his debating skill led to an easy conquest over the neoclassical paradigm. That his pure theory is pure nonsense only makes the victory perfect.

Keynes would be extremely active in government during and after World War II for the years remaining to him after publication, but those services would be exquisitely irrelevant to *The General Theory*. Nevertheless they would have great public relations value in winning opinion for it. By way of his fully lived life in theory he was revolutionizing economic science and the economies under its sway.

NOTES

1. Letter to Bernard Swithinbank, 13 May 1908, quoted, Harrod, *The Life*, 20.

2. David Garnett, *Flowers of the Forest* (London, 1955), 144–45.

3. Letter, JMK to Duncan Grant, 3 October 1911, BL, Add. MSS 57930.

4. Skidelsky, *JMK*, 2: 238, 239, quoting Keynes's lecture, "Economic Possibilities for Our Grandchildren," *CW*, 9: 330.

5. Felix Frankfurter, *From the Diaries of Felix Frankfurter*. With a Biographical Essay by Joseph P. Lash (New York, 1975), 24.

6. Quoted, Quentin Bell, *Virginia Woolf*, 2: 2, 4; editorial note quoting Quentin Bell, Leonard Woolf, *Letters of LW*, 470; letter, Marie Woolf to LW, 7 August 1912, and editorial note, *Letters of LW*, 178, 157.

7. Skidelsky, *JMK*, 2: 664, endnote 60.

8. JMK's letter to Max Radin, 12 September 1933, KP, L/33; Skidelsky, *JMK*, 2: 239.

9. "Dr. Melchior: A Defeated Enemy," *CW*, 10: 389–429; quotations, 395, 403, 414, 415.

10. Entry, 5 February 1921 (dating the meeting as Wednesday, 2 February), Virginia Woolf, *The Diary*, 2: 90.

11. "Dr. Melchior," *CW*, 10: 422.

12. Articles dated 10 April, 6 July 1922, *CW*, 17: 373, 436.

13. Memoir, "My Visit to Berlin" (dated 22 June 1926), previously unpublished sketch, found in JMK's papers, ibid., 10: 382–84.

14. Editorial note, Virginia Woolf, *The Diary*, 5: 193.

15. 28 July 1917, CP.

16. Virginia Woolf, *The Diary*, 5: 179.

17. JMK to LL, 4 November, 4 February 1934; 7 May, 17 November, 29 October 1933, KP, PP/45/190.

18. JMK to LL, 14 November 1924, ibid.

19. Harrod, *The Life*, 20.

20. 15 November 1931, KP, PP/45/190.

21. Virginia Woolf had charitably spent three weeks campaigning for Eliot as literary editor of *The Nation* when JMK was taking it over, but Eliot was fearful of the risks, the position falling to Leonard Woolf, entry, 23 March 1923, *The Diary*, 2: 240.

22. Copy in JMK–Labordère correspondence, KP, PP/45/177.

23. Peter Gay, *Freud: A Life for Our Time* (New York, 1988), 55–61, 101–2; quotation, 101.

24. Letter to Kahn, 5 May 1938, *CW*, 12: 100–101.

25. Letter to JMK, 16 December 1928, KP, PP/45/177.

26. Letter and typescript, 13 February 1937, ibid.

27. Letter, 7 May 1937, ibid.

28. Last surviving letters, JMK-Labordère, Labordère-JMK, 28 March, 5 April 1945, ibid.

29. The reader is reminded that we are concerned here with JMK's *life* in theory and not the theory en soi. Although independently responsible for elucidating its basic sense, this discussion draws on the specifics of my analysis in *Biography of an Idea*, ch. 4: "Theorizing of the Middle Period: *A Treatise on Money*," 67–83.

30. JMK–DHR correspondence on their respective books, *CW*, 13: 29–41.

31. Robertson, *Banking Policy and the Price Level* (London, 1926), 40, 47.

32. JMK objected to DHR's view of inflation as inducing saving, letter to DHR, 31 May 1925, *CW*, 13: 34–35.

33. Robertson, *Banking Policy*, 81–83, 22.

34. Table of contents, related correspondence, and other data, *CW*, 13: 15–117. On the subject in general see Eprime Eshag, *From Marshall to Keynes: An Essay on the Monetary Theory of the Cambridge School* (London, 1963).

35. *CW*, 5 (*Treatise on Money*), 1: 120.

36. Ibid., 6: 4–5; ibid., 5: 241–47.

37. Ibid., 5: 124–125.

38. Ibid., 3–43, 217.

39. Hawtrey, "Mr. Keynes's *Treatise on Money*" in his *Art of Central Banking* (London, 1962: 1st ed.: 1932), 332–411; quotation, 359.

40. Robertson, "Mr. Keynes's Theory of Money," *Economic Journal* 41 (September 1931): 395–411.

41. *CW*, 13: 238.

42. Friedrich von Hayek, "Reflections on the Pure Theory of Money of Mr. J. M. Keynes," *Economica* 11 (August 1931): 270–90, and 12 (February 1932): 22–44; quotations, *Economica* 11, 270, 271; comment on capital theory, ibid., 279–80.

43. Editorial note and quotation, *CW*, 13: 243.

44. Keynes, "The Pure Theory of Money," *Economica*, November 1931, ibid., 243–56; quotation, 252.

45. Hayek, "A Rejoinder to Mr. Keynes," *Economica* 11 (November 1931): 398–403; quotation, 398.

46. Piero Sraffa, "Dr. Hayek on Money and Capital," *Economic Journal* 42 (March 1932): 42–53; quotations, 42, 53.

47. E.g., Hawtrey, *The Art of Central Banking*, 363.

48. See chs. 4, 5, "Capital and Employment," in Hawtrey, *Capital and Employment* (London, 1952; 1st ed.: 1937), 55–131.

49. Friedrich A. Hayek, *Prices and Production* (London, 1935; 1st ed.: 1931), 133–34.

50. "Historical Illustrations," *CW*, 6: 132–86.

51. Ibid., 5: 158–60.

52. Ibid., 6: 338–47.

53. Ibid., 5: xvii.

54. Joan Robinson, "A Parable on Savings and Investment," *Economica* 13 (February 1932): 75–84. On the *Treatise*'s constant output during a depression she argued, "It was naturally hard for [the reader] to . . . visualize an acute slump with full employment, and a trade boom without any increase in output, but once he sees his way through this difficulty, it ceases to be very important" (83–84).

55. See editorial note on the Circus, *CW*, 13: 337–43, and on the whole process, ibid., 337–65 passim.

56. Vol. 41, 173–98.

57. Letters, JMK–Joan Robinson, JR–JMK, 29 November, 2 December 1935, *CW*, 13: 612, 612–13; and JR–JMK, 29 May 1936, ibid., 14: 34–35.

58. Letters, JMK–LL, 1 February 1932, 13 October 1933, KP, PP/45/190.

59. Letters, 25 March, 9 September 1934, KP, PP/45/168.

60. Letters, 24, 30 March 1933, October (?) 1935, *CW*, 13: 413, 414, 637.

61. Ibid., 527–65 passim.

62. Letter to JMK, 10 February 1935, ibid., 506.

63. Harrod, *The Life*, 453.

64. JMK–Roy Harrod, 10 September 1935, *CW*, 13: 557–59.

65. JNK–JMK, 13 August 1914, KP, PP/45/168.

66. Clive Bell, *Civilization and Old Friends* (Chicago, 1973), 59.

67. The sum entitled "An Economic Analysis of Unemployment," *CW*, 13: 343–67. At seminars JMK also discussed wage cuts, which he disliked, as an unemployment remedy, some of his comments, ibid., 367–73. See also other documents, ch. 6, "An American Visit," ibid., 12: 529–88.

68. Reprinted, ibid., 9 (*Essays in Persuasion*): 335–66; quotation, 336.

69. Published, *The Listener* 5 (14 January 1931): 46–47.

70. "President Roosevelt Is Magnificently Right," *Daily Mail*, 4 July 1933, *CW*, 20: 273–79.

71. On the JMK–FDR meeting, JMK's notes, Harrod, *The Life*, 20; Frances Perkins, *The Roosevelt I Knew* (New York, 1946), 225.

72. See his talk to American Political Economy Club, *CW*, 13: 457–68.

73. KP, PP/45/190.

74. *CW*, 13: 485–92; quotations, 488, 489, 488.

75. Ibid., 28: 42.

76. Ibid., 489.

77. Felix, *Biography of an Idea*, 131–203, following ch. 6 on the theorizing leading to it, 105–29.

78. *CW*, 7 (*The General Theory*): 97.

79. Jacob Viner, "Mr. Keynes on the Causes of Unemployment," *Quarterly Journal of Economics* 51 (November 1936): 147–67.

80. Ibid., 167. The whole argument, ch. 13, "The General Theory of the Rate of Interest," ibid., 165–74. JMK goes on to discuss the three motives into which he breaks down liquidity preference: transactions, speculative, and precautionary, but this does not explain how the *transaction* with the entrepreneurial-borrower takes place.

81. Karl Marx, "On the Jewish Question," in Marx and Friedrich Engels, *Collected Works* (New York, 1975), 3: 146–74; "True trading nations exist in the ancient world only in the interstices, like the gods of Epicurus, or like the Jews in the pores of Polish society," Marx, *Capital* (New York, 1947), 1: 51.

82. "Theory of Exchange," W. Stanley Jevons, *The Theory of Political Economy* (New York, 1957: 5th ed.; 1st ed.: 1871), 75–166; catena, 165; diagram relating two commodities to each other, 97. JMK's talk, 21 April 1936 at Royal Statistical Society, reprinted, *CW*, 10 (*Essays in Biography*): 109–50; catena, 131.

83. JMK's discussion, ch. 14. "The Classical Theory of the Rate of Interest," *CW*, 7: 175–85; diagram, 180. He classified classicals like Adam Smith and David Ricardo together with neoclassicals like Jevons and Marshall, all in the category "classical."

84. Discussion of diagram of neoclassical interest rate determination, Felix, *Biography of an Idea*, 174–80.

85. JMK's critique of neoclassical interest theory, *CW*, 7: 179–82; question of its being "determinate," 181.

86. "Book I," ibid., 3–34.

87. Ibid., 20.

88. Reflecting the thought of these Keynesians, effective demand is seen as JMK's great epiphany in the two penultimate chapters of (the historian) Peter Clarke, *The Keynesian Revolution in the Making 1924–1936*, 256–310.

89. Bertrand Russell, *The Autobiography of Bertrand Russell* (London, 1978), 1: 72.

90. Harrod, *The Life*, 437.

91. B. R. Mitchell, *European Historical Statistics 1750–1970*, 380, 416.

92. 17 February 1937, BL, Add. MSS 57923.

93. E. A. G. Robinson, "John Maynard Keynes," *Economic Journal*, 57: 41.

94. "The General Theory of Employment," *CW*, 14: 109–23.

95. JMK's major articles, correspondence on the issues, and a few of his opponents' comments, ibid., 185–233.

96. In "Alternative Theories . . . Three Rejoinders," *Economic Journal* 47 (September 1937): 427, 431.

97. Joseph A. Schumpeter, *Ten Great Economists* (London, 1965), 287–88.

98. Paul A. Samuelson and William D. Nordhaus, *Economics* (New York, 1998). From 1948 Samuelson published eleven editions on his own; from 1985 he has had Nordhaus as collaborator.

99. Thomas S. Kuhn, *The Structure of Scientific Revolutions* (Chicago, 1970, 2nd ed., enlarged; 1st ed.: 1962), vii, 151.

CHAPTER 10

Afterlife

Although he did not die until Easter Sunday 1946, Keynes had long since risen to an appropriately appointed British heaven. The ascension had begun in 1937 with his successful defense of *The General Theory* and its acceptance as the Bible of the new economic order-in-becoming. When Roosevelt's administration, in a last access of classical insecurity, sharply reduced expenditures, the Recession of 1937–38 and the recovery from it on a policy reversal combined to give a persuasive lesson in applied economics according to Keynes. The developing war economies of Germany and Great Britain, however different in style, were also proceeding in a similarly Keynesian sense. While the pedants boringly and mysteriously objected, *The General Theory* converged in practice with the real political economy of the time.

Keynes's recovery from his heart attack always remained qualified, but, except for a very few moments of insight, he would refuse to conceive of a worst-case hypothesis. He could live on and enjoy an exquisite sense of vindication, extraordinary for a Cassandra. Having said all that he wanted to say in theory, he could move on into practice and find himself richly engaged as applied economist again in the dignity, furthermore, of a Very Important Person. Approaching and entering into World War II, he naturally bombarded public and government with articles and memoranda drawing on his extraordinarily apt experience. Inevitably, on 28 June 1940, the chancellor of the exchequeur named him to the Treasury's newly established Consultative Council, meant to exploit the experience of unsalaried war horses like him. He had first reassuringly ex-

In his Treasury office a mortally fatigued Lord Keynes prepares to undertake the fifth of his six wartime missions to the United States, 24 August 1945. Photo courtesy of the Associated Press.

plained to his mother that his consulting amounted to a "small job of work . . . without involving strain," but in a week wrote her that he would use the council to "establish helpful relations with the permanent Treasury people to persuade them to make use of me." One month later, on 10 August, he exuberantly reported that he had been "put in a small high up body which is to control generally the major decisions of what was my old department in the last war." Moreover, "I am to have a room in the building, and even the sharing of a private secretary!" He granted, "It means more work," but insisted, with his magical even-handedness, that he had been feeling "extremely well," although he had become feverish and his vulnerable tonsils were troublesome.[1]

Keynes was vouchsafed other, purer honors. He always managed to contribute hard work wherever possible in those cases as well. The two most gratifying, most glittering honors raised him to the Court (as its board of directors was called) of the Bank of England and to the House of Lords.

On 6 September 1941 Keynes wrote his mother that the chancellor of the exchequeur had invited him to become a director of the Bank of England, where Governor Montagu Norman had so consistently ignored his advice: "Rather appalling, I feel, such respectability! . . . It will be regarded as a symbol." He might be in danger of becoming bishop or dean of York![2] At the bank he was replacing his good professional friend, Josiah Stamp, killed when a bomb struck Stamp's Kentish country house. Another old friend, Gerald Shove, celebrated perfectly: "Well, well, well. . . . Another of the forts of folly taken. What a triumph. . . . But nobody but you could have brought it off."[3] The war was a great unifying factor and, conscientiously doing his committee work at the bank, Keynes found little cause for aggressions against Governor Norman and the other directors. His influence at the Treasury sufficed. Furthermore, the government and its major departments had joined him in appreciating the excellences of low interest rates.

On 21 May 1942 Keynes's fellow clubman Winston Churchill, who had never taken his *Economic Consequences of Mr. Churchill* and other strictures tragically, wrote in his own hand from 10 Downing Street, "My dear Keynes," followed by a typescript announcing his intention to "submit your name to the King with a recommendation that His Majesty may be graciously pleased to approve that the dignity of a Barony of the United Kingdom be conferred on you." Courteously, he asked to be informed if that was agreeable.[4] Florence wrote to Maynard, "our joy and pride—my heart overflows." A few days later Maynard reported he was being treated as a "star," normally Lydia's prerogative, receiving "dozens and dozens of letters and telegrams," including one from Lloyd George: "So I suppose we must regard the latest quarrel as made up." Also, "Winston proposed my health at dinner [at] the Other Club—Winston's inner guard of friends."[5] At the Other Club during the Battle of Britain a year and a half earlier, he had sat "next to Winston," whom he found "serene, full of normal feelings, and completely uninflated." He had two to three hours of conversation with the prime minister: two great Englishmen carrying on. Maynard had remarked about Churchill: "Perhaps this moment is the height of his power and glory."[6] Maynard could share some of that. Now he informed Florence that his formal entry into the House of Lords would take place on 8 July: "You could go with Lydia."[7] Of course she went. It rained other honors.

Earlier, in October 1940, Keynes had been named a fellow of Eton as member of its Governing Body. He had found Eton's finances ill-managed for the past half-century,[8] a situation calling up his most pleasurable aggressions. One member, the banker Sir Jasper Ridley, expostulated on one occasion that he preferred to do without "your little lecture," and the provost found the meetings, given Keynes's initiatives, "very entertaining. I like to hear the naked covetousness with which you recommend Southern Preferred Stock, the austere puritanism with which [Cecil] Lubbock [a former deputy governor of the Bank of England] meets such suggestions and the tergiversation of Ridley, who, agreeing with Lubbock, nevertheless votes with you because it is a poor heart that never rejoices and one must have a flutter sometimes."[9] Keynes also found the meetings entertaining and expended too much of his energy on his homework for them.

Then there were the arts. If the London Artists' Association and the Camargo Society were part of the past, Bloomsbury, Lydia, and his yearning toward the aesthetic kept his interest passionately contemporary. On 30 October 1941, writing from the Treasury, he happily wrote his mother that Churchill had asked him to serve as a trustee of the National Gallery: "A very pleasant and honorable mild job."[10] In April 1942, even more appropriately, because drawing on his executive skills and thus demanding more of him, he took the chairmanship of the Committee for the Encouragement of Music and the Arts (CEMA), which would be reorganized in July 1945 largely on his prescription as the Arts Council of Great Britain. (It was in committeee and council that Kenneth Clark, then director of the National Gallery and functioning as vice-chairman under Keynes, observed his less attractive bullying of weaker persons.) Under Keynes CEMA and the Arts Council most valuably increased and rationalized the support of the arts. In mid-course, in 1943, Keynes was complaining of the inevitable to one correspondent: "My work in connection with CEMA has lately got so heavy as to be incompatible with my other duties, which are not decreasing." Indeed it seemed they were increasing exponentially, while, as he boasted to the chief Russian delegate to the Bretton Woods conference, "I can almost boast that I am the Commissar for Fine Arts in my country!"[11] At one point Keynes was even threatening to resign because of overwork, but then Kenneth Clark relieved him of much of the burden, particularly during his absences as Treasury negotiator in America. But then, in 1944, Keynes became chairman of a new committee managing the Royal Opera House, Covent Garden! Under his direction the new Covent Garden presented its first production, *The Sleeping Beauty*—Lydia's old triumph, now with Margot Fonteyn—on 20 February 1946. His health problems stalking him all the while, he was not well enough to attend.[12]

One might gratuitously mention that Keynes was awarded honorary doctorates by Manchester (May 1942) and Edinburgh universities (April 1945) and, in January 1945, the Sorbonne and his own Cambridge University, this last, the Honorary Doctorate of Science echoing John Neville Keynes's scholarly Doctorate of Science. Keynes failed quite to achieve the Royal Society, the oldest scientific society in continuous existence, but it was only his own mortality that defeated him. On 11 April 1946 Vivian Hill, his brother-in-law and a member, wrote him formally that the society, on his assent, would like to elect him. A great admirer of Isaac Newton, who was famously associated with the society, and a collector of Newton first editions, Keynes returned four days later, "I cannot imagine a nicer proposal than that. I am honored and delighted about it." The election would have taken place at the next meeting, 2 May.[13]

Whatever his achievements or distinctions in that period, the most important events in Keynes's life since May 1937 were the fluctuations in his health. The extravagantly voluminous record of his activities cannot deny the bare, elementary fact of his illness: he was a cardiac sufferer under the threat of "sudden death," in his doctor-uncle's words.

After his heart attack Maynard remained at Harvey Road for a month. A former colleague had recommended Ruthin Castle in Wales, a sanitorium for those who could afford it, and on 19 June an ambulance took him there. He remained for three months. As he wrote his brother, the Ruthin Castle doctors discovered pathological details their uncle had missed. His tonsils, inhabited by threatening microscopic creatures, were in a "shocking condition."[14] His stay effected some improvement, but he needed better diagnosis and treatment before he could function satisfactorily. He remained optimistic.

Of course Lydia went to Ruthin with Maynard. She returned to London a few days after their arrival to make a BBC broadcast, however, and Maynard wrote her on 24 June, "Now that the well-filled morning is over, I miss the expectation of your visits." He reassured her, "But I shall soon fall into a routine when the days slip by unnnoticed." That day he also sent a telegram, "Thank you so much for your tender and uncomplaining care all these weeks. But I hope I shall return from the garage a good second-hand machine in running order which can live and move with you a bit." The next day he wrote in pencil that he had acquired a radio to hear her broadcast, insisting, "I am in outrageously good *general* health and my little details are also improving."[15] He economically reused the extravagant first half of the sentence in a letter to his mother, beginning, "I am looking forward to seeing you tomorrow."[16] Florence Ada and John Neville would spell Lydia in keeping him company. Writing of his parents' arrival, he told Lydia, "But *don't* hurry back—time will slip by innocent and unregarded." The next day he wrote that he had been so moved by the plight of Basque children, victims of bombings in the Spanish Civil War, that he had sent £100 for their relief. It was a few days before Julian Bell would be killed in Spain. Maynard wrote his rigorously comforting letter to Vanessa from Ruthin Castle. On Tuesday, 29 June, reporting on her broadcast, he wrote Lydia hearteningly as ever, "It was perfectly done. . . . Your breathing and tempo were perfect—no criticisms at all.'' About himself, he said his Uncle Walter, still prescribing, had forbidden movement, with freedom promised for mind first, body second: ''But they can't take my thoughts away from me. . . . I shall have to confess that I have written a letter this morning to the Chancellor of the Exchequeur.'' Again, ''Don't hurry back if you are enjoying London. I suggest (say) Saturday.'' On Wednesday, responding to her letter, he was worried about ''your bad sleeping. We must try to experiment to find a cure for it.'' Virginia's novel, *The Years*, was leading the list of U.S. best-sellers.[17] One month later he told his mother that he had been allowed to walk for the first time. Also, ''Lydia now rules over a vast hen party of [Ruthin] Castle widows—seven of them sit round'' and compare notes on their husbands' progress.[18] Lydia's sleeping was no longer a problem.

Still an invalid, Maynard was released from Ruthin on 23 September 1937 and, after a week at Gordon Square, went on to Tilton. There, in October, he enjoyed a visit of Margaret and Vivian Hill. He was walking more and continued to interpret his situation as optimistically as possible, financial considerations being added to the physical. Later in October he had to report to his mother, ''The panic on Wall Street was necessarily rather an anxiety. There had been ''[b]ig losses, many decisions to make, many telephone [calls].'' He had sold his parents' English stock and bought American ''at the bottom of the market,'' in two days gaining a profit of £500 for them.[19] These small gains could not make up for the losses. Actually, the resources of his parents also suffering, he experienced the greatest speculative disaster of his life in 1937, his capital going from £506,522 to £220,619.[20] Later in the year he suffered more cardiac distress. In his Christmas letter of 1937 he tried to put the latter, at least, behind him and assured Florence that he was ''completely recovered from my setback (in spite of two letters to *The Times*).'' Lydia was giving presents to forty-five persons in their Tilton community, the Woolfs were coming for the annual Christmas dinner of the two couples, and he was writing a long review of a book on Adam Smith.[21] The alternation of acknowledged setbacks and modest recovery continued through 1938 into early 1939.

In 1938, closely monitored by Lydia, Maynard permitted himself measured rations of activity. On 23 February he gave his annual speech at the National Mutual Life Assurance Society, but he was unhappy about the pessimism of the board majority and its rejection of his advice during the Recession of 1937–38. In October he thought to free himself for more agreeable work and resigned. (He remained with the more sympathetic Provincial Insurance Company.) The day after the National Mutual meeting, meanwhile, he could attend a meeting of the council of the Royal Economic Society because it was held at 46 Gordon Square. Still, he found it exhausting. In May he resumed attending meetings of the Committee of Economic Information, which was modestly carrying on the activities of the moribund Economic Advisory Council of 1930. In March and again in May he went up to Cambridge on faculty affairs. In the fall he settled there in the apartment he had created for Lydia, now most convenient for him in his condition, and could pleasurably busy himself with the Arts Theatre and bursarial work. Of course he was still active editor of the *Economic Journal*. Also, in the face of the threat of war and responding to his instinct for critical points, he wrote a premonitory paper on commodity storage, which the journal later published, for the British Association for the Advancement of Science. He did not go to the meeting, held in Cambridge in August while he was back at Tilton, Gerald Shove reading it for him.[22] At Tilton at summer's end he could pleasurably soak mind, feelings, and body in a warm bath of Bloomsbury. On 11 September, reclining comfortably, he gave his important paper, "My Early Beliefs,"[23] his account of the Apostolic–Mooreian philosophy that he still retained, to Bloomsbury's Memoir Club. He could enjoy his closest Bloomsbury friends, Clive and Vanessa Bell, Duncan Grant, Leonard and Virginia Woolf, Desmond and Molly MacCarthy, Bunny Garnett, and E. M.—Morgan—Forster. Present also were members of the next generation: Quentin and Angelica Bell, and Janie Bussy, daughter of Lytton's sister Dorothy and the French painter, Simon Bussy. (In memoriam: Lytton Strachey and Roger Fry had died.) Maynard and Bloomsbury, his friends responding feelingly to his tranquil reminiscence of thoughts past, were still vital and vital to each other. The ruthlessly critical Virginia found his paper "very ... profound and impressive. ... I was impressed by Maynard."[24]

At the end of February 1939 severe influenza, fortunately as it turned out, once again befell Maynard. He was in London, unable to consult the Cambridge physician he had been seeing in addition to his uncle, and fell into the hands of Janos Plesch, a Hungarian (-Jewish?) internal medicine specialist, prudently resettled in London from a premier situation in Berlin, where he had treated such distinguished patients as Maynard's old flirt, Albert Einstein. As Maynard explained to the Cambridge doctor on 14 March, Plesch had put him on a saltless diet to reduce body fluid and packed his chest in ice for three hours daily. It made him "very chilly" and left him wondering "whether there is really anything in these drastic methods."[25] One month later he reported to Dr. Plesch that he was feeling much better: "Nerves a great deal better. ... The main thing is that, to all appearances, the improvement of the heart is enormous. I remain completely free from all subjective symptoms whatever. Yesterday, I walked for a mile and a half. ... So very many thanks indeed."[26] Before then Maynard had adopted Plesch as his friendly life-giving "ogre," so named in letters to his mother[27] and others, and consulted with him intimately and frequently. ("Ogre" is a good translation of the wonder-working "golem" of Jewish legend.) As Maynard's "improvement" letter indicated, he and Plesch agreed on his psychosomatic pathology. Although a cardiac specialist of recent years would command better understanding and techniques (and stop Maynard's smoking), the elimination of salt, the limits on activities, the empathy, and perhaps the ice were all life-saving. Like Lydia, Plesch understood that Maynard had to be flexibly restrained in his compulsiveness. Responding to his patient's confession, thus, Plesch wrote, "It was very wrong from [*sic*] you to run for a train. Please

the next time use your car. You never ought to be in a hurry." He promised a
"cure" in one and a half years, but only if earned.[28] At least Maynard achieved
a verisimilitude of normal functioning on the doctor's schedule.

Part of the cure consisted of Maynard's playing host to Plesch, accompanied
by wife and son, in Cambridge in the spring of 1939. The entertainment comprised an undergraduate revue in the Arts Theatre and, as Maynard promised,
"English church music in its most exquisite form and in the grandest possible
environment"—King's College Chapel. In all honesty he had to grant that,
unlike most, he found the music "lifeless and even moribund and always falls
on my emotions flatter than I expect," but trusted Plesch would join the appreciative majority. That spring of 1939, examining tripos candidates and attending
committee meetings, Keynes was functioning as a conscientious King's fellow.
Indeed, the day before Plesch arrived, he wrote him that he was "standing up
most successfully to heavy work." But, as he recounted, "I had however two
very bad nights" the previous week and, before that, "a bad attack of cramps
in the heart [after] a very difficult and emotionally straining conversation, which
I was compelled to break off in order to recover."[29] Obviously Maynard had
not recovered as much as he persisted in believing, but he got a good rest in
Tilton that summer and, in August, went off to Royat in south-central France.
"Royat did me a lot of good," he reported after the outbreak of war forced him
to return, the cure half accomplished, to a "good deal of anxiety and work [and]
getting very tired."[30] And so it went. But Keynes was going to do his duty.
After 1940, despite anxiety, more and more work, and his being bombed out of
Gordon Square during the Battle of Britain, his letters to Plesch thin out; the
archive has none between July 1942 and March 1945. (Of course some may
have been lost.) The correspondence then resuming, Plesch would get him
through the war.

Keynes had approached the war diffidently. Mentally strangulated by his sense
of the power realities, he had, along with the great majority of the British people,
accepted appeasement and its expression in the Munich Conference of September 1938 as a nasty, humiliating necessity. An insecure Machiavellian, he had
earlier trusted that Hitler's Germany would respect the British fleet and expand
eastward.[31] As Virginia Woolf recorded, he dismissed Munich as a sham: "All
a put-up job between [Prime Minister Neville] Chamberlain and Hitler. Never
had been any chance of war."[32] He was not reasoning very coherently about
the disorderly succession of disasters, but then who was? The aggressions continuing, Keynes began to wrench his thinking around to an acceptance of the
need to fight. In this war Bloomsbury, Julian Bell having anticipated his elders,
agreed with him. On 14 August 1939 Keynes wrote Richard Kahn that he still
did not expect war.[33] His trip to Royat, beginning the next day, expressed his
last wishful thinking. The Nazi-Soviet Non-Aggression Pact of 23 August gave
the alarm and he then regretfully cut his planned three-week cure short by one
week. Of course he was ready to do his duty. What was it?

Keynes's first idea was self-abnegating and innocently inauthentic. On 7 September he wrote Roy Harrod from King's College, "My plan is to come up here to run a good part of the bursary of the college, the *Economic Journal*, and teaching in the Economic Faculty, which in due course will release more active people."[34] A week later he hoisted his true colors.

On 15 September Keynes sent a memorandum to his old associates, Josiah Stamp and Hubert Henderson, both already in government service, and to the Treasury, on price policy in war.[35] A letter to Stamp tried to moderate his initiative; he saw committee work, "quiet drafting in my own room, and occasional visits to London" as the "sort of thing I might be fit for."[36] But his price policy memorandum led to meetings with his friendly old antagonist, Richard Hopkins in the Treasury, now second secretary, and Under-Secretary Frederick Phillips, and, on 24 September, to another memorandum, "Notes on Exchange Control." Keynes then blew up a blizzard of more memoranda and letters to the editor, articles, talks to groups of MP's and union leaders, among others, broadcasts, and, summarizing his most urgent ideas, the pamphlet *How to Pay for the War* (February 1940).[37] A cardiac invalid and middle-aged, Keynes was replicating the actions of the youthful don he had been at the beginning of World War I, a quarter of a century before. He had descended from his lofty tower of theory and, transforming himself back into an applied economist (and insatiable child), was canvassing for a job.

On 23 June 1942, well launched in his new activities and just turned fifty-nine, Keynes would write Oswald Falk, his old partner in speculation, what was evidently the last letter of their correspondence: "I am getting too elderly to have any fresh ideas well in advance of the times. I have run as fast as I could and am now out of breath." It was an extraordinary statement for a man burdened with too many ideas. But then how could any new ones compete with his culminating *General Theory* and its unerring anticipation of the times? One such idea was enough for any person: he was his own greatest competition and anyway the need was for implementing, and not foundational, conceptions. He continued, "Certainly no help to transfer to monkish rumination. That . . . is not playing the same game in a different way. It is a different game altogether."[38] Monkish rumination was never an option but the intense activity of an applied economist, however threatening to his health, was both different and appropriate to his and his nation's needs. For an uncharacteristic moment he had faltered and fallen into modesty.

Keynes did not rest on his memoranda and other expressions of advice. In late September 1939 he became ringleader of World War I war horses—he and Lydia insisted on calling them "old dogs"—who began meeting at 46 Gordon Square to focus their efforts to influence policy and place themselves in its implementation. They included William Beveridge, who would go on to his eponymous plan, among other interventions; Walter Layton, who would discharge important responsibilities guiding war supply and production, and Arthur

Salter, a civil servant and financial expert with experience at the League of Nations, who would, like Keynes, serve his country on mission in the United States. Keynes launched himself in several directions.

Both Keynes and the government had to pick among an embarrassment of choices. Which, among his many capacities, did he want to offer and which could the government best use? The problem was never definitively solved, but perhaps *that* was the solution, Keynes becoming fluently protean as new situations developed. His character as busybody expanded without limit.

Keynes restrained himself in one direction. Since the early 1920s he had been repeatedly invited to stand for Parliament on his splendid notoriety. Increasingly honored respectability replacing the notoriety, it happened once again, in October 1939, when an opening occurred for a Cambridge University M.P. The master of Magdalen College, who was chairman of the University Conservative Committee, brushing past the candidate's deep-dyed identity as Liberal, made the offer in a most inviting way by achieving his group's nomination of Keynes and getting the agreement of the two other party committees. As before, Keynes was divided between the compulsion for both service *and* distinction, and his revulsion before the vulgar hurly-burly of the House of Commons. When he resisted on grounds of health, the master went to the authority, Dr. Plesch. As Keynes wrote him in mock recrimination, "I gather you let me down completely." Perhaps Plesch had great faith in his curative powers; perhaps he did not want to give Keynes reason for worry. After discussing his condition with him, Plesch sent him a "Pathological Report" by another doctor: "The examinations reveal a remarkable improvement."[39] The report actually fudged his real condition because it affirmed a relative and not necessarily a definitive improvement, but assuming the best, Keynes had to face another reality: what did he really want to do about the nomination? He wrote the master, "I have never had a more difficult decision to make and have been torn both ways to a truly tormenting degree." He had to see and admit: "The active political life is not my right and true activity. I am an extremely active publicist. . . . I can only operate usefully and have my full influence if I am aloof from the day to day life of Westminster."[40] This can be seen as a negative critical point in his life and career, which Keynes judged as correctly as the great positive points. Any compromise here, say a half-hearted attendance in the House of Commons, would have diminished his effectiveness and led him into mistakes of tact or, at the very least, wasted time. His eventual ascent to the House of Lords, a very different body, was another matter. In any case obliged to spend little time with them, he could abide his fellow lords more easily than the Commons masses.

One distracting use of Keynes's time cannot be accounted a waste. When France fell in June 1940 the British authorities began to intern nationals of enemy countries on the Isle of Man. These included Piero Sraffa and another Cambridge economist, one Erwin Rothbarth, among others. Friendship and fairness drove Keynes to intense efforts to free them. "Interned refugees seem to be becoming a whole-time occupation as far as I am concerned, even though there are only five in whom I am interested!'' he wrote to Sir John Anderson, the powerful and sympathetic home secretary. ''The exhaustion of time and energy on your Rothbarth must be almost beyond contemplation.''[41] He succeeded in freeing his charges at more cost to his health.

Keynes's conquest of a room in the Treasury on 10 August 1940 had established him in London during the Battle of Britain, which began officially three days later. Leaving Lydia at Tilton, he wrote to her reassuringly, but could not deny the reality of the bombing, nor his need to run down and up the stairs at the Treasury to and from its safer basement.[42] In the third week of September Maynard's letters to her recounted a crescendo of his experiences. On Monday, 16 September, writing from Gordon Square, he reported: ''A quiet and uneventful day. Raid warnings most of the time, but I have not heard a sound either of guns or bombs.'' His niece, Polly Hill, was working in London and had no safe place to stay: ''So I have asked her here. . . . I am to sleep in the kitchen. . . . Polly sleeps in the cellar,'' his chauffeur was placed in the passageway, and his secretary in the pantry. Maynard wrote the next day, ''We were all very comfortable last night and I slept beautifully.'' There had been ''one big noise before midnight but long quiet intervals. . . . It's not as bad as it sounds. But the warnings are continuous.'' A second letter that day specified that ''two bombs we heard whistling past us last night landed in Fitzroy Square and Fitzroy Street. Tell Vanessa and Duncan that their studios [at the rear of 8 Fitzroy Street] are still intact, although those higher up the street have disappeared.'' He insisted on being ''consoled to find that even if the bombs had fallen on 46, we should have been all right in the basement.'' On Wednesday, 18 September, he evidently dictated a typed letter from the Treasury Chambers reporting that everything was fine at Gordon Square, but ''not for London as a whole. . . . We all slept well in our bunks, rather like life on board ship.''[43] Later on Wednesday, when Maynard was dining with his fellow inhabitants, a loud noise exploded at the other end of the square, shattering the house's windows but leaving everyone unhurt. A time bomb discovered in the vicinity prevented repairs, and Maynard first took temporary quarters in the Treasury and then retreated to Tilton. It was just as well.

''Bloomsbury all round has suffered severely and few have escaped,'' Maynard wrote his mother on 27 September. Another attack had now demolished Duncan's and Vanessa's studios, and the area was ''a mess.'' Maynard was now commuting to Tilton and enduring a ''terrifically long day.'' He had breakfast at 8 A.M. and did not get back until 8:30 P.M. He was, however, staying Fridays and Saturdays at Tilton, where ''I can compose the more important memoranda quietly.'' He took the occasion to tell her of his election to the Eton Governing Body.[44] Writing to Dr. Plesch two days later he had himself starting breakfast at 7 and out of the house before 8 A.M. Although he had reported ''bothersome'' tonsils and weight loss six weeks earlier, he had ''no distressing symptoms'' at the moment.[45] The Battle of Britain subsided.

The memoranda of the applied economist Keynes, given extra force by his operations as publicist, appeared almost everywhere in the Treasury files and, from there, in the working papers of other government departments. Convinced he was always right and the responsibles wrong, he fired his counsel, replicated shotgun fashion in many carbon copies, on almost any subject, minor as well as major. He was profound and prescient on allocation of resources and war finance, while gratuitously detailed on such subjects as war damage compensation, the nationalization of electric power, and corporate taxation.[46] His formidable opinions were often ''polemic in tone [and] full of factual inaccuracies,'' as one civil servant remembered: ''Just as we feared: Maynard had got it all wrong, but this was going to cause a lot of trouble before it was finished with.'' In the British embassy in Washington another official received ''instructions to deliver a rather cockeyed ultimatum'' on Bolivian tin to members of the U.S. cabinet.[47] In November 1939 Keynes composed ''Notes on the War for the President,'' which instructed Roosevelt to ''break off diplomatic relations with Germany and declare a state of nonintercourse.'' The point was ''not to conquer Germany, but to convert her. . . . Her lapse is partly our fault. For twenty years we have behaved like asses.''[48] The fact that much of ''Notes'' was reasonable only emphasized his cockeyed tactlessness. In 1938, after their 1934 meeting, Keynes had pursued Roosevelt with advice in two letters, but the president responded coolly to the first and evidently not at all to the second.[49] In these instances, as in many others, Keynes made more sense than contemporary politics could endure.

Keynes's pamphlet, *How to Pay for the War*, baldly reversed the depression doctrine of *The General Theory* constructed around weak demand and confronted the excessive demand created by war. Although he retained his distaste for rationing and advised against it as a ''pseudo-remedy,'' he did hit on a good way to deal with inflation—and, furthermore, anticipate and counter the weakening of demand expected with the peace. This was compulsory savings or, put more tactfully, ''deferred pay.'' The idea was that the national budget would allow for deferred pay of £550 million annually, the money to be released after the war.[50] Labor, however, was not going to permit the deprivations to continue after so many meager depression years. Once again, as on the economic terms of the peace of 1919 or the return to the gold standard, Keynes found himself too far in advance of public opinion. The 1941 budget, which significantly incorporated other, hugely important ideas of his, provided for only some £125 million of deferred pay. Harrod had to concede that instead of being ''the centrepiece of war finance,'' the scheme was at best ''an interesting experiment, but only played a minor part in the whole situation.''[51] It amounted to less than that, while Keynes had to see stringent rationing introduced. He continued to mix right and wrong creatively and constructively.

Keynes's attempt to address President Roosevelt, although ill-fitting at the time, pointed unerringly in the right direction: the finances, industrial power, and, ultimately, the totality of the United States. Keynes *knew* that the United

States, however infra dig, had to make this war its own and save his world. His efforts converged on Washington.

In an association that would seem more and more natural and inevitable, Keynes would make six trips to the United States between 1941 and 1946. He spent thirteen months there or traveling to and fro. His first mission, from the beginning of May to late July 1941, dealt with Lend-Lease aid; the second and third, in 1943 and 1944, the Bretton Woods agreements for the The International Monetary Fund and the International Bank for Reconstruction and Development ("World Bank"); the fourth, in late 1944, financial arrangements of the period, known as Stage II, between the German and Japanese defeats; the fifth, a post-war loan for Britain, and the last, a month from late February into March 1946, the formal inauguration of the Bretton Woods institutions, meant to be a relaxing vacation for Keynes, but providing him the occasion for another stressful battle, this one typically over matters not worth the trouble. With his range of experience and skill, and his insistence on minding everybody's business, Keynes became a negotiator on all major financial matters with the United States. One cannot imagine a half-dozen other persons doing as much and getting to the point—or missing it—as often. The relation between the United States and Great Britain, Keynes traveling the whole route, underwent various stages from sympathetic help gingerly given an increasingly desperate combatant power by a friendly but neutral nation to an intimate, irritable alliance of equally embattled, if unequal, partners.

Keynes got to the United States by getting to the critical point, identified in fluent memoranda, before anyone else. In August 1940, named a member of the Exchange Control Conference, composed of Treasury and Bank of England personnel, he determined the agenda of its first meeting by presenting it with a study he had made on foreign exchange control and the payments problem.[52] The problem was paying for great war materiel orders already made in the United States, and Keynes was fertile with suggestions on borrowing dollars against the security of British firms in the country and other sources. U.S. neutrality legislation, although relaxed, required cash payment, impossible in the disastrous year 1940 and not much easier until the United States entered the war. Roosevelt, however, was reelected in November 1940, and, leading a reluctant country toward its great international position, presently advanced the idea, which he himself conceived, of the Lend-Lease Agreement. Becoming law in March 1941, it would permit the "loan" of military equipment against vague future compensation (and the American "leasing" of British bases in the Western Hemisphere, a significant strategic advantage for Britain as well). Although providing $7 billion, a magnificent sum, to be followed by more billions, the law, however, did not cover the orders made before. In early 1941 Keynes found himself discussing ways of easing payment for these orders, and also entering questions ranging from surplus commodities to war aims. His interlocutors were U.S. Ambassador John G. Winant and his adviser Benjamin V. Cohen, a major drafter of New Deal legislation earlier. (With his genius for apt relations, Keynes had dined with Thomas G. Corcoran, Cohen's associate in that drafting, during his 1934 Washington visit.)[53] In mid-April 1941, in a richly informative letter to his mother on the 1941 budget, among other matters, Keynes mentioned talk of sending him to the United States soon; the ambassador, evidently given the idea by by Cohen, was urging it. Keynes, with his command of the British *and* American situations, was obviously the man to remove misunderstandings. (One should not forget this genius for creating them as well.)

On 1 May Maynard wrote Florence Ada that he and Lydia were off to Bournemouth on the south coast to fly to Lisbon the next day en route to the United States. He had resolved ''1) not to talk too fast, 2) never once speak my mind or tell the truth, 3) not to drink cocktails, 4) to obey Lydia in all matters.''[54] A veteran of the Battle of Britain, he evidently did not worry about the flight. Staying actually in the resort of Estoril for two days while awaiting the flying boat, the busybody Keynes took the occasion to join in negotiations for a monetary agreement with Portugal.[55] His flight got him to New York on 8 May by way of a stop in the Azores. The U.S. negotiations were a proliferating tangle and Keynes stayed two and a half months before flying back. (He found that flight particularly exhausting and, with the exception of a New York–London air trip in 1943, was able to enjoy the relaxation, combined agreeably with memoranda-drafting and editing of the *Economic Journal*, of sea voyages.)

The first North American trip set the pattern of the half-dozen: intense, depleting negotiations conducted by a man with a weakened heart; warm acquaintanceships, if not friendships, as both sides perhaps thought; Keynesian expressions of arrogance made good by his sparkling intelligence and underlying kindness; unendurable misunderstandings as either party defended its embattled or triumphant ego and, as in the military alliance, remarkably effective cooperation despite errors of detail and grand confusions. The importance of Keynes's contribution to the general results, compared with that of his *General Theory*, remains to be examined. We should not forget that the book was now making its way, while requiring and receiving lessening help from its author, into the economic thought and policy of the West.

''On overseas issues both wartime and postwar . . . Keynes soon became the dominant force in the Treasury, determining grand strategy and a high proportion of the tactics,'' Donald Moggridge, who has written about this period of his life in the greatest detail, would have it. Yet, in regard to this first trip, Moggridge had to concede that Keynes had got the Americans *perhaps* ''to stretch slightly the promise of $300–$400 million relief on the old commitments'' given to the earlier British negotiators before he had arrived.[56] In any case Keynes's influence on the British Treasury, whether dominant or less so, could have little effect on U.S. power. Although Roosevelt and his experts had a realistic sense of British desperation, the Congress and the American people were only gradually emerging from their old isolationism and Depression-generated sense of penury. The result was terrific strains on all those engaged in the negotiations.

The Jewish Harry Dexter White, the acting assistant secretary of the Treasury and trusted deputy of the famously Jewish Secretary Henry Morgenthau Jr., became Keynes's fate in drafting the Bretton Woods Agreements, the most important, most Keynesian part of his financial diplomacy. His intellectual parentage of Bretton Woods is overwhelmingly documented. His *Treatise on Money* had projected the idea of an internationalizing world bank. For the World Economic Conference of 1933 he had conceived of a variant, with a special currency equivalent to $5 billion to attack the Depression. He had, however, seen President Roosevelt, astride economic nationalism, annihilate the conference, his bank scheme vanishing with it. In terms of his own statesmanship Keynes, balancing the competing advantages, had then approved Roosevelt's action. Now, a decade later, he had to act the statesman vis-à-vis Harry White.

On 8 September 1941, with his usual dispatch and building on his earlier ideas, Keynes had produced a completely developed plan of a Clearing Union, as he called it, to operate as an international central bank.[57] This was less than a month and a half after his return from the Lend-Lease negotiations. He would make endless changes to accomodate suggestions and objections, but kept the essence of the scheme—until the Americans produced theirs.[58] The Clearing Union would provide liquidity expressed in a currency called *bancor* and equivalent to gold measured in dollars, the only truly convertible major currency of the period, totaling $26 billion. So financed, it would stabilize the various currencies against each other. Because every nation except the United States was poor or in deep deficit, Keynes developed an intricate system of safeguards meant to protect the union against excessive demands for funds. But this only emphasized the magnitude of the problem without providing a solution.

The United States, the world's creditor of the last resort, meanwhile, bestirred itself. On 14 December 1941 Henry Morgenthau instructed Harry White to design a "stabilization fund" to do essentially what Keynes's Clearing Union would do. Producing three drafts of his plan by early 1942, White did more than that. More Keynesian than Keynes, he would achieve two different, comparably hopeful objectives. Besides the fund Morgenthau demanded, White also conceived of a bank to finance postwar reconstruction. Yet, although it was a duplex scheme compared with Keynes's singular conception, it was more modest in financial scope, the fund to be capitalized at $5 billion and the bank at $10 billion. Over the next months Keynes and White, developing newer variants of their plans, dueled with each other until their first grand confrontation in Washington in September–October 1943.

By the time of the Washington meeting the Realpolitiker Keynes had bowed graciously to U.S. power. In April 1943 he put it this way to Frederick Phillips at the Treasury: "I have been quite conscious that we were in a sense propagating for the Harry White scheme by pressing the Clearing Union the way we have." With perfect vision he saw that the details were not as important as an American commitment: "The real risk is that there will be no plan at all and that Congress will run away from their own proposal."[59] By the time he went to Washington Keynes was simply attempting to add minor Keynesian modifications to the White plan.

If Keynes, with his long practice in English elitist manners, was exquisitely rude, White, American in his drive and unencumbered by manners, was rude and crude. Once again, as with Leonard Woolf, Keynes balanced his ambivalences toward a Jew and arrived at a fair verdict. He found White "overbearing, a bad colleague [without] the faintest conception of how to behave." Yet, "I have a very great respect and even liking for him. In many respects he is the best man here."[60] Under cover of verbal violences Keynes surrendered so superbly to White that James Meade found his own leader "a menace in international negotiations." Among other imprecations, in one of a number of anti-semitic remarks, Keynes denounced a White proposal as "yet another Talmud. We had better break off negotiations." Meade drew the scene: "What absolute Bedlam these discussions are! Keynes and White . . . go for each other in a strident duet of discord which after a crescendo of abuse on either side leads up to a chaotic adjournment."[61] White's biographer offered another perspective capturing Keynes's contradictory feelings: "Behind the scenes the authors of the White Plan and the Keynes Plan eventually became cronies and went off to the baseball game together."[62] Virginia Woolf had used the word "cronies" to pair Leonard and Maynard. The Keynes–White cooperative duel continued at the Bretton Woods conference, held in a salubrious New Hampshire resort, in July 1944.

If White represented American power mercilessly, Keynes was a virtuoso of English culture—and impotence. Lionel Robbins had endured Keynes's bullying when, as a member of the Committee of Economists in 1930, he frustrated his chairman's demand for a unanimous recommendation on tariff policy. Now, as a supportive, still minor colleague in a common cause, he could easily admire a great man. At a meeting preliminary to Bretton Woods in Atlantic City (held there instead of Washington to accomodate Keynes's ailing heart) Robbins observed Keynes in action: "Keynes must be one of the most remarkable men that have ever lived—the quick logic, the birdlike swoop of intuition, the vivid fancy, the wide vision, above all the incomparable sense of the fitness of words." Robbins could compare him only to Churchill, who possessed the "traditional qualities of our race raised to the scale of grandeur. Whereas the special qualities of Keynes are something outside of all that . . . a unique unearthly quality of which one can only say it is pure genius." Robbins recorded the apotheosis: "The Americans sat entranced as the God-like visitor sang and the golden light played round." Then, at Bretton Wods, "At the end Keynes capped the proceedings by one of his most felicitous speeches, and the delegates paid tribute by rising and applauding again and again. In a way, this is one of the greatest triumphs of his life."[63]

Keynes's triumph must be qualified—on balance to his credit. His ultimate conception, and Harry White's no less so, built on an aggressively false assumption about the global political economy. A true international central bank would have worked only in an homogenous, more or less unitary world of essentially equal well-being and similar political behavior. Only these conditions would have permitted equal responsibility and power among all its national members. A deception might have got closer to becoming a practical operation, thus a kind of neocolonialism in which the more advanced nations dominated the poorer ones and imposed a general financial order. Keynes, Churchill, and the British people had adumbrated something of the sort in their dream of an Anglo-American partnership in the postwar world. But, humiliatingly, Britain was too far from being an equal of the United States, World War II having accelerated the dissolution of empire and its empire specifically. Actually, the only realistic possibility was the one that the International Monetary Fund (IMF) and the World Bank, as the Bretton Woods institutions, actually incorporated, a suggestion—but only a suggestion—of a limited and reluctantly assumed global financial hegemony exercised by a benificent United States. Harry White had appropriately designed the IMF and the bank in this sense while limiting them to mediocrity. They have been less than that. In more recent years the IMF, after giving up its impossible mission of global monetary stabilization, has usefully aided the more viable of the former Soviet nations toward a rational economic order while rescuing others, and the World Bank has provided development loans to less advanced countries. Useful, but hardly inspiring.

Keynes's vision did project ultimate goals which could guide the preliminary steps of 1944. In a more practical manner this genius of applied economics tried to slip through an absolutely necessary solution to an immediate, impossible problem. It was the crying need of the leading national survivors of the war in relation to the wealth of the United States and the threat, given extra force by its repressed and even greater need, of the Soviet Union. According to his biographer, the terrifically competent Harry White, always as alert as Keynes, knew what his opposite number was about, specifically trying to smuggle into his plan a way of financing postwar relief.[64] Keynes's Clearing Union had allowed for "unlimited liability," in theory permitting any member to draw on its projected fund of $26 billion to an unlimited extent. The U.S. government, contributing $3 billion, might have seen withdrawals of the rest, thus $23 billion, to meet the urgent financial requirements of the poorer nations—all the others. It might then have been invited to pour more funds into the Clearing Union rather than see it implode. On the face of it Keynes's deception was too patently absurd to be taken seriously. White's IMF limited withdrawals to the size of a given nation's contribution. So much for that.

But Keynes was as correct as White, indeed on a much higher level of statesmanship. Furthermore, as his biographer indicates, White may have had a pro-Soviet agenda that was also absurd and hence unlikely to be harmful. As it happened, White disappeared from the scene too quickly to do any damage while his scheme made its practical, if limited, contribution to the postwar order.[65]

The new threat of the Cold War, Winston Churchill making his "Iron Curtain" speech on 15 March 1946, drove the United States to the unimagined generosity and practical sense of the Marshall Plan. Secretary of State George C. Marshall (the victorious U.S. Army chief of staff) proposed it at the Harvard University commencement on 5 June 1947 (Keynes's birthday!). In the following years the plan and aid programs succeeding it gave away an approximation of the billions Keynes had hoped to draw out of the Clearing Union with U.S. financial backing. Restoring economic viability very quickly, the Marshall Plan halted the Soviet thrust into the heart of Europe.

Keynes's instincts were also acute, as circumstances would show, in his opposition to the Morgenthau Plan, which would have reduced Germany to the "status of a fifth-rate power" in White's words. An expert examiner of his stewardship put it: "Morgenthau considered the eradication of Nazism and the destruction of German military power the first requisite of peace . . . and he deemed postwar friendship with Great Britian and Russia a second essential." White, again according to his biographer, appears to have supported his chief determinedly out of sympathy for Soviet aims, among other possible reasons.[66] Keynes, consistent with his earlier advice to President Roosevelt not to condemn the Germans out of hand, opposed efforts, as he had in 1919, to overwhelm the country with crushing sanctions. At one point, finding the plan "pretty mad," Keynes asked White how the Ruhr inhabitants "were to be kept from starving," and was less than relieved by White's assurance that they could survive "on a very low level of subsistence."[67] The onset of the Cold War swept away the Morgenthau Plan even as it led to the inclusion of (West) Germany within the aid program of the Marshall Plan.

How much had Keynes accomplished on his American missions besides exercising his imagination so prophetically and inspiringly? We have seen that his pre-Lend-Lease negotiations had perhaps eased matters but changed little in the sum granted Britain. Similarly, following his ultimately gracious surrender on the Bretton Woods Agreements, he had no visible effect on the magnitude of the Stage II funds allocated Great Britain between the German and Japanese defeats, a period of less than four months anyway. Similarly, he went to the United States a year after Bretton Woods in late August 1945, with the war ending, to beg for a grant-in-aid of $6 billion. His mission ended with a much smaller and humiliating, Shylock's *loan* of $3.75 billion. Actually he had gotten close to that point when the new Labour government, in power since July, refused to believe he had moved the Americans sufficiently and sent a Treasury permanent secretary to supersede him—and accept those terms.[68] The loan had its stop-gap value, but it melted away very fast because, inter alia, of the government's Keynesian low interest rate policy. But the Soviet danger and the Marshall Plan, the latter announced a year and a half after the loan agreement, changed everything, incidentally sweeping away Britain's obligation to pay. And so Harry White's IMF and World Bank, in all their mediocrity, were the most substantial results of Keynes's efforts in America. In sum, substantially speaking, he need not have bothered.[69]

Although Keynes's Herculean labors in and about the United States had achieved so little, he himself did little to assist his *General Theory*, following his great defense of it in the *Quarterly Journal of Economics* and the *Economic Journal*. Without him, it went on to gain its ascendancy over economic thought and policy in the non-Communist world. But then he had performed magnificently in shaping its politically correct message, converting able followers, and managing the personnel to implement his ideas. That sufficed: the founder was no longer necessary to the Keynesian Revolution. In one minor but illustrative case Joan Robinson, partnered by Richard Kahn, extended the conversion process by organizing a joint seminar for students of Cambridge University and the London School of Economics in 1935, even before *The General Theory* was published. One seminar member, the future Professor G. L. S. Shackle of the University of Liverpool, experienced a ''staggering and thrilling flood of light'' and went on to propagate the new gospel in his lectures and books.[70] In 1940 Arthur Pigou complained to Keynes about the Cambridge economics students' ''parrot-like treatment of your stuff [as effected by] the lectures or supervisions of the beautiful Mrs. Robinson—a magpie breeding innumerable parrots!''[71] American textbooks, expanding American hegemony, would soon generalize and regularize the new paradigm as it was being transformed into policy.

Important agents of Keynesian policy were Lionel Robbins, recanting from the rigidity of his neoclassical theory without, however, becoming a Keynesian; James Meade, happily pursuing his Circus thoughts to further realization; Richard Hopkins of the Treasury, who was always open to Keynes's remedies if they were practicable, and William Beveridge, head of an Oxford college after serving as director of the London School of Economics. An important agency of Keynesian policy was the Economic Section of the War Cabinet Offices, successor of the Economic Advisory Council and the Committee on Economic Information. The Economic Section became a fair approximation of the economic general staff Keynes had urged in 1929 (ch. 6), which had been Beveridge's original idea back in 1923 anyway.[72] Robbins became the section's director in September 1941, with Meade a member and his postwar successor. Keynes, distracted by his burgeoning activities, could passively, for the most part, observe as these very competent and dedicated persons made his ideas part of the machinery of government.

In 1940 Meade wrote a paper arguing for the objective of high employment as part of the Keynesian ''regulation of national expenditure as a whole,'' Robbins has recorded.[73] The paper excited the undoctrinaire Hopkins, eager to avoid another depression, and he urged Meade on, with the collaboration of the decreasingly doctrinaire Robbins, to the White Paper on budget policy of the next year. The White Paper, providing the accounting framework for the British budget of 1941, shifted the criterion from a governmental budgetary balance to a macroeconomic balance of the economy as a whole. This ended the old, rigid imposition of pure accounting principles in government at the cost of employment and general well-being. It was a major aspect of the quiet Keynesian Revolution and, if it did not need Keynes, he nevertheless worked one day for thirteen hours on that budget. In a letter to his mother he wrote that Dr. Plesch, who could hardly prescribe retroactively, had ruled "no harm done" when he reported that labor to him. More reasonably, Keynes could take satisfaction, as he confided to his mother, that "the logical structure and method of the wartime budget . . . together with the new White Paper [meant] a revolution in public finance." (If he had failed with his deferred pay scheme, he knew where to take his just satisfaction.) In this letter he mentioned the U.S. ambassador's request that he go to America.[74] With his domestic policy moving along nicely he could depart light-heartedly.

The later development of Keynesian policy during the war years owed even less to its author's direct contemporary efforts. With Keynes frequently away, the socialist Meade and the flexible neoclassical theorist Robbins later collaborated on another, major Keynesian White Paper, *Economic Policy*, submitted on 26 May 1944. The opening statement established unequivocally: "This Government accept as one of their primary aims . . . the maintenance of a high and stable level of employment after the war."[75] Perversely hearkening to his own never completely abandoned neoclassical principles, Keynes, however, had suggested revisions the day before he left for the Bretton Woods conference and tried to qualify the Meade-Robbins attack on unemployment. With appreciative humor the reformed Robbins found that "doubtless something of the verve and attack of the original paper had been lost: there was a great deal of waffling ambiguity about some of the sections, oddly enough even those which had passed through Keynes's hands."[76]

William Beveridge, meanwhile, was developing his welfare and health plan. Keynes chose to welcome it, writing him on 17 March 1942 that his memoranda on the subject "leave me in a state of wild enthusiasm. . . . I think it a vast constructive reform of real importance."[77] Keynes had seen that the Beveridge Plan could play a countercyclical role within his general framework of a macroeconomically guided economy. At the same time he was aware that he and Beveridge were competing in their designs for postwar Britain. In 1943, as his team of Robbins and Meade were pondering its attack on unemployment in the new paper, Keynes had told Arthur Pigou that Beveridge seemed to have a monopoly on the issue.[78] Hearing of the paper's pending appearance, Beveridge defended his monopoly by rushing into print with his book, *Full Employment in a Free Society* (1944).[79] Now in 1944 Keynes chose to see the book as supportive of *his* policy and congratulated Beveridge on it. Again leaning toward his more conservative side, he objected only in finding Beveridge excessively Keynesian in the announced objective. In his congratulatory note Keynes added in a postscript: "No harm in aiming at three per cent unemployment, but I shall be surprised if we succeed."[80] Indeed *The General Theory*'s effective denial of the danger of inflation had licensed Beveridge to recommend the impossible. Keynes was wrong about the success and the harm, the latter taking the form of persistent inflation accompanying very low unemployment and generous social services. For better or worse Keynes and Beveridge jointly shaped postwar Britain.

Beyond Britain, the United States quickly accepted Keynes's lead on domestic economic policy. As early as 1943 his American followers began to draft an employment measure. The eventual Employment Act of 1946 proposed to ''promote maximum employment, production, and purchasing power,'' creating the Council of Economic Advisers as the president's modest economic general staff.[81] Similarly converted, Canada, Australia, Sweden, France (with the Monnet Plan, inter alia), and other advanced nations took similar actions.

Keynes's grand conception proved crucially important, indeed essential, in the Cold War, which began to envelop the world when he died and which confirmed his view of himself as Karl Marx's rival. With the war ended, the Western nations, still insecure because of the mysterious force of the Depression, feared a great rise in unemployment after the end of war-generated demand. Keynes gave them the hope and the tools to manage their economies effectively. Without a Keynesian strategy the West might have well suffered greater defeats before the monolithic Marxian power of the Soviet system, which the war had hammered into a dangerous, operative unity, however much weakness was repressed within it. For almost a half century Keynes and Marx divided the world between them—until Keynes could claim a second triumph.[82]

Thus, by way of his *General Theory*, Keynes had won victories of world-historical magnitude in two movements, first against doctrinaire capitalism and then against doctrinaire communism. His stature is much greater than the epigones of the pure theorist prefer to imagine. Seeing him as merely correct in economic theory, they blind themselves to the way he generated a seductive power out of his deceptions: a pied piper of theory become statesman. This view permits us to evaluate the sense of his final activities more justly.

Had Keynes died afer the defense of *The General Theory*, the world would have been insignificantly different. Inessential for the book's success after his heart attack in 1937, he accomplished little of substance during the rest of his life. His six American missions served only to provide a distinguished decor for British submission to U.S. hegemony. Of course his expanded public personality had a certain, but less than essential, public relations effect in selling his theory. Perversely, however, the best value of his prominence was personal to him: his activities kept him alive while incrementally killing him. Since boyhood he had been pursued by his demonic ''natural sadness'' and escaped only by compulsive work and the associated ego satisfaction. Had he not entered totally into Britain's battle of survival—another critical point—had he been confined to observing passively, he would have quickly collapsed into himself. Naturally veering too closely to an excess of action, he lived his last years teetering enjoyably on the edge of the abyss.

On his first trip, as he recounted to his mother, Maynard had dined out forty-seven times in five weeks. It was "much more dangerous than the Blitz." His health, he insisted, was better than ever, "Yet I shouldn't have survived without Lydia—who provides constant rest, discipline, and comfort." He was writing from the hills of Virginia, where they had escaped the dangerous Washington heat. In this "tortuous and suspicious, yet kindly, Washington world" they had "made some good friends."[83] In a letter to a Treasury official he specified, "The (I suppose rather highbrow) group where Lydia and I are most comfortable are the Walter Lippmanns, Dean Achesons [he was then assistant secretary of state] and the Archie McLeishes (the Librarian of Congress and poet)." Keynes failed to mention Felix Frankfurter, by then on the Supreme Court, who celebrated his Washington presence with a party. Keynes was also seeing "quite a lot of Pasvolsky (Leo—economist)" of the State Department, the "extremely suspicious and jealous" Lauchlin Currie, economist and administrative assistant to Roosevelt, and, of course, Harry White.[84] (One notes the Jews, generating in Keynes a sense of comfortable familiarity but also outbursts of negative feelings.) Acheson, while remarking on White's "capacity for rudeness," recalled "an evening when he joined the Keyneses for dinner at the Whites," when White was exceptionally "pleasant and amusing."[85] All this served Keynes's financial diplomacy well.

Yet on both sides the connection was superficial personally. These were good professional relationships on a level with Keynes's City friendships at home but further reduced to his limited stays in Washington. He had made the acquaintance of Lippmann and Frankfurter at the Paris Peace Conference and had seen them both in England in the 1930s. Lippmann did say, "My friendship with Keynes was one of the happiest of my life,"[86] but this leaves one wondering about the quality of friendship in his life. According to the Keynes Papers, Keynes and Lippmann each wrote the other seven letters, all impersonal and functional, from 1935 to 1946. In January 1935, in the only interesting letter, Lippmann reports the U.S. government "deliberately running deficits large enough to give work . . . to the able-bodied unemployed," a gratifyingly Keynesian policy. A little later that year Lippmann, as chairman of the Harvard Board of Overseers, inquires into Keynes's opinion of the distinguished Gottfried Haberler, an expert in international trade, and Keynes rates him "B+ if not A."[87] (Haberler became professor of economics at Harvard from 1936 to 1971.) The 1919 encounters of Keynes with Lippmann and Frankfurter had not amounted to much. At the time Frankfurter, writing to Lippmann, referred to him distantly as "Keynes (you may have met him, he was the financial adviser to the British)."[88] The renewals of the old contacts and the new ones meant little more personal depth. Acheson recalled seeing Keynes in Washington in May 1941 as "a representative of Mr. Churchill," an inaccurate impression that Keynes may well have suggested to him. Acheson found him "not only one of the most delightful and engaging men I have ever known but also . . . one of the most brillilant." He granted, "But not all felt his charm; to some he appeared arrogant.''[89] Research as much as personal contact seems behind these comments. Acheson's memoirs mentioned many other persons in an equally—and distantly—friendly and diplomatic manner. The Keynes–McLeish relationship is documented in the Keynes Papers by one letter from McLeish to Keynes in 1941.[90]

However successful he was or was not, Keynes's style remained marvelously contradictory—Keynesian—in the United States as well. On his American missions, he insensibly joined his ambivalences about Jews and the country. During his first experience there in 1917 he had furiously confronted its terrific economic superiority and even greater potentials. He reacted then, as he would in Acheson's time, in a manner ''rude, dogmatic, and disobliging,'' as a friend of his felt impelled to report. ''He made a terrible reputation for rudeness.''[91] To Duncan Grant, Maynard had written on that first visit: ''The only sympathetic and original thing in America is the niggers, who are charming.''[92] The American hospitality shown him and his *General Theory* softened this attitude considerably but not completely. In the 1940s he had found his American friends, Jewish or not, not only enjoyable but also select. Still, as in the case of international Jewry, he retained his arbitrary, hostile theories about the United States. In 1943 James Meade recorded his remarks on the train taking them from New York to Washington for the preliminary talks on the Bretton Woods Agreements: ''There was a flow of acid comments on the American countryside, their air-raid precautions, lack of birds, and sterility of the land!'' Those oddments derived from a view recalled in 1948 by Maynard's old friend Bernard Swithinbank to be passed on to Roy Harrod, then writing his Keynes biography: ''He was attracted to the theory that the human race could not thrive in North America (when it was 'discovered,' the population was extraordinarily small) and that it would gradually die out.'' The small bird population that Keynes perceived was consistent with this theory. Furthermore, Swithinbank remembered, Keynes had laid down an ultimate condemnation of the Americans: ''[H]e said they seemed to have no intuition.''[93] (Harrod chose not to use this information.) Keynes's sense of distance from the American scene was then emphasized, as Meade's account suggested, by his dismissing the subject and plunging into a ''tremendous discussion on modern painting and the whole journey was rounded off by Lydia singing the Casse-Noisette [Nutcracker Suite] music at the top of her voice and dancing it with her hands. We had been instructed to slip into Washington unnoticed.''[94]

Like all persons famous in their time, Keynes was a public personality, his Washington relationships expressing it even more purely than comparable English connections. These included, for example, his City associates and such other public personalities as Lloyd George, Winston Churchill, George Bernard Shaw, H. G. Wells, and Beatrice and Sidney Webb. Yet one feels in Keynes none of the windy emptiness emanating from some public individuals. Even the warmly expressive Franklin Roosevelt remains elusive despite family and lover(s); it is hard to imagine him whole outside of politics. Churchill, spending expansive hours in club and House of Commons Smoking Room and limited ones at home, is another such example of the public man. Outside of politics can one imagine Richard Nixon at all? Maynard Keynes, however, was rooted in the personal. We have seen his intense and enduring relationships with his own, always cherished, family, his Cambridge world, Bloomsbury, and ultimately and limitlessly with Lydia. The Maynard–Duncan attachment remained absolute while Maynard persisted in adoring Vanessa. His connection with the Woolves, however striated with dislike, was always a thorough and complex friendship. After Vanessa wrote Virginia, then traveling, about his heart attack, Virginia noted in her diary, "Anxious about Maynard to the extent of dreading post or buying a paper."[95] But then, on 1 April 1941, a little less than four years later, Maynard wrote his mother, "We have been much upset by the sad fate of our dear friend Virginia Woolf. Her old troubles came back on her, and she drowned herself. . . . We rang up . . . to ask her over to tea and got this answer." He mentioned "the devoted care of her husband Leonard." Pathetically, if wishfully, he added, "The two of them were our dearest friends."[96] Leonard continued to come to Tilton for their Christmas reunion. Loving perhaps more than loved, but so validating his life thoroughly enough, Maynard clung to his people.

To affirm his closeness to his family Maynard had first to measure out a given amount of separating space. That helps explain his brief professional excursion into the India Office. Returned to Cambridge in 1908, he continued to expand that space precisely because of the renewed physical closeness. His brother Geoffrey was doubtless correct, when, going through Maynard's papers, he found an unkind letter about himself and tried not to be hurt. "Geoffrey is *hopeless*, more irredeemably hopeless than anyone I've ever met," Maynard had written to Duncan Grant from the Pyrenees, where he had joined his parents and Geoffrey. In his memoirs Geoffrey could interpret that he was being made the scapegoat for his brother's reaction to the family: "He had been mistaken to come on this family holiday . . . and he never made the same mistake again."[97] Geoffrey did not mention another unkind reference, also in a letter to Duncan, a year later. Maynard reported having enjoyed lunch with his sister Margaret, who was "charming," gratuitously adding, "much nicer than your horrid Geoffrey."[98] Distance then well established, Maynard could begin to enjoy his family anew, Geoffrey eventually included. He could look with increasing favor on his brother's accomplishments, which brought credit to the family without threatening his position. Their bibliophile interests brought them closer together, but the turning point was the presence of the exotic Lydia, who perversely tightened the Keynes family bonds generally. Geoffey's adoration of Lydia established, "Maynard's attitude changed instantly; from that time onward he became a kind and affectionate brother."[99]

Maynard and Geoffrey had a great deal in common as long as neither emphasized the differences. If Maynard had first denigrated Geoffrey, Geoffrey, although a more genuine aesthete, made a point of denying membership in Bloomsbury and rejecting the group en soi, although he liked Duncan, Vanessa, and Leonard Woolf (while detesting Clive Bell). He had, in fact, occupied a room in the prewar Brunswick Square establishment. This was when Virginia, on 9 September 1913, took an overdose of veronal in an early suicide attempt and he "spent part of the night washing out our patient's stomach."[100] That represented the extent of Geoffrey's involvement in Bloomsbury.

Early on the brothers were sending each other catalogues and buying books for each other's collections. In 1915, from the ambulance train where he practiced gory battle surgery, Geoffrey wrote, "Thanks for sending me that Lowe catalogue, but it has caused me sleepless nights" (because of the decisions required). When, from Ruthin Castle, Maynard reported on the shocking condition of his tonsils to Geoffrey, he also asked him to buy certain books at given price limits.[101] In 1939, two weeks after World War II had started, Maynard asked Geoffrey to come round to Gordon Square; he wanted to arrange a £100 annual gift to his older son similar to one for Margaret's sons. Geoffrey and his wife had become "constant guests" at 46 Gordon Square and Tilton, often staying at Tilton by themselves until they got their own country place in 1932.[102] Maynard may have been more generous with his resources than his presence, but the brothers' relations were easy and included equal shares in responsibility, along with Margaret, for their aging parents.

Although both Neville and Florence almost achieved a century of life (as did Neville's elder half-sister precisely), Neville showed the effects of aging rather soon after his numerous complaints of early maturity. In November 1914, when Neville was sixty-two years old, Geoffrey, after thanking Maynard for books sent him, wrote that he was "not altogether reassured by your description of Father's mental condition." He had heard from their Uncle Walter, who reported no physical signs but the "change [is] a subtle thing, not due to any vascular deterioration, but more a tiredness of the brain cells." Perhaps propped up as he had propped up his seniors, Neville functioned well enough to continue as Cambridge University registrary for more than a decade, but he was indeed giving off more signs of a mental tiredness and withdrawing more and more. In 1938, at eighty-six, he was suffering from a "tired heart" and a breathing problem with exertion, Geoffrey reported to Maynard after a visit to Harvey Road. "I think he may get better with care [but] I feel he may just die at any moment without warning, although he seemed more mentally alert and less deaf than usual." But Neville was able to enjoy the King's College celebration Maynard had arranged for his ninetieth birthday and his (and Florence's) diamond wedding anniversary in 1942. In 1946 he "walked the aisle with a firm tread" at the memorial service for his son in Westminster Abbey.[103]

The day after the King's College event Florence wrote to thank Maynard for the "wonderful time on Sunday." Of course she chose not to take note of the cool, patronizing social scientist's dissertation on the "elegant, mid-Victorian highbrow . . . rather rich, rather pleasure-loving."[104] She directed her attention elsewhere: "You had caught the spirit of his earlier life . . . it was almost too beautiful to bear." She had to say, "What you mean to us is beyond words."

In a trembling hand Neville added, "You have been a joy to us from the day you were born."[105] Less than a year later Geoffrey urged their parents to accept Margaret's invitation to stay at her home in Highgate, north of London, Florence's "muscular debility" having been worsened caring for Neville. In another letter Geoffrey reported to Maynard, after seeing them at Margaret's, that Neville had "deteriorated since I last saw him." He was "more dim and shambling." He was also buying up stamps recklessly, to the extent of £750 worth.[106] It was later determined that Neville had made entirely sensible, indeed profitable, purchases. He was permitted to continue.

In late October 1945 Geoffrey wrote to Maynard, then in Washington on the loan negotiations, that he and Margaret had visited their parents at Florence's request. For their mother to ask for help was extraordinary, and Geoffrey found their father in a "rather pitiful state of senility difficult to control when he is awake . . . needs a constant attendant." Today one thinks: Alzheimer's. As for their mother, "She is wonderful and equal to everything." Geoffrey appended thirteen x's for Lydia. Maynard wrote that he hoped to board the Queen Mary on 30 November; he wanted to see his father as soon as possible because of the "dismaying report." He added that it had looked bad for him but, with his resilient optimism, now felt entirely recovered.[107] He did not report that, exceptionally, Lydia, under the strain of caring for him, had been feeling unwell herself.

Missions to America notwithstanding, Maynard clung to Bloomsbury as much as to family. In 1941, a few weeks after returning from his first trip, he summarized his manifold activities in the letter to his mother reporting his nomination to the Court of the Bank of England. He was "writing a heavy memorandum on postwar international currency plans" (his Clearing Union), but had to interrupt it when the Treasury called him in. He had bought the farm area contiguous to Vanessa's Charleston and an additional 170 lambs for it, making more than 200 sheep in all. Further, "We are feasting the Charlestonians tonight on five partridges, [?] bottles of champagne, and a bottle of 1896 port."[108] (Since the episode of the exiguous grouse, he had evidently learned to provide enough for true feasting.) "Despite all the vicissitudes of their relationship, the irritations, and Vanessa's undeniable dislike of certain aspects of Maynard's character," as her biographer justly put it, "their friendship survived, based is it was on deep affection and respect."[109]

Spinning out more bonds in their relations, Tilton and Charleston joined in making the best of things during the war. Vanessa, wisely anticipating it and deciding she preferred country living, had shifted her household and her (and Duncan's) painting completely to Charleston by the summer of 1939. Beginning in the spring of 1943, Quentin Bell, having been rejected for military service because of tuberculosis, worked as a farm hand at Tilton for two periods. Vanessa was delighted to have him there close and safe. In June 1944 Maynard advised her and Duncan to avoid London because of the new flying bombs; preparing to go to the United States on the first of his two trips that year, he told Duncan he could lodge his mother and aunt in the safety of Tilton that summer.[110] At year's end, on Boxing Day (the day after Christmas, when presents were traditionally given to employees) the Charlestonians attended a Tilton party for Maynard's people and their families. Besides addressing vast supplies of chicken, turkey, and cakes, each of the forty guests found a present under the Christmas tree, the presents including silk stockings and other useful items brought back by Lydia from America's vast larder. (She had actually brought 120 pairs of stockings for others as well.) "The evening ended with songs and recitations, and a performance of Little Red Riding Hood by Duncan and Clive."[111] In late August 1945 Maynard wrote to Vanessa, "Lydia and I are off to America tomorrow. I hope the Memoir Club will be able to wait until we are back. . . . This is the toughest mission yet [on the loan] and I need your prayers."[112] The Memoir Club waited. Upon the Keyneses' return Charleston again came to Tilton to celebrate Christmas—and peace. The Charlestonians, Duncan acting the part of a bishop, performed a version of a popular radio program.[113]

For the survivors the Bloomsbury spirit lived on, perhaps a bit stiffly, in the Memoir Club. In November 1945 Molly MacCarthy wrote, "Dearest Maynard, Love to both of you. And welcome home. I long to see you and to have our Memoir Club going strong again." Quite deaf, she might not hear a word, but this long-lived Bloomsbury institution, which she had founded, was important to her and the others. After another note from her, making up for sparse and belated communications, Maynard wrote a long letter touching on his last Washington negotiations and explaining that he wanted to get the Charlestonians' agreement on the date of a meeting, which could be 23 January. It had been planned that Morgan Forster or Leonard Woolf (who had been at Tilton for the Christmas dinner "as usual") would speak, but Maynard suggested Clive Bell as another possibility. (As it turned out, it was Clive who gave his paper that January.) On her own authority, as she reported, Molly had enrolled Janie Bussy, representing the next generation, in the club. The younger people were replacing the departed; Maynard accepted her decision: "I approve of the Führer-prinzip." He added that Lydia would provide dinner. After the meeting Molly wrote to thank Maynard for sending his car for her and Desmond. The dinner was "*exquise*." Sensitively, she noted that Lydia looked exhausted and recommended a doctor. A last letter to "Dearest Lydia and Maynard" thanked them for the "wonderful present . . . wine!" Long troubled with asthma, Desmond had been lately depressed after an influenza attack, but now felt better; for herself Molly wrote, "I am weak." (Both would die, we recall, in the early 1950s.) Molly was planning another meeting in February, when Leonard and Morgan would give the papers originally planned.[114]

Maynard had also kept up with Bunny Garnett, at least until 1942. In March 1921 Bunny had married Ray (Rachel) Marshall, a sister of Frances Marshall (eventual wife of Ralph Partridge) and had two sons with her. In another act of his fluent generosity, Maynard had pressed money on his younger friend for the boys' education.[115] In 1940 Bunny entered Richard, his eldest son, in King's College, Maynard responding by encouraging him strongly and recommending Richard to the provost, his friend John Sheppard. Bunny thereupon wrote that he was sending Richard up to King's, could he visit at Tilton? "I want so much to see you."[116] By the spring of 1938 Bunny, twenty-six years older, had undertaken an affair with Angelica, which Vanessa tolerated as possibly helping her daughter through the shock of Julian's death.[117] In March 1941 Ray Garnett died of cancer. A year later, in the last letter of their correspondence in the archive, Bunny wrote Maynard, "This is to announce that Angelica and I are being married tomorrow. We send you and Lydia our warmest love."[118] Angelica later thought that Maynard "appealed to him not to go on with the marriage."[119] If so, Maynard changed his mind after writing Geoffrey: "No I cannot say I approve of the Bunny marriage. But, as you say, it is their affair . . . and we must wish them the best of happiness."[120] Vanessa was appalled but reconciled herself and richly enjoyed the grandchildren produced, four girls, the last two, twins.

Still immature and undefined, Angelica found she had left a possessive mother and an inoperative father for a self-centered asynchronous husband given to "shattering rages," and slipped into depression. Her well-written memoir, a worthy Bloomsbury document on which these references draw, seems an effort to understand and contend with her feelings.[121] In defending itself against parental errors, Bloomsbury had often been hard on its children. But then Maynard could have filed as grave a complaint as Angelica. That was not, however, the case with Baron Keynes of Tilton.

Maynard's American experiences and other activities were keeping him alive at great cost. He had to spend time at Tilton to recover from the fatigue of his first mission as exacerbated by round-trip air travel. Yet the recovery had to coexist with his active expansion of farm operations as overseen by Logan Thompson. On his second mission, in 1943, he was "horribly overworked" and, while claiming that the Washington climate—it was mid-September— "does agree with my heart," reported himself "overexhausted one day and had to take a day off to recoup."[122] The Bretton Woods conference of 1944, direly followed by the similarly intense Stage II financial negotiations later that year, was particularly damaging. Maynard experienced seven cardiac incidents in less than a month. How many deserved the name of "heart attack," however "slight," as they were sometimes defined, remains conjectural. The entry of 19 July 1944 in Lionel Robbins' diary recorded a "slight attack," further described as "not serious and no doctor," when Keynes had dined with Henry Morgenthau and then run upstairs to keep another appointment. But the entry continued: "There was one evening of prostration at Atlantic City [the preliminary conference, in late June], two the first week here [from 1 July, Bretton Woods], three last week; and now I feel that it is a race between the exhaustion of his powers and the termination of the conference."[123] During the Stage II negotiations, on 6 October 1944, Keynes had a "slight" heart attack, according to a

Treasury colleague, who later, in November, found him successively "very nervy and difficult to deal with" and "in bed shaken and white."[124] In his letter to his doctor Keynes reported similar incidents on his last two missions.

On 5 January 1946, upon his "belated New Year's greeting from Lydia and me," Keynes wrote Dr. Plesch that the loan negotiations had been "a very severe strain." He had been mediating between American resistance to British requests and British incomprehension of American parsimony. The result was "war on two fronts and suffering the greatest responsibilities and irritations, I began to give way." He experienced "symptons . . . which made Lydia very cross," specifically heart spasms. He recovered to an extent by lying down with Plesch-commanded bags of ice. The voyage back was restful but then he went from the ship, stopping briefly at Gordon Square, to the House of Lords, where the loan debate was taking place. The next day he then made his "big speech [which] shook me up a bit."[125] He was gallantly defending a loan that he agreed was a wretched and humiliating substitute for a grant. Lionel Robbins hyperbolically thought Keynes "almost single-handedly saved the Government."[126] It was a superb speech, but the House of Commons had already approved acceptance of the loan, and the lords followed suit grumpily but ineluctably. At more cost to his heart Keynes had simply made passage easier and less humiliating to the government.

Following this exercise in heroism, Keynes indulged in silliness compounded on his last American trip in February–March 1946. At the inauguration of the Bretton Woods institutions in Savannah he wasted too much intense emotion to protest and lose on two minor points. The Americans got the general agreement to locate both the IMF and World Bank in Washington and give representatives of the major nations considerable power over the Fund's decisions. Keynes, arguing that this would politicalize them excessively, wanted them located in New York close to the United Nations headquarters and the Wall Street financial center, with the IMF obedient to a professional staff and sheltered from national intrigues. His effort to sanitize the politics out of both institutions had been as utopian as it was futile, reminiscent of the young Keynes's waste of energy trying to micromanage the Indian currency issue in 1913.[127] He then got on the night train to New York and drove himself into another cardiac incident. As he wrote Plesch in the archive's last letter of their correspondence, he had walked an enormous distance "down the swaying carriages" to the restaurant car: "I was quite knocked out, and so remained for about an hour," this followed by "a certain measure of distress . . . for much longer." He wanted to see Plesch. The letter was dated a month before he died.[128]

Pressing resolutely on to the end, Keynes seems to have denied the abyss always at his feet—with one clear exception. In early 1945 he heard again from Marcel Labordère, his French correspondent, after the wartime interruption. He had been afraid his friend might not have survived. Calling up his "very affectionate respects," he had found it a delightful and "great . . . surprise to see the handwriting on the envelope . . . exactly as usual." Labordère was in poor health while comparably Keynes reported, "[M]y heart is very deficient in strength . . . and I cannot walk. I find it profitable to spend about 12 hours in ever[y] 24 in a horizontal position in bed." No other letter in the archive, surely not to his Dr. Plesch, described his condition in nearly such dire terms. Nobly, stoically, Labordère returned, "Since one year or so I have had to forsake every kind of activity, continuous decline." He was seventy-five: "More and more I am enticed towards what is eternal: the permanent properties of each individual substance as it occurs ever the same in the stars. Humble and most grateful respects of your old, frenzied crank."[129] Nos moraturi.

On New Year's Day 1946 Keynes was contemplating leaving the government although the inauguration of the Bretton Woods institutions was still before him. That day he announced his intention "to step out of the Treasury" to two persons, but with the equilibrating intention, as he wrote to two others as well, of returning in force to Cambridge. More characteristically, he was ignoring his earlier admission of distress and proposing to exchange one demanding responsibility for another. Having labored cordially with Lord Halifax, ambassador to the United States, on the American loan, Keynes wrote him a long, shrewd review of the economic and political situation. Expressing his discontent with the Labour government, he veered off into his facile anti-semitism, as aroused now by the its "socialist advisers . . . who, like so many Jews, are either Nazi or Communist at least." He concluded, "Being of a resigning temperament, I shall not last long in this galère in any case."[130] In the event he lasted as long as he lived.

On that New Year's Day Maynard also wrote to Dennis Robertson, who had earlier been a great help to him on the Bretton Woods negotiations with his "intellectual subtlety and patience of mind and tenacity of character," as he had made a point of recognizing in a letter to Richard Hopkins of the Treasury.[131] Referring now to the more recent loan negotiations, Maynard thanked Dennis "for your letter of greeting—I needed a little comfort then." Although their deep differences in theory remained, their joint war work had brought them closer together. He mentioned his intention to quit the Treasury and added that he was "hoping to be at Cambridge next term more days than I have been for many a year past."[132] This was a formal statement to the responsible faculty member: with Maynard's approval Dennis had succeeded Arthur Pigou as Cambridge University professor of political economy in 1944. His sense of responsibility to college and university as strong as ever, Maynard joined easily with Dennis in concerning himself about their well-being.

In return, college and university still wanted Maynard, indeed loved him. In December 1942 Joan Robinson had privately, pleadingly written him; would he take the political-economy professorship if it entailed no residence or other requirements? He replied that he would not accept special conditions, felt too much bound by other postwar commitments, and preferred to be free to recommend other candidates for the position. In January 1944 the university's Board of Electors passed the unanimous resolution to offer it to him while recognizing other demands on his time. Keynes responded, "[M]y answer must be nolo episcopari." He mentioned his "uncertain state of health" and dislike of being an exception.[133] So Dennis took it.

On 23 December 1945 Dadie Rylands wrote Maynard:

I feel moved to send you both messages of admiration, affection, and sympathy. I have felt anxious and agitated over you for many months. Thank God that you are safe back . . . and not too mentally fatigued to turn over the leaves of Jacobean play-books with a decanter of claret beside you.

The College has ambled along. Undergraduates abound. They are either 17 or 25. . . .

No answer to this on any account. It is only a greeting and the best of wishes to you and to Lydia for a year in which I hope you will not be sacrificed entirely to your country. Yours ever, Dadie.[134]

Throughout the war, whatever the distractions, Maynard had kept his connection with Cambridge alive, and it would be easy to slip back into greater activity there—God willing. Indeed, on that New Year's Day he had also written to Gerald Shove, still an active fellow, and John Sheppard, still King's College provost. To the first he said that he had "made some pretty good progress" in negotiating with the Rockefeller Foundation for a grant to support a department of applied economics at Cambridge, an old project delayed by the war.[135] He wrote to Sheppard that he proposed to donate an old etching of a Cambridge music party to the college.[136] Dennis Robertson had also taken over Maynard's Political Economy Club, and invited Maynard, now as distinguished guest speaker, to give a talk to it on 2 February. Published posthumously in the *Economic Journal*, it would be his last significant contribution to college and university.

In the memory of a competent observer, Keynes, "sitting right beside Robertson's hearth fire, gave us a very elegant talk . . . every sentence a piece of good English prose and every paragraph cadenced—just a wonderful performance." Robertson, however, later remarked that "the impishness of his mind" was missing[137]—it was two and a half months before the fatal Easter morning. With his marvelously persuasive and prophetically fertile wrongheadedness, Keynes was predicting that the great American trade, hence dollar, surplus would soon obey the dictates of equilibrium and become manageable for Britain and other trading partners of the United States. He referred to his House of Lords speech defending the American loan and the neoclassical economic laws, the latter of which *The General Theory* had spurned. In a sudden relapse characteristic of his contradictory nature, he had arrived at an appeal to "the wisdom of Adam Smith."[138] Actually, the trade imbalance lasted well into the 1950s, but, as in the case of his attempt to smuggle American aid into his aborted Clearing Union, Keynes's sense of the global *political* economy was impeccable. Intuitively he knew that the United States, in due time, would make the political decision not to permit the pure economic laws to rule, thus the Marshall Plan and the equilibrating restoration of bearable conditions for international trade. It was a perfect *Ave atque Vale*.

Keynes's engagement diaries for 1946, beginning with Wednesday, 9 January, are dense with his varied activities. (There is no diary in the archive for 1945, and the diaries from 1942 through 1944 and the diary of 1946, although busy, do not record his appointments in the United States.) In January, besides seeing Dr. Plesch twice, he attended meetings of the House of Lords, the Bank of England, the King's College bursary, the Eton fellows, and the Budget Commission of the Treasury. After the interruption occasioned by his American trip, the 1946 diary resumed in force on Thursday, 28 March, when Keynes had appointments at the Bank of England, and Friday, 29 March, with the chancellor of the exchequeur, among others. In the first week in April, from Monday 1 April, he had appointments at the Bank of England, Provincial Insurance Company, and the Other Club. In the second week, from Monday, 8 April he was very busy with the Budget Commission, the Bank, the Provincial, the French Ballet, and the National Gallery trustees.[139] On Tuesday, 9 April, as Easter approached, he wrote his mother from Gordon Square suggesting that she come there on Thursday evening and go on to Tilton with Lydia on Friday.[140] Perhaps he had an appointment in London on Friday and planned to go later, but it is not listed. The diary is blank for the Tilton period, thus for the weekend and, following it, the week beginning Monday, 15 April, but it noted appointments to be kept from Friday, 26 April, to Tuesday, 13 August. The last was a meeting at the National Gallery, but it is crossed out, after "Glyndebourne," on Friday, 26 July.[141]

Roy Harrod wrote that Keynes "spent the whole week before Easter" at Tilton. "He could not abandon work completely. Each morning brought the pouch from the Treasury, which demanded his attention for at least a couple of hours." In the "beautiful English spring weather," he strolled about his domain and, one morning, "took his mother to see the supply of meat provided for an Easter feast in all the cottages on the estate." On Tuesday, 18 April, Maynard went to tea at Charleston; Clive Bell was there as well as Vanessa and Duncan. Three times that week he rode up to the top of Firle Beacon on the Sussex Downs, with its exhilerating view of the sea. On Saturday, 20 April, he sent his mother back in the car and, feeling invigorated, walked down to Tilton with Lydia. "Early next morning his mother heard a sound of coughing in his room. She went to seek Lydia. . . . In a few minutes all was over."[142]

NOTES

1. JMK to FAK, 28 June, 5 July, 10 August 1940, KP, PP/45/168.
2. Ibid.
3. Quoted, Hession, *JMK*, 326.
4. KP, PP/45/168.
5. Letters, 4, 14 June 1942, ibid.

6. Letter, 6 September 1940, ibid.

7. Letter, 1 July 1942, ibid.

8. Letter, JMK to Lord Quickswood (the provost), 19 February 1942, *CW*, 12: 110.

9. Letters, Ridley, Quickswood to JMK, 8 March 1944, 17 December 1943, ibid., 112, 113–14.

10. KP, PP/45/168.

11. Letters, 2 July 1943, 18 July 1944, quoted, Moggridge, *MK*, 702, 705.

12. Harrod, *The Life*, 592.

13. Letters, Hill to JMK, JMK to Hill, 11, 15 April 1946, KP, PP/45/142.

14. JMK to GLK, 10 July 1937, KP, PP/45/167.

15. KP, PP/45/190.

16. Letter, 25 June 1937, KP, PP/45/168.

17. Letters, 27, 28, 29, 30 June 1937, KP, PP/45/190.

18. Letter, 27 July 1937, KP, PP/45/168.

19. JMK to FAK, 10, 21 October 1937, ibid.

20. Table, JMK's assets, 1922–46, *CW*, 12 (*Economic Articles and Correspondence: Investment and Editorial*): 11.

21. KP, PP/45/168.

22. Editorial note, *CW*, 21 (*Activities 1931–1939; World Crises and Politics in Britain and America*): 456; "The Policy of Government Storage of Foodstuffs and Raw Materials," *Economic Journal*, September 1938, ibid., 456–70.

23. "My Early Beliefs," *CW*, 10 (*Essays in Biography*): 433–50.

24. Virginia Woolf, *The Diary*, 5: 168–69.

25. JMK to Dr. H. Hanton, KP, PP/45/255.

26. Letter, 13 April 1939, ibid.

27. E.g., 10 April, 14 July 1939, KP, PP/45/168.

28. Letter, dated only "Sunday," but in response to a letter of JMK, KP, PP/45/255.

29. Letters, 28 May, 9 June 1939, ibid.

30. Letter, JMK to Janos Plesch, October 1929, ibid.

31. JMK to W. W. Stewart (an American associate), 14 November 1937, *CW*, 21: 426–29.

32. Virginia Woolf, *The Diary*, 5: 179.

33. Editorial note, *CW*, 22 (*Activities 1929–45: Internal War Finance*): 3.

34. Quoted, Harrod, *The Life*, 487–88.

35. Editorial note (as above), *CW*, 22: 33; "Price Policy," ibid., 4–9.

36. 15 September 1939, quoted, Harrod, *The Life*, n. 488.

37. *CW*, 22: 9–15; ch. 2, "How to Pay for the War," 40–155.

38. BL, Add. MSS 57923.

39. Letter, 18 October 1939, and "Pathological Report," n.d., KP, PP/45/255.

40. Letter to A. B. Ramsay, 24 November 1939, *CW*, 22: 38–39.

41. 31 July 1940, KP, University Affairs (hereafter UA)/5/5. Other letters on the internees in this file.

42. JMK to FAK, 15 September 1940, KP, PP/45/168.

43. KP, PP/45/190.

44. KP, PP/45/168.

45. 29 September, 12 August 1940, KP, PP/45/255.

46. See ch. 7, "Miscellaneous Activities," *CW*, 22: 432–86.

47. Quoted, Moggridge, *MK*, 639.

48. "Notes on the War," 2 November 1939, *CW*, 22: 23–29; quotations, 25, 24.

49. JMK's letters, 1 February, 25 March 1938, and Roosevelt's reply, 3 March 1938, ibid., 21: 434–39, 440, 439.

50. As first expressed in the two-part article, "Paying for the War," *The Times*, 14, 15 November 1939, ibid., 22: 41–51; "pseudo-remedy," 43.

51. Harrod, *The Life*, 494. See also Moggridge, *MK*, 645–47.

52. Editorial note, *CW*, 23 (*Activities 1940–1943: External War Finance*):1; discussion, 2–10.

53. Moggridge, *MK*, 582.

54. JMK to FAK, 14 April, 1 May 1941, KP, PP/45/168.

55. Harrod, *The Life*, 505.

56. Moggridge, *MK*, 663, 657.

57. In two memoranda, "Post-War Currency Policy" and "Proposals for an International Currency Union," *CW*, 25 (*Activities 1940–1944: Shaping the Post-War World: The Clearing Union*): 21–32, 33–40. For JMK's plans in the context of U.S. and international action, see J. Keith Horsefield, *The International Monetary Fund 1945–1965*, 3 vols. (Washington, 1969). Vol. 3 (*Documents*) reprints the final two of five of JMK's draft plans, and two drafts of the successfully competitive U.S. plan.

58. See *CW*, 25: 1–237, passim.

59. Ibid., 242.

60. In a long account of the negotiations to Wilfred Eady, Treasury joint second secretary, 3 October 1943, ibid., 352–57; quotation, 356.

61. Entries, 9, 4 October 1943, Robbins and Meade, *The Wartime Diaries of Lionel Robbins and James Meade*, Susan Howson and Donald Moggridge, eds. (London, 1990), 139, 127.

62. David Rees, *Harry Dexter White: A Study in Paradox* (New York, 1973), 230.

63. Entries, 24 June, 22 July 1944, Robbins and Meade, *The Wartime Diaries*, 158–59, 191.

64. Rees, *Harry Dexter White*, 148.

65. His biographer records the fact that White, accused of acting as a Soviet spy, resigned precipitously as U.S. executive director of the IMF at the end of March 1947, and died of a possibly self-induced heart attack on 16 August 1948, ibid., 10.

66. General account, ch. 15, "The Carthaginian Peace," Rees, *Harry Dexter White*, 239–65; "status of a fifth-rate power," 248. On Morgenthau, John Morton Blum, *From the Morgenthau Diaries*, 3: *Years of War 1941–1945* (Boston, 1967); quotation, vi.

67. JMK's report to the chancellor of the exchequeur, *CW*, 24 (*Activities 1944–1946: The Transition to Peace*): 133–34; see also "Recommendations of British . . . Committee on Reparation and Economic Security," 28 September 1943, which JMK may have drafted, ibid., 26 (*Activities 1941–1946: Shaping the Post-War World: Bretton Woods and Reparations*) : 348–73.

68. Specifics on loan, which carried 1.6 percent interest, *CW*, 24: editorial note, 603–4; on loan in general, "The Loan Negotiations," ibid., 420–628. Another of JMK's wide swings between desire and reality is documented by his projected demands on U.S. aid in his memorandum, "Overseas Financial Policy in Stage IV," original draft, 18 March, and draft submitted to the cabinet, 15 May 1945, ibid., 256–95. Quickly discarded when he got to Washington, they proposed that the United States would *give* Britain a $3 billion grant to pay for pre-Lend-Lease purchases, a comparable postwar grant, and a credit of $5 billion, while Canada, besides giving it a $500 million credit, would join

other allies in canceling Britain's substantial debts to them. Marshalling King's College's hospitality, Keynes entranced, but failed to persuade, a Canadian delegation with this plan during a long Cambridge weekend, 18–21 May 1945, Douglas LePan, *Bright Glass of Memory*, (Toronto, 1979), 53–110.

69. A recent article asked in its title, "Is There a Good Case for a New Bretton Woods International Monetary System?", and concluded that it was "dubious." By Michael D. Bordo, Papers and Proceedings, *American Economic Review* 85 (May 1995): 317–22.

70. G. L. S. Shackle, *The Nature of Economic Thought* (Cambridge, 1966), 53. Shackle went on to write the Keynesian paean, *The Years of High Theory* (Cambridge, 1983; 1st ed.: 1967).

71. Letter, June 1940, KP, PP/45/254.

72. "An Economic General Staff," in JMK's *Nation*, 29 December 1923 and 5 January 1924; see Felix, *Biography of an Idea*, 90.

73. Lionel Robbins, *Autobiography*, 186. See "Post-War Planning," 186–212, ibid., on these developments.

74. JMK to FAK, 14 April 1941, KP, PP/45/168.

75. Quoted, Moggridge, *MK*, 714.

76. Robbins, *Autobiography*, 187–88.

77. *CW*, 27 (*Activities 1940–1946: Shaping the Post-War World: Employment and Commodities*): 203–8; quotation, 203.

78. Letter, JMK to Pigou, 25 April 1943, KP, PP/45/254.

79. Robbins, *Autobiography*, 189.

80. Letter, JMK to Beveridge, 16 December 1944, *CW*, 27: 381.

81. Quoted, Robert Lekachman, *The Age of Keynes* (New York, 1966), 171.

82. Comparison of the statesmanship of JMK and Marx, Felix, "Marx and Keynes: The Primacy of Politics," *Biography* 18 (Summer 1995): 219–27.

83. JMK to FAK, 28 June 1941, KP, PP/45/168.

84. JMK's report of 3 October 1943 to Wilfred Eady on his negotiations with Harry White (as above, n. 60), *CW*, 25: 354, 356.

85. Dean Acheson, *Present at the Creation: My Years in the State Department* (New York, 1969), 82.

86. Quoted from the Oral History Collection, Yale Lippmann Collection, Ronald Steel, *Walter Lippmann and the American Century* (Boston, 1980), 306.

87. Lippmann to JMK, 9, 21 January 1935; JMK to Lippmann, 5 February 1935. KP, PP/45/187.

88. Quoted from the biographical essay by Joseph P. Lash, Felix Frankfurter, *From the Diaries of Felix Frankfurter*, 28.

89. Acheson, *Present at the Creation*, 29.

90. KP, PP/45/204.

91. The friend was Basil P. Blackett of the Treasury, writing to the private secretary of the chancellor of the exchequeur, 1 January 1918, quoted, editorial note, *CW*, 16 (*Activities 1914–1919: The Treasury and Versailles*): 264.

92. JMK to Grant, 17 October 1917, BL, Add. MSS 57931.

93. Letter, Swithinbank to "Robin," 9 March 1948, KP, PP/45/321.

94. Entry by James Meade, 11 September 1943, Robbins and Meade, *The Wartime Diaries*, 100.

95. Virginia Woolf, *The Diary*, 25 May 1937, 5: 90.

96. JMK to FAK, PP/45/168.

97. Geoffrey Keynes, *The Gates of Memory*, 196. Quoting the letters, Geoffrey left off everything after the word *"hopeless,"* JMK to DG, 28 June 1909, BL, Add. MSS 57930.

98. JMK to DG, 1 July 1910, ibid.

99. Geoffrey Keynes, *The Gates of Memory*, 196 (as in note 97).

100. Geoffrey Keynes, *The Gates of Memory*, 115.

101. GLK to JMK, 7 March 1915, JMK to GLK, 10 July 1937 (as in note 14), KP, PP/45/167.

102. JMK to GLK, 17 September 1939, KP, PP/45/167; Geoffrey Keynes, *The Gates of Memory*, 196 (as in notes 97 and 99).

103. GLK to JMK, 18 December 1938, KP, PP/45/167; Harrod, *The Life*, 643.

104. KP, PP/20 (referred to in ch. 1 et seq.).

105. Letter, 31 August 1942, KP, PP/45/168.

106. GLK to JMK, 13 May, 14 June 1943, KP, PP/45/167.

107. GLK to JMK, JMK to GLK, 25 October, 23 November 1945, ibid.

108. 6 September 1941, KP, PP/45/168 (as in note 2).

109. Frances Spalding, *Vanessa Bell*, 331.

110. Ibid., 313–14, 323.

111. Ibid., 324, 325.

112. Quoted, ibid., 331.

113. Ibid.

114. Molly MacCarthy to JMK, 22 November 1945, 1 January, 4 February 1946, n.d. [1946]; JMK to Molly MacCarthy, 2 January 1946, KP, PP/45/198.

115. David Garnett, *Great Friends* (London, 1979), 146–47.

116. Letter, David Garnett to JMK, August 1940, n. d., but following JMK's response; JMK to Garnett, 6 August 1940, KP, PP/45/116.

117. Frances Spalding, *Vanessa Bell*, 306.

118. 7 May 1942, KP, PP/45/116.

119. Angelica Garnett, *Deceived with Kindness*, 154.

120. JMK to GLK, 13 May 1942, KP, PP/45/167.

121. Angelica Garnett, *Deceived with Kindness*, 162.

122. Also in the report to Wilfred Eady of the Treasury, noted above twice, *CW*, 25: 353–54.

123. Robbins and Meade, *The Wartime Diaries*, 190–91. JMK also called the incident of 19 July a "heart attack," letter to John Anderson, 21 July 1944, *CW*, 26: 107.

124. Diary of Frederic Harmer, assistant secretary, Treasury, quoted, Moggridge, *MK*, 803, 809; "slight heart attack" is Moggridge's term.

125. JMK to Plesch, KP, PP/45/255. The letter had JMK giving his "big speech . . . almost as I slipped off the boat" and did not mention that the speech came a day after he had silently listened to the debate.

126. Robbins, *Autobiography*, 211; JMK's speech, 18 December 1945, *CW*, 24: 608–24.

127. JMK's report to the Treasury opposing locating the IMF and the World Bank in Washington, 7 March 1946, *CW*, 26: 211–13; JMK's letter to Richard Kahn arguing that the Americans did not know how "to make these institutions into operating international concerns," 13 March 1946, ibid, 217.

128. 20 March 1946, KP, PP/45/255.

129. JMK to Labordère, Labordère to JMK, 28 March, 5 April 1945, KP, PP/45/177.

130. *CW*, 24: 625–28; quotations, 628, 626, 628.

131. 22 July 1944, *CW*, 26: 109.

132. KP, UA/5/6.

133. Letters, Joan Robinson to JMK and JMK to her, 7, 12 December 1942, and the vice chancellor to JMK and JMK to him, 22, 24 January 1944, ibid.

134. KP, PP/45/278.

135. KP, UA/5/4.

136. KP, PP/45/293.

137. Harry G. Johnson, "Cambridge in the 1950s," in Elizabeth S. and Harry G. Johnson, *The Shadow of Keynes* (Chicago, 1978), 133, 134 (quoting DHR). Johnson was a distinguished, non-Keynesian monetary economist.

138. JMK, "The Balance of Payments of the United States," *CW*, 22: 186.

139. KP, PP/41.

140. KP, PP/45/168.

141. KP, PP/41.

142. Harrod, *The Life*, 641–43; tea at Charleston, Spalding, *Vanessa Bell*, 331.

CHAPTER 11

Afterword

Where can we situate Keynes's life and works in the waning moments of the twentieth century? The answer, consistent with his effects during his lifetime, is marvelously ambiguous, almost to the point of giving new meaning to the word. We have seen how he stretched sense to anti-sense, how he reversed and rereversed direction. His followers and critics have planted new settlements on terra incognita-until-Keynes and, like him, moved on and back, and dynamically flung the ambiguities further in four dimensions at least. We find Keynes again, creatively ambiguous, at another critical point in the global political economy.

Keynes was important, although surely not uniquely responsible, in shattering the unity of economic science. The marginalists Jevons, Menger, and Walras had created neoclassical economics in the 1870s, Walras conceiving of a general equilibrium that helped establish that unity and giving it a mathematical structure extending to all markets. From the Cambridge of John Neville Keynes, Alfred Marshall's partial equilibrium, although drawn from a different perspective in his *Principles of Economics* of 1890, further consolidated neoclassical theory on broadly acceptable terms. From the 1870s to the Keynesian revolution of the 1930s, the professional economists recognized themselves as a community speaking a common language although agreement was, of course, neither total nor absolute. Beyond that community the German Historical School, suspecting all theory, amassed mysteriously selected historical instances in economic developments, but it had isolated itself from functional thinking about, and acting upon, economic reality. Paralleling it, the Marxian system, stubbornly classical, raised itself in partial opposition to the old classicals and blank rejection of the neoclassicals. Undisturbed, the neoclassicals could challenge the first to produce *reasoned* policies and recognize the second as a philosophically interesting antithesis to reason in economics. Then there were the other less systematic underconsumptionists and the monetary cranks claiming, like the Marxists, a vision unvouchsafed to the conventionally sighted. But until the Soviet area built its Marxist–Leninist institutes, and only then and there, students of economics either went to school in neoclassical theory or huddled in odd corners with other odd men and women out.

Keynes was symptom as well as cause of the shattered unity. In the early 1930s he and Friedrich von Hayek debated each other as neoclassicals, both attempting, as we have seen, to develop a dynamic version of the neoclassical. Both slipped away. Joined by Ludwig von Mises, his Austrian colleague, Hayek went on to recreate the economics of the great Carl Menger as *neo*-Austrian economics.[1] In his masterpiece of concision and vastness of view, *Principles of Economics* (1871), Menger had applied a profound clarity of pure theory to the dense solidity of the factual.[2] It was too nearly perfect for Hayek and Mises, who preferred to adventure in empyrean theoretical reaches. Emphasizing great blanks in the information available to economic agents and an entrepreneurial-driven dynamics-cum-uncertainty, they saw the economy too much driven to settle in the old equilibrium of the neoclassical founders, and concentrated on the pre- or postequilibrium phases.

Mises, particularly, emphasized subjectivity and reason washed clean of empirical impurities: "What we know about the fundamental categories of action . . . is not derived from experience. We conceive of all this from within."[3] While defending the purest freedom of pure enterprise and opposing Keynes variously, Hayek and Mises moved toward him on uncertainty and subjectivity and, one might add, in generating symmetrical confusions. In the process these talented theorists theorized themselves out of economics, Mises entering into sociological and epistemological questions, while Hayek, as mentioned here earlier, launched into philosophical and related concerns. Like Keynes, they were drawn to the United States, where, despite their departure from economics, they inspired the neo-Austrian school, which has attempted to make something of their aerated conceptions. Keynes and his critics, past and present, had joined in replacing unity with diversity.[4]

Behold the other schools:

§The mainstream Keynesians, who attempt to hold together the "neoclassical synthesis," which Paul Samuelson claimed to have invented in his textbook. Allowing half its space to neoclassical microeconomics, he raised up in the other half a dominating Keynesian macroeconomics, which he said would produce the full employment needed for the microeconomics to function. He was literally papering over the absolute contradictions between neoclassical and Keynesian thought.

§The traditional neoclassicals, with an important center at the University of

Chicago, known as the Chicago school. They are content to exploit and widen the wisdom of the founders, although the wide-ranging monetarist Milton Friedman has freshened that wisdom in untraditional ways. He has, for example, played *with* and *against* Keynesian theory.

§Still another neoclassical group takes its position near the neo-Austrians. Founded by the American James M. Buchanan in the 1960s, public choice is actually political science theory attempting to do justice to the economy by protecting it against Keynesianism allied with state. Believing that the truly free economy functions perfectly well on its own, public choice proposes to use government against government when it interferes. Thus Buchanan (and a collaborator) have advocated a budget-balancing amendment to the Constitution which would prevent the Keynesian corruption of deficit-financing.[5]

§The Marxists clinging to the master's labor theory of value and the sense of capitalistic exploitation and decline. They have lately been further marginalized by the collapse of the Soviet Union, although they can argue that the fault lies in the mistaken implementation of Marxian truth.

§The Post-Keynesians, founded by Joan Robinson, who became enamoured of Marxism and tried, offending Keynes, to link it to Keynesianism.[6] Remaining tinged with Marxian ideas, they advocate thorough governmental action to prevent the anticipated capitalistic disaster. They follow Mrs. Robinson in taking as their text Keynes's article, "The General Theory of Employment," his ultimate defense of his General Theory, with its order-annihilating uncertainty.[7] For Robinson and those susceptible to her views, Marxism could reestablish certainty and order.

§The rational expectations ("ratex") theorists (also called the New Classical school), who began arguing in the 1960s that countervailing private action could frustrate Keynesian policies. Thus providers of investment funds, seeing the government increase the money supply to reduce interest rates, would demand a premium to compensate them for the expected loss in the value of the money to be repaid them. The rational expectationists, concentrating on policy, have not, however, attempted to debate Keynesian *theory* itself besides referring back to the Walrasian general equilibrium.

§In the 1980s a new group calling themselves New Keynesians reacted against the ratex people and, while ignoring the Post-Keynesians as faded and failing, have attempted to defend and extend Keynesianism. Their views have been conveniently articulated in the two-volume *New Keynesian Economics* (1991). Like their ratex opponents, however, they have made no effort to examine the roots of Keynes's system and confined their arguments to policy questions. Loyal to Keynes, they have emphasized the informational gaps in the economy (emphasized also by the neo-Austrians) as generators of excessive uncertainty. As a result of *dis*information, they argue, the *General Theory*'s conception of *dis*equilibrium can be restored.[8] (This is another of the instances where groups otherwise hostile to each other find themselves in embarrassed agreement.)

As radical Keynesians, the New Keynesians have given themselves the assignment of providing the microfoundations of Keynesian macroeconomics, an objective which previous generations of Keynesians have failed to reach. With this the new group may have endowed themselves with everlasting life because Keynes's macroeconomics, denying equilibrium and supply-and-demand price determination, is incompatible with the microeconomic laws. In the event, besides existing as a tiny group, they are threatened by defections from their leadership.

The great service of the smaller groups is to expose the weaknesses of the major ones, thus the Keynesian tendency toward fiscal and monetary irresponsibility, and the neoclassical failure to credit the importance of government as *economic* agent. Meanwhile, all the groups, large and small, represent a chaos of theory in their absolute disagreement. The situation has been repetitively defined as a crisis, recognition of which might lead toward resolution and a reunification of economic science. Perversely, a few negative indications might be encouraging. The Keynesian consensus has been shaken while neoclassical economics has been reasserting itself. Yet neither side is prepared to surrender any of its strategic positions. Real though it is, the crisis seems interminably protracted. A few more or less recent events suggest its character.

In April 1973 John R. Hicks, appalled at what he had wrought as a leader in the Keynesian revolution, pointed to *The Crisis in Keynesian Economics*, the title of a series of lectures published the next year.[9] In 1980 the neo-Conservative social-policy periodical *The Public Interest*, broadening the charge to all economics, devoted an entire issue to *The Crisis in Economic Theory*, published as a book in 1981. In that year, for good measure, it carried the article "The Retreat from Keynesian Economics" by Martin Feldstein of Harvard, president of the National Bureau of Economic Research and soon to be chairman (1982–84) of the Council of Economic Advisers.[10] The articles in the special issue, written by economists of the various persuasions, only reaffirmed their divisions—the *Crisis*.

Other events, both real and mental, persistently support and deny the thesis of a breakdown of the Keynesian consensus. The inflationary burst of the 1960s and 1970s suggests the failure of Keynesian *policies*, particularly because they had been accompanied by stagflation, a condition defying all theory. More recently, on the terrain of thought, a retreat of Keynesianism would seem to be signaled by the appearances of an ambitious new economics textbook and the fifteenth edition of Samuelson's famous older one. In midlife his *Economics* had begun to reduce out its explicit Keynesian message while the new one has gone further in this direction. The latter is N. Gregory Mankiw's *Principles of Economics* (1998), which its publishers hoped would invade the market where Samuelson's text has so long reigned. The Mankiw book was written for the most part in a neoclassical vein while appending three final chapters of mild Keynesian qualifications. Yet Mankiw was one of the two editors of the radical *New Keynesian Economics*, mentioned previously. Mankiw's enterprise would appear to confirm even more resoundingly the somewhat pending, somewhat achieved, revival of neoclassical economics. At this point, approaching the end of the twentieth century, these increasingly complex ambiguities proclaim that Keynes's theory is alive but not well.

Keynes, still vital as a *force* in economic thought, has his responsibility for the present as well as the past situation: economists seem mentally fatigued by the effort to work with or through a theory still important in the textbooks and econometric models while defeating understanding. The profession seems to prefer to discuss theory *applications* or policy, which do not demand rethinking of the fundamentals of theory. This is shown in the subject matter of articles published in the three organs of the American Economic Association, the *American Economic Review* (*AER*), the *Journal of Economic Literature* (*JEL*), and the *Journal of Economic Perspectives* (*JEP*), the *JEL*'s book reviews recording books of the same kind. Here is a recent sampling: "Interactions Between Seasonal and Business Cycles in Production and Inventories" (*AER*, December 1997), "Simulation-Based Estimation" (*JEL*, December 1997), and "Meddling Through: Regulating Local Telephone Competition in the United States" (*JEP*, Fall 1997). If all of the *AER* articles are similarly technical, those of the other journals are somewhat less so, the *JEL* issue carrying "Hayek and Socialism" while the *JEP* issue published two articles on neo-Austrian and neoclassical economics. But these penetrations into theory fail to penetrate very far; they prefer to apply long-established economic philosophies to carefully circumscribed areas of theory. None of the articles (or books reviewed), although worthy exercises dealing with problems requiring solution, visibly advances economic science or illuminates the tense relation between pure theory and practical action. The *Economic Journal*, Keynes's old strong point in Britain, is no different.

Another failing of contemporary economic thinking, expressing the shyness before theory, is the refusal of the various schools to engage each other in serious dialogue. Every school refuses to submit its basic theses to question. Instead, it uses its beliefs to test and find wanting the beliefs of the other groups. Intergroup debates, failing to threaten theory, tend to revolve around policy. In 1986, on the fiftieth anniversary of *The General Theory*, I organized a panel discussion on it with a leading mainstream Keynesian and Post-Keynesian; both ignored the book-and-theory (and my efforts to discuss it) and collegially debated the policy questions of the moment. These included the long since faded ideas of strengthening consumption and minimizing the importance of deficits. A recent dialogue in the *JEP* promised to philosophize about grander questions but only avoided them.

Here, also, the superbly ubiquitous Paul Samuelson makes his presence felt. In the spring 1997 issue the neo-Austrian Mark Skousen deplored "The Perseverance of Paul Samuelson's *Economics*" and its assistance to Keynesian persuasions, but carefully delimited the terrain of discourse: "The discussion here will spend little time on pure microeconomics and will focus on macroeconomics and policy advice." He was denying himself microeconomic reasoning, the best instrument for understanding and criticizing Keynes's theory. In his "Credo of a Lucky Textbook Author" Samuelson could blithely join with his critic on the terrain so safely delimited. Dangerously, however, Samuelson did indeed grant the existence of the "post-1965 decline in Keynesianism's esteem," which he attributed to "the onset of stagflation . . . a scourge difficult to prescribe for by any of the competing macro paradigms." But then, given Skousen's invitation to confine his discussion to policy and unplumbed macro formulas, he could elude theoretical considerations and propose his solution in the form of a trial-and-error *policy* of "alternative mixes of central bank money/credit configurations and fiscal expenditure/tax configurations."[11] Critic and defender of Keynesian theory had united in extruding thought. Similarly, Feldstein, occupying a position between Samuelson and Skousen, had ignored theory in his 1981 article and specified three policy reasons for the retreat from Keynesianism, namely, its tendency to increase unemployment, reduce saving and capital investment, and encourage excessive governmental activism.[12]

Actually, Keynes, revising the advice designed for the 1930s emergency, suggested how to confront reality with *balanced* theory and policy. As recounted in the previous chapter, his last economic statement, made to his old Political Economy Club shortly before he died, had returned resiliently to the old neoclassical verities that he had never quite deserted. Addressing Britain's difficult position in February 1946 he was "moved . . . to remind contemporary economists that the classical teaching embodied some permanent truths of great significance." There were "natural forces . . . operating towards equilibrium." And so he swept away the foundation of the General Theory in disequilibrium and denial of the function of supply and demand. But then he qualified: "I do not suppose that the classical medicine will work by itself."[13] He had provided the pragmatic formula for the mixed economy: give due importance both to the economic laws and the growing importance of government.

Skousen and his inspirations in economics, Mises and Hayek, have refused to admit that neoclassical theory, elegant and irrefutable on its own ground, suffers from its failure to recognize the economic force in government for good as well as ill. Keynes concurring, this suggests a compromise. The economic laws should be permitted to work themselves out as freely as possible in accord with neoclassical theory, while policy would correct, in measured Keynesian style, for the inevitable shocks with which society and polity assault the economic system. Of course, Keynes shutting his eyes, economic science should give up the nonsense perpetrated in *The General Theory* to jump start the economy in the 1930s. This should be a great relief to the surviving Keynesian loyalists. With this one can at least envision the end of the crisis in economic theory.

If this sounds too neat, we should take careful account of both the positives and negatives of the government's role—and the fact that it is ineluctably growing. (Privatization will remain an enlivening and healthy palliation, nothing more.) In 1900 governments in the advanced world took about 5 percent of the gross domestic product (GDP); in Keynes's day, about 20 percent. By the 1990s government had become the biggest business in the economy, taking more than 50 percent of GDP in Sweden and Great Britain, for example, if perhaps a few points less than 40 percent in backward United States. The area in which neo-classical economics can actually work has thus been narrowed to about half. Furthermore the economic process in the "free enterprise" part is not that free. Economies of scale are manufacturing more and more larger and larger con-glomerates: the growth of government is partly a necessary defensive measure against overweening corporate power. In the United States the situation is in-stitutionalized in the form of the Council of Economic Advisers, the National Economic Council, the Treasury's and the Federal Reserve System's operations, the "military-industrial complex," and incessant legislative action: the govern-ment effectively leads the economy, as it must. Even when it gives no explicit orders, private business has learned to look over its shoulder to inquire what Washington has in mind. Keynes honestly and presciently called himself a "democratic socialist," and the mixed economies of the advanced nations have plenty of socialism mixed into them. This certainly means a threat to liberty, as economy-governing bureaucracies burgeon, and to efficiency, with the erosion of the bottom line and competition.

Presciently, also, Keynes had seen the threat and hoped for a solution he could not quite see. In June 1944, sailing to America for the Bretton Woods negotiations, he wrote to his old and friendly opponent Hayek to congratulate him on his "grand book," *The Road to Serfdom*, with its warnings of socialism's negative effects. Keynes hoped that people operating from Hayek's "moral po-sition" would resist them. For himself Keynes was in "a deeply moved agree-ment" with Hayek.[14] Of course it would take more than morality but with his encouragement, if not specific guidance, economists (and responsible citizens) must address this great present and future problem. Variously, Keynes lives!

NOTES

1. See, e.g., Friedrich von Hayek, "Competition as a Discovery Procedure," in *New Studies in Philosophy, Politics, Economics, and the History of Ideas* (Chicago, 1978), 139–90; and Ludwig von Mises, *Epistemological Problems of Economics* (New York and London, 1981).

2. Carl Menger, *Principles of Economics* (New York and London, 1981; translation of *Grundsätze der Volkswirtschaftlehre*, 1871).

3. Mises, "The Task and Scope of the Science of Human Action," in *Epistemolog-ical Problems*, 13–14.

4. See, e.g., Israel M. Kirzner, "Entrepreneurial Discovery and the Competitive Mar-ket Process: An Austrian Approach," *Journal of Economic Literature* 35 (March 1997): 60–85.

5. James M. Buchanan and Richard E. Wagner, *Democracy in Deficit: The Political*

Legacy of Lord Keynes (New York, 1977), 173–83; see also Buchanan, *Theory of Public Choice* (Ann Arbor, Mich., 1972).

6. In, e.g., Joan Robinson, *An Essay on Marxian Economics* (London, 1942).

7. *CW*, 14: 109–23.

8. See N. Gregory Mankiw and David Romer, eds., *New Keynesian Economics*, 2 vols. (Cambridge, Mass., 1991), especially the editors' introduction, 1: 1–26.

9. John R. Hicks, *The Crisis in Keynesian Economics* (New York, 1974).

10. Daniel Bell and Irving Kristol, eds., *The Crisis in Economic Theory* (New York, 1981); Martin Feldstein, "The Retreat from Keynesian Economics," *The Public Interest* 21 (Summer 1981): 92–105.

11. *Journal of Economic Perspectives* 11 (Spring 1997): 138, 156, 155.

12. Feldstein, "The Retreat," 97–102.

13. "The Balance of Payments of the United States," *CW*, 27 (*Activities 1940–46: Shaping the Post-War World*): 444, 445.

14. Keynes to Hayek, letter, 28 June 1944, ibid., 385, 387.

Bibliography

ARCHIVAL SOURCES

Berg Collection, New York Public Library: Keynes–Lytton Strachey Correspondence; Keynes–Virginia Woolf Correspondence; Strachey–Leonard Woolf Correspondence.

British Library, London: Keynes–Duncan Grant Correspondence; Keynes–Oswald T. Falk Correspondence.

Cambridge University Library: J. N. Keynes Diary.

Modern Archive Centre, King's College, Cambridge: Keynes Papers; Charleston Papers (photocopies and a few original letters).

Public Record Office, London/Kew Gardens: Cabinet Papers; Committee on Finance and Industry: Discussions; Economic Advisory Council: Memoranda, Minutes of Meetings, Notes; Committee on Economic Information: Memoranda, Minutes of Meetings; Treasury Papers.

PUBLISHED SOURCES

Acheson, Dean. *Present at the Creation: My Years in the State Department*. New York: Norton, 1969.

Allan, Walter, ed. *A Critique of Keynesian Economics*. New York: St. Martin, 1993.

Annan, Noel. *Leslie Stephen: The Godless Victorian*. New York: Random House, 1984.

Bagchi, Amiya Komar. *The Presidency Banks and the Indian Economy*. Calcutta: Oxford University Press, 1989.

Bairoch, Paul. *Economics and World History: Myths and Paradoxes*. Chicago: University of Chicago Press, 1993.

Bateman, Bradley W. *Keynes's Uncertain Revolution*. Ann Arbor: University of Michigan Press, 1996.

Bedford, Sybille. *Aldous Huxley: A Biography*. New York: Carroll & Graf, 1985 (1st ed.: 1973).

Bell, Clive. *Art*. London: Chatto & Windus, 1915.

———. *Civilization and Old Friends*. Chicago: University of Chicago Press, 1973.

Bell, Daniel, and Irving Kristol, eds. *The Crisis in Economic Theory*. New York: Basic Books, 1981.

Bell, Quentin. *Bloomsbury*. London: Weidenfeld & Nicolson, 1968.

———. *Elders and Betters*. London: John Murray, 1995.

———. *Virginia Woolf: A Biography*. New York: Harcourt Brace Jovanovich, 1974.

Bell, Vanessa. *Selected Letters of Vanessa Bell*, ed. Regina Marler. New York: Pantheon, 1993.

Beveridge, William H. "An Economic General Staff," parts 1, 2. *The Nation* 34 (29 December 1923; 5 January 1924): 485–86, 509–10.

Blum, John Morton. *From the Morgenthau Diaries*, vol. 2: *Years of Urgency 1938–1941*. Boston: Houghton Mifflin, 1965.

———. *From the Morgenthau Diaries*, vol. 3: *Years of War 1941–1945*. Boston: Houghton Mifflin, 1967.

Boettke, Peter J. "Where Did Economics Go Wrong? Modern Economics as a Flight from Reality," *Critical Review* 11 (Winter 1997): 11–64.

Born, Karl Erich. *Die deutsche Bankenkrise*. Munich: Piper, 1967.

Brown, Neville. *Dissenting Forbears: The Maternal Ancestors of J. M. Keynes*. Chichester, Sussex: Phillimore, 1988.

Browning, Oscar. *Memories of Sixty Years at Eton, Cambridge and Elsewhere*. London: John Lane, 1910.

Buchanan, James M. and Richard E. Wagner. *Democracy in Deficit: The Political Legacy of Lord Keynes*. New York: Academic Press, 1977.

———. *The Theory of Public Choice*. Ann Arbor: University of Michigan Press, 1972.

Burnett, Philip M. *Reparations at the Paris Peace Conference*. 2 vols. New York: Columbia University Press, 1940.

Burton, John, ed. *Keynes's* General Theory: *Fifty Years On*. London: Institute of Economic Affairs, 1986.

Cecil, Hugh and Mirabel Cecil. *Clever Hearts: Desmond and Molly MacCarthy: A Biography*. London: Gollancz, 1990.

Chandavakar, Anand. *Keynes and India: A Study in Economics and Biography*. London: Macmillan, 1989.

Clark, Kenneth. *The Other Half: A Self-Portrait*. London: John Murray, 1977.

Clarke, Peter. *The Keynesian Revolution in the Making, 1924–1936*. Oxford: Clarendon Press, 1988.

Colander, David C. and Harry Landreth, eds. *The Coming of Keynesianism to America*. Brookfield, Vt.: Elgar, 1996.

Committee on Finance and Industry. *Report*. (Cmd. 3897). London: H. M. Stationery Office, 1969 (reprint).

———. *Minutes of Evidence Taken before the Committee on Finance and Industry*. 2 Vols. London: H. M. Stationery Office, 1931.

Connolly, Cyril. *Enemies of Promise*. Boston: Little, Brown, 1979.

Crick, Bernard. *George Orwell: A Life*. Boston: Little, Brown, 1981.

Davenport, Nicholas. *Memoirs of a City Radical.* London: Weidenfeld & Nicolson, 1974.

Davis, John B. *Keynes's Philosophical Development.* New York: Columbia University Press, 1994.

Deacon, Richard. *The Cambridge Apostles.* New York: Farrar, Straus and Giroux, 1985.

Delany, Paul. *The Neo-Pagans: Rupert Brooke and the Ordeal of Youth.* New York: Free Press, 1987.

Deutscher, Patrick. *R. G. Hawtrey and the Development of Macroeconomics.* London: Macmillan, 1990.

Dow, Sheila and John Hilliard, eds. *Keynes, Knowledge and Uncertainty.* Aldershot, Hants: Elgar, 1995.

Dunn, Jane. *A Very Close Conspiracy: Vanessa Bell and Virginia Woolf.* Boston: Little, Brown, 1990.

Edel, Leon. *Bloomsbury: A House of Lions.* Philadelphia: Lippincott, 1979.

Escoffier, Jeffrey. *John Maynard Keynes.* Lives of Notable Gay Men and Lesbians, ed. Martin Duberman. New York and Philadelphia: Chelsea House, 1995.

Eshag, Eprime. *From Marshall to Keynes: An Essay on the Monetary Theory of the Cambridge School.* London: Basil Blackwell, 1963.

Feldman, David. *Englishmen and Jews: Social Relations and Political Culture 1840–1914.* New Haven: Yale University Press, 1994.

Felix, David. *Biography of an Idea: John Maynard Keynes and* The General Theory. New Brunswick, N.J.: Transaction, 1995.

———. "Marx and Keynes: The Primacy of Politics." *Biography* 18 (Summer 1995): 219–27.

———. *Marx as Politician.* Carbondale: Southern Illinois University Press, 1983.

———. *Walther Rathenau and the Weimar Republic: The Politics of Reparations.* Baltimore: Johns Hopkins Press, 1971.

Fetter, Frank W. "Lenin, Keynes, and Inflation." *Economica* 44 (February 1977): 77–80.

Fink, Carole. *The Genoa Conference.* Chapel Hill: University of North Carolina Press, 1984.

Fitzgerald, Penelope. *The Knox Brothers.* London: Macmillan, 1977.

Fitzgibbons, Athol. *Keynes's Vision: A New Political Economy.* Oxford: Clarendon Press, 1988.

Ford, J. L. *G. L. S. Shackle: The Dissenting Economist's Economist.* Aldershot, Hants: Elgar, 1994.

Forster, E. M. *Two Cheers for Democracy.* New York: Harcourt, Brace, 1951.

Frankfurter, Felix. *From the Diaries of Felix Frankfurter.* With a Biographical Essay . . . by Joseph P. Lash. New York: Norton, 1975.

Freeden, Michael. *Liberalism Divided: A Study in British Political Thought 1914–1939.* Oxford: Clarendon Press, 1986.

Freud, Sigmund. "A Child is Being Beaten: A Contribution to the Study of the Origin of Sexual Perversions," in *The Standard Edition of the Complete Works of Sigmund Freud,* tr. James Strachey, vol. 17 (1917–1919). London: Hogarth Press and the Institute of Psychoanalysis, 1955.

Galbraith, John Kenneth. "How Keynes Came to America," in *A Contemporary Guide to Economics, Peace and Laughter.* Boston: Houghton Mifflin, 1971.

———. *A Journey Through Economic Time.* Boston: Houghton Mifflin, 1994.

Garnett, Angelica. *Deceived with Kindness: A Bloomsbury Childhood.* London: Chatto & Windus-Hogarth Press, 1984.

Garnett, David. *The Familiar Faces.* London: Chatto & Windus, 1962.

————. *The Flowers of the Forest.* London: Chatto & Windus, 1955.

————. *The Golden Echo.* London: Chatto & Windus, 1954.

————. *Great Friends: Portraits of Seventeen Writers.* London: Macmillan, 1979.

Garraty, John A. *Unemployment in History: Economic Thought and Public Policy.* New York: Harper & Row, 1978.

Gay, Peter. *Freud: A Life for Our Time.* New York: Norton, 1988.

Gerzina, Gretchen. *Carrington.* London: John Murray, 1989.

Glendinning, Victoria. *Vita: The Life of Vita Sackville-West.* New York: Knopf, 1983.

Grigg, P. J. *Prejudice and Judgment.* London: Jonathan Cape, 1948.

Hansen, Alvin H. *A Guide to Keynes.* New York: McGraw-Hill, 1953.

Harrod, Roy F. *The Life of John Maynard Keynes.* New York: Norton, 1982 (1st ed.: 1951).

Hawtrey, Ralph G. *The Art of Central Banking.* London: Frank Cass, 1962 (1st ed.: 1932).

————. *Capital and Employment.* London: Longmans, Green, 1937.

Hayek, Friedrich A. von. ''Competition as a Discovery Procedure,'' in *New Studies in Philosophy, Politics, Economics, and the History of Ideas.* Chicago: University of Chicago Press, 1985 (1st ed.: 1978): 179–90.

————. *Contra Keynes and Cambridge: Essays, Correspondence,* vol. 9: *The Collected Works of F. A. Hayek,* ed. Bruce Caldwell. Chicago: University of Chicago Press, 1995.

————. *Prices and Production.* London: George Routledge, 1935 (2nd, revised, enlarged edition).

————. ''Reflections on the Pure Theory of Money of Mr. J. M. Keynes,'' parts 1, 2. *Economica* 11 (old series: August 1931): 270–95; 12 (o.s.: February 1932): 22–44.

Hazlitt, Henry, ed. *The Critics of Keynesian Economics.* New Rochelle, N.Y.: Arlington House, 1977.

Hession, Charles H. *John Maynard Keynes: A Personal Biography . . .* New York, Macmillan, 1984.

Hicks, John R. *Collected Essays on Economic Theory.* 3 vols. Cambridge, Mass.: Harvard University Press, 1981–83.

————. *The Crisis in Keynesian Economics.* New York: Basic Books, 1974.

Hollis, Christopher. *Eton: A History.* London: Hollis & Carter, 1960.

Holroyd, Michael. *Lytton Strachey.* 2 vols. New York: Holt, Rinehart and Winston, 1968.

————. *Lytton Strachey: The New Biography.* New York: Farrar, Straus and Giroux, 1995.

Horsefield, J. Keith. *The International Monetary Fund 1945–1965.* 3 Vols. Washington: IMF, 1969.

Howarth, T. E. B. *Cambridge Between Two Wars.* London: Collins, 1978.

Howson, Susan, and Donald Winch. *The Economic Advisory Council 1930–1939.* Cambridge: Cambridge University Press, 1977.

Hubback, David. *No Ordinary Press Baron: A Life of Walter Layton.* London: Weidenfeld & Nicolson, 1985.

Jevons, W. Stanley. *The Theory of Political Economy*. New York: Kelley & Millman, 1957 (5th ed.).

Johnson, Elizabeth S. and Harry G. Johnson. *The Shadow of Keynes*. Chicago: University of Chicago Press, 1978.

Johnstone, John K. *The Bloomsbury Group*. New York: Farrar, Straus and Giroux, 1978 (1st ed.: 1954).

Kavanagh, Julie. *Secret Muses: The Life of Frederick Ashton*. London: Faber and Faber, 1996.

Keynes, Florence Ada. *Gathering up the Threads: A Study in Family Biography*. Cambridge: Heffer, 1950.

Keynes, Geoffrey. *The Gates of Memory*. Oxford: Clarendon Press, 1981.

Keynes, John Maynard. *The Collected Writings of John Maynard Keynes*, 30 Vols., ed. Sir Austin Robinson and Donald E. Moggridge. London: Published for the Royal Economic Society by Macmillan, 1971–89.

———— and Lydia Lopokova. *The Letters of John Maynard Keynes and Lydia Lopokova*, ed. Polly Hill and Richard Keynes. New York: Charles Scribner's Sons, 1989.

Keynes, John Neville. *The Scope and Method of Political Economy*. New York: Kelley & Millman, 1955 (1st ed.: 1891).

————. *Studies and Exercises in Formal Logic*. London: Macmillan, 1906 (1st ed.: 1884).

Keynes, Milo, ed. *Essays on John Maynard Keynes*. Cambridge: Cambridge University Press, 1975.

————, ed. *Lydia Lopokova*. London: Weidenfeld & Nicolson, 1983.

King, James. *Virginia Woolf*. London: Hamish Hamilton, 1994.

Kirzner, Israel M. ''Entrepreneurial Discovery and the Competitive Market Process: An Austrian Approach.'' *Journal of Economic Literature* 35 (March 1997): 60–85.

Kuhn, Thomas S. *The Structure of Scientific Revolutions*. Chicago: University of Chicago Press, 1970 (2nd, enlarged ed.; 1st. ed.: 1962).

Lee, Hermione. *Virginia Woolf*. London: Chatto & Windus, 1996.

Lehmann, John. *The Whispering Gallery*. New York: Harcourt Brace, 1955.

Lekachman, Robert. *The Age of Keynes*. New York: Random House, 1966.

LePan, Douglas. *Bright Glass of Memory*. Toronto: McGraw-Hill Ryerson, 1979.

Levy, Paul. *G. E. Moore and the Cambridge Apostles*. London: Weidenfeld & Nicolson, 1979.

Liberal Industrial Inquiry. *Britain's Industrial Future*. London: Ernest Benn, 1928.

MacCarthy, Desmond. *Memories*. London: MacGibbon & Kee, 1953.

MacWeeney, Alen and Sue Allison. *Bloomsbury Reflections*. New York: Norton, 1990.

Magnus, Philip. *Gladstone: A Biography*. London: John Murray, 1970 (1st ed.: 1954).

Mankiw, N. Gregory. *Principles of Economics*. New York: Harcourt Brace/Dryden Press, 1998.

Mankiw, N. Gregory and David Romer, eds. *New Keynesian Economics*. 2 vols. Cambridge: MIT Press, 1991.

Marler, Regina. *Bloomsbury Pie: The Making of the Bloomsbury Boom*. New York: Henry Holt, 1997.

Marshall, Alfred. *Principles of Economics*, ed. C. W. Guillebaud, 2 Vols. London: Macmillan, 1961 (9th variorum ed.; 1st ed.: 1890).

Marx, Karl. *Capital*, vol. 1. New York: International, 1947 (1st ed.: 1887).

————. "On the Jewish Question," in *Collected Works*, vol. 3. New York: International, 1975.

Mason, Richard, ed. *Cambridge Minds*. Cambridge: Cambridge University Press, 1994.

Medlicott, W. N. *Contemporary England 1914–1964*. London: Longman, 1976 (1st ed.: 1967).

Menger, Carl. *Principles of Economics*. New York: New York University Press, 1981 (1st German ed.: 1871).

Mini, Piero V. *John Maynard Keynes: A Study in the Psychology of Original Work*. New York: St. Martin's Press, 1994.

————. *Keynes, Bloomsbury and* The General Theory. London: Macmillan, 1991.

Mises, Ludwig. *Epistemological Problems of Economics*. New York: New York University Press, 1981.

Mitchell, B. R. *European Historical Statistics, 1750–1970*. Abridged edition. New York: Columbia University Press, 1978.

Moggridge, Donald E. *British Monetary Policy 1924–1931: The Norman Conquest of $4.86*. Cambridge: Cambridge University Press, 1972.

————. *Maynard Keynes: An Economist's Biography*. London and New York: Routledge, 1992.

Monk, Ray. *Ludwig Wittgenstein: The Duty of Genius*. London: Jonathan Cape, 1990.

Moore, G. E. *Principia Ethica*. Cambridge: Cambridge University Press, 1962 (1st ed.: 1903).

Morgan, E. V. *Studies in British Financial Policy, 1914–1925*. London: Macmillan, 1952.

Mosley, Sir Oswald. *My Life*. London: Nelson, 1968.

O'Brien, Dennis P. *Lionel Robbins*. London: Macmillan, 1988.

O'Donnell, R. M. *Keynes: Philosophy, Economics & Politics*. New York: St. Martin's Press, 1989.

————. "The Unwritten Books and Papers of J. M. Keynes," *History of Political Economy* 24 (Winter 1992): 769–817.

Ohlin, Bertil. "The Reparation Problem: A Discussion," "A Rejoinder from Prof. Ohlin," *Economic Journal* 39 (June, September 1929): 172–82, 400–404.

————. "Some Notes on the Stockholm Theory of Savings and Interest," *Economic Journal* 47, part 1 (March 1937): 53–69; part 2 (June 1937): 221–40.

Ollard, Richard. *An English Education: A Perspective of Eton*. London: Collins, 1982.

Palatsky, Eugene. "Lord John Maynard Keynes: Economist and Balletomane," *Dance Magazine*, 35 (October 1961): 44–46, 60.

Partridge, Frances. *Love in Bloomsbury: Memories*. Boston: Little, Brown, 1981.

Patinkin, Don. *Anticipations of the* General Theory? *And Other Essays on Keynes*. Chicago: University of Chicago Press, 1984.

Perkins, Frances. *The Roosevelt I Knew*. New York: Viking, 1946.

Peter, Matthias. *John Maynard Keynes und die Britische Deutschlandpolitik*. Munich: Oldenbourg, 1997.

Pritchard, Jane. "London's Favorite Ballerina," *Dancing Times*, 58 (December 1989): 243–45.

Rees, David. *Harry Dexter White: A Study in Paradox*. New York: Coward, McCann & Geoghegan, 1973.

Robbins, Lionel. *Autobiography of an Economist*. London: Macmillan, 1971.

————. *The Great Depression*. London: Macmillan, 1934.

────── and James Meade. *The Wartime Diaries of Lionel Robbins and James Meade*, ed. Susan Howson and Donald E. Moggridge. London: Macmillan, 1990.

Robertson, Dennis H. *Banking Policy and the Price Level*. London: P. S. King, 1926.

──────. "Mr. Keynes's Theory of Money," *Economic Journal* 41 (September 1931): 395–411.

──────. Review of *The Economic Consequences of the Peace*. *Economic Journal* 30 (March 1920): 77–84.

──────. "Some Notes on Mr. Keynes's General Theory of Employment." *Quarterly Journal of Economics* 51 (November 1936): 168–91.

Robinson, E. A. G. "John Maynard Keynes." *Economic Journal* 57 (March 1947): 1–68.

Robinson, Joan. *Collected Economic Papers*. 5 Vols. Oxford: Basil Blackwell, 1951–79.

──────. *An Essay on Marxian Economics*. London: Macmillan, 1942.

──────. "A Parable on Savings and Investment." *Economica* 13 (old series: February 1932): 75–84.

Rosen, Sherwin. "Austrian and Neoclassical Economics: Any Gains from Trade?" *Journal of Economic Perspectives* 11 (Fall 1997): 139–52.

Rosenbaum, S. P., ed. *The Bloomsbury Group*. Toronto: University of Toronto Press, 1975.

Rueff, Jacques. "A Criticism by Mr. Jacques Rueff." *Economic Journal* 39 (September 1929): 388–99.

Russell, Bertrand. *The Autobiography of Bertrand Russell*, vol. 1. London: Allen & Unwin, 1978.

Samuelson, Paul A. *Economics*, 1st, 9th, 10th eds. New York: McGraw-Hill, 1948, 1973, 1976.

──────. "Credo of a Lucky Textbook Author." *Journal of Economic Perspectives* 11 (Spring 1997): 153–60.

────── and William D. Nordhaus. *Economics*, 12th, 13th, 14th, 15th, 16th eds. New York: McGraw-Hill, 1985, 1989, 1992, 1995, 1998.

Sayers, R. S. *The Bank of England 1891–1944*. 3 Vols. Cambridge: Cambridge University Press, 1976.

Schumpeter, Joseph A. *Ten Great Economists*. London: Allen & Unwin, 1965.

──────. *History of Economic Analysis*. New York: Oxford University Press, 1954.

Scrase, David, and Peter Croft. *Maynard Keynes Collection of Pictures, Books and Manuscripts*. Catalogue of exhibition, Fitzwilliam Museum, Cambridge, 1983. Cambridge: Provost and Scholars of King's College, 1983.

Seymour, Miranda. *Ottoline Morrell: Life on the Grand Scale*. New York: Farrar, Straus and Giroux, 1993.

Shackle, G. L. S. *The Nature of Economic Thought*. Selected Papers 1955–64. Cambridge: Cambridge University Press, 1966.

──────. *The Years of High Theory: Invention and Tradition in Economic Thought 1926–1939*. Cambridge: Cambridge University Press, 1983 (1st ed.: 1967).

Shone, Richard. *Bloomsbury Portraits: Vanessa Bell, Duncan Grant, and their Circle*. Oxford: Phaidon/New York: E. P. Dutton, 1976.

Skidelsky, Robert. *John Maynard Keynes*, vol. 1: *Hopes Betrayed 1883–1920*. New York: Viking, 1986 (1st ed.: 1983); vol. 2: *The Economist as Saviour 1920–1937*. London: Macmillan, 1992.

──────. *Keynes*. Past Masters. Oxford: Oxford University Press, 1996.

———. *Oswald Mosley*. London: Macmillan, 1975.

Skousen, Mark. "The Perseverance of Paul Samuelson's *Economics.*" *Journal of Economic Perspectives* 11 (Spring 1997): 137–52.

———, ed. *Dissent on Keynes: A Critical Appraisal of Keynesian Economics*. New York: Praeger, 1992.

Spalding, Frances. *Duncan Grant*. London: Chatto & Windus, 1997.

———. *Roger Fry: Art and Life*. Berkeley: University of California Press, 1980.

———. *Vanessa Bell*. New York: Ticknor and Fields, 1983.

Spater, George and Ian Parsons. *A Marriage of True Minds: An Intimate Portrait of Leonard and Virginia Woolf*. London: Jonathan Cape–Hogarth Press, 1977.

Sraffa, Piero. "Dr. Hayek on Money and Capital." *Economic Journal* 42 (March 1932): 42–53.

Stansky, Peter. *On or About December 1910: Early Bloomsbury and Its Intimate World*. Cambridge, Mass.: Harvard University Press, 1996.

Steel, Ronald. *Walter Lippmann and the American Century*. Boston: Little, Brown, 1980.

Strachey, James. *Bloomsbury/Freud: The Letters of James and Alix Strachey 1924–1925*, ed. Perry Meisel and Walter Kendrick. New York: Basic Books, 1985.

Strachey, Lytton. *Elizabeth and Essex: A Tragic History*. London: Chatto & Windus, 1928.

———. *Eminent Victorians*. London: Chatto & Windus, 1918.

———. *Queen Victoria*. London: Chatto & Windus, 1921.

Turnbaugh, Douglas Blair. *Duncan Grant and the Bloomsbury Group*. London: Bloomsbury, 1987.

Viner, Jacob. "Mr. Keynes on the Causes of Unemployment." *Quarterly Journal of Economics* 51 (November 1936): 147–67.

Watney, Simon. *The Art of Duncan Grant*. London: John Murray, 1990.

Webb, Beatrice. *The Diary of Beatrice Webb*, vol. 4: *1924–1943: "The Wheel of Life,"* ed. Norman and Jeanne MacKenzie. London: Virago, 1985.

Weill-Raynal, Étienne. *Les réparations allemandes et la France*. 3 Vols. Paris: Nouvelles éditions latines, 1938–47.

Weintraub, E. Roy. Editor's Introduction, "Minisymposium: Keynes Lives in Several Communities." *History of Political Economy* 26 (Spring 1994): 97–98.

Wicksell, Knut. *Interest and Prices*, tr. R. F. Kahn. London: Macmillan, 1936 (German ed.: 1898).

Wilkinson, L. P. *A Century of King's 1873–1972*. Cambridge: Provost and Fellows of King's College, 1980.

Wilson, Francesca M. *Rebel Daughter of a Country House: The Life of Eglantyne Jebb*. London: Allen & Unwin, 1967.

Wood, John Cunningham, ed. *John Maynard Keynes: Critical Assessments*. 4 Vols. Canberra and London: Croom Helm, 1983.

Woolf, Leonard. *After the Deluge*, vols. 1, 2: *A Study of Communal Psychology*. London: Hogarth Press, 1931, 1939.

———. *Beginning Again: An Autobiography of the Years 1911–1918*. London: Hogarth Press, 1964.

———. *Downhill All the Way: An Autobiography of the Years 1919–1939*. London: Hogarth Press, 1967.

———. *Ethica Politica*. London: Hogarth Press, 1953.

————. *Letters of Leonard Woolf*, ed. Frederic Spotts. New York: Harcourt Brace Jovanovich, 1989.

Woolf, Virginia. *The Diary of Virginia Woolf*, ed. Anne Olivier Bell. 5 Vols. London: Hogarth Press, 1977–84.

————. *Jacob's Room*. New York: Harcourt Brace, 1923 (1st ed.: 1922).

————. *The Letters of Virginia Woolf*, ed. Nigel Nicolson. 6 Vols. London: Hogarth Press, 1975–80.

————. *Mrs. Dalloway*. New York: Harcourt Brace, 1925.

————. *A Room of One's Own and Three Guineas*. London: Chatto & Windus–Hogarth Press, 1989.

————. *To the Lighthouse*. New York: Harcourt Brace, 1927.

————. *The Virginia Woolf Reader*, ed. Mitchell A. Leaska. New York: Harcourt Brace Jovanovich, 1984.

————. *The Waves*. New York: Harcourt Brace, 1931.

Yeager, Leland B. "Austrian Economics, Neoclassicism, and the Market Test." *Journal of Economic Perspectives* 11 (Fall 1997): 153–65.

Young, Warren. *Interpreting Mr. Keynes: The IS–LM Enigma*. Cambridge: Polity Press, 1987.

Index

About the Author

DAVID FELIX is Professor Emeritus of History at the City University of New York. He is the author of several books including, most recently, *Biography of an Idea: John Maynard Keynes and The General Theory of Employment, Interest, and Money* (1995).

ISBN 0-313-28827-5

90000>

HARDCOVER BAR CODE